The publisher of Muhammad Abu Zahra's inspiring book, *The Four Imams* are deeply grateful to His *Excellency, Mr. Easa Saleh Al-Gurg, CBE*, for his generosity in making the publication of the book possible. In these days of high production costs of even the most valuable texts, such help as given by *His Excellency* is greatly valued as it enables the book to reach a wider readership.

In the Name of Allah,
The Merciful, The Most Beneficent

THE FOUR IMAMS
The Lives and Teaching of their Founders

Muhammad Abu Zahra

Dar Al-Taqwa

© Dar Al Taqwa Ltd. 2001

ISBN 1-870582-41-1

Translation: Aisha Bewley

Editors: Abdalhaqq Bewley and Muhammad Isa Waley

Production: Bookwork, Norwich

Published by:
Dar Al Taqwa Ltd.
7A Melcombe Street
Baker Street
London NW1 6AE

Website   www@daraltaqwa.com
E-Mail   info@daraltaqwa.com

Printed and bound in Great Britain by
Redwood Books, Trowbridge, Wiltshire.

Foreword

I am delighted to have this opportunity to be able to contribute in some way to the publication of *The Four Imams*. I congratulate the publishers, **Dar Al-Taqwa** on their initiative in the translating and publishing of such an important book, which shall inspire and fulfil the aspirations of the scholar and student alike in their research of the different schools of thought.

The Imams devoted their life's in studying the sunna and the knowledge of Islam and its fiqh through the transmission from the Prophet (s.a.w) at a time when there were questions connected to the dogma, raised by the Muslim sects and disseminated among the majority of the Muslims. As today, Muslims rely on the knowledge of the hadith (fuqaha) scholars whom were the only ones able to remove the uncertainty that these questions provoked. *The Four Imams* is a book of revelation into the intellectual opinions and sincere quest of knowledge stimulated by a heart free of the impurities of this world and desire of high ideals and truth. The Imams sought knowledge for the sake of Allah alone, in their quest of the Straight Path.

The well-renowned contemporary scholar of the book, Imam Mohammad Abu Zahra, educated at Al-Azhar University, dedicated his life to the study of the different legal schools of thought and Islamic law. May this work help all people to understand the significance of the lives of the imams as models for us to follow as we, insha Allah, continue to be as witness to the Message and the Messenger.

Easa Saleh Al-Gurg, CBE.

Foreword

This is book is a compilation of four books which deal with the lives and work of the Imams who founded the four great canonical Schools of Islamic *Fiqh* written in Arabic by the great Egyptian scholar and theologian, Muhammad Abu Zahra, and presented in translation to give English-speaking readers for the first time an in-depth analysis of these pivotal figures of Islamic history. Such a work is long overdue in the English language.

The first part is about Imam Malik, who lived his whole life in Madina where much of the Qur'an was revealed and most of the legal practices of Islam established, spent his life studying, recording and clarifying the legal parameters and precedents which had been passed down to him by the two generations who had lived in Madina since the Prophet's death, may Allah bless him and grant him peace, and were, therefore, the direct inheritors of the perfected form of Islam he left there.

It deals with not only the biographical details of the Imam's life but also puts it in its historical context and, most importantly, shows us the methods he used in reaching his legal conclusions which played such a vital part in preserving exactly that legacy of pure Divine Guidance left by the Prophet and his Companions.

The second part explores both the *fiqh* and the life and times of Imam Abu Hanifa, who died in 150/767. He met Companions of the Prophet and is counted amongst the *Tabi'un* (Followers). He is renowned for his piercing intellect as a *faqih*, his scrupulousness and integrity of character, and his resoluteness in the face of oppression.

His school, through its historical association with the Abbasid and Ottoman khalifates and Moghul rule in India, is the most widespread of all the schools of *fiqh*. This makes this study particularly important for English-speaking Muslims since it gives

i

them an in-depth appreciation of the school followed by the great majority of Muslims in the West.

The third Imam is Imam ash-Shafi'i. He is remarkable in that he resolved the different strands of opinion which had emerged in the still evolving Muslim community and brought them together in probably the most brilliant legal synthesis in the whole history of mankind.

Abu Zahra looks at his life and traces the development of his thought. He talks of his teachers and his followers and shows how the system he devised grew out of the intellectual and political currents of his time. He also gives an in depth historical analysis of the various movements and sects which formed the background to the Islamic world in which he lived

Ahmad ibn Hanbal is chronologically the last of the four Imams and lived just after the first three formative generations of the Islamic community, thus confronting a slightly different situation from that faced by his three illustrious forebears. This necessitated a fresh approach to the legal issues arising out of the situation of rapidly expanding urban development and imperial government which had become the day-to-day reality of so much of the Muslim community.

Abu Zahra shows how Imam Ahmad, through his incredible personal integrity and scrupulous adherence to sound tradition, was able to chart a course through the stormy period in which he lived and how his example provided his followers with the legal bases of what later became the Hanbali *madhhab*.

The present publisher has decided to combine the four original books into one volume so that for the first time in English there is a comprehensive, in depth analysis of the four *Sunni madhhabs* and their founders. This is particularly important and relevant in the world today when many thousands of Muslims find themselves in a situation where there is no traditional allegiance to a particular *madhhab* and where adherents of all four schools frequently pray together in a single mosque.

Table of Contents

Malik ibn Anas

Chapter Four

The Opinions and *Fiqh* of ash-Shafi'i

Chapter Five

The Principles of ash-Shafi'i

Malik ibn Anas

(93-179/712-795)

The Life of Malik ibn Anas
(93-179/712-795)

Malik's birth and lineage

Scholars disagree about the year in which Malik was born. Different accounts mention 90, 93, 94, 95, 96 and 98 AH. The most widely accepted date is 93. Indeed, it is reported that Malik himself said, "I was born in 93."

He was born and lived his whole life in Madina and saw the traces of the Companions and Followers and the grave of the Prophet, may Allah bless him and grant him peace, and all the great places there. He felt an enormous esteem for Madina and all it contained which marked his life from his earliest childhood. He knew it to be the cradle of knowledge, the fountain of light and the spring of gnosis. He maintained this deep-rooted respect until his death and it had a profound impact on his thought, his *fiqh* and his life in general. He never rode in Madina and he gave great importance to the practice of its people in his *ijtihad*. Indeed, the principle of the 'Practice of the People of Madina' was one of the foundations of his legal method, as we will show.

Malik was descended from a Yemeni tribe, Dhu Asbah. His full name was Malik ibn Anas ibn Malik ibn Abi 'Amir al-Asbahi al-Yamani. His mother was al-'Aliyya bint Sharik al-Azdiyya. His father and mother were both Yemeni Arabs. But there are two disputed matters in this regard which should be cleared up at this juncture. The first is that there is one transmission which states that his mother was a client and that her name was Tulayha and that she was the client of 'Abdullah ibn Ma'mar. That is not the accepted position since she was in fact a Yemeni Azdite, and so this unsubstantiated report is generally ignored.

The second point is that some biographers claim that Malik and his whole family were clients and therefore not pure members of an Arab tribe. They state that his great-grandfather, Abu 'Amir, was a client[1] of the Banu Taym, the sub-tribe to which Abu Bakr belonged. According to this, he would be Qurayshi by clientage. We find that al-Bukhari mentions that Abu Suhayl was a client and Ibn Hajar states that this Abu Suhayl was the uncle of Malik. It is said that Ibn Shihab az-Zuhri, the shaykh of Malik, considered Malik to be one of the clients of the Banu Taym since his uncle was so considered. Malik denied that and made it clear that his lineage was pure Arab. It appears that the source of this report was Muhammad ibn Ishaq, the author of the *Sira*. That is why its transmission is not accepted: because he is not considered reliable, the statement is baseless. The erroneous impression arose because of his alliance with Banu Taym.

Abu Suhayl, Malik's uncle, said, "We are people from Dhu As'hab. Our grandfather came to Madina and married among the Taymis. He was with them and was ascribed to them." This indicates that they formed an alliance with Abu 'Amir. An alliance is a natural consequence of the relationship by marriage between the parties, which results in mutual support.

There is some question about when Abu 'Amir settled in Madina and married into the Banu Taym, which led to the mutual alliance. According to some historians he settled in Madina after the Battle of Badr while the Prophet was still alive, and was present with the Prophet in all the expeditions except that of Badr. Qadi ibn al-'Ala' al-Qushayri mentioned that Abu 'Amir, the grandfather of Malik's father, was one of the Companions of the Prophet. He said, "We went on all the expeditions with the Prophet, except that of Badr." His son Malik, whose *kunya* was Abu Anas, was Malik's grandfather. He was one of the great *Tabi'un*. More than one person mentioned that he related from 'Umar, Talha, 'A'isha, Abu Hurayra and Hassan ibn Thabit. He was one of the four men who carried 'Uthman to his grave and shrouded him.

1. The plural of *mawla*, a person with whom a tie of *wala'* has been established, originally by having been a slave and then set free. It is also used for a type of political patronage extended to non-Arab Muslims.

Some sources say something different: that Abu 'Amir settled in Madina after the death of the Messenger of Allah, and so was alive while the Prophet was alive but did not meet him. He met his Companions and studied with them and so on that basis he is a Follower.

According to another source it was Malik, the grandfather of the Imam, who came to Madina: "Malik ibn Abi 'Amir came to Madina complaining about one of the governors in Yemen. He inclined to one of the Banu Taym ibn Murra and made an alliance with them and joined them." From this it is understood that the family of Abu 'Amir was from Yemen and that the first of them to come to Madina was the grandfather of Malik, not Abu 'Amir.

It is clear to us, then, that there are three transmissions: one is that Abu 'Amir was alive in the time of the Prophet and was present at all the expeditions except Badr; another, that he came to Madina after the death of the Prophet and married into the Banu Taym; and the third is that the first of this family to come to Madina was Malik ibn Abi 'Amir, not Abu 'Amir. We prefer the second of these because it agrees with what is related about Abu Suhayl.

Malik's youth and studies

Malik grew up in a household which was engaged in the science of Traditions and *hadith*. His family was interested in the knowledge of the reports and traditions of the Companions and their *fatwas*. His grandfather, Malik ibn Abi 'Amir, was one of the great men of knowledge of the *Tabi'un*. He related from many Companions. It is clear, however, that Anas ibn Malik,[1] Malik's father, was not greatly concerned with *hadith* since it is not known that Malik related anything from him, although Malik's grandfather and uncles were. His family was well-known for their devotion to knowledge. Malik was originally known as 'the brother of an-Nadr', a brother of his who was esteemed for his knowledge.

---

1. He should not be confused with the famous Companion, Anas ibn Malik al-Ansari al-Khazraji.

Then his own desire to seek knowledge grew to such an extent that people began to say, 'an-Nadr, the brother of Malik.'

The general ambience of the place where he lived was one of knowledge and learning. It was the city of the Messenger, may Allah bless him and grant him peace, and the place to which he emigrated, the land of the *Shari'a*, the fount of the Light of the *Deen* and the stronghold of Islamic governance and the capital of Islam as a whole during the time of Abu Bakr, 'Umar, and 'Uthman. The period of 'Umar was crucial for the implementation of the guidance of the Qur'an and the Messenger and the many legal judgements which that entailed.

Madina in the time of the Umayyads remained a pivotal source of the *Shari'a* and point of reference for scholars, even for the Companions themselves who were living in other places. It is related that 'Abdullah ibn Mas'ud would be asked about something in Iraq and give a *fatwa* about it. If he came to Madina and found that the ruling on the matter was different there, he would return to Iraq and not dismount until he had gone to the one to whom he had given the *fatwa* and informed him of the difference. 'Abdullah ibn 'Umar was consulted by 'Abdullah ibn az-Zubayr and 'Abdu'l-Malik ibn Marwan who were contending over the leadership. He wrote to them, "If you both desire advice then you must come to the land of the *Hijra*, the cradle of the *Sunna*."

Malik grew up while Madina still held this position, so that when 'Umar ibn 'Abdu'l-'Aziz wrote to the cities to instruct them in the *Sunna* and *fiqh* he wrote to Madina to ask them about their practices. He wrote to Abu Bakr ibn Hazm in Madina asking him to compile the practices of the *Sunna* for him and to record them for him, but then 'Umar ibn 'Abdu'l-'Aziz died. Ibn Hazm had written some letters to him but he died before he could publish them.

Such was Madina in the time when Malik was growing up: it was the cradle of the *Sunna* and the home of *fatwa*. The first masters of the people of knowledge among the Companions gathered there, as did their students after them, until Malik came and inherited that noble legacy of knowledge, *hadith* and *fatwas* which they had kept alive. His natural gifts flourished under its aegis. He grew

4

up there, memorising the Noble Qur'an in his early youth as many young Muslims do. After memorising the Qur'an he devoted himself to memorising *hadith,* which was much encouraged in the environment of Madina. Malik went to the assemblies of scholars to write down what they taught and study it. He told his mother that he wanted to go and study, and she dressed him in his best clothes and turban and then said, "Go and write now." She said, "Go to Rabi'a and learn his knowledge before learning his *adab.*"

It is clear that this encouragement from his mother led him to sit with Rabi'a first, and he studied with him and learned *fiqh.* He started studying while he was still very young. One of his contemporaries said about him, "I saw Malik in the circle of Rabi'a when there was an earring in his ear." That indicates how young he was. He was eager from his earliest youth to memorise everything he learned. When he was studying, he would move round to stay within the shade of a tree so that he could finish what he wanted to finish. His sister said to her father, "This brother of mine does not go to visit people." He said, "My daughter, he is memorising the *hadiths* of the Messenger of Allah."

Malik sought knowledge in various gatherings and constantly kept the company of *fuqaha'* and men of knowledge. He said, "I had a brother the same age as Ibn Shihab. My father put a question to us one day and my brother was right and I was wrong. My father said to me, 'Have the pigeons distracted you from the quest for knowledge?' So I became angry and devoted myself to Ibn Hurmuz for seven years (one version has eight years) and I did not go to anyone else. I used to put some dates in my sleeve and I gave them to his children, telling them, 'If anyone asks about the shaykh, say that he is busy.'" One day Ibn Hurmuz said to his slavegirl, "Who is at the door?" She could only see Malik. She came back and told him, "It is only that ruddy-skinned one." He said, "Let him be. That is the man of knowledge of this people." Malik used to put on short padded trousers to sit at the door of Ibn Hurmuz to protect himself from the cold of the stones there.

This report indicates how Malik devoted himself to knowledge from an early age and sought it out from the people of knowledge in Madina. He confined himself to two areas of knowledge: *hadith* and *fiqh*. He did not like to argue about the reports of the various sects regarding matters about which people become confused and disagree. That was not due to any ignorance of their positions but was based on knowledge and clear evidence because he saw that delving into such things had no benefit.

According to *Tartib al-Madarik,* a Mu'tazilite critic said, "I came to Malik ibn Anas, and I asked him in the presence of the people about a question dealing with predestination. He indicated that I should be silent. When the assembly was over, he said to me, 'Ask now.' He did not want to answer me in the presence of other people.'" The Mu'tazilite stated that he asked him about every one of their positions and Malik refuted them all and established the falseness of their school. It can be seen from this that Malik did not teach all that he knew, but taught the best of what he knew.

He had various teachers among the *Tabi'un* in Madina. It was Ibn Hurmuz who taught him about the disagreements between people and how to refute the adherents of the various sects. He also went to Nafi', the client of Ibn 'Umar, and sat with him. Malik said, "I used to come to Nafi' for half of the day. As long as the tree shaded me from the sun, I would wait for him to come out. When he came out, I left him alone for a time as if I had not noticed him. Then I would turn to him and greet him and then leave him again until he entered the courtyard. Then I would say to him, 'What did Ibn 'Umar say about such-and-such?' and he would answer me. Then I would withdraw from him. He was prone to be a little irritable."

Malik also studied with Ibn Shihab az-Zuhri. It is related that he said, "Az-Zuhri visited us so we went to see him. Rabi'a was with us. He gave us about forty *hadiths*, and then we went to him again the following day. He said, 'Look for a book so I may give you *hadiths* from that. Do you think that you have retained any of the *hadiths* I gave you yesterday?' Rabi'a said to him, 'Here is someone who will repeat to you all the *hadiths* you gave him yesterday.' He said, 'Who is it?' He replied, 'Ibn Abi 'Amir.' He said, 'Go on.' Then I repeated the forty *hadiths* he had given us. Az-Zuhri then said, 'I did not think that there was anyone capable of memorising in this way except for me.'"

6

Malik was as eager to benefit from the transmission of az-Zuhri as he had been to benefit previously from the knowledge of Ibn Hurmuz and the knowledge of Nafi'. He went to his house to wait for him to come out, as he had gone to Nafi''s house in al-Baqi' at midday, to wait for him to come out. He went to him when he had finished his public teaching in order to learn in a calm atmosphere without the distraction of the group.

Malik said, "I was at the 'Id prayer and I said, 'This is the day on which Ibn Shihab retires,' so I left the place of the prayer and went and sat at his door. I heard him say to his slavegirl, 'Look and see who is at the door.' She looked and I heard her say, 'It is your ruddy-skinned friend, Malik.' He said, 'Bring him in,' so I went in. He remarked, 'I do not see you going to your home after the prayer.' I said, 'No.' 'Have you eaten anything?' he asked. 'No,' I replied. He said, 'Eat!' I replied, 'I have no need of it.' He asked, 'What do you want then?' I said, 'I want you to give me hadith.' He told me, 'Come on then!' So I brought out my slates and he gave me forty hadiths. I said to him, 'More!' He told me, 'That is enough for you. If you can relate these hadiths, you are one of the huffaz.' I said, 'I have memorised them.' He pulled the slates from my hand and then he said, 'Speak then!' so I related them and he repeated them to me. He said, 'Get up. You are one of the vessels of knowledge.'"

He mentioned that because of his desire for the hadiths of Ibn Shihab when he sat with him, he kept a thread with him. Whenever Ibn Shihab gave a hadith, Malik tied a knot in the thread to keep track of the number of hadiths he had learned.

From the time of his youth Malik showed great respect for the hadiths of the Messenger of Allah, may Allah bless him and grant him peace, and would only teach them in a state of calm and gravity out of respect for them and the desire to be precise in them. He would not teach them while standing or while he was anxious or agitated. We are told in al-Madarik, "Malik was asked whether he had listened to 'Amr ibn Dinar. He said, "I saw him giving hadith and the people were writing standing up. I did not like to write down a hadith of the Messenger of Allah, may Allah bless him and grant him peace, while standing." Another time Malik passed by

7

Abu'z-Zinad while he was relating *hadith* and he did not sit with him. He met him after that and asked, 'What kept you from sitting with me?' He said, 'The place was crowded and I did not want to take a *hadith* of the Messenger of Allah, may Allah bless him and grant him peace, while standing.'"

We mentioned these anecdotes about Malik's quest for *hadiths* and what has been said about his shaykhs in order to bring out three points. Firstly, at that time knowledge was taken by learning directly from the mouths of men and not from books in which knowledge was recorded. This is why the memory of students was so sharp: they were entirely dependent on it and were eager not to lose anything they heard. Malik kept track of the number of *hadiths* he learned by tying knots in a length of thread. If he forgot a *hadith*, he would return to hear it again. No reproach or rebuke would stop him, but even so he would only miss the odd one.

The second thing we learn is that scholars had begun to record their knowledge in writing, even if they did not rely on what was written. Ibn Shihab encouraged his students to write down what they heard, out of fear that they might forget it. Malik went to him with slates in hand on which he wrote down what he heard. That did not prevent him from memorising what he wrote. So when Ibn Shihab took away the slates he could repeat what was on them.

Thirdly, we gather from these extracts that Malik was tirelessly devoted to seeking knowledge and applied himself to it with an earnestness, energy and patience rarely emulated in the history of Islam. Undeterred by intense heat, he would leave his home and wait for the time when scholars left their houses for the mosque, and not even the irascibility of some of them prevented him from learning from them. He endured criticism for that at times but he kept at it until he managed to achieve his aim.

We should at this point elaborate on the different branches of knowledge that Malik studied in his pursuit of learning. He sought knowledge in four areas which are part and parcel of the formation of the complete scholar and *faqih* who knows the sources properly, who is able to derive rulings from them correctly, who is in touch with the spirit of his time and has true understanding of what is

8

happening around him, and has the ability to disseminate among people the knowledges which he thinks are beneficial for them.

Firstly he learned how to refute adherents of deviant sects and how to resolve people's disagreements and clarify their disputes in respect of *fiqh* and other matters. He studied that with Ibn Hurmuz, as he himself said. He took from him much knowledge which he did not spread publicly. But when there was an occasion where it was necessary to impart it, he did so.

It seems that Malik divided knowledge into two kinds: knowledge to be taught to people in general, which was not to be confined to anyone since there was no harm in it for anyone and all intellects could accept it and listen to it and benefit from it; and another kind of knowledge which should be reserved for the elite. He did not teach that kind to ordinary people because it would harm some people more than help them. This was the case with the refutation of the adherents of sects, which can be difficult for people and even cause some people to deviate themselves.

Secondly he learned the *fatwas* of the Companions from the *Tabi'un* and the *Tabi'i't-Tabi'in*[1]. He learned 'Umar's *fatwas* and those of Ibn Umar, 'A'isha and other Companions. He learned the *fatwas* of Ibn al-Musayyab and other great *Tabi'un*. Their *fatwas* are the source of much of Maliki *fiqh*.

Thirdly he learned *fiqh ar-ra'y* (understanding by mental perception) from Rabi'a ibn 'Abdi'r-Rahman who was known as Rabi'a ar-Ra'y. It is evident that the method he learned from Rabi'a was not the same as analogy. Its basis was harmonisation of different texts with the best interests of people and how they could best be benefited. That is why, according to *al-Madarik*, "Malik was asked whether they used to use analogy in the assembly of Rabi'a and discuss a lot with one another. He said, 'No, by Allah.'" From this we can see that Malik did not understand *fiqh ar-ra'y* as meaning opinion in which there is a lot of analogy and analysis because that might have led to involvement in the kind of hypothetical *fiqh* which was so common in Iraq and which resulted

---

1. The *Tabi'un* or 'Followers' are the generation after the Companions of the Prophet and the *Tabi'i't-Tabi'in* or 'Followers of the Followers' are the third generation.

from the excessive use of analogy. Rabi'a's basic principle was the best interests of the people.

Fourthly he learned the *hadiths* of the Messenger, may Allah bless him and grant him peace; he sought out all who transmitted the Messenger's words and selected the most reliable among them. He was given great insight into men's understanding and the power of their intellects. It is reported that he said, "This knowledge is vital to the *Deen,* so look to the one from whom you take it. I have met seventy people who said, 'The Messenger of Allah, may Allah bless him and grant him peace, said' within these pillars," and he pointed to the mosque, "and I did not take anything from them. Had any of them been entrusted with a treasure, they would have proved trustworthy, but they were not worthy to undertake this business."

Malik's sessions of teaching and giving legal rulings

After Malik completed his studies he took a place in the mosque of the Prophet to teach and give *fatwas.* There is no doubt that he used to sit in the place of those *Tabi'un* and their followers to whom people came from east and west. This must mean that he had both great knowledge and also the respect and esteem of the people and that made him the focus of students of *fiqh* and those who sought *fatwas* on many different subjects. This is why he said to clarify his position when he set up to teach and give *fatwa*: "No one who desires to sit in the mosque to teach *hadith* and *fatwa* can do so until he has consulted people of soundness and excellence and the people in charge of the mosque. Only when they consider him worthy of it may he sit there. I did not sit until seventy shaykhs of the people of knowledge had testified that I was ready to do so."

A man came to ask Malik about something and Ibn al-Qasim promptly gave him a *fatwa*. Malik turned on him with an angry expression and told him, "You dare to give *fatwa*, 'Abdu'r-Rahman? I did not give a *fatwa* until I had asked myself whether I was ready to do so." When his anger had abated, he was asked,

"Whom did you ask?" He replied, "Az-Zuhri and Rabi'a." There are sound reports that Malik did not think anyone should give *fatwa* until he was fully mature. He applied that to himself: he did not give *fatwa* until he was mature and seventy reliable men had testified to his readiness to do so.

The question arises how old he was when he began to give *fatwas*. There are no sound reports mentioning his age at that time and we must assume it to be the age of full manhood. No one reached the level of being able to give *fatwa* in the midst of those profound scholars before reaching manhood. It would not have been correct for a young boy, however great his reputation and intelligence, to sit to teach *hadith* and give *fatwa* in the Mosque of the Prophet, may Allah bless him and grant him peace, and in the midst of those great shaykhs who were teaching. But there are some partisan Malikis who insist on saying that he started teaching and giving *fatwa* when he was only seventeen years old, and it appears that they mean to make something miraculous of it.

As regards his age, they rely on a report ascribed to Sufyan ibn 'Uyayna who said: "A question passed around the assembly of Rabi'a. Malik was asked about it, and Rabi'a spoke some critical words. Malik left in anger and sat alone at the *Dhuhr* prayer and people sat with him. After *Maghrib* had been prayed, there were fifty or more gathered around him. In the morning there were many. He was seventeen at the time."

We do not accept this report. That is because no one of seventeen would have had the necessary importance to be able to carry that off. It is inconceivable that people would have left Ibn Shihab, Nafi' and others of their stature for a mere lad. Furthermore, we find various other things which refute this report.

It is mentioned that the reason that Malik sat to give *fatwa* was that he had left Rabi'a's assembly in anger although the sound transmissions say that before he sat to teach and give *fatwa* he had consulted his shaykhs, among whom he mentioned Ibn Shihab and Rabi'a. So Rabi'a was one of those who gave him permission to sit to give *fatwa*. This does not tally with the story that the reason he sat to give *fatwa* was that he became angry with Rabi'a. We think that he did leave Rabi'a but did not sit to give *fatwa* immediately.

That was not because of criticism but because of a disagreement between them; and he was not seventeen at the time.

There are sound traditions about his staying with Ibn Hurmuz for seven or eight years and then going to others for similar periods. The reason why Malik stayed with Ibn Hurmuz has already been mentioned: his father asked him a question which he was unable to answer correctly while his brother was right. It is unlikely that he would have been criticised for being wrong while under the age of ten. Thus he was at least ten when he went to study with Ibn Hurmuz, and he spent seven years with him so that his age at the end of that time would have been at least seventeen. So when did he study with his other shaykhs, since he said that he was with Ibn Hurmuz alone for seven years?

Sound transmissions state that he did not sit to give *fatwa* until after he had consulted seventy of his shaykhs. It is not reasonable to suppose that seventy shaykhs could have given an *ijaza* for *fatwa* and *hadith* of the Messenger of Allah, may Allah bless him and grant him peace, in the mosque of Madina to a lad of seventeen, unless there were miracles to support him. That may be why the people who say this added various miraculous events in their accounts of Malik's life.

Other sound transmissions mention that he was in Rabi'a's company when he first met Ibn Shihab, and that it was Rabi'a who told Malik to repeat by heart the *hadiths* he had heard from Ibn Shihab when he criticised him for not writing them down. There is no doubt at this stage that he had not yet sat to give *fatwa* because he had not learned the necessary number of *hadiths* to make him a *faqih* who was famous for his complete knowledge of tradition before he sat with Ibn Shihab; and there are many reports about how often he went to Ibn Shihab.

The reports that mention Malik teaching while Nafi' was still alive are unsure as to whether it is Nafi' or Rabi'a who is intended. Nafi' died in 117 and Rabi'a in 136. The transmission that he gave *fatwa* a year after Nafi''s death is more likely. So we do not know precisely at what age he first sat to teach. We can say that he was mature and that it was while Rabi'a was still alive. Rabi'a died in

136 and Malik was born probably in 93, so he would have been forty-three when he died. He was giving *fatwa* before that.

Malik did not continue to study with Rabi'a until his death. He left him because of a disagreement with him about certain opinions which he disliked in some of his *fatwas*. We read in the letter al-Layth wrote to Malik:

> There was a disagreement with Rabi'a about something which happened. I knew about it, being present, and heard what you said along with what was said by those qualified to give an opinion among the people of Madina: Yahya ibn Sa'id, 'Ubaydullah ibn 'Umar, Kathir ibn Farqad, and many others senior to Rabi'a. Eventually what you disliked in his assembly compelled you to leave it. I remember some of the criticism you and 'Abdu'l-'Aziz ibn 'Abdullah had about Rabi'a concerning that matter, and you two were among those who agreed about the same thing I disapproved of. You dislike what I dislike. In spite of that, Allah be praised, Rabi'a is an excellent man and has a fine intellect, an eloquent tongue, clear virtue, an excellent path in Islam, and true love for his brothers.[1]

This makes it clear that Malik left Rabi'a's assembly of because of a disagreement with him about something he related which was contrary to what one of the *Tabi'un* had passed down. It is not strange that Malik should have a separate teaching group during the lifetime of Rabi'a if both of them had a different opinions. But the main point is that Malik reached an appropriate age to teach and give *fatwa* during Rabi'a's lifetime.

Malik sat to teach, once he was mature and adult, in the Mosque of the Messenger of Allah, may Allah bless him and grant him peace, and gave *fatwa* there. Students of *hadith* related from him. He sat in the Mosque of the Prophet, in the seat where 'Umar ibn al-Khattab had sat for consultation and judgement. It is as though by choosing that spot, Malik were preferring 'Umar and

---

1. From the version of al-Layth's letter in *I'lam al-Muwaqqi'in* by Ibn al-Qayyim.

giving precedence to his *fatwas* which Ibn al-Musayyab and other *Tabi'un* related from him. It was as if the physical was inspired by the spiritual. The same might be said to have applied to the where place he lived, since he lived in the house of 'Abdullah ibn Mas'ud. According to one report, "The house in which Malik ibn Anas lived in Madina was the house of 'Abdullah ibn Mas'ud. His place in the Mosque was that of 'Umar ibn al-Khattab."

Malik lived surrounded by the traces of the *Tabi'un* and Companions, and he learned the *fatwas* of the Companions from the *Tabi'un* and singled out those whose opinions were best. He investigated the reports of 'Umar and Ibn Mas'ud and other *fuqaha'* of the Companions, studying their cases and rulings. He was eager to learn precedents in order to follow what had gone before and not to innovate. He thought that the actions, weights, measures, *waqfs* and reports of the people of Madina were sufficient to illuminate any *faqih* who followed their guidance and borrowed from their light.

According to most reports Malik ibn Anas died in the year 179. He had many students and his *fiqh* spread and wide and there are many stories about him. He did not stay teaching in the mosque for his entire life but moved his teaching circle to his house when he became ill with incontinence, as some of the transmitters mention. All agree that he was ill and for that reason moved from the mosque to his house and ceased going out to people. However, he did not cease studying, speaking, teaching and giving *fatwa*.

It is reported in *ad-Dibaj* that "Malik used to come to mosque and attend the prayers, *Jumu'a*, and funerals, visit the sick, and sit in the mosque; and his Companions would join him there. Then he ceased to sit in the mosque. He did not attend funerals but would go to his companions and console them. Then he ceased doing even those things. He did not attend the prayers in the mosque or go to *Jumu'a* or go to console anyone. But he continued to see people until he died." Most people agree that he died in 179, on the night of the 14th of Rabi' ath-Thani, at well over eighty years of age.

Malik's way of life and relationship with the rulers of the time

While discussing Malik's life, we must mention his livelihood, his studies and his relationship with the rulers of his time, his behaviour towards them and the difficulties he suffered at their hands. We will first discuss his livelihood. The books do not mention how Malik earned his living but there are various reports which shed light on it. Scholars have noted that his father made arrows. Did his son follow this craft, as often happens in many families? The books do not mention that he did so: in fact, they indicate otherwise.

There are many reports that he devoted himself completely to knowledge at an early age. That was not new in his family. His grandfather and uncles were noted transmitters of *hadith* and tradition. Since he turned to knowledge when young, it seems most unlikely that he became an arrow-maker.

We find that the books mention that Malik's brother an-Nadr traded in cloth and Malik became a partner with him and traded in it. There is nothing to prevent someone combining commerce and the quest for knowledge. An-Nadr himself was one of those interested in knowledge and seeking *hadith*. It seems likely that Malik earned some money from commerce and indeed that is explicitly stated in some books. Ibn al-Qasim, his student, said that Malik had four hundred dinars with which he traded to support himself.

This, then, was the probable source of Malik's basic livelihood. In addition to this, he accepted gifts from the khalifs. He had no doubt that it was lawful to accept such gifts, whereas Abu Hanifa, his contemporary, was unsure and did not accept gifts from khalifs. Although Malik did not refuse to take gifts from khalifs, he would not take from lesser officials. When asked about taking from khalifs, he said: "There is no harm in taking from the khalifs. There is some doubt about those under them."

Some people made much of his acceptance of these gifts. It is related that ar-Rashid allotted him 3000 dinars and he was asked, "Abu 'Abdullah! Do you take 3000 from the Amir al-Mu'minin?" Malik replied, "If it is the amount which he would have given if he had a just Imam who was equitable to the people of virtue, I do not see any harm in it." It is clear that he accepted it to preserve his manliness and to satisfy his needs and what his social position demanded to enable him to look after the requirements of poor students and satisfy the needs of the poor. He accepted the gifts of the khalifs with that intention. It is clear that his intention in doing this was entirely good. That was why he forbade others from accepting such gifts: out of the fear that they would not have the same intention. He was often asked about the gifts of the Sultan and he told the enquirer, "Do not take it." But you take it," people would object. He said, "Do you want to burden me with my wrong action and your wrong action?"

Early in his life as a teacher he was in great hardship, to the extent that his daughter sometimes wept out of hunger. He once admonished the khalif, al-Mansur, telling him to look into the circumstances of the people. Al-Mansur said to him, "Is it not the case that when your daughter weeps from hunger you make your servant move the millstone so that the neighbours will not hear her?" Malik said, "By Allah, no one knows this except Allah." Al-Mansur asked him, "Could I know this and not know the state of the people?"

It is clear that this hardship was the result of devoting himself to knowledge and neglecting his livelihood. This was so much the case that Ibn al-Qasim said, "The quest for knowledge compelled Malik to dismantle the roof of his house and sell the wood in it. Then later on this world inclined towards him." In both states he praised Allah for His blessings.

Qadi 'Iyad said, "There are many different stories which we have told and will tell about his different states in respect of this world. It varied with time and indeed states change, for the state of a man at the beginning of his life is different from his state at the end. Malik lived for nearly ninety years and was an Imam for some seventy of them who related *hadiths*, who gave *fatwa*, and whose words were listened to. His states changed continually and he acquired increasing majesty. He advanced every day in his excellence and leadership until his death. He was unique for years and obtained the leadership of the *Deen* and this world without dispute. Do not object then to any report you may hear about his different states. Allah is the One who gives success." (*ad-Dibaj*, p. 110.)

After Allah expanded his livelihood he lived a more comfortable life and the blessing showed on him in his food, dress and lodging. He said, "I do not like a man whom Allah has blessed not to show the effect of the blessing on him, especially the people of knowledge." He used to say, "I like it when a Qur'an reciter wears white garments."

As for his food, he did not eat the cheapest type of food. He sought the best without being extravagant. He ate a great deal of meat. Meat was cheap in the Hijaz and he was keen to eat two dirhams' worth of meat a day. He enjoyed food and liked to choose between its varieties. He liked bananas and said there was nothing closer to the fruit of Paradise than them.

He was concerned with his dress, preferring white, and used to wear new clothes. According to *Tartib al-Madarik*: "Malik used to wear good garments from Aden and Khorasan, and white Egyptian garments of fine quality. He put on fine scent and used to say, 'I do not like anyone to be given blessings by Allah and then not see the traces of His blessing on him, particularly on scholars.'"

In his home, he was concerned with its furniture and decoration and aimed for things that make for comfort, such as carpets and cushions on which to sit. Part of his concern for such things was to give ease and encourage tranquillity and to delight the eye and calm the mind. He liked perfume like musk and other scents.

Malik's Teaching

Malik taught first in the mosque and then later in his house and, as we have already heard, the reason for that move was the illness which he did not make public. When teaching Malik had gravity and tranquillity and was far from frivolity and any behaviour not fitting to knowledge. He did not think that frivolity should accompany the seeker of knowledge. It is related that he advised one of his nephews, saying, "It is a duty for anyone who seeks knowledge

17

to have gravity, tranquillity and fear. He should follow in the footsteps of those who have gone before. The people of knowledge should dispense with joking, particularly if they have some renown in knowledge."

He took strong account of himself so that he remained giving lessons and relating *hadiths* for more than fifty years. Not a single laugh is recounted from him in all this time, such were his gravity and fear throughout all those years. That was not due to any acerbity in himself or his nature. He forced himself to be serious out of respect for teaching and *hadith*. One of his students said, "When Malik was with us, it was as if he were one of us. He was cheerful with us in conversation and we had the greatest humility towards him. When he began the *hadith*, his words filled us with awe. It was as if he did not recognise us and we did not recognise him."

He had noble behaviour in all his scholarly states, whether he was giving *fatwa* or relating *hadiths*. When he taught *hadith*, he would always perform *wudu'* and prepare and put on his best garments and sit on the dais. One of his students said, "When people came to Malik, his slavegirl went out to them and said to them, 'The shaykh asks you, "Do you want *hadith* or do you have questions?"' If they said, 'Questions,' he would come out to them and give them *fatwas*. If they said, '*Hadith*,' he would tell them, 'Sit down,' and he went into the bathroom and performed a major ablution, he put on some scent and a turban on his head and a dais would be set out for him. He went out to them dressed and scented, full of humility. He burned aloes wood until he had finished relating the *hadiths* of the Messenger of Allah, may Allah bless him and grant him peace."

When he taught in the mosque, whoever wished could listen to him and no one would be expelled, even if he did not observe the proper behaviour in listening. When he was in his house, he first selected his companions for study and then after that he gave permission for the common people to come and he would relate to them. He related to each according to their ability.

People from every land came to visit him during the *Hajj* season, and so during the festival he commanded his doorman to give permission first to the people of Madina, then to all people, and sometimes, if there was a large crowd at his door, to people from particular areas by turn. Al-Hasan ibn ar-Rabi' says in *al-Madarik*, "I was at Malik's door, and a caller called out, 'Let the people of the Hijaz enter.' Only they entered. Then he called for the people of Syria, and then the people of Iraq. I was the last to enter. Hammad ibn Hanifa was among us."

There are two further important points to add when discussing Malik's knowledge. The first is that Imam Malik was concerned in his teaching only to talk about things that had actually happened and not to theorise about what had not happened. Sometimes his students tried to make him answer theoretical questions because their intellectual eagerness and desire to apply the basic principles moved them to go beyond actual events and into the realms of surmise and conjecture. Malik did not pay any attention to them. He stopped with real cases. Once man asked him about a theoretical situation and he replied, "Ask about what exists and leave what does not." Another asked him and he did not answer. He was told, "If you had asked him about something that would benefit you, he would have answered you."

His student Ibn al-Qasim said, "Malik used almost not answer us at all, and so his companions would resort to tricks. A man would present a question the answer to which they wanted to know as if it were a question of urgency, and he would answer it." He was wary on two counts: firstly, that people's tendency to hypothesise and theorise might lead them beyond the proper scope of thought and logic, which in turn might lead to opposing some traditions and giving *fatwa* without knowledge or authority from the Book or *Sunna*; and secondly because giving *fatwa* is a test and trial of the scholar whose only goal is to guide people in their actions.

In his *fatwas*, Malik was afraid of erring and so he gave few answers because he knew that this knowledge is the *deen* and it is not valid to speak about the *deen* without evidence. He would begin his answer by saying, "What Allah wills. There is no strength except by Allah." He often said, "I do not know." He would often follow a *fatwa* by stating, "This is simply an opinion and we are not certain."

19

Ibn Mahdi said, "A man asked Malik about a question and he mentioned that he had been sent for that purpose on a six-month journey from Morocco. Malik told him, 'Tell the one who sent you that I have no knowledge of it.' He said, 'Then who knows it?' He said, 'Whomever Allah has taught about it.'"

A man asked him about a question which the people of the Maghrib had entrusted to him. He said, "I do not know. We have not been tested with this matter in our land and have not heard any of our shaykhs speak about it, so you can go back." The next day the man came and he had loaded his baggage on a mule he was leading. He said, "My question?" Malik said, "I do not know. What is it?" The man said, Abu 'Abdullah! I have left behind me people who say that there is no one on the face of the earth with more knowledge than you!" Malik replied without any distaste, "When you return, tell them that I do not think that it is true."

The second thing is that it must be clarified whether or not his companions wrote down his *fatwas* and whether or not they recorded what he dictated them to them. There is no doubt that in his relating *hadith* Malik relied on what he had heard and written down from the transmitters who taught him. He wrote down the *hadiths* of the Messenger of Allah, may Allah bless him and grant him peace, listening without that weakening his memorisation of them. He both memorised and recorded them.

It is evident that in respect of *hadiths* he encouraged his companions to do what he had done. He wrote down *hadiths* and presented them to them. They were read to them in his presence and his student Habib would read the *hadith* back to him. If he erred in the reading, Malik stopped and corrected him. Writing down the *hadiths* and reading them back in this way was the best way to preserve them.

As for writing down his *fatwas*, it is clear from the collection of reports that survived that he used to encourage his students to write them down and did not prevent them from doing so. Sometimes he objected to them writing down everything he said.

Ibn al-Madini said, "I asked Yahya, 'Did Malik dictate to you?' He replied, 'I used to write in his presence.'" His student Mus'ab said, "Malik would see a man writing in his presence and he did

not forbid him but he did not answer him nor let him consult him."
This indicates his dislike for much of what his students wrote from
him. His student Ma'n said that he heard Malik say, "I am a man
who is sometimes right and sometimes wrong. Not all that I say
should be written down." Ashhab said, "He saw me write down his
answer to a question and he said, "Do not write it down. I do not
know whether I will remain firm in it or not."

So it is clear that Malik disliked his students' writing down all
that he said and did not want all his *fatwas* to be written down, for
fear that he might later retract some of them. When he gave a
fatwa about a question and was completely satisfied with it or followed it with a definitive text on it or a clear *hadith* confirming its
judgement he did not forbid it being written down. But when he
answered a question and was not sure of the absolute soundness of
the *fatwa*, he forbade that it be written down.

Malik's relationship with khalifs and governors

As Malik was born in 93/712 and died in 179/795, he saw both
Umayyad and Abbasid governments during the course of his life.
He was born in the reign of al-Walid ibn 'Abdu'l-Malik (86-
96/705-715) so he only experienced dynastic and hereditary rule.
He saw that those who rebelled against the government were no
more just than those they rebelled against and that rebellion
entailed chaos, loss of life, and injustice.

The khalifate of 'Umar ibn 'Abdu'l-'Aziz (99-101/717-720),
for whom Malik had great respect, coincided with his late childhood. Malik regarded him as a true example of good governance,
taking 'Umar ibn al-Khattab as his model. 'Umar ibn 'Abdi'l-Aziz
took care of people's rights and protected their honour, lives and
property. Unfortunately, his rule did not last long. The khalifs after
him did not behave so well and the community experienced hardships.

Malik saw those rulers; he also saw the rebellion of the
Kharijites and the uprising of the 'Alawites[1] and the damage which

1. This was the Shi'ite revolt against the Abbasid khalif, al-Mansur, in
762/145 in the Hijaz and Basra led by Muhammad the Pure Soul and his brother

that inflicted on the Muslim community without it resulting in any benefit or justice whatsoever. He learned from the mouths of his shaykhs who had witnessed past events; he heard accounts of the events from them and how after the Battle of Harra (63/683) Madina, the sanctuary of the Prophet, had been violated and the children of the Ansar humiliated and shackled in chains. This was a result of the civil war between Ibn az-Zubayr and 'Abdu'l-Malik and the battles in which the *Haram* of Allah was violated, the Ka'ba bombarded, and the whole Hijaz devastated.

That was why Malik did not think that people should revolt against their rulers, even if they were unjust, because the evils of civil war and unlawful shedding of blood were so much worse. In such cases, "the one who sits is better than the one who stands, and the one who stands is better than the one who runs," as Abu Musa al-Ash'ari reported from the Prophet, may Allah bless him and grant him peace.

When he was nearly forty years old he witnessed an uprising by the Kharijites in the Hijaz. Abu Hamza al-Khariji attacked while the *hajjis* were at 'Arafa and the Kharijites made a truce with the governor of Makka until the people had departed. A group of noble *hajjis* went to him which included Rabi'a ibn 'Abdu'r-Rahman, Malik's shaykh. They made a peace agreement. Then in 130/746 Abu Hamza entered Madina after a battle between him and the people of Madina and killed many of them, especially Qurayshites.

Through all the turmoil and upheavals, Malik clung to the community: he did not consider that people should cease obeying their ruler and did not move to rebellion nor did he abet it. Nor did he call people to support the governors and khalifs of the time. He sought to remain neutral and did not rally people to anyone when rebellion or unrest occurred. He did not think that the ruler was acting in accordance with the laws of Islam and the guidance of the Qur'an, but he was content with obedience because of the great good there was in it. At the same time he did not countenance wrongdoing on the part of the rulers, but his resistance to injustice

---

Ibrahim respectively. They were descendants of al-Hasan ibn 'Ali.

was achieved through admonition and speaking the truth. It was the task of the scholars to teach the people these things.

He was asked about fighting those who revolted against the khalif and he replied, "Only if they attack someone like 'Umar ibn 'Abdu'l-Aziz." "And if he is not like him?" came the response. "Leave them," Malik is said to have replied, "Allah will punish the unjust by means of the unjust and then take revenge on both of them." It is not clear which dynasty he was speaking about, but the Abbasids were ruling at that time.

Some of Malik's views on these matters were recorded for posterity. One of the 'Alawites asked him, "Who is the best of people after the Messenger of Allah, may Allah bless him and grant him peace?" He replied, "Abu Bakr." The 'Alawite said, "Then who?" Malik said, "Then 'Umar." The 'Alawite said, "Then who?" Malik replied, "The wrongfully slain khalif, 'Uthman." Mus'ab said that after he mentioned 'Uthman, he was asked, "Then who?" He replied, "People stop here. These are the best of the Companions of the Messenger of Allah, may Allah bless him and grant him peace. He put Abu Bakr in charge of the prayer and Abu Bakr chose 'Umar. 'Umar gave the choice to six men and they chose 'Uthman. Therefore people stop there." He added in one variant, "Someone who seeks leadership is not equal to someone who does not seek it."

From this it is clear that Malik placed Abu Bakr, 'Umar and 'Uthman at a higher rank than the other Companions and ranked 'Ali with the rest of the Companions. In that respect Malik differed from two other contemporary Imams, one older who died before him – Abu Hanifa – and one younger than him – his student ash-Shafi'i. Abu Hanifa did not consider 'Ali to be on the same level as the rest of the Companions but elevated him to the rank of the rightly-guided, advancing him in rank over 'Uthman. Ash-Shafi'i proclaimed his love for 'Ali and deemed that his opponents were rebels so much so that he was suspected of being a Shi'ite. Nevertheless he put Abu Bakr above 'Ali.

Why did Malik not give 'Ali this rank and stop at 'Uthman, saying, "After him people are equal" if 'Ali was not like the rest of the people? It was not that Malik was ignorant of 'Ali's personal

23

virtues, which he fully acknowledged, but he was responding to a question related to khalifate. There are a number of justifications for his answer, even if one may not agree with it. In his view, 'Ali sought the khalifate and so was not of the same rank as those who did not seek it. One transmission has, "Someone who seeks leadership is not like someone who does not seek it."

Further, the khalifate of Abu Bakr was by command of the Prophet, may Allah bless him and grant him peace, and the khalifate of 'Umar was the choice of Abu Bakr whom the Prophet had put in command. 'Uthman was chosen by the six to whom 'Umar delegated the duty of consultation. 'Ali was chosen by the murderers of 'Uthman; and hence his selection was not like that of his predecessors. Finally, Malik was a realist in his view of matters: he judged by actions and nothing else. The period of 'Ali as khalif was full of wars and disturbances, something which Malik hated.

Some of Malik's contemporaries remarked that he did not relate many *hadiths* from 'Ali and Ibn 'Abbas, and for that reason he was suspected of an Umayyad bias. He was asked about that and answered that he had not met their companions and so could not relate from them. He related from those who had met other Companions. The person who asked was Harun ar-Rashid. We find in the commentary on the *Muwatta'* by az-Zurqani: "Ar-Rashid said to Malik, 'We do not see either 'Ali or Ibn 'Abbas mentioned in your book.' He responded, 'They were not in my home town and I did not meet their transmitters.'"

'Ali ruled from Iraq during the last part of his life and he is buried there. Ibn 'Abbas had his school in Makka where he taught, concentrating on *tafsir*. This is why transmitters from 'Ali and Ibn 'Abbas were numerous in Iraq and Makka but few in Madina.

Malik was also one of those who did not delve into politics or rebellions and was disturbed by civil unrest. He accepted the gifts from khalifs. If he was inclined to the Umayyads, that did not move him to either word or deed in their favour.

Malik's ordeal at the hands of al-Mansur

Although Malik kept himself apart from all rebellions and any encouragement of them and from seditions and any involvement in them, he was nevertheless forced to undergo an ordeal in the Abbasid era, during the reign of al-Mansur. Historians agree that this took place and most say it was in 147/763. He was whipped during this ordeal and his arms were racked to the point that his shoulder became dislocated. There is disagreement about the reason for this event and three theories have been advanced as to why this outrage took place.

The weakest theory is that Malik openly stated his opposition to the Abbasids with regard to temporary marriage and stated that it was unlawful. This report is not reliable because the sources that mention it say that it took place in Baghdad and it is not known that Malik ever left the Hijaz. It is also weak because all scholars except for the Shi'ites agree that temporary marriage is invalid.

The second theory mentioned by historians is that Malik preferred 'Uthman over 'Ali and people reported him to the governor of Madina for doing so. This is found in the text of *Tartib al-Madarik,* which states: "Ibn Bukayr said, 'Malik was flogged purely because he preferred 'Uthman over 'Ali. The Talibites did give up until he was flogged.'" It was said to Ibn Bukayr, "You differ from your companions. They say it was about the allegiance." He replied, "I know better than my companions." It is unlikely that al-Mansur would have punished a *faqih* for a *fatwa* of this nature at that time.

The third well-known theory is that the punishment meted out to Malik was on account of his recounting the *hadith,* "There is no divorce for anyone who is compelled." People involved in the rebellion are supposed to have taken this as proof of the invalidity of oaths of allegiance made to al-Mansur under duress. This happened at the time the rebellion was in progress. Al-Mansur forbade Malik to relate it and then someone enticed him into relating it and so he was beaten. It is also related that he gave a *fatwa* about giving allegiance to Muhammad ibn 'Abdullah (the Pure Soul).

It seems most likely that he was in fact flogged for relating this *hadith* at the time of the rebellion in Madina, though he did not do so for the reason attributed to him. We believe that he related it and people transmitted it from him and others found that they could use it to throw off their allegiance to al-Mansur by claiming that it was only given under duress. Ibn 'Abdu'l-Barr said, "Malik was summoned, consulted, listened to, and his statement accepted and people objected to him and envied him. When Ja'far ibn Sulayman was appointed over Madina, they spoke to him a lot about Malik and said, 'He thinks nothing of oaths of allegiance made to you. He accepts the *hadith* related from Thabit ibn al-Ahnaf about forced divorces not being allowed...'"

This indicates the existence of schemers depicting Malik as a rebel by relating this *hadith*. So it seems likely that the reason for his punishment was that he related this *hadith* at a time of civil unrest and the rebels used it to encourage people to go out, exploiting the position of Malik in knowledge and *fatwa*. This understanding agrees with the statement of the majority and is also consistent with what is known of Malik throughout his life. He did not encourage rebellion nor did he conceal knowledge.

To sum up, after consulting various sources, the reason for the ordeal was his recounting that particular *hadith* at the time of the rebellion while certain people were working against him. How did it happen? Many transmitters say that it came from the governor of Madina, Ja'far ibn Sulayman. The question is whether al-Mansur had a hand in it or not. Sources, including *Tartib al-Madarik*, indicate that the governor did it without the knowledge of al-Mansur because it happened after the sedition had occurred.

It is clear that when the people of Madina saw their Imam subjected to this punishment they were incensed against the Abbasids and their governors, especially since it was unjust. Malik had not encouraged sedition or rebellion nor had he exceeded the limits of *fatwa,* and he did not alter his course before or after the injury was inflicted. He continued to teach and did not encourage unrest. That increased the people's rancour against their rulers. The rulers began to regret what they had done, especially al-Mansur. A favourable opportunity to make amends transpired when the khalif came to the Hijaz on *hajj*. He went to Malik to apologise. The event was reported by Malik:

> When I came to Abu Ja'far (al-Mansur), and he obliged me to come to him at the Festival, he said to me, 'By Allah, there is no god but Him, I did not desire what happened nor did I know of it. The people of the two *Harams* (Makka and Madina) will continue to profit so long as you are among them. I believe that you are a security for them from the punishment of Allah and that Allah has lifted a terrible blow from them because of you. They are the swiftest of people to rebel and I have commanded the enemy of Allah (the governor who ordered the punishment) to be brought from Madina to Iraq on a pack-saddle. I have ordered him to be imprisoned and humiliated. I must give him a punishment many times more than what you received from him!' I said, 'May Allah preserve the Amir al-Mu'minin and increase his reward! I declared him free of responsibility for what happened and have said to him that I have pardoned him for it because of his kinship with the Messenger of Allah, may Allah bless him and grant him peace.' He said to me, 'And you, may Allah pardon you and your relations.'"

Malik's admonition and counsel to the khalifs

Malik did not think that the khalifs of his time were ruling according to the laws of Islam; but nor did he think that it was permissible to remove them by force, because the result of civil strife was inevitably corruption and disorder. He therefore considered it his duty to guide the khalifs and reform them because he was a man who looked at actual facts. Perhaps they would be moved to right guidance.

That is why he used to visit amirs and khalifs and admonish them and guide them to the good. He used to say, "It is a duty for every Muslim (or man) in whose breast Allah has put any knowledge and *fiqh* to go to those with power to command them to do

27

what is right and forbid them from doing what is wrong so that the station of a man of knowledge will be clear to others. If that is the case, then it is an excellence which is unsurpassed."

One of his students said to him: "People keep saying that you visit the rulers." He said, "That is a burden on myself. I do it because otherwise he might consult those whom he should not consult." He took it on himself to go to them to order what is the right and forbid the wrong, and to guide them. He said, "If I had not gone to them, you would not see any *Sunna* of the Prophet, may Allah bless him and grant him peace, acted upon in this city."

He used to admonish the khalifs when they came to the Hijaz during *hajj*. One example is what he said to Harun ar-Rashid: "It has been reported to me that 'Umar ibn al-Khattab, in spite of his excellence and position, would blow for people on the ashes of the fire under the pots until smoke came from his beard. People are pleased with you doing less than that."

Malik told one of the governors, "Investigate the affairs of the people. You are responsible for them. 'Umar ibn al-Khattab said, 'By the One in whose hand is my soul, if a camel had died from neglect on the banks of the Euphrates, I would think that I should be questioned about it on the Day of Rising'."

Respect was shown to Malik by them. When the khalif al-Mahdi came to Madina, people came to him to pledge allegiance to him. When they took their places, Malik asked for permission to enter and people said, "Today Malik will sit at the far end of the gathering." When he came near and looked at the crowd of people, he said "Amir al-Mu'minin, where shall your shaykh, Malik, sit?" He called to him, "With me, Abu 'Abdullah!" The people moved aside so that he was able to reach him and al-Mahdi lifted his right knee and made him sit down next to him."

Malik did not confine his advice to speaking but also wrote letters to rulers. He said in one of them:

> Know that Allah Almighty has singled you out for my warning to you by what good counsel I have given you previously. In it I have explained for you what I hope Allah will make a means of happiness for you and a matter which He will make your path to Him in Paradise. There-

fore – may Allah have mercy on us and you! – it lies in what I have written to you about establishing the command of Allah and what Allah has said about being responsible for His flock. According to a *hadith,* 'Guardians will be brought with their hands tied to their necks. Only justice will set them free.'

'Umar ibn al-Khattab, may Allah be pleased with him, said, 'By Allah, if a lamb died on the bank of the Euphrates, I would think that Allah Almighty would ask 'Umar about it.' He went on *hajj* for ten years, and I am told that he only spent twelve dinars on his *hajj*. He would alight in the shade of a tree and carry his whip on his neck and go around in the markets to inquire about the news of those who were present and absent (from Madina).

We are told that when he was struck down, those Companions of the Prophet, may Allah bless him and grant him peace, who were present praised him. He said to them, 'Deceived is the one who deceives. If I had any gold on the face on the earth, I would give it in ransom for the terror of what is coming.'

'Umar, may Allah have mercy on him, was insistent on being corrected – even though the Prophet, may Allah bless him and grant him peace, had testified that he was one of the people of the Garden. In spite of that, he was fearful since he had taken the affairs of the Muslims upon himself. So then how is it with what you know? You must pay attention to what will bring you near to Allah and what will rescue you from Him tomorrow. Beware of a Day when only your actions will save you. You have an example in those who passed away before you. You must show fear of Allah. Make it your first consideration and read what I have written to you in all your moments. Make yourself take on its responsibilities and assume them. Model your *adab* on it and ask Allah for success and right guidance if Allah Almighty wills.

One of the things Malik feared for rulers was flattery and syco-phancy which would make their actions seem good to them. He became angry with those who praised rulers in their presence. Thus it is related that once in Malik's presence someone praised the governor. Malik became angry and said, "Beware lest these people beguile you through their praise of you. Whoever praises you and says good about you which is not in you is just as likely to say evil about you which is not in you. Be on your guard about claiming for yourself or being pleased with what one of them says to your face. You know yourself better than they do. I have heard that a man praised another man in the presence of the Prophet and the Prophet said to him, 'You have cut his back' or 'his neck'. If he had heard it, he would not have prospered. The Prophet said, 'Throw dirt in the faces of people who praise too much.'"

Malik's Great Knowledge

We have given a brief outline of the life of Malik ibn Anas and mentioned some of the difficulties he encountered. Now we must examine Malik's knowledge and sources in more detail and from that we will see how great his knowledge was. Malik reached the pinnacle of knowledge and *fiqh* to the extent that he was known as the Unique *Faqih* of the Hijaz, which region was, after all, the source of all knowledge of Islam.

His knowledge covered both *hadith* and *fiqh* and he was an Imam of hadith transmitters. He is considered the first recorder of the science of *hadith*, and his book *al-Muwatta'* was the first sound collection of *hadith*. Malik was a perceptive *faqih* and his *fiqh* was devoted to clarifying the pure and ensuring people's best interests. Thus he takes account of both the spiritual and the worldly, using the criterion of *masalih mursala* (considerations of public interest), which he considered to be one of the basic principles of *fiqh*.

He was praised by all the scholars of his time – the *fuqaha'* of opinion as well as the scholars of *hadith*. His contemporary, Sufyan ibn 'Uyayna, said, "May Allah have mercy on Malik. He was exceedingly careful in the way he selected narrators." He also said, "We used to follow in Malik's footsteps. When Malik used a shaykh as a source, we would also do so. He only conveyed sound *hadiths* and only related from reliable men. I think that Madina will disintegrate after Malik goes."

Ash-Shafi'i said, "When a tradition comes to you from Malik, hold on to it tightly. When a tradition comes to you from him know that Malik is the star. When scholars are mentioned know that Malik is the star. No one reached the level that Malik did in knowledge through his memory, his proficiency and his scrupulousness. Whoever wants sound *hadith* must have Malik."

31

Ahmad ibn Hanbal said, "Malik is the master of the masters of knowledge, and he is their Imam in *hadith* and *fiqh*."

Malik's character

He was utterly sincere in his quest for knowledge and sought it for the sake of Allah alone, not desiring elevation, pride or reputation. Sincerity is a light which shines in the soul and illuminates reflection. It is reported that he used to say, "Knowledge is a light which can only reside in a godfearing heart." Sincerity and abandoning the pleasures and appetites of this world illuminate the path for the seeker of knowledge so he used to say, "No one makes do with little in this world without Allah making him speak with wisdom." He said to his student Ibn Wahb, "If you desire to gain what is with Allah by your quest, then you have obtained what will benefit you. If you desire to gain this world by your learning, your hands will remain empty."

His sincerity in the quest for knowledge made him cling to certain things and remain aloof from others. He clung to the *Sunna* and clear matters. He used to say, "The best of matters are those which are clear and evident. If you are unsure about two things, take the more reliable." He continued to give *fatwas* about questions without imposing them on people, out of the fear of misleading them from the *Sunna* of the Messenger of Allah, may Allah bless him and grant him peace, and making things difficult for people. He always thought deeply about a judicial decision and did not rush to give it.

He remarked to his student Ibn al-Qasim, "I have been reflecting on one question for some twenty years and even now I do not have an opinion on it." Ibn 'Abdu'l-Hakam said: "When Malik was asked about a question, he told the asker, "Go away so that I can look into it." The man would go away and come back again several times about it. We spoke to him about that. He wept and said, "I fear that I will be asked such questions on a Day – and what a Day!" Malik was asked about something and the asker said, "It is a simple matter." Malik got angry and said, "A light, simple question! There is nothing light in knowledge! Have you not heard the words of Allah, *'We will cast a weighty word on you"*? (73: 5) All knowledge is weighty and especially what we will be asked about on the Day of Rising."

Because of his sincerity towards the Book and the *Sunna*, Malik was very careful about declaring anything lawful or unlawful without an explicit text to that effect. If his opinion was not based on an explicit text in the Book or the *Sunna*, he would make it clear that it was simply his opinion and would not make the thing categorically unlawful. He would often say afterwards, "It is only an opinion and we are not certain."

In doing this he was following the *Salaf*, as he himself made clear:

> Nothing is harder for me than when I am asked a question about the *halal* and the *haram* because this is absolute in the judgement of Allah. I met the people of knowledge and *fiqh* in our land and if one of them was asked such a question, it was as if death were dearer to him. But I see the people of this time desiring to discuss it and give *fatwa*. If they had understood what it is that they are heading for Tomorrow, they would have done little of this. As for 'Umar ibn al-Khattab, 'Ali and 'Alqama, the best of the Companions, and the best generation to whom the Prophet, may Allah bless him and grant him peace, was sent, when questions came to them, they would gather together the Companions of the Prophet, may Allah bless him and grant him peace, and ask. Then and only then would they give a *fatwa* on it.
>
> The people of our time now pride themselves in their *fatwas* and the knowledge they have. It was not the way of the people nor of those who passed away before us who are followed and on whom Islam is based to say, 'This is *halal* and this is *haram*': they would say, 'I dislike this' and 'I think this.' But as for the *halal* and the *haram*, that is inventing things against Allah. I have heard the words of Allah: *"Say: 'Tell me, what do you think about the*

33

*things Allah has sent down to you as provision and which
you have then designated as lawful and unlawful?'"*
(10:59) because the *halal* is what Allah and His
Messenger have made *halal* and the *haram* is what they
have made *haram*." (*Tartib al-Madarik*, p. 158)

Malik's sincerity often led him to say "I do not know" when he
was asked for a *fatwa*. He was famous for that. He would be asked
about twenty matters and would only answer two of them and
announce that he did not know the rest. This did not arise from any
lack of ability on his part, as some people suspect, but he would
say "I do not know" when he did not want to make something public or did not find anything about the matter from the Companions.
His reluctance was due to his intense fear of Allah.

This sincerity also led him to eschew argument and debate,
because that is a form of conflict and the *Deen* of Allah is too
exalted to be the subject of conflict. Conflict also often leads people to fanaticism. He did not consider that argumentation befitted
the nobility of people of knowledge. When Abu Yusuf asked ar-
Rashid to command Malik to debate with him Malik replied,
"Knowledge is not like baiting beasts and cocks."

He forbade arguing about the *Deen*. He said, "Quarrelling and
argument in matters of knowledge remove the light of belief from
the heart," and "Disputation hardens people's hearts and brings
about rancour." Az-Zuhri said, "I saw Malik when some people
were arguing in his presence. He got up and changed his cloak,
saying, 'You are war.'" Malik was asked, "Should a man with
knowledge of the *Sunna* argue about it?" He said, "No. He should
inform people about the *Sunna* if they will accept it from him.
Otherwise he should remain silent." This does not preclude active
discussion of matters of *fiqh* for the sake of discovering the truth
but it does exclude debate for the sake of debate.

He also did not answer questions about judgements (*qada'*) that
had been made. Ibn Wahb said, "When he was asked about a question of judgement, he said, 'This is part of the property of the
Sultan.' I heard him criticise a scholar for giving too many
answers since it would expose the judgements to criticism or

scrutiny." In this he differed from the approach of Abu Hanifa who insisted on scrutinising judgements. This was out of Malik's desire to avoid anything that might lead to rebellion.

Another of Malik's gifts was that of insight into the heart of things and into people's selves, so that he knew what they were like from the way they moved and the timbre of their voices. This knowledge, called *firasa* in Arabic, has to do with impressions, the penetration of insight, and careful attention to outward movements and how they are connected to psychological traits.

He also inspired respect and awe in people. Sa'id ibn Abi Hind said, "I was never in awe of anyone in the way I was in awe of 'Abdu'r-Rahman ibn Mu'awiya – meaning the Sultan of Andalusia – until I went on *hajj* and met Malik. He filled me with an intense awe which made my awe of Mu'awiya's son seem insignificant." Sometimes this feeling was so intense that even his students could not put questions to him. Ibn Wahb said, "I came to Madina and people asked me to question Malik about hermaphrodites. They gathered around him and I was supposed to ask on their behalf. I was too awed to ask him and all who were in the assembly were too awed to ask the question." Ash-Shafi'i said, "I have never been in awe of anyone as I was of Malik ibn Anas."

Madina

There are reliable reports that the Messenger of Allah, may Allah bless him and grant him peace, said, "The time is fast approaching when people will urge on their animals in quest of knowledge. They will not find a man with more knowledge than the scholar of Madina." This is clear evidence of the excellence of the knowledge existing in Madina and the distinction and extensive knowledge of its scholars. There were none who knew the *Sunna* of the Messenger of Allah, may Allah bless him and grant him peace, better than the scholars of Madina.

The excellence of Madina in the time of the Companions and the Followers and those after them is something which no one can deny. Madina was the place to which the Messenger of Allah emigrated and where the *Shari'a* of Islam was revealed, and in Madina the basis of rule was the Law of Allah Almighty. All the laws except for those pertaining to faith and to the prayer were revealed in Madina; and the *Sunna* of the Messenger of Allah was actualised there in judging by the Qur'an, clarifying it and explaining it and proclaiming its ordinances to people.

When the Prophet died, may Allah bless him and grant him peace, Madina was the capital of Islamic governance and the site of the Khalifate and in it the understanding of the Companions was made manifest. It is there that judgements were arrived at on many social questions after the early conquests. 'Umar ibn al-Khattab kept most of the *fuqaha'* of the Companions near him in Madina to consult them and ask for their opinions. They comprised his consultative assembly. When he was murdered and the khalifate passed to 'Uthman, he allowed the Companions whom 'Umar had kept in Madina to travel to the conquered areas and they were a light and a source of knowledge there.

Malik grew up in this environment and he studied with about one hundred shaykhs. He studied with people as long as they were trustworthy and scrupulous and critical about those from whom they had taken knowledge. Thus it is reported that he took from Ja'far as-Sadiq even though he knew that he was approved of by the Shi'ites, with whose Path he disagreed. Malik said, "I used to frequent him for a time. I only saw him doing three things: praying, fasting or reciting Qur'an. I never saw him relate from the Messenger of Allah, may Allah bless him and grant him peace, except in a state of purity, or speak about what did not concern him. He was one of the men of knowledge, worship and *zuhd* who feared Allah and I never came to him without him removing the cushion he was sitting on and giving it to me to sit on."

Malik was particularly eager to learn about the *fatwas* of 'Umar. The period of his khalifate was the time in which Islam flourished and expanded and many conquests took place. He was also keen on the *fatwas* of Zayd ibn Thabit and 'Abdullah ibn 'Umar. One of the scholars of tradition said, "The Imam of the people with us after 'Umar ibn al-Khattab was Zayd ibn Thabit, and the Imam of the people after Zayd ibn Thabit was 'Abdullah ibn 'Umar. Twenty-one men took from Zayd. Then the knowledge of all these went to three men: Ibn Shihab, Bukayr ibn 'Abdullah ibn al-Ashajj, and Abu'z-Zinad. Then the knowledge of all these went to Malik ibn Anas."

As we have already stated, Malik's main teachers were five: Ibn Hurmuz, Abu'z-Zinad, Yahya ibn Sa'id al-Ansari, Rabi'a, and Ibn Shihab. We can add a sixth to these: Nafi', the client of 'Abdullah ibn 'Umar. These men are all described as having knowledge of *hadith* and the traditions of the Followers. Of course, they varied in this. Some were more concerned with *hadith* and traditions, like Nafi', Abu'z-Zinad and Ibn Shihab az-Zuhri. Some were more interested in *fiqh*, like Rabi'a ar-Ra'y and Yahya ibn Sa'id. Thus he had two categories of shaykhs, one being the source of his *fiqh* and investigation and the other the source of his *hadith*.

As an illustration of Malik's great esteem for Madina and its learning, we have his letter to al-Layth ibn Sa'd:

From Malik ibn Anas to al-Layth ibn Sa'd. Peace be upon you. I praise Allah to you. There is no god but He. As for what follows: may Allah hold us and you to His obedience both secretly and openly and preserve us and you from every disliked thing! Know, may Allah have mercy on you, that I have been informed that you give people *fatwas* which are contrary to what is done by our community and in our city. You are Imam and have importance and position with the people of your city and they need you and rely on what they get from you. Therefore you ought to fear for yourself and follow that whose pursuit you hope will bring you salvation.

Allah Almighty says in His Mighty Book, '*The out-strippers, the first of the Muhajirun and the Ansar.*' (9:100) Allah Almighty further says, "*So give good news to My slaves, those who listen well to what is said and then follow the best of it.*' (39:18) It is essential to follow the People of Madina. The *Hijra* was made to it, the Qur'an was sent down in it, and the *halal* was made *halal* and the *haram* was made *haram* there. The Messenger of Allah was among them and they were present when the Revelation was revealed. He commanded them and they obeyed him. He made the *Sunna* for them and they followed it until Allah caused him to die and chose for him what is with Him. May the blessings of Allah and His mercy and blessing be upon him.

Then after his death, the Muslims followed those from among his community who were given authority after him. When something happened to them that they knew how to deal with, they carried it out. If they had no knowledge on the subject, they asked about it and then they followed the most best line that they could deduce by *ijtihad*. In this they were helped by having been until recently in personal contact (with the Prophet). If someone opposed them or proposed an alternative view which was stronger and better than the ruling they had made , they left the former and acted upon the latter.

Then the *Tabi'un* after them travelled this Path and followed those *sunan*. If there is a practice which is clearly acted upon in Madina, I do not think that anyone may oppose it because of the inheritance they had received which no one is allowed to plagiarise or lay claim to. If the people of other cities were to say, 'This is the practice in our city,' and 'This is what those before us used to do,' that would not be permissible for them.[1]

Investigate for yourself, may Allah have mercy on you, what I have written to you. Know that I hope that what has impelled me to write this for you was only good counsel for the sake of Allah alone. Investigation is up to you and your opinion is up to you. Put my letter to you in that position. If you do that, you will know that I have not neglected to give you good counsel. May Allah give us and you success in obeying Him and obeying His Messenger in every matter and in every state. Peace be upon you and the mercy and blessing of Allah.

Al-Layth replied at length to this letter and some of his reply follows here:

"Peace be upon you. I praise Allah to you. There is no god but Him...

It has reached you that I have given *fatwas* different from those your community agrees on and that I must fear for myself because those near me rely on my *fatwas,* whereas people should follow the people of Madina to which the *Hijra* was made and where the Qur'an was revealed. You are correct in what you wrote about that, Allah willing, and it came to me in a way which I do not dislike. No one is more strongly inclined than I am to prefer the knowledge of the people of Madina who have passed away and no one acknowledges their *fatwas* more readily than I do. Praise be to Allah, the Lord of the worlds, who has no partner.

---

1. Here Malik is pointing out the authoritative nature of the practice (*'amal*) of Madina as a source of law. See page 101.

As for what you mentioned about the Messenger of Allah, may Allah bless him and grant him peace, residing in Madina, the Qur'an being sent down to him among the Companions and what Allah taught them from him and that people became their followers, it is as you have stated.

As for what you mentioned from the words of the Almighty, *'The Outstrippers, the first of the Muhajirun and the Ansar, and those who have followed them in doing good: Allah is pleased with them and they are pleased with Him. He has prepared Gardens for them with rivers flowing under them, remaining in them timelessly, forever without end. That is the great triumph,'* (9:100) many of those Outstrippers went out to do *jihad* in the Way of Allah, seeking Allah's pleasure, and they formed military garrisons and people flocked to them. They made known the Book of Allah and the *Sunna* of His Prophet and they did not conceal anything that they knew.

There were some in every group who taught the Book of Allah and the *Sunna* of the Prophet and exercised *ijtihad* in respect of anything which the Book and *Sunna* did not explain to them. They were headed by Abu Bakr, 'Umar and 'Uthman, whom the Muslims chose for themselves. These three did not neglect the armies, nor were they heedless of them. They wrote what was necessary to establish the *Deen* and warned against disagreement about the Book of Allah and the *Sunna* of His Prophet. They did not abandon any command explained by the Qur'an or carried out by the Prophet, may Allah bless him and grant him peace: they taught it and made it understood. When a command came, the Companions of the Messenger of Allah acted on it in Egypt, Syria and Iraq in the time of Abu Bakr, 'Umar and 'Uthman, and continued to do so until they died.

However, the Companions of the Messenger of Allah, may Allah bless him and grant him peace, disagreed in their *fatwas* about many things, as you well know. Then the Followers disagreed strongly about things after the

Companions of Messenger of Allah: Sa'id ibn al-Musayyab and people like him. Then those after them disagreed and they are present today in Madina. Their leaders are Ibn Shihab and Rabi'a ibn Abi 'Abdu'r-Rahman.

You know and were present when Rabi'a disagreed with some of what happened. I heard what you said about it and what was said by those of people among the people of Madina – Yahya ibn Sa'id, 'Ubaydullah ibn 'Umar, Kathir ibn Farqad, and many others older than him – until it reached the point where you were compelled to part from him because of what you disliked in what he said. Nonetheless, there is much good in Rabi'a.

Ibn Shihab issued several varying statements which were sometimes contradictory. This is what led me to abandon what you object to my abandoning...

These two letters illustrate the discussion on the question which Malik made one of the fundamental principles of his method: that of the Practice of the People of Madina. Malik holds to it in his letter and al-Layth disagrees because of the dispersal of the Companions of the Messenger of Allah, may Allah bless him and grant him peace, to other cities. Nonetheless, both showed the utmost respect and courtesy towards one another.

'Umar ibn 'Abdu'l-'Aziz said, "Islam has limits and laws and *sunan*. Whoever acts according to them has complete faith. Whoever does not act according to them does not have complete faith. If I live, I will teach them to you and make you implement them. If I die, I am not eager for your company." In the course of that teaching that just leader followed two paths, both of which began with the guidance he found in Madina.

Firstly he commanded the scholars of Madina to disperse throughout the lands of Islam to instruct and guide people. They clarified for them the limits and laws of Islam, and the *fiqh* of Madina was disseminated in this way. Right guidance became widespread through them. It is perhaps those Followers who were sent from Madina who made the Muslims in North Africa love the knowledge of Madina so that only Malik was followed when his *madhhab* was founded, Madina being the source of its knowledge.

Secondly 'Umar ibn 'Abdu'l-'Aziz commanded that the well-known *sunan* of Madina be written down and he wrote to its qadi, Abu Bakr ibn Hazm, asking him to record them. According to the *Muwatta'* 'Umar ibn 'Abdu'l-'Aziz wrote to Abu Bakr ibn Hazm, "See what *hadiths* or *sunan* of the Messenger of Allah, may Allah bless him and grant him peace, you have and record them for me. I fear that knowledge may become extinct and men of knowledge disappear."

It is not correct to say that *fiqh* and the *Sunna* were only to be found in Madina. The Companions of the Messenger of Allah, may Allah bless him and grant him peace, dispersed to the various cities. Wherever they settled, they were a source of light and knowledge. But Madina had the lion's share. There were the greatest number of Companions and Followers there as well as clear guides to the Islamic *Shari'a* and its methods. Naming those among the Companions and their students who gave *fatwa*, Ibn al-Qayyim said, "The *Deen* and *fiqh* spread in the Community from the followers of Ibn Mas'ud, the followers of Zayd ibn Thabit and Ibn 'Umar, and the followers of 'Abdullah ibn 'Abbas. People's knowledge, on the whole, came from those four. The knowledge of people of Madina came from the followers of Zayd ibn Thabit and 'Abdullah ibn 'Umar; the knowledge of the people of Makka came from the followers of 'Abdullah ibn 'Abbas; and the knowledge of the people of Iraq came from the followers of 'Abdullah ibn Mas'ud."

Ibn al-Qayyim quoted at-Tabari as follows: "It is said that Ibn 'Umar and a group of those after him in Madina among the Companions of the Messenger of Allah, may Allah bless him and grant him peace gave *fatwa* according to the school of Zayd ibn Thabit and what they had learned through him from those who had learned it from the Messenger of Allah, may Allah bless him and grant him peace." (*I'lam al-Muwaqqi'in*, vol. 1, p. 16)

In fact this is a vast underestimate and there were, of course, many Companions besides those mentioned above who were responsible for passing on the rulings of the *Deen*, most of whom remained in Madina. 'Umar, may Allah be pleased with him, was one of the most learned of the Companions of the Messenger of Allah, if not the most learned. Mujahid said, "When people disagreed about something, they looked to see what 'Umar had done and they followed that." Ibn al-Musayyab said, "I do not know of anyone with more knowledge, after the Messenger of Allah, than 'Umar ibn al-Khattab."

'Uthman ibn 'Affan gave *fatwas* and judgements. 'Ali gave *fatwas* and judgements. 'A'isha gave *fatwas* and was prominent in knowledge. Al-Qasim, the son of her brother, Muhammad ibn Abi Bakr, took from her as did 'Urwa ibn az-Zubayr, the son of her sister Asma'.

It is true that the followers of the four whom we mentioned related the *fiqh* of those four and transmitted with it the *fiqh* of many of the other Companions, may Allah be pleased with them. 'Abdullah ibn 'Umar transmitted the *fiqh* of his father. The followers of Ibn Mas'ud in Kufa transmitted the *fiqh* of 'Ali ibn Abi Talib as well as Ibn Mas'ud's opinions. It is true that Ibn Mas'ud, Ibn 'Umar and Zayd ibn Thabit all took from 'Umar and they shared with him in many of his opinions and judgements.

'Umar, may Allah be pleased with him, acted according to his opinion – or his opinion coincided with that of many of the Companions in his time and those who were especially part of his consultative council, such as 'Ali, Zayd, Ibn Mas'ud, Ibn 'Abbas and other exalted Companions. Whoever related the *fiqh* of 'Umar related the *fiqh* of the people with him. The transmitters of the *fiqh* of 'Umar in Madina were his son and Zayd and others.

They transmitted that *fiqh,* made deductions based on it, and followed 'Umar in his methods of deduction. Scholars particularly mention seven *fuqaha'* of Madina and state that they were the Followers whose renown was famous and who transmitted the knowledge of Zayd, 'Umar, Ibn 'Umar and 'A'isha. They were: Sa'id ibn al-Musayyab, 'Urwa ibn az-Zubayr, al-Qasim ibn Muhammad, Kharija ibn Zayd, Abu Bakr ibn 'Ubayd ibn 'Abdu'r-Rahman, Sulayman ibn Yasar, and 'Ubaydullah ibn 'Abdullah. Malik considered the seven *fuqaha'* to include Salim and Abu Salama, and not Abu Bakr ibn 'Ubayd or 'Ubaydullah ibn 'Abdullah. Some did not include Sulayman ibn Yasar.

The fact is that it is not possible to enumerate the seven *Tabi'un* who transmitted the *fiqh* of the Companions and be correct from all aspects. The transmitters were many and those distinguished among them were more than seven. Each chose the seven who he thought had the greatest effect. They agreed on a number of them like Sa'id ibn al-Musayyab, 'Urwa and al-Qasim. The *fiqh* of the seven was learned by Ibn Shihab, Nafi' the client of 'Umar, Abu'z-Zinad 'Abdullah ibn Dhakwan, Rabi'a ar-Ra'y, and Yahya ibn Sa'id.

The Seven *Fuqaha'* of Madina

We should briefly mention the seven *fuqaha'* since they were largely responsible for the transmission of knowledge of Madina and were the source of most of Malik's knowledge. Indeed we are indebted to them for much of the knowledge of Islam and the *Sunna* which we possess today. Malik mentioned them as being the *fuqaha'* and the bearers of knowledge.

1. Sa'id ibn al-Musayyab

The first of them in position and importance in knowledge was Sa'id ibn al-Musayyab, may Allah be pleased with him. He was from Makhzum, the sub-tribe of Quraysh. He was born during the khalifate of 'Umar ibn al-Khattab and died in 93 AH, so he lived through the rule of 'Uthman, 'Ali, Mu'awiya, Yazid, Marwan, and 'Abdu'l-Malik.

He completely devoted himself to *fiqh*. He was not concerned with *tafsir* of the Qur'an as was 'Ikrima, the client and student of Ibn 'Abbas and transmitter of his *fiqh* and *tafsir*. According to the *tafsir* of at-Tabari, "Yazid ibn Abi Yazid said: 'We used to ask Sa'id ibn al-Musayyab about the lawful and unlawful; he was the most knowledgeable of people. We asked him about the *tafsir* of an *ayat* of the Qur'an and he said, 'Do not ask me about any *ayat* of the Qur'an. Ask the one who claims that none of it is hidden from him,' meaning 'Ikrima."

Sa'id met a great number of the Companions, and took from them and studied with them. What he especially sought were the judgements of the Messenger of Allah, may Allah bless him and grant him peace, and the judgements of Abu Bakr, 'Umar and 'Uthman. He took half of his knowledge from Zayd ibn Thabit, and most of his transmission was from Abu Hurayra, his father-in-law, since Sa'id was married to his daughter.

He learned the *fiqh* of 'Umar from his companions to such an extent that he was considered the main transmitter of the *fiqh* of 'Umar. Ibn al-Qayyim called him "the transmitter of 'Umar and the bearer of his knowledge." Ja'far ibn Rabi'a said, "I asked 'Irak ibn Malik, 'Who among Malik's sources has the most *fiqh*?' He replied, 'The one among them with the most *fiqh* and knowledge of the judgements of the Messenger of Allah, may Allah bless him and grant him peace, the judgements of 'Umar, and the judgements of 'Uthman, and the one with the knowledge of what people did is Sa'id ibn al-Musayyab. The one with the most *hadiths* is 'Urwa ibn az-Zubayr. You could not wish for a greater ocean than 'Ubaydullah (ibn 'Abdullah ibn 'Utba),' 'Irak continued, 'I think that the one among them with the most *fiqh* is Ibn Shihab because he joined their knowledge to his.'

Az-Zuhri said, 'I used to seek knowledge from three men: Sa'id ibn al-Musayyab, who had the most *fiqh* of all, 'Urwa ibn az-Zubayr, who was a bottomless ocean, and if you wish to find a kind of knowledge not found with anyone else you would find it with 'Ubaydullah.'" (*I'lam*, vol. 1, p. 18)

Ibn al-Musayyab concentrated on *fiqh*. His concern with *hadith* was to learn the judgements of the Prophet, may Allah bless him and grant him peace, and he also learned the traditions containing the judgements of the khalifs since he was concerned to know the judgements and *fatwas* of the khalifs. The most prominent in his transmission of the knowledge of the *fiqh* of the Companions was 'Umar ibn al-Khattab, for his time was the pre-eminent time of

45

fiqh, judgements and *fatwas* because the state was expanding and events occurred which made them necessary.

Since Ibn al-Musayyab followed the traditions of 'Umar in judgement and *fiqh*, *ra'y* (opinion) had great importance in his view because 'Umar frequently formed an opinion on matters about which there was no explicit text in the Book of Allah or the *Sunna* of the Messenger. So Ibn al-Musayyab also used *ijtihad* (independent reasoning) to answer problems presented to him about matters on which there was no explicit text from the Book or *Sunna* or judgement or *fatwa* of a Companion: he would give a *fatwa* based on his opinion which did not exceed what was proper. That is why it is transmitted that he used to give *fatwa* when others feared to do so.

He was the Imam of the *fuqaha'* of Madina in the time of the *Tabi'un*. He did not refuse to give a *fatwa* when there was need for one. His opinion was based on the firm pillars of *fiqh*: the Qur'an and *hadith*, and the judgements of the Prophet and Rightly-Guided Khalifs.

2. 'Urwa ibn az-Zubayr

The second of the seven *fuqaha'* who formulated the *fiqh* of Madina in the time of the *Tabi'un* was 'Urwa ibn az-Zubayr ibn al-'Awwam. He was the brother of 'Abdullah ibn az-Zubayr and the nephew of 'A'isha, may Allah be pleased with her. He was born in the khalifate of 'Uthman ibn 'Affan and died in 94 AH. He lived through the seditions which occurred after the murder of 'Uthman until authority was settled with the Marwanids. Although his brother, 'Abdullah ibn az-Zubayr, wrested the rule from 'Abdu'l-Malik ibn Marwan, and the conflict became intense between them, it is not known that he became involved in the business or helped his brother in any way. It is clear that he completely devoted himself to study, studying *fiqh* and *hadith*. In *hadith* he was, as his student Ibn Shihab said, "a sea undiminished by buckets." Ibn al-Musayyab had the most *fiqh* of the *Tabi'un* in Madina. 'Urwa had the most *hadiths*. He learned the *fiqh* of the *deen* from a group of the Companions, particularly 'A'isha, the Mother of the Faithful. She was foremost in general knowledge, rules for the apportionment of shares of inheritance and rulings. Al-Qasim ibn Muhammad, the son of her brother, took knowledge from her as did 'Urwa, the son of her sister Asma'.

'Urwa was the person with the greatest knowledge of the *hadiths* of 'A'isha. He said, "Before 'A'isha died, I saw that I had become one of four authorities. I said, 'If she dies, there will be no *hadith* which will be lost from those she knows. I have memorised all of them."

It is clear that 'Urwa was concerned with recording the *fiqh* and *hadith* he learned and it is related that he wrote books; but he was afraid that they might become books alongside the Book of Allah and so he destroyed them. His son Hisham related that he had books which he burned on the day of the Battle of Harra. He later he regretted that, however, and used to say, "I would rather have them in my possession than my family and property twice over."

He was a *hadith* transmitter and a *faqih* who followed the path of tradition and he did not give *fatwas* in the way that Ibn al-Musayyab did.

3. Abu Bakr ibn 'Abdu'r-Rahman

The third of the those *fuqaha'* was Abu Bakr ibn 'Abdu'r-Rahman ibn al-Harith. He died in 94 AH. He was devout and devoted to worship and asceticism to the extent that he was called 'the Monk of Quraysh'. He related from 'A'isha and Umm Salama. He was a *faqih* and *hadith* transmitter. He also did not give *fatwa* as Ibn al-Musayyab did. Tradition dominated his *fiqh*.

4. Al-Qasim ibn Muhammad ibn Abi Bakr

The fourth of the seven was al-Qasim ibn Muhammad ibn Abi Bakr, the nephew of 'A'isha, may Allah be pleased with her. He died in 108 AH. He learned *hadith* and *fiqh* from his aunt and from

Ibn 'Abbas. He was a *hadith* transmitter. He criticised the use of a *hadith* if its text was put before the Book of Allah and the well-known *Sunna*. He was a *faqih* and so he had both *fiqh* and *hadith*. His famous student, Abu'z-Zinad 'Abdullah ibn Dhakwan said about him, "I never saw a *faqih* with more knowledge than al-Qasim. I never saw anyone who had more knowledge of the *Sunna* than him." It is clear that as well as piety he had aspiration (*himma*) and cleverness, and resolve in things. That is why Malik related that 'Umar ibn 'Abdu'l-'Aziz said, "If I had authority in the matter, I would appoint the blind one of Banu Taym," meaning al-Qasim ibn Muhammad.

5. 'Ubaydullah ibn 'Abdullah ibn 'Utba ibn Mas'ud

The fifth of those *fuqaha'* was 'Ubaydullah ibn 'Abdullah ibn 'Utba. He transmitted from Ibn 'Abbas, 'A'isha, and Abu Hurayra. He was a teacher of 'Umar ibn 'Abdu'l-'Aziz and had a profound effect on his intellect and person. In addition to his knowledge of *fiqh* and *hadith* and his good character, he composed poetry. He died in 98 or 99 AH. It is also said that it was earlier than that, in 94 AH.

6. Sulayman ibn Yasar

The sixth was Sulayman ibn Yasar. He was a client of Maymuna bint al-Harith, the wife of the Prophet, may Allah bless him and grant him peace. It is said that she gave him a *kitaba* contract and stipulated an amount of money he must pay for his freedom. It is reported that he asked permission to visit 'A'isha. He said, "She recognised my voice. She said, 'Is it Sulayman?' Then she asked, 'Have you paid what she stipulated for you?' I said, 'Yes, nearly. There is only a small amount outstanding.' She said, 'Come in. You are still owned as long as you still owe anything.'"[1] He transmitted from Zayd ibn Thabit, 'Abdullah ibn 'Umar, Abu

---

1. Slaves are allowed to visit women because they are not subject to the rules regarding unrelated men.

Hurayra, and the wives of the Prophet, Maymuna, A'isha, and Umm Salama. Sulayman had fine understanding. His knowledge and understanding of *fiqh* were increased by his study of people's affairs and knowledge of their states. He was the overseer of the Market of Madina when 'Umar ibn 'Abdu'l-'Aziz was its governor. He died in 100 AH.

7. Kharija ibn Zayd ibn Thabit

The seventh was Kharija ibn Zayd ibn Thabit who died in 100 AH. He was a *faqih* in legal opinion (*ra'y*), like his father Zayd well-known for that and the science of shares of inheritance. That is why Kharija had few *hadiths,* and many *fatwas* based on opinion. Because of his great knowledge of the shares of inheritance, he used to distribute people's inheritances according to the Book of Allah Almighty. Mus'ab ibn 'Abdullah said, "Kharija and Talha ibn 'Abdu'r-Rahman gave *fatwa* in their time. People accepted their statements and they distributed people's inheritance - houses, palm-trees and property – and they wrote out documents for people."

In addition to his knowledge, *fiqh* and *fatwa* and his connection to people at the beginning of his life, Kharija was one of the devout worshippers of Madina. Worship moved him at the end of his life to withdraw and be alone, which is why not much of his *fiqh* and knowledge spread.

Those are the seven *fuqaha'* who, together with those of their generation who also knew the *fiqh* of the Companions and the Prophet, formed the school which formulated the *fiqh* of Madina and gave it a distinctive character. Its basis was giving *fatwa* according to the *fatwas* of the Companions of the Messenger of Allah, may Allah bless him and grant him peace, and proceeding in their own way in respect of deriving judgements when they did not find a directly relevant *fatwa* which had been passed down. Sometimes they would exercise *ijtihad* according to their own opinions but only in the way in which the Companions had done; and they did not complicate the ramifications of problems in the way that the people of Iraq did.

It should be pointed out that those *fuqaha'* were not traditionists in all respects. They were traditionists and legists who studied the *fiqh* of the First Generation, and they deduced from it and gave *fatwas* when they did not find a tradition from the Prophet or his Companions, using their intellects to arrive at a deduction based well-known judgements of the Prophet, may Allah bless him and grant him peace. Some of them had mainly knowledge of *hadith* and little *fiqh* and *fatwa*, like 'Urwa ibn az-Zubayr, but most of them concentrated on *fatwa* and *fiqh*.

This would seem to suggest that the *fiqh* of opinion had a prominent position among them, which would in turn tend to make them seem similar to the people of Iraq. However, the difference between their opinion and that of the scholars of Iraq lies in the fact that the scholars of Iraq used to give *fatwas* on whatever questions came up as well as in respect of things which had not even occurred, in the form of hypothetical questions which they devised. Furthermore, their opinion was not confined to deduction based firmly on transmitted judgements of the Companions.

The Madinans only gave *fatwas* about matters which had actually arisen. The *fiqh* of opinion was used by them only to derive principles from the *fatwas* of the Companions and the judgements of the Prophet, may Allah bless him and grant him peace, which had been transmitted to them and were being acted upon on a daily basis around them in the city of Madina where they had been made.

The *fiqh* of those seven scholars was learned by Ibn Shihab, Rabi'a and all of their generation. Then Malik learned from that generation. His shaykhs included some for whom *fiqh* and opinion was predominant and others for whom *hadith* was predominant. *Hadith* dominated the *fiqh* of Ibn Shihab, and opinion rather than *hadith* came first for Rabi'a ar-Ra'y and Yahya ibn Sa'id. Thus it is not strange that we find that opinion played a large role in Malik's *fiqh*.

Opinion (*Ra'y*) and *Hadith*

Ash-Shahrastani states in *al-Milal wa'n-Nihal*, "Events and cases regarding acts of worship and general conduct are innumerable. We know absolutely that there is no explicit text dealing with every event that occurs; nor is such a thing even conceivable. Explicit texts are limited while events are endless.... Thus it is apparent absolutely that *ijtihad* and analogy must be considered so that there can be a ruling in the case of every new event."

After the death of the Prophet, may Allah bless him and grant him peace, the Companions were faced with innumerable new events. They had the Book of Allah Almighty and the *Sunna* and decisions of the Messenger of Allah, may Allah bless him and grant him peace. They had recourse to the Book in the case of new events. If they found a clear judgement in it, they acted by it. If they did not find a clear judgement in the Book, they turned to what was transmitted from the Messenger of Allah, may Allah bless him and grant him peace, and consulted the memories of his Companions so that they could state what the judgement of the Prophet was in similar cases.

If there was nothing relevant then they practised *ijtihad* with their own opinions to come to an appropriate judgement on the basis of everything they knew. That is like the case of a *qadi* limited to explicit texts: if he cannot find anything in the texts on which to make a judgement, he applies what is like it or what he considers just and fair. That is how they behaved.

We read in a letter of 'Umar to Abu Musa al-Ash'ari about coming to judgement: "Understanding: understanding is what speaks in your heart about subjects which are not in the Book or the *Sunna*. Recognise resemblances and similarities and compare matters in that case." So the Companions made use of opinion but they varied in the extent to which they used it. Some used it a lot and some a little. This was only done when there was no explicit text on the matter. All that continued with the next generation, the Followers. Those who used *ra'y* little thought that protection against temptations and seditions lay in taking the explicit *Sunna*. The others felt that many false *hadiths* had been attributed to the

Messenger and that the reason for it was the imperative of giving judgement on cases. Hence there are two types of *fiqh*: *fiqh* of opinion and *fiqh* of tradition. There were renowned *fuqaha'* in both groups.

The basis of this difference between the two groups was not in using the *Sunna* as a proof nor in accepting it when it was sound. The basis was in giving *fatwa* based on opinion and in the divergence as to what questions should be subject to it. The people of tradition used *ra'y* only when absolutely necessary, as when a Muslim is compelled by necessity to eat pork. They sought to give judgements only for things which had actually occurred. The people of opinion, on the other hand, pronounced many *fatwas* on all kinds of matters about which there was no definitive text.

Some of them were not content merely to give judgements about actual incidents but also devised theoretical questions and issued judgements on them based on their opinions. It was said by scholars that most of the people of *hadith* were in the Hijaz and most of the people of *ra'y* were in Iraq. The basis for that is that the *fuqaha'* of Madina criticised the *fuqaha'* of Iraq for being far from the *Sunna* and giving judgements based on their opinions alone, while the Iraqis denied that.

The differences between the two groups can be seen in three main areas. The Madinans had the judgements and *fatwas* of Abu Bakr, 'Umar and 'Uthman, the *fatwas* of Ibn 'Abbas and 'A'isha, and the *hadiths* of Abu Hurayra. The Iraqis had the *hadiths* and *fatwas* of Ibn Mas'ud, the *hadiths*, judgements and *fatwas* of 'Ali, the judgements of Abu Musa al-Ash'ari, and the judgements of Shurayh. In cases where the actual judgements of these great Companions were applied the differences were of shaykh, not of method.

The legacy of traditions was greater with the Madinans and so they relied more on traditions. The subject of *fiqh* based on tradition is formed from the judgements and *fatwas* of the Companions, and opinions are based on those traditions or derived from them. The people of Madina had a living tradition of this handed down from the time of the Prophet, may Allah bless him and grant him peace.

For this reason the *fatwas* of the Followers were of great importance to the People of Madina. They were respected by them and followed in many cases, whereas they were not considered binding by the people of Iraq. That is why it is reported that Abu Hanifa limited himself to the opinion of the Companions, ignoring that of the Followers. He considered them men who strove to reach an opinion in the same way that he did, not taking into account the weight of tradition in Madina.

What we can see from this is that opinion existed among the people of Madina and was not lacking, since *fiqh* necessarily involves deriving rulings from texts which may not specifically refer to the case in hand, and opinion is bound to be used in that. Madinan opinions, however, were derived from transmitted reports and traditional practices. Opinion was more widely used by the scholars of Iraq than by those of Madina, since the Madinans had access to many traditions while the Iraqis had access only to a few and because they allowed themselves to make freer use of their opinions.

It may be that Iraqi opinion relied on analogy and *istihsan* (equitable preference to find a just solution) and the usage of the people of Iraq while Madinan opinion did not rely much on logical analogy; rather it was based on public interest and the customary practice of the people of Madina. The difference between the custom of Madina and the custom of Iraq was like the difference between Madina and Iraq. Iraq was a place of sects and erroneous ideas and people of innovation, being a place where various religions were practised, whereas Madina was the place of Islam where it first developed and had been protected. There is no doubt that its custom was derived from Islam alone.

Malik inherited all the knowledge of the Madinans. Ad-Dihlawi said about him, "Malik was the strongest of them in the *hadiths* of the Madinans from the Messenger of Allah, may Allah bless him and grant him peace, and had the most reliable *isnads* and the most knowledge of the judgements of 'Umar and the statements of 'Abdullah ibn 'Umar, 'A'isha and their companions among the seven *fuqaha'*."

A Word About Sects

In Malik's time there were a many political upheavals but he refused to have anything to do with them and enjoyed the calm of a thoughtful scholar. In his time there were also many arguments about the *fatwas* of the Companions and the Followers and their various merits. Malik preferred the position of the People of Madina. He made holding to it one of the basic principles of his method which he taught in his lessons and wrote about in his letters, as we saw in his letter to al-Layth. It was in his time, too, that various sects and erroneous ideas arose which we should note briefly along with Malik's view of them.

The Createdness of the Qur'an

During this time the nature of the Qur'an became the subject of great dispute among the Muslims – is it created or not? One group maintained that the Qur'an is the timeless, uncreated Word of Allah, another hesitated, and a third said that it is created because it consists of words articulated by the reader. The position of the createdness of the Qur'an was adopted as the official position under three of the Abbasid khalifs: al-Ma'mun, al-Mu'tasim and al-Wathiq.

Political Groups: the Shi'a, Kharijites and others

The Shi'a are considered to be the oldest Islamic sect. They believe that 'Ali was the Muslim most entitled to be khalif after the Messenger of Allah, may Allah bless him and grant him peace.

They form various groups, some of them going to extremes in their sanctification of 'Ali.

The Kharijites appeared in the army of 'Ali after he agreed to arbitration at the Battle of Siffin.[1] They then rebelled against him and declared that anyone who agreed to arbitration was an unbeliever. They also had several sub-groups.

There were also the Murji'ites who mixed politics with the fundamentals of the *deen*. There were the Jabariyya or Jahmiyya, who believed in total predestination, and the Qadariyya, who believed in unlimited free will.

Malik's opinions and *fiqh*

Malik was a *muhaddith* and *faqih* and did not apply any other term to himself because he did not seek anything but knowledge of the Book and *Sunna* and the Path that the righteous early Muslims had followed. Thus he derived his opinions first from the Book of Allah, then from the *Sunna*, and then from the statements and judgements of the Companions and those who followed them. He studied events in the light of what he knew with an ample intellect. He avoided the people of opinions and did not mention them.

In fact, the only science in Madina was that which Malik loved: the science of *hadiths* and the science of *fiqh* based on that transmitted legacy left by the Companions of the Prophet, may Allah bless him and grant him peace, and their Followers. It was free of the extrapolations from outside which proliferated in places like Basra and Kufa, and elsewhere. Nonetheless, in view of the fact that the *hajjis* came to the Hijaz every year, news of these ideas did reach Madina, and indeed Madina was at one point subject to the depredations of the Kharijites and experienced the Shi'ite rebellion of Muhammad ibn 'Abdullah, the Pure Soul, in 145/762. Hence Malik did mention some of those topics.

---

1. The battle between Mu'awiya and 'Ali in 38/657.

Malik's position on doctrines

Malik reported: "'Umar ibn 'Abdu'l-'Aziz said, 'The Messenger of Allah made a *sunna* and those with authority after him made *sunan*. To accept that is to follow the Book of Allah and the perfection of obedience to Allah and strength in the *Deen* of Allah. No one after these may change the *sunan* or look into anything which opposes them. Whoever is guided by the *sunan* will be guided. Whoever seeks help by them will be helped. Whoever leaves them will not be following the Path of the believers. Allah will assign him what he has taken and he will roast in Hell. What an evil return!'" When Malik uttered this, he shook with joy.

A man asked Malik, "Who are the people of the *Sunna*, Abu 'Abdullah?" He replied, "Those who do not have any name by which they are known – who are not Jahmis, Rafidites (Shi'ites) or Qadaris."

When he was asked about certain questions into which sects were delving, he would say very little so that that would not lead to argumentation and the very delving he was trying to avoid. His answer directed people to rely on what is transmitted and to distance themselves from that for which there is no precedent in the Book or *Sunna*.

Sufyan ibn 'Uyayna said, "A man questioned Malik as follows, '*"The Merciful settles on the Throne."* How can He settle anywhere, Abu 'Abdullah?' Malik was silent for a long time until he began to sweat profusely. I had never seen Malik grieve at anything the way that he did at these words. People began to look to see what position he would take. Then he regained his composure and said, 'His settling is well-known. The "how" of it is beyond our comprehension. Asking about it is innovation. Belief in it is obligatory. I think you are misguided. Get him out!' The man called out to him, 'Abu 'Abdullah! By Allah, and there is no god but He! I asked the people of Basra, Kufa and Iraq about this question, and I did not find anyone who dealt with it as successfully as you have.'"

Malik's teaching, then, stopped at what the text indicated and he did not exceed the evident meaning in any text in the Book or *Sunna*, especially where doctrines were concerned.

In Malik's day there was much discussion about the nature of faith and whether it increases or decreases and whether its reality was word or action or simply faith itself. There was also discussion about the actions of the human being, about whether committing major wrong actions makes people unbelievers and whether or not Allah will actually be seen on the Day of Rising. He was asked about these matters in his lessons and his method was to stop where the *Salaf* stopped: with the explicit text. He did not get involved in theoretical debates.

What Malik said about Faith

Malik thought that faith was not only a matter of belief but also involved action. He used to say, "Belief is both word and deed." He considered that acts of obedience were part of faith, so that performing the prayer was an integral part of faith. His evidence for this was that when the *qibla* was changed from Jerusalem to the House of Allah, some of the believers were afraid that their previous prayers would be lost; but Allah revealed, *"Allah would not let your faith go to waste."* (2:143) This indicates that the prayer and faith are inseparable and since prayer is action, faith must involve both word and deed.

Since faith is both word and deed, it increases through action. That is why it is reported that Malik said that faith is subject to increase. His view is based on clear *ayats* which indicate that and is a logical corollary of considering action to be part of faith. But Malik forbade people to call those who did not agree with this unbelievers.

Zuhayr ibn 'Abbad told Malik that there were two groups in Syria who disagreed concerning faith. One said that it was subject to increase and decrease; the other said that it always remains constant. Zuhayr asked him, "What should the two groups say?" He replied, "They should say, 'We are believers' and then refrain from going beyond those words. The Prophet, may Allah bless him and grant him peace, said, 'I am commanded to fight the people until they say, "There is no god but Allah." Once they say it, their blood and property are protected except when there is a legal right.' The Almighty says, *"Do not say 'You are not a believer' to someone who gives you the Muslim greeting."* (4:94) Zuhayr told him that the two groups attacked one another.' He said, 'We belong to Allah and to Him we return!'"

Malik believed that faith is subject to increase and decrease because anything which can increase can also decrease. But because he found that the *ayats* of the Qur'an only mention increase, he refrained from speaking about its decrease. We find in *Tartib al-Madarik* that more than one person heard Malik say, "Faith consists in words and action, and it increases and decreases." Ibn al-Qasim said, "Malik used to say 'Faith increases' and refrained from mentioning decrease. He said, 'Allah mentioned its increase in more than one place. He did not speak of its decrease.' He refrained from doing so."

What Malik said about Destiny (*Qadar*) and man's actions

The subject of Destiny is connected to man's will. Do we have freedom of choice in what we do so that we are responsible for our good and bad actions or do we have no freedom? Discussion of this matter began at the end of the *Rashidun* period and was widespread in the Umayyad period and led eventually to two opposing groups: the Jabriyya, led by Jahm ibn Safwan who believed that man had no will in what he did and no choice in the actions ascribed to him, and the Qadariyya, led by Ghaylan ad-Dimishqi and others who believed that man had complete freedom of will in respect of his actions and that furthermore man created his own actions by his free will. A group of Muslims took a position in between and held that man's actions are created by Allah Almighty and not by man, but that man acquires them and advances to them, which is how he becomes responsible for them.

Malik detested the Qadariyya who claimed that we create our own actions. He refrained from speaking to them and forbade them to sit with him. He stated, "All the believers in complete free will I have seen embody imbecility, levity and contrivance." He said, "'Umar ibn 'Abdu'l-Aziz used to say, 'If Allah had willed that He should not be disobeyed, he would not have created Iblis, who is the head of wrong actions.' What could be clearer and stronger than this *ayat* as evidence against the Qadariyya? *'Had We so willed We could have given guidance to everybody, but now My pronouncement has been carried out: that I shall fill up Hell entirely with jinn and human beings.'* (32:13)" Malik's dislike of them and the damage they might do to the *deen* was so great that he forbade his students to marry them, attend their funeral processions, or pray over them.

Malik was asked about the people of *Qadar*, "Should one keep out of their discussions?" He said, "Yes, when one recognises their position. We command them to what is correct and forbid them what is incorrect. We inform them of their opposition to the truth and we do not continue to speak with them or pray over them or attend their funerals. And I do not think that others should marry them. Allah says, *'A believing slave is better than an idolater.'* One must not pray behind them nor transmit *hadith* from them. If you come across them in a place, dislodge them from it."

Malik's opinion about those who commit grave wrong actions

The position of those who commit wrong actions was also one with which the Muslims were concerned in the time of Malik. It was the basis for the Kharijites attacking 'Ali previously. The Kharijites said that anyone who committed a major wrong action was a unbeliever. This opinion of theirs was their hallmark by which they differed from the rest of the Muslims and it occupied the minds of many in the Umayyad period. The 'Ibadites among them thought that such people were merely ungrateful for Allah's blessings, not unbelievers in a legal sense. The Mu'tazilites, led by

Wasil ibn 'Ata', a contemporary of Malik, held that they occupied a position in between believers and unbelievers and would be forever in the Fire unless they repented. They did not forbid calling them Muslims. The Murji'ites claimed that they were believers in every sense, but were divided into two groups. One held that they were rebellious believers who could hope for Allah's forgiveness and Allah's all-embracing mercy; the other, that rebellion did not impair belief in any way, just as acts of obedience bring no benefit to anyone who does not believe.

Most Muslims held that those who commit a major wrong action are degenerate believers. If Allah wishes, He will forgive them. If He punishes them, it is for their wrong action, not for disbelief. That was the opinion of Abu Hanifa and others, which is why he was accused of being a Murji'ite. It is clear that that was also the opinion of Malik. It is reported in the *Madarik* that al-Farawi said, "I heard the son of Abu Hanifa tell Malik, 'We have an opinion which we will put to you. If you think it is good, we will continue in it. If you think that it is bad, we will turn from it. We do not call anyone an unbeliever because of a wrong action. Wrongdoers are still Muslims.' He replied, 'I see no harm in that.'"

The nature of the Qur'an

In the time of Malik many Muslims, influenced by rationalism, began to say that the Qur'an was created. This doctrine was embraced by the Qadariyya and the Mu'tazilites, who began to spread it among the generality of Muslims. It was a question which had not been discussed by the early Muslims. Malik avoided discussing it but said, "The Qur'an is the Word of Allah. Anyone who says that the Qur'an is created should be beaten and imprisoned until he repents."

The Vision of Allah

The Mu'tazilites stirred up the issue of the Vision of Allah, saying that it is impossible because it demands that Allah Almighty be in a place but Allah has no place since only bodies can occupy space. Allah Almighty is free of corporeality and from any of the attributes of temporal things since He is the Necessarily Existent. He can only described by what is appropriate to the Necessarily Existent. The Almighty said, *"There is nothing like Him and He is the All-Hearing, the All-Seeing."* If He could be seen, He must have a body and all other bodies would be like Him in respect of their corporeality. It is also because Allah Almighty said to Musa when he asked for the vision, *"You will not see me..."* This indicates that the prohibition is eternal and vision is impossible.

The Mu'tazilites took this position, which Malik thought was contrary to the Path of the early Muslims and was deducing from the Qur'an something different from its clear text. He rejected it, affirming the vision of Allah Almighty in the Next World, not in this world. Ashhab said, "Abu 'Abdullah! *'Faces on that day are radiant, looking at their Lord.'* Do they look at Allah?" He said, "Yes, with these eyes." Ashhab continued, "Some people say that one does not look at Allah and that *nadhira* (looking) means *muntadhira* (waiting) for the reward." He answered, "They have lied. One looks at Allah. Have you not heard what Musa, peace be upon him, said: 'Lord, let me look at You'? Do you think that Musa would ask his Lord for something impossible? Allah Almighty says 'You will not see Me' in this world because it is a transient realm. The eternal cannot seen by the temporal. When people go to the Abode of Eternity, they will look and see the eternal by the eternal. Allah Almighty said, *'No, on that Day they will be veiled from their Lord.'"*

Malik's opinion about politics

In Malik's time there were Kharijites, Shi'ites, Umayyads and then Abbasids. Some of them permitted vilification of the early

61

Companions. The Shi'ites attacked Abu Bakr, 'Umar and 'Uthman. The Kharijites attacked 'Uthman, 'Ali, 'Amr ibn al-'As and Mu'awiya and accused them of disbelief. The Shi'ites claimed the khalifate for 'Ali and his sons by Fatima. Some of them, the Kaysaniyya, included his other son Muhammad ibn al-Hanafiyya as a possible candidate. The Kharijites claimed that the khalifate was the right of whoever was entitled to it among the Muslims, not being limited to any tribe or family. The Abbasids claimed that the khalifate was reserved for the clan of al-'Abbas from the clan of Hashim. The Umayyads and others claimed that any of Quraysh were entitled to it.

So what was Malik's opinion in the midst of the muddle of all these divergent positions? What did he say about vilifying the Companions, about the people from whom the khalif should be chosen, about who should pledge allegiance, about obedience to rulers if they were unworthy, and about rebellion in general? We will briefly mention his position on these matters.

On vilifying the Companions

Malik objected to vilifying the Companions of the Messenger of Allah, may Allah bless him and grant him peace, and considered that to be a terrible sin. He declared that anyone who cursed the Companions should be expelled from Madina since they no longer had any right to live there. It is related that he said that people who cursed the Companions of the Messenger of Allah, may Allah bless him and grant him peace, had no right to any of the booty. He used *Sura al-Hashr* (59):8-10 as evidence for that.

He also avoided any discussion about who was the best of them because of the political repercussions inherent in that. He said, "They are all equal except for three: Abu Bakr, 'Umar, and 'Uthman." An 'Alawi asked him, "Who is the best of mankind after the Messenger of Allah, may Allah bless him and grant him peace?" He replied, "Abu Bakr." The 'Alawite said, "Then who?" Malik said, "Then 'Umar." The 'Alawite said, "Then who?" Malik said, "The wrongly-slain khalif, 'Uthman." The 'Alawite said, "By

Allah, I will never sit with you!" Malik said to him, "That is your choice."

Ibn Wahb said, "He said, 'The best of people were Abu Bakr and 'Umar.' I said, 'Then who?' Malik hesitated. I said, 'I am someone who imitates you in my *deen*.' He said, 'And 'Uthman.'" He based this on transmission: the Prophet, may Allah bless him and grant him peace, appointed Abu Bakr to lead the prayer, that being his personal preference, and Abu Bakr chose 'Umar. 'Umar chose six men and they chose 'Uthman. Malik considered that the basis of that was the action by which Prophet selected Abu Bakr.

The House of the Khalifate

Malik said very little about anything which was not connected to *fiqh* and *hadith* since his sole concern was the *deen* and he did not want it to be become a matter of dispute. Thus we do not have any explicit statements from him about the khalifate, and his viewpoint must be deduced from other sources.

We know for certain that he did not think that the khalifate was confined to the Hashimite house or the family of 'Ali, because of his view that the position of Abu Bakr, 'Umar and 'Uthman was based on Prophetic choice. None of them were Hashimites: they were from Quraysh. Malik did not include 'Ali, and he was Hashimite. All he said about him was, "One who seeks command is not like one who does not seek it."

Ibn Hazm mentioned that the position of all the people of the *Sunna* and the Community is that the Imamate belongs to Quraysh, based on *mutawatir* transmission, and it is evident that Malik, who followed the Path of the people of the *Sunna*, would take that position.

The method of selecting the Khalif

The method of selecting the khalif was a topic of dispute among the Muslims. The Shi'ites believed it was by stipulation from the Prophet to 'Ali and from 'Ali to his successor and so on, each Imam appointing his own successor. The Umayyads said it was by virtue of power and the allegiance of people. Many objected to Mu'awiya appointing his successor because it turned the khalifate into hereditary kingship.

The majority of Muslims believe that the khalif should be chosen from those entitled to the khalifate. There is nothing to stop the khalif designating his successor as long as it is not by caprice, since Abu Bakr designated 'Umar and 'Umar appointed the council.

Malik's opinion was between these opinions. It appears that he affirmed the system of appointment when caprice was not the motive, based on what Abu Bakr and 'Umar did. The khalifate is only binding by the free allegiance between the khalif and the Muslims. But did that entail universal allegiance from all areas?

Malik said that the allegiance of the people of Makka and Madina is sufficient to constitute the allegiance which entitles the khalif to be Imam of the Muslims, because they are the bearers of the *Sunna* of the Prophet and so they are the people entitled to make the contract. Ibn Nafi' said, "Malik used to relate that when the people of the two *Harams* (Makka and Madina) paid allegiance, that allegiance was binding on all the people of Islam."

Obeying the less excellent person

When someone overcomes the Muslims and so is not initially appointed by acceptance, but is just and people are content with his rule, it is evident that the position of Malik is that it is not valid to rebel against him and he must be obeyed because only justice is demanded and it has been achieved in this instance. Even if he were not just, Malik would not permit rebellion against him. The Muslims must be steadfast and strive to correct him. They should not help Kharijites against him. If he was unjust, it was for Allah to punish him by means of another tyrant and then take revenge on both of them.

That is the position of Malik. The thing he feared most was civil war and the corruption and disturbance which resulted from it, and he cited the fact that 'Umar ibn 'Abdu'l-'Aziz refused to appoint a righteous man after him for fear that it would provoke Yazid ibn 'Abdu'l-Malik to insurrection. When someone rebelled against al-Mansur and asked Malik to pray for him and said to him, "The people of the *Haramayn* have given me homage; have you decided for the injustice of Abu Ja'far?" Malik asked him, "Do you know what kept 'Umar ibn Abdu'l-'Aziz from appointing a righteous man after him?" "No.," said the man. Malik said, "The khalifate had been given to Yazid and 'Umar feared that if he pledged allegiance to another man, Yazid would start a civil war and people would fight and thus that action would sow dissension."

Such was Malik's view of policy – a view which looked both to the highest model of judgement and to the pragmatic solution which would serve the best interests of the people. One must consider the state of the Community and the events of history and avoid civil war. That is also the position of the Maliki school, and they say that it is the opinion represented in the *Sunna*. The patience for which Malik calls is not that of someone who is humbled and cannot object to injustice and is content with it. It is the steadfastness of someone who seeks people's welfare, and who sees that there is corruption in taking the way of insurrection and that the proper course lies in compelling the tyrant to justice through admonition, good advice, guidance, and reminding him of the commands of the *Deen*. If that is impossible, then one has as little to do with him as possible.

This does not, however, remove the obligation to follow him if he orders a *jihad* in the Way of Allah. Ibn al-Qasim said, "I do not see anything wrong in fighting the Greeks under these rulers."

Malik's *Fiqh*

To find out about Malik's *fiqh* is one of the main objectives of our study of Malik, may Allah be pleased with him, and in this section we will study Malik the *hadith* scholar and Malik the *faqih*. Knowledge of *hadith* and *fiqh* were not distinct disciplines then but were closely interrelated.

A *faqih* relates the *hadiths* on which his deduction is based and he relates what has been transmitted to him. Nevertheless, some *fuqaha'* are more distinguished for giving *fatwa* than for transmitting *hadith*. Whoever derives judgements from the Qur'an and from *hadiths* after knowing how to verify their soundness is a *faqih*. Someone who simply knows sound from unsound *hadiths* and how to assess their transmitters is a *muhaddith*. In Malik's time, the two were not completely distinct. Malik had command of both disciplines.

When we direct our attention to the *fiqh* of Imam Malik we must first look at certain things so that we can ascertain his methods of deriving rulings and his basic principles and the branches of *fiqh* in which he gave judgements. We find that Malik did not record his principles in detail, although he did mention the general outline of his method many times in the *Muwatta'* and in other statements related from him by his students and contemporaries. So we must analyse them to discover his method.

Malik's books

Those who made rulings in the time of the Companions refused to record their *fatwas* or *ijtihad*. They even refused to write down the *Sunna*. But then it become necessary to record the *Sunna*, and many *fatwas* and decisions were also recorded. The *fuqaha'* of the

Hijaz collected the *fatwas* of 'Abdullah ibn 'Umar, 'A'isha, and Ibn 'Abbas, and of the *Tabi'un* after them in Madina. The Iraqis collected the *fatwas* of 'Abdullah ibn Mas'ud and the judgements and *fatwas* of 'Ali and the judgements of Shurayh and other *qadis* of Kufa. There were collections made by Ibrahim an-Nakha'i and Hammad, the shaykh of Abu Hanifa.

These were not actually distributed as books: they were more like personal notes which the *mujtahid* would consult to refresh his memory. Nonetheless there were instances of written records among the Companions. For instance, 'Ali ibn Abi Talib is reported to have had a paper which contained judicial judgements. However, the first actual book, or the earliest one that is known, was the *Muwatta'* of Imam Malik, may Allah be pleased with him.

The *Muwatta'* was not Malik's only book. There are other works ascribed to him which are mentioned in books about him. Several books are mentioned. For instance, as-Suyuti says in *Tazyin al-Mamalik*, "Reports indicate that Malik wrote several books besides the *Muwatta'*. I saw a fine *tafsir* by him. I saw that Ibn Wahb has the *Book of Assemblies* from Malik, which contained what was heard from Malik in his assemblies. It contains many *hadiths*, traditions, rules of proper behaviour (*adab*) and the like."

Qadi 'Iyad said in *Tartib al-Madarik*:

> Know, may Allah give you success, that Malik had noble books related from him. Most of them were with sound *isnads* in other sciences of knowledge. However, none of them are well known except the *Muwatta'*... All of his works were related from him by the one who wrote them for him or asked him about them or by one of his companions, not all of whom related them. One of the most famous is his letter to Ibn Wahb about *Qadar* and the refutation of the Qadariyya. One of the best letters on this subject, it shows the vastness of his knowledge of the subject... There is also his book on the stars, *"The Reckoning of the Passage of Time and the Stages of the Moon"*, which is a very good and useful treatise indeed. People rely on it in this subject and use it as a basis... There is

also the Treatise of Malik in ten parts on Judgements, which he addressed to a certain *qadi*.... There is also his famous letter to Abu Ghassan Muhammad ibn Mutarrif on *fatwa*. ...There is his treatise on the *tafsir* of the unusual words of the Qur'an which Khalid ibn 'Abdu'r-Rahman al-Makhzumi related....A book is also ascribed to Malik called *Kitab as-Sirr* as transmitted by Ibn al-Qasim.

It should be noted that they were not related from Malik with a well-known transmission but go back to only one or two of his companions. These books did not achieve any popularity among people. But there is one letter which is in circulation and was published in Egypt, which is read by preachers and guides. This is his letter to ar-Rshsid and so we should pay some attention to it.

In *Tartib al-Madarik*, Qadi 'Iyad discussed the contents of this letter: "One item is his famous letter to Harun ar-Rashid about *adab* and admonition. It was first related in Andalusia by Ibn Habib from its transmitters from Malik. Then later it was related by Abu Ja'far ibn 'Awnullah and the Qadi Abu 'Abdullah ibn Mufarrij from Ahmad ibn Zaydawayh ad-Dimishqi, although the *isnad* is not continuous."

Some Malikis have stated that it was not Malik who wrote the letter. This is because of its *isnad* and because it contains *hadiths* which Malik disacknowledged and judgements which are contrary to the school of Malik. After close examination, we are forced to conclude that not all of what the published letter contains can be ascribed to Malik because Malik was an intelligent man and he knew the proper usage of words. Nonetheless, it would appear that the preface of this letter, which is found elsewhere, can actually be ascribed to Malik.

The following is its text as found in *Tartib al-Madarik*:

According to Sa'id ibn Abi Zanbar, Malik wrote a letter to one of the khalifs in which he admonished him:

"As for what follows, I am writing a letter to you in which I do not hold back right guidance and I do not omit counsel. It contains the praise of Allah Almighty and the *adab* of His Messenger, may Allah bless him and grant him peace. So consider that with your intellect, turn your eyes to it, and devote your hearing to it. Understand it with your intellect and apply your understanding. Do not allow your mind to let it slip away. It contains excellence in this world and the good reward of Allah Almighty in the Next.

Remind yourself of the throes of death and its grief, and what will happen to you when it comes, and what you know follows after death: being presented before Allah Almighty, and then the Reckoning, and then remaining forever either in the Garden or the Fire. Prepare for it something to make the terrors of those sights and their distress easy for you.

If you were to see the people who incur wrath of Allah Almighty and the myriad punishments they are heading to and the severity of the vengeance of Allah, and if you were to hear their moaning in the Fire and their groaning with their livid faces and the length of their grief and their being turned over on their faces in its bottom levels where they cannot hear or see while calling out for utter and final destruction – and the most terrible thing of all for them is the pain when Allah Almighty turns away from them and their hope is cut off from Him and His answer to them after the long drawn-out sorrow is *'Slink down in it and do not speak.'* If you remind yourself of this, nothing of this world will seem of any importance to you. You will want to be saved from that. You have no security from its terror. Even if you were to offer all that the people of this world have to seek deliverance, that would be little.

If you were to see the people who obey Allah and what they are destined to receive by way of honour from Allah, their position of nearness to Allah Almighty, the freshness of their faces and the light of their colours, their joy in looking at Him, and having a place with Him and their rank in His sight along with nearness to Him, those things of this world which you seek and which appear immense in your eyes would then seem insignificant.

Be careful not to allow your lower self to beguile you. Deal with your lower self before it gets the better of you and remember the distress it will feel when death alights. Contend with your soul for Allah Almighty while you still have time. If Allah permits, you will be able to bring benefit to yourself and avert the punishment from yourself before Allah takes charge of your Reckoning. Once it comes you will not be able to avert from your soul that which it will hate nor bring any benefit to it. Give Allah Almighty a portion of your time by night and day.

It also appears that the letter was not addressed to ar-Rashid. It was a text which has had pieces added to it. In any case none of these letters are used as a text for *fiqh* in the school of Malik. What reveals his method in *fiqh* is the record of *hadiths* and tradition he considered to be definitive: the *Muwatta'*.

The *Muwatta'*

There is no doubt that *al-Muwatta'* is considered to be the first book of reliable ascription which was circulated widely within the Islamic world and it has been passed down to us generation after generation to the present day. It is soundly and authentically ascribed to Imam Malik. It is considered to be both the first book written on *hadith* and the first on *fiqh*. Previously people had put more reliance on oral transmission than on written texts. In the preface to *Fath al-Bari*, his commentary on the *Sahih* of Muslim, Ibn Hajar says:

Know, may Allah teach us and you, that the traditions of the Prophet, may Allah bless him and grant him peace, were not recorded in collections in the time of the Companions and the great *Tabi'un* and they were not systematised, for two reasons. The first reason was that, as is confirmed in the *Sahih* of Muslim, there was a real fear that some *hadiths* might become mixed up with the text of

70

the Qur'an. The second reason was the extraordinary capacity of those men's memory and the agility of their minds which made writing unnecessary, together with the fact that many of them did not know how to write in any case.

Then at the end of the time of the *Tabi'un*, traditions began to be systematically recorded under various headings since the scholars had spread throughout the cities of Islam. When innovations which emanated from the Kharijites, extreme Shi'ites and those who denied the Divine Decree became widespread, the first to deal with that were ar-Rabi' ibn Sabih, Sa'id ibn Abi 'Aruba, and others who wrote on each subject individually. Then the great people of the third generation came and wrote down their judgements. Imam Malik compiled the *Muwatta'*, in which he used strong *hadiths* of the people of the Hijaz, statements of the Companions and the *fatwas* of the *Tabi'un* and those after them.

We have nothing older than Malik's *Muwatta'* in *fiqh* or *hadith*. It was in his time that it became necessary to record things. The impetus to collect and record the statements of the Companions and the Followers and the *hadiths* of the Messenger of Allah, may Allah bless him and grant him peace, began before Malik. His contemporaries collected *hadiths* on specific subjects and recorded them. The first to make a *Muwatta'* – to collect together what the people of Madina agreed upon – was 'Abdu'l-'Aziz ibn al-Majishun. Malik examined it and criticised the fact that he did not begin with *hadiths*. Malik said, 'How excellent is his work! But if it had been me, I would have begun with traditions. Then I would have supplemented them with further sayings."

So there were various stimuli and also a model available for Malik when he put together the *Muwatta'*; and the areas of *fiqh* agreed upon by the people of Madina had already been delineated. It was clear that the time had come for such a book, so he formulated his *Muwatta'*. Malik was told, "You have occupied yourself with composing this book while people share with you in this task

71

and are making ones like it." Malik said, 'Bring them to me!' He looked at them and said, 'You should know that I am doing this purely to please Allah.'"

The appearance of the *Muwatta'*, then, was dictated by the necessities of the time and by various factors, since the interest of men of knowledge before Malik had already been turned towards collecting the knowledge of Madina. It was necessary to remove any grounds for dispute, and the knowledge of the Imam of the Hijaz was not disputed by anyone.

It is reported that the khalif, Abu Ja'far al-Mansur, said to Malik while he was at Makka, "Make all knowledge into one knowledge, Abu 'Abdullah." He said, "Amir al-Mu'minin, the Companions of the Messenger of Allah, may Allah bless him and grant him peace, scattered throughout the lands and each of them made *fatwas* in the city to which he went as he thought best. So the people of the various regions each have a position, and the people of Madina have a position. The people of Iraq have a position in which they overstep their authority." Al-Mansur said, "As for the people of Iraq, I do not take either my religious obligations or supererogatory actions from them. True knowledge is the knowledge of the people of Madina, so write down knowledge for people." Malik said, "The people of Iraq are not content with our knowledge." Abu Ja'far said, "Their common folk will be driven to it with the sword and their backs will be broken to it by whips."

Thus al-Mansur had the same idea that 'Umar ibn 'Abdu'l-'Aziz had – to compile the knowledge of Madina to be a definitive compilation of the knowledge of Islam. 'Umar ibn 'Abdu'l-'Aziz had commanded Abu Bakr ibn Hazm to do this and al-Mansur commanded Malik to do it. But the *Muwatta'* was not completed during the lifetime of al-Mansur. It was completed around 159 AH after his death, or perhaps at the very end of his life, just as Abu Bakr ibn Hazm did not complete his work until after the death of 'Umar ibn 'Abdu'l-'Aziz. It appears that Malik took a long time to write and edit the *Muwatta'* before he was able to present it to people. The initial request had been made in 148.

The khalifs after al-Mansur, however, had the same idea. According to *al-Madarik,* "Al-Mahdi told Malik, 'Write a book that I will make the community adopt.' Malik said to him, 'As for the region, i.e. Maghrib, I have spared you from it. As for Syria, al-Awza'i is there. As for the people of Iraq, they are the people of Iraq.'"

As-Suyuti tells us in his book *The Virtues of Malik*:

> Abu Nu'aym transmitted in *al-Hilya* that 'Abdullah ibn 'Abdu'l-Hakam said, "I heard Malik ibn Anas say, 'Harun ar-Rashid consulted me about three things: whether the *Muwatta'* should be hung in the Ka'ba and people compelled to follow what it contains; whether the *minbar* of the Prophet, may Allah bless him and grant him peace, should be dismantled and rebuilt with jewels and gold and silver; and whether Nafi' ibn Abi Nu'aym should be made Imam to lead the people in prayer in the mosque of the Messenger of Allah. I replied, 'Amir al-Mu'minin, as for hanging the *Muwatta'* in the Ka'ba, the Companions of the Messenger of Allah disagreed about the branches of knowledge. They dispersed throughout the lands of Islam and each one did what he thought correct. As for dismantling the *minbar*, I do not think that you should deny people the relics of the Messenger of Allah. As for promoting Nafi' to lead the people in the prayer, Nafi' is an Imam in recitation and he is not safe from making a mistake in the *mihrab*, so protect him.' Harun said, 'May Allah give you success, Abu 'Abdullah!'"

It is clear that Malik was not unduly disturbed by the difference in judgements and decisions in various places which so alarmed some Abbasid officials. He saw that divergence was inevitable and that judgements should be in harmony with the customs of every area so long as they did not contravene any explicit text of the Book or the *Sunna*. People should not be constricted. Malik once told Harun ar-Rashid, when he repeated his request about the *Muwatta'*, "O Amir al-Mu'minin, the differences of the people of knowledge are a mercy from Allah to this community. Each follows what he considers to be sound, each is rightly guided, and each desires to please Allah."

Malik's method in his book is in harmony with the intention behind its compilation. His goal was not to simply record some of the *hadiths* he considered to be sound, as was the case in the *Sahih* collections of *hadith* compiled after his time. The intention of his book was to collect Madinan *fiqh* and the foundations on which it was based. So it is a book of *hadith*, *Sunna* and *fiqh*. That is why we find that he mentioned under the heading of *fiqh* the *hadiths* and then the practice of the people of Madina which was agreed upon, and then the opinion of the *Tabi'un* and people of *fiqh,* and well-known current opinions in Madina. If the question in hand had not been dealt with before then he exercised his own opinion in the light of the *hadiths*, *fatwas* and decisions he knew, with the aim of reaching that decision which best served the public interest.

Malik was well known for his critical approach to transmitters of *hadith*. He measured the *hadiths* he heard against the Book of Allah and what was well known in the *Sunna* and what he considered to be agreed upon by the people of Madina. It may well be that Malik was the first scholar to be strongly concerned with studying the men who transmitted *hadith:* this became a separate branch of knowledge which was pursued by others after him. Even if someone was righteous and godfearing, Malik might still not relate from him because he was known not to memorise accurately. Malik said, "This knowledge concerns the *deen*, so make sure about those from whom you take it. I have met seventy people who said, 'The Messenger of Allah, may Allah bless him and grant him peace, said' within these pillars," and he pointed to the mosque, "but from whom I did not accept anything. Had one of them been entrusted with a treasure, he would have proved trustworthy, but they were not reliable authorities for this business.'"

As far as the *fiqh* in the *Muwatta'* is concerned, some of it is derived from *hadith*, some is clarification of matters agreed upon in Madina, some is clarification of the opinions of the *Tabi'un* whom Malik met, some is opinion that he selected from the sum of their opinions, and some is opinion based on analogy, which was based on what Malik himself knew of the Book and *Sunna* of the

Messenger of Allah, may Allah bless him and grant him peace, and the consensus of the people of Madina and what was transmitted from the people of knowledge among the *Tabi'un* and Companions.

Malik himself described the *fiqh* he utilises in the *Muwatta'*:

> Most of what is in the book is my opinion but, by my life, it is not mere opinion since I heard it from more than one of the people of knowledge and excellence and the Imams who are followed from whom I took knowledge. They are the ones who showed great fear of Allah. It became too repetitive for me (to mention all that), so I said, 'my opinion'. My opinion is the same as their opinion, which was the same as the opinion of the Companions, which they found with them and subsequently I found that with them. This is an inheritance which was passed on from generation to generation down to our time. So it is the opinion of the previous Imams.[1]
>
> As for 'the agreed-upon business', it is what the people of *fiqh* and knowledge agreed upon without dispute. When I say, 'the business with me', that refers to what the people here among us do and concerning which judgements have passed, and which both the common man and the man of knowledge know. The same applies when I say 'in our land'; and when I say 'one of the people of knowledge,' it denotes something I liked in the words of the men of knowledge.
>
> For questions on which I have heard no judgements reported from them, I have striven and investigated according to the method of those I have met until I felt that I had reached the truth or something close to it, so that it would not depart from the school of the people of Madina and their opinions, even if I had not heard that itself. I have stated it as my opinion after exercising *ijtihad* according to the *Sunna,* the actions of the people of

---

1. In other words, what he is presenting is the prevailing consensus of his predecessors in Madina.

knowledge who are followed, and the practice which has been acted upon among us since the time of the Messenger of Allah, may Allah bless him and grant him peace, and the rightly-guided Khalifs, and those I have met. That is their opinion and I have not departed from it in favour of of anyone else's opinion.

This is a clear summary of the method which Imam Malik, may Allah be pleased with him, followed when making *ijtihad* when there was no text. He looked at what the people of knowledge of Madina were agreed upon and then at what the people of Madina acted on and at matters on which judgements had been given and which was known by the common and the elite in Madina. If he did not find any position agreed upon by scholars, or on which there were already judgements in place, he took what seemed good to him from the words of the scholars. If none existed, then he practised *ijtihad* in the light of what he knew, making analogies with similar cases which did exist.

Examples of Malik's method in the *Muwatta'*:

One example of Malik's transmission of *hadiths* and deducing judgement from them is what we find in the *Muwatta'* about asking an apostate to repent before he is killed: (see 36.18.15)

> Malik related from Zayd ibn Aslam that the Messenger of Allah, may Allah bless him and grant him peace, said, 'If someone changes his religion, then strike off his head.' The meaning of the statement of the Prophet, may Allah bless him and grant him peace, in our opinion – and Allah knows best – is that the words 'If someone changes his religion, then strike off his head!' refer to those who leave Islam for something else – heretics and such like who are known to have abandoned Islam (but remain outwardly Muslims). They are killed without being called to repent because their repentance is not recognised. They were concealing their disbelief and making their Islam public,

so I do not think that one should call such people to repent and one does not accept their word.

A person who abandons Islam for something else and divulges the fact is called on to repent. If he does not turn in repentance, he is to be killed. If there are people in that situation, I think that one should call them to Islam and call on them to repent. If they repent, that is accepted from them. If they do not repent, they are killed.

That does not refer, in our view, and Allah knows best, to those who convert from Judaism to Christianity or from Christianity to Judaism, nor to someone who changes his religion from any of the various forms of religion except for Islam. It is the people who leave Islam for something else and make that fact known who are being referred to, and Allah knows best.

Here we see an excellent example of deriving a ruling from a *hadith*. Malik limits the judgement by applying logic in order to arrive at an opinion; consequently he explains "change of religion" as meaning leaving Islam for another religion, thus not including everyone who changes his religion. If it were general, it would also include people who leave paganism for Islam, which clearly is not intended. Since generality does not apply here, Malik explains that what is meant is to protect Islam from the mockery of some corrupters who enter it and leave it with the intention of harming it, or of those who enter Islam with a worldly aim, not believing in its reality, and then leave it.

He makes the command of killing subject to asking for repentance, except in the case of those suspected of heresy who pretend to practise Islam in order to corrupt people. When such people reveal their true state by either action or word, they should be killed without being asked to repent because asking them to repent will only enable them to make a public display of repentance while the heretics are still inwardly committed to disbelief.

Malik also takes the *fatwas* and decisions of the Companions and records them in the *Muwatta'*. An example of this is the divorce of someone suffering from a fatal illness and whose wife inherited from him in spite of the finality of the divorce. He says:

Malik related from Ibn Shihab that Talha ibn 'Abdullah ibn 'Awf reported, and he knew better than them, from Abu Salama ibn 'Abdu'r-Rahman ibn 'Awf that 'Abdu'r-Rahman ibn 'Awf divorced his wife irrevocably when he was terminally ill but 'Uthman ibn 'Affan allowed her to inherit after the end of her *'idda*.

Malik heard from 'Abdullah ibn al-Fadl from al-A'raj that 'Uthman ibn 'Affan made the wives of Ibn Mukmil inherit from him, although he had divorced them when he was terminally ill...

Malik heard Ibn Shihab say, "Even if a man who is terminally ill divorces his wife three times, she inherits from him."

Malik said, "If he divorces her when he is terminally ill but before he has consummated the marriage, she receives half of the dowry and inherits and she does not have to wait through an *'idda*. If he has consummated the marriage she receives all the dowry and also inherits. A virgin and a previously married woman are the same in this situation, in our view. (29:16)

As you see, Malik relates the *fatwas* of the Companions letting the wife inherit in this case. Then he derives from the sum of what he has related that the divorce takes place and the amount of the dowry that is obliged by that divorce, depending on whether the marriage has been consummated or not, and then that the wife is absolutely entitled to inherit, whether she has an *'idda* or not, and whether her *'idda* has ended or not.

He accepts the statement of some of the lesser Companions, which is the Practice of Madina, about accepting the testimony of children in certain cases. He states in the *Muwatta'*:

Malik reported from Hisham ibn 'Urwa that 'Abdullah ibn az-Zubayr gave judgement based on the testimony of children concerning injuries they inflict on each other. Malik said, "The generally accepted practice in our community is that the testimony of children is allowed concerning injuries they inflict on each other but not on any other subject. It is only acceptable if they make their testimony before they leave the scene of the incident and have not been in a position to be deceived or instructed. If they leave the scene, they cannot give testimony unless they call just witnesses to support their testimony about what happened before they left. (36.7.9)

We can see from this that Malik adopted the consensus of the people of Madina on this subject. He was familiar with the words of 'Abdullah ibn az-Zubayr about the testimony of children which was adjudged as correct by Mu'awiya, and 'Umar ibn 'Abdu'l-'Aziz, Sa'id ibn al-Musayyab, 'Urwa and Muhammad al-Baqir all gave *fatwas* on that basis.

The *Muwatta'* also contains a report of the consensus of the people of Madina about the inheritance of full sisters and half-brothers from one father.

The generally accepted practice among us is that full brothers and sisters do not inherit anything if there are sons, or grandsons through a son, or if there is a father. They do inherit if there are daughters or grand-daughters through a son, when the deceased does not have a paternal grandfather still alive. They are considered as paternal relations in any property that is left over. One begins with the people who are allotted fixed shares. They are given their shares. If there is anything left over after that, it belongs to the full brothers and sisters. They divide it between themselves according to the Book of Allah, whether they are male or female. The male receives twice the portion a female. If there is nothing left over, they get nothing. (27.5)

We see that this statement takes the consensus of the people of Madina alone as evidence and then proceeds to the branches on the basis of that agreement.

There are *fatwas* of the Companions which Malik takes and recommends and then uses as a basis for analogy when others disagree with them. Then he derives branches based on them, as happened in the case of the wives of missing men.

> Malik related from Yahya ibn Sa'id from Sa'id ibn al-Musayyab that 'Umar ibn al-Khattab said: "A woman who loses her husband and does not know where he is must wait for four years; wait through an *'idda* of four months; and then she is free to marry." Malik said, "If she marries after her *'idda* is over, regardless of whether the new husband has consummated the marriage or not, her first husband has no right of access to her. That is what is done among us. If her husband reaches her before she has remarried, he is more entitled to her. I have met people who disapprove of one person's statement, attributed by somebody to 'Umar ibn al-Khattab, that he said, "Her first husband can choose, if he comes, between her dowry and taking back his wife."
>
> He said, "In the case of a woman whose husband divorced her while he was absent from her and then took her back; news of his taking her back had not reached her while the news of his divorcing her had, and so she had married again, I have heard that 'Umar ibn al-Khattab said, 'Her first husband who divorced her has no right of access to her whether or not the new husband has consummated the marriage.'" Malik said, "This is what I like best of what I have heard about missing husbands." (29.20.52)

Several things can be seen from this. Malik chose the opinion of 'Umar from among other opinions regarding the wives of missing men and people who divorce their wives while they are away and then want to take them back.

There are subsidiary judgements which result from that opinion. If the husband reappears after the period of four years and four months has passed, she is his if she has not remarried. If she has remarried she belongs to the second husband whether or not the marriage has been consummated. But Malik revised his opinion a year before his death, saying that she belonged to the first husband if the second marriage had not been consummated or if the second husband consummated it knowing that her husband was alive.

An analogy is made between the case of a man adjudged to be dead after four years and one who takes his wife back without her knowing it. 'Umar gave a *fatwa* that in the second case the wife belongs to the second husband whether or not the second marriage has been consummated. Malik made an analogy between this and someone who returns after his wife has observed the *'idda* for his death and has remarried.

From all these various examples it is clear that the *Muwatta'* is a book of both *fiqh* and *hadiths,* and that the purpose of the *hadiths* quoted is to derive judgements of *fiqh* from their texts and to derive further rulings which accord with them. For this reason Malik does not confine himself to *hadiths* but also mentions the judgements made by the Companions, choosing what he believes to be most appropriate and beneficial in the particular case in hand. He mentions the action agreed upon in Madina and the judgements in cases there. When there is no previous ruling he makes an analogy from what he knows of the cases decided by the Companions.

There are two main transmitted recensions of the *Muwatta'*. One is from Muhammad ibn al-Hasan ash-Shaybani, the companion of Abu Hanifa, and the other is from Yahya ibn Yahya al-Laythi al-Andalusi (d. 234), one of Malik's students, who emigrated to Andalusia and was called "the intellectual leader of the Andalusians". He was a leader in *fiqh* and it was through him that the school of Malik spread there and countless individuals learned it. He was offered the job of *qadi* there, but refused it. The recension from Muhammad ibn al-Hasan ash-Shaybani has fewer chapters. Some people prefer one and some the other. Muhammad sometimes mentions opinions of his own which contradicts that of Malik in questions of *fiqh*, just as he did with his own shaykh, Abu Hanifa. The differences between the two versions are very minor which indicates that they came from a common source.

Some of Malik's Students

Maliki *fiqh* was transmitted in two ways. One was by the books which Malik wrote and which are related from him and the soundness and strongest of those is the *Muwatta'* as we have made clear. The second was through his students. They transmitted his *fiqh*, and many books were transmitted from them.

No other Imam is known to have had such a large number of students as Malik. They were very numerous indeed and came from all over the world. He had students from Khorasan, Iraq, and Syria, although most of them were from Madina, Egypt, or North Africa.

The reason for that is that he resided in the Hijaz and particularly in Madina al-Munawwara. He only left it to perform *Hajj* and he is not known ever to have left the land of the Hijaz at all. Madina was the home of the Prophet, may Allah bless him and grant him peace. People from all over the world went there after making *Hajj* to the House of Allah. Malik lived to be well over eighty and taught for about sixty years of his life. This was another factor in the number of his students.

The importance of the role of Malik's students can be gauged from the fact that the *Muwatta'* reports only a small number of the topics which he taught and on which he gave *fatwa*. However, his students used to record his *fatwas*. Indeed, he sometimes forbade them to go too far in writing them down. It would be impossible to deal fully and comprehensively with all his students, so we will just mention a few of the more important ones in brief.

'Abdullah ibn Wahb

This man was a Berber allied to Quraysh. He stayed with Malik
for about twenty years, and disseminated his *fiqh* in Egypt. He
studied not only with Malik but also with many of the companions
of az-Zuhri. He also took from more than 400 shaykhs of *hadith* in
Egypt, the Hijaz and Iraq, including Sufyan ath-Thawri, Ibn
'Uyayna, Ibn Jurayj, 'Abdu'r-Rahman ibn Ziyad al-Ifriqi, Sa'id
ibn Abi Ayyub, and others. Many related from him. Asbagh, one
of the students of the companions of Malik, said "Ibn Wahb was
the companion of Malik with the most knowledge of the *Sunna*
and traditions although he related from men who were weak."

Ibn Wahb himself recognised that some of his *hadiths* were
weak. He said, "If it had not been that Allah rescued me through
Malik and al-Layth, I would have been lost." He was asked, "How
is that?" He replied, "I knew many *hadiths,* and that confused me.
I used to present them to Malik and al-Layth and they would say,
'Take this and leave that.'"

Malik esteemed and loved him. He did not spare any of his
companions criticism except for Ibn Wahb. He used to call him
"the *faqih*" when he wrote to him. Ibn Wahb was one of those who
spread Malik's school in Egypt and the Maghrib. People travelled
to him to learn Malik's *fiqh* both during Malik's lifetime and after
his death. He left many excellent books, including what he heard
from Malik which took up about 30 volumes. He died in 197 AH
at the age of 72.

'Abdu'r-Rahman ibn al-Qasim

This scholar was one of the companions of Malik who had a
tremendous influence in recording his school since he was the
source for Sahnun in his record of the teaching of Malik. In the
school of Malik he has the same position as Muhammad ibn al-
Hasan ash-Shaybani has in the school of Abu Hanifa. There is a
complete correspondence between the two men. Both of them

transmitted the school and made free use of *ijtihad*. Ibn al-Qasim had opinions which differed from those of his shaykh, Malik, so that it was said that he was dominated by opinion. Ibn 'Abdu'l-Barr said of him, "He was a *faqih* dominated by opinion. He was a righteous, poor, steadfast man."

He met Malik after Ibn Wahb and kept his company for a long time – about twenty years. He learned his *fiqh*. He also met al-Layth, 'Abdu'l-'Aziz ibn al-Majishun and Muslim ibn Khalid al-Zanji. Many people related from him and consulted him about Malik's *fatwas*. Ibn Wahb used to say, "If you want this business – meaning the *fiqh* of Malik – you must have Ibn al-Qasim. He is unique in it." His transmission of the *Muwatta'* is the soundest and Sahnun learned the contents of the *Mudawwana,* the most comprehensive collection of Maliki *fiqh*, from him. Thus he can be considered as the main transmitter of Maliki *fiqh,* for the *Mudawwana* is its chief source.

He was a generous and abstemious man. He did not accept the stipends of any ruler and he said, "There is no good in the proximity of rulers." He frequented them at first, but then he kept away from them. He died in 191 at the age of 63.

Ashhab ibn 'Abdu'l-'Aziz al-'Amiri

Ashhab studied with al-Layth, Yahya ibn Ayyub, and Ibn Lahi'a. He kept Malik's company and learned his *fiqh*, and was one of those who transmitted his *fiqh*. He had a collection called the *Mudawwana* of Ashhab or the Books of Ashhab. He was a contemporary of Ibn al-Qasim, but was younger than him. Sahnun was the student of both of them and was asked which of them knew more *fiqh*. He replied, "They were like two horses neck and neck. Sometimes this one was successful and that one unsuccessful, and sometimes it was the reverse."

Ibn al-Qasim and Ashhab once disagreed about what Malik had said about a particular matter and each of them swore to refute what the other said. They asked Ibn Wahb, who was an older companion than they were; and he told them that Malik had made both statements. Ash-Shafi'i met Ashhab and said, "I have not seen anyone with more *fiqh* than Ashhab. He achieved supremacy in *fiqh* in Egypt."

Ashhab compiled a book called *al-Mudawwana,* which was not the *Mudawwana* of Sahnun. Qadi 'Iyad said of it, "It is a large majestic book containing much knowledge." Ibn Harith said, "When the *Asadiyya* [the basis for the *Mudawwana* of Sahnun] was completed, Ashhab took it and edited it, having objected to some of it. He produced a noble book. When Ibn al-Qasim heard that, he commented that he had found a complete book and then built on it. Ashhab said to him, 'You scooped from one spring and I from many springs.' So Ibn al-Qasim answered him, 'Your springs are turbid but my spring is clear.'"

Sahnun was a student of both Ashhab and Ibn al-Qasim and so he took from both of them. Ashhab left other books as well. He was born in 140 AH and died in 204, a few days after ash-Shafi'i.

Asad ibn al-Furat

Asad's origins lay in Khorasan although he was born at Harran. Then his father moved with him to Tunis, although some say that he was born in Tunis. He memorised the Qur'an and then studied *fiqh.* He travelled to the east and heard the *Muwatta'* and other teachings from Malik. He then went to Iraq and met Abu Yusuf and Muhammad ibn al-Hasan ash-Shaybani.

Asad then combined the *fiqh* of Iraq and the *fiqh* of Madina. He had studied with both Muhammad ibn al-Hasan and Malik. The student of Malik who took the most from him later was Ibn al-Qasim.

According to the *Madarik:* "When Asad came to Egypt, he went to Ibn Wahb and said, 'These are the books of Abu Hanifa,' and he asked him to answer them according to the school of Malik. Ibn Wahb was too scrupulous and refused. Asad he went to Ibn al-Qasim, who answered the questions he asked from what he remembered of Malik's actual words. When he was unsure, Ibn al-Qasim said, 'I imagine,' 'I suppose' and 'I think'. On one occasion he said, 'I heard him speak on such-and-such a question and your question is similar to it.' On other occasions, he spoke according to his own *ijtihad* based on what Malik had said. He collected those answers into books which were called *al-Asadiyya*."

The *Asadiyya* was the basis for the *Mudawwana* of Sahnun. Asad was appointed *qadi* of Qayrawan. He died in 212 in the siege of Syracuse while he was the commander and *qadi* of the army. He was born in 145.

The Major Works of the Maliki School

Ibn Khaldun reports about the books of the Maliki school: "'Abdu'l-Malik ibn Habib travelled from Andalusia and took from Ibn al-Qasim. He then disseminated what he learned and so the school of Malik spread in Andalusia. He wrote a book on it called *al-Wadiha*. Next one of his students, al-'Utbi, wrote *al-'Utbiyya*. Asad ibn Furat travelled from North Africa and wrote first from the people of Abu Hanifa and before moving to the school of Malik. Ibn al-Qasim brought his book to Qayrawan and called it *al-Asadiyya*. Sahnun read it to Asad and then travelled east and met Ibn al-Qasim. He took from him and reviewed with him the questions of the *Asadiyya,* much of which he retracted. Then Sahnun wrote out its questions, put them in order, and produced *al-Mudawwana*. People then abandoned the *Asadiyya* and adopted Sahnun's book. The people of Qayrawan relied on this *Mudawwana* and the people of Andalusia on *al-Wadiha* and *al-'Utbiyya*. Then Ibn Abi Zayd summarised *al-Mudawwana* and *al-Mukhtalita* in a book called *al-Mukhtasar*. A synopsis of it, entitled *at-Tahdhib,* was also made by one of the *fuqaha'* of Qayrawan, Abu Sa'id al-Baradhi'i. The shaykhs of North Africa came to rely on it and adopted it, abandoning other books. Similarly, the people of Andalusia relied on *al-'Utbiyya* and left *al-Wadiha* and the other books."

The position of Maliki *fiqh* in respect of *ijtihad*

As we know Malik, learned the *fiqh* of the seven *fuqaha'* of
Madina and others. He learned *hadiths* from them and others.
Then he passed on the *hadiths* he had learned to his students and
gave them *fatwas* on questions which arose. The method of Malik,
in short, is to take first the Book of Allah and the *Sunna* of the
Messenger of Allah, may Allah bless him and grant him peace,
and the *fatwas* of the Companions, and then *ijtihad* with opinion
using analogy and *masalih mursala* (considerations of public interest) and other techniques as we will explain below when outlining
the fundamental principles of his school, Allah willing. They are
the results of a sound investigation directed to seeking out the truth
without ignoring the value of action or belittling the right of the
doer or undervaluing transmitted sources.

A group of orientalists, however, who looked at Islamic *fiqh*
from a different viewpoint from ours, have said that Malik did not
originate a new school of *fiqh*. According to them he confined
himself to only two methods. He wrote down what was found dispersed in various sources on questions of *fiqh* and collected legal
customs which were known to the people of Madina, endowing
them with a religious authority whereas in fact those customs were
merely old Arab usages. That is their view of the *fiqh* of Malik.
They separate it from its source, which is the Book of Allah and
the *Sunna* of His Messenger, and consider that it consists of Arab
customs clothed in a religious garment and that he merely wrote
down dispersed information. But this is a very short-sighted view
indeed.

Malik did not leave the arena open to doubt. He used a clear
methodology in *fiqh;* related *hadiths* with *isnads* which were *muttasil, mursal* or *munqati';* and derived judgements from their texts
and expounded them. In view of what we have mentioned, it is
necessary to examine the principles on which his *fiqh* was based.

The Fundamental Principles of Malik's *fiqh*

Malik did not record the fundamental principles on which he based his school and on whose basis he derived his judgements and to which he limited himself in the derivation of his rulings. In that respect he resembled his contemporary, Abu Hanifa, but not his student, ash-Shafi'i, who did record the principles he used in derivation and defined them precisely, specifying the motives which moved him to consider them and their position in deduction.

Nonetheless, Malik did indicate the principles he used in some of his *fatwas*, questions and the *hadiths* which had *muttasil* (uninterrupted), *munqati'* (broken),or *mursal* (link missing) *isnads* and *balaghat* (without *isnad*) *hadith*, even if he did not precisely explain his method or defend it or explain the motives which moved him to adopt it and why he used that method rather than another.

For instance, the *Muwatta'* makes it clear to us that Malik uses *mursal, munqati'* and *balaghat hadiths* but does not explain how he chose them because it does not go into the problems concerning the *isnads*. The reason for this is that Malik only transmitted from people in whose *mursal* and *balaghat hadith* he had absolute confidence. That is why his great concern was with the choice of transmitter. When he had confidence in the character, intelligence and knowledge of the transmitter he dispensed with the chain of narration.

Malik clearly stated that he took the practice of the people of Madina as a source and explained the motives which led him to do so. The *Muwatta'* shows that he used it in making analogy, as he when he made an analogy between the wife of a missing man when he returns to her after she has married someone else and

88

someone who divorces his wife with a revocable divorce and then takes her back when she knows about the divorce but not the taking back and consequently remarries.

The author of *al-Madarik* mentions the general foundations of Islamic *fiqh,* which are the Noble Qur'an, its texts, its outward meanings and understood meanings, the *Sunna* – *mutawatir, mashhur* and single – then consensus, and then analogy. Next he mentions the principles used by Malik and his position.

> If you look straight away at the methods of these Imams and the establishment of their principles in *fiqh* and *ijtihad* in the *Shari'a,* you will find that Malik pursued a clear methodology in respect of these principles and ordered them according to their respective ranks. He put the Book of Allah first and put the traditions with it, placing them before analogy and opinion. He left anything which was not considered probable by reliable men known for their sound knowledge, or when he found that the great majority of the people of Madina did something different and contrary to it. He did not pay any attention to those who interpreted things according to their own opinions: explicitly declared that such rulings were false and baseless. (*Tartib al-Madarik*, p. 16)

Qadi 'Iyad also lists the basic foundations of the school of Malik as being the Book and *Sunna,* the practice of the people of Madina and *qiyas* (analogy), but he does not mention any others. He does not mention *ijma'* (consensus) or the other methodological principles which distinguish the Maliki school, such as *masalih mursala, sadd adh-dhara'i',* custom, and certain other principles which other people have mentioned.

The most precise enumeration of the principles of the Maliki school is that given by al-Qarafi in his book *Tanqih al-Usul.* He stated that the foundational principles of the school are: the Qur'an, the *Sunna,* the consensus of the people of Madina, analogy, the statement of the Companions, together with *masalih mursala* (considerations of public interest), *'urf* (custom), *'adat* (common usage), *sadd adh-dhara'i'* (blocking the means), *istishab* (presumption of continuity), and *istihsan* (discretion).

The Qur'an

According to ash-Shatibi al-Maliki in *al-Muwafaqat*:

> The Qur'an is the whole of the *Shari'a*, the support of religion, the fount of wisdom, the sign of Prophethood and the light of the eyes and the heart. There is no way to Allah except through it and there is no salvation by any other means. You must not hold to anything that contradicts it. None of this needs affirmation or deduction because it is known to the *deen* of the Community. Since that is the case, whoever wants complete knowledge of the *Shari'a* and desires to perceive its aims and be joined to its adherents must necessarily take the Qur'an as his constant companion and make it his intimate, night and day, in both investigation and action.

Malik viewed the Qur'an in the same way. So he was only seen reciting the Qur'an or relating *hadiths* or deriving *fatwas* from them to answer questions which were directed to him. He did not look at the Qur'an with the eye of a debater. It is not reported that he ever said that the Qur'an consisted of both words and meaning or meaning only; or did he engage in any discussion of the *mutakallimun* about the Qur'an being created since he did not consider such subjects to be debatable.

Malik knew that the Qur'an contains all the *Shari'a* and that the *Sunna* is simply its exposition. The *Sunna* is the straight way to grasp the meanings of the Book. That is why it is not correct to hold only to the Qur'an without seeking help in its explanation, meaning the *Sunna*. He disliked including any Biblical or Jewish (Talmudic) material in its explanation.

We will now discuss different aspects of Qur'anic evidence.

Explicit texts (*nass*) and apparent (*dhahir*) texts

Rulings are taken from the Book of Allah but not all Qur'anic texts are the same as regards whether one may derive rulings from them. The scholars of the Maliki principles say that there is a difference between explicit, unequivocal texts (*nass*) and apparent texts (*dhahir*) in that *nass* texts are not open to interpretation whereas *dhahir* texts can be interpreted. That is something which ash-Shafi'i did not discuss in his *Risala*, as he considered *nass* and *dhahir* to be basically interchangeable. In the Maliki position, the *nass* is stronger than the *dhahir*. A *dhahir* text can mean one of two or more things and requires further exposition from the *Sunna* or Qur'an.

The *Sunna*

There is no dispute that Malik was an Imam in *hadith* and *fiqh*: a transmitter of the first rank in *hadith* and a *faqih* with insight into *fatwa* and the deduction of judgements. His transmission of *hadith* is also considered one of the soundest of transmissions, particularly in his choice of transmitters and knowledge of the accuracy of their transmission. There are three ways in which the *Sunna* clarifies and complements the Qur'an.

It directly confirms the judgements of the Qur'an; in this case it adds nothing new whatsoever, nor does it clarify something unclear or limit something which is unrestricted or specify something referred to in general terms.

The *Sunna* also casts light on the intention of the Qur'an and limits some things which are unrestricted in the Book and gives detailed form to some matters which are undefined by the Book. One example of that is the sound *hadith* of the Prophet, may Allah bless him and grant him peace, which clarifies the *ayat*: *"Those who believe and do not mix their belief with any wrongdoing."* (6:82) in which he makes it clear that "wrongdoing" in this context means *shirk*. Another example is the way that the *Sunna* delineates the details of the prayer, *zakat* and *hajj*. The Noble

Qur'an deals with these acts of worship in general. It prescribes the prayer but does not give details of its pillars and times. The Prophet expounded them by action and said, "Pray as you saw me pray." The Qur'an commands us to pay *zakat* but the *Sunna* gives us its details, specifying the *zakat* to be paid on gold and silver, on crops and fruits, and on livestock. The same applies to the *hajj*. It is referred to in general terms in the Qur'an but it is the *Sunna* of the Prophet which clarifies its practices for us.

The *Sunna* also clarifies the *hudud* in the same way. Allah says: *"As for both male thieves and female thieves, cut off their hands as payment for what they have earned: an object lesson from Allah."* (5:38) The *ayat* does not define the minimum for which the hand is cut off, or its preconditions. That is left to the *Sunna*. There are, of course, a great many other situations in which the *Sunna* amplifies Qur'anic texts in the same way.

The third way in which the *Sunna* complements the Qur'an is in judgements about which the Book is silent. An example of this is Malik's position of rendering judgement with only one witness and an oath when a claimant does not have two witnesses. The testimony of one witness is heard and the oath of the claimant takes the place of the second witness. This procedure is based on a tradition which Malik considers sound. Another example is inheritance by a grandmother, which is not mentioned in the Qur'an.

According to Malik, however, if the *Sunna* is not supported by consensus, the practice of the people of Madina or analogy, the text must be taken literally and any *sunna* which contradicts that literal text is rejected if it is transmitted via a single tradition. When it comes through multiple transmissions (*mutawatir*), the *Sunna* can be raised to the level of abrogating the Qur'an in Malik's opinion. So Malik preferred the *dhahir* text over a single tradition, even one considered sound, if it was not reinforced by consensus or practice. On this basis he rejected the report "If a dog drinks out of one of your vessels, you should wash it seven times, once with earth" because it clashes with the apparent meaning of the Qur'an in the words of the Almighty, *"what is caught for you by hunting animals which you have trained."* (5:4) According to this, anything caught by hunting dogs is permitted, which indicates its purity and refutes the idea suggested by the report that it is impure.

Ibn Rushd divided the *Sunna* in the Maliki view into four categories according to the strength of its methods of transmission and its subject matter.

- A *sunna* whose rejection is a mark of unbelief. If someone does reject it they are asked to repent. If they do not, they are to be killed as unbelievers. This applies to *sunnas* which have been transmitted by multiple transmission. Acquiring knowledge of such a *sunna* is obligatory: like wine being unlawful, the prayers being five, the Messenger of Allah, may Allah bless him and grant him peace, commanding the calling of the *adhan*, and other similar things.

- A *sunna* which only people of deviation, error and denial reject and which all the People of the *Sunna* agree to be sound: such as the *hadiths* of intercession, the Vision, the punishment in the grave, and similar things connected with faith, even if they are not *mutawatir* in their *isnad*.

- A *sunna* which it is obligatory to know and to act on, even if some of the opponents of the People of *Sunna* oppose it, such as wiping over leather socks, because it is known that it is acted upon by the vast majority of the Muslims and its opponents are very few.

- A *sunna* which it is obligatory to act on, being one which is transmitted by a reliable source from a reliable source. They are numerous in all the categories of law and it is obligatory to act by them. An example of this is judging by the testimony of two witnesses of good character, even if they might lie or be suspect in their testimony.

Opinion and *Hadith*

It might be imagined that Malik was lacking in opinion, to judge from the statements of those who have written about the history of Islamic *fiqh* and divided *fiqh* into *fiqh* of tradition and *fiqh* of opinion, considering Madina to be the place of the first and Iraq the place of the second and stating that Malik was a *faqih* of tradition and Abu Hanifa a *faqih* of opinion.

We see that this is not true of Malik but is true of Abu Hanifa. We find, for instance, that Ibn Qutayba considered Malik to be a *faqih* of opinion. We mentioned in our account of the life of Malik that his contemporaries considered him to be a *faqih* of opinion so that one of them asked in his time, "Who is capable of formulating an opinion in Madina now that Rabi'a and Yahya ibn Sa'id have gone?" The reply was "Malik".

Malik used to study questions of *fiqh* with the eyes of an expert who could compare them against the measure of people's best interests and compare them by means of analogy, and study the *hadiths* of the Prophet in the light of these things, and compare them against the general meaning of the Noble Qur'an. He explored all these matters with a profound and precise examination. In this study we see that Malik was the *faqih* whose opinion did not swerve from the *deen* just as we have seen that he was a *hadith* scholar with reliable transmissions.

The extent of Malik's use of opinion is shown clearly by two things: firstly the considerable number of questions in dealing with which he relied on opinion, whether it was reached by analogy or *istihsan, masalih mursala, istihsan* or by *sadd adh-dhara'i'*. There were many and if you open the *Mudawwana* you will see that clearly. The methods by which Malik reaches opinions are more numerous than those used by others and that shows the great importance of opinion in his work. Its frequency is a clear indication of his reliance on it and that he clearly made use of it.

Secondly we find that when there is a conflict between single traditions and analogy, which is one kind of opinion, we find that many of the Malikis confirm that he preferred analogy, and they all mention that sometimes he used analogy and rejected traditions if they came from a single source.

That makes Malik one of the most distinguished *fuqaha'* of opinion. It does not in any way detract from him being the Imam of the *Sunna*. Rather it makes that Imamate more impressive, because the Imam of the *Sunna* is not someone who simply follows every tradition which comes to him without investigating its *isnad* and the text. Malik investigated the *isnads* and was most particular about the people from whom he related and rigorous in examining their states.

In the same way he examined the texts of the traditions and weighed them very finely. He would weigh them against other general Islamic principles which are derived from its texts and goals and attested to by various judgements from the secondary rulings. If everything about them was in order with them, he would accept them. If anything was not right, he would reject them.

We should state at this point that if a single tradition was reinforced by the practice of the people of Madina, that would raise it from being merely an isolated report to the rank of consensus. In this case it cannot be rejected, for if the practice of the people of Madina reinforces a single tradition it is preferred even to an apparent text of the Qur'an.

As we said, this does not indicate that Malik forsook the *Sunna* in any way: it simply indicates that he used individual opinion (*ra'y*) and that this was the method of some of the righteous *Salaf*. For instance, 'A'isha and Ibn 'Abbas, may Allah be pleased with them, rejected the tradition of Abu Hurayra about washing the hands before putting them into a *wudu'* jug under the general established principle of removing constriction from the *deen*. Neither 'A'isha nor Ibn 'Abbas ever forsook the *Sunna* or abandoned any sound and established statement of the Prophet, may Allah bless him and grant him peace. But when they saw a tradition which clashed with a general confirmed principle on which there is no doubt, they left it and judged that its ascription to the Prophet, may Allah bless him and grant him peace, was not sound. They did not abandon the statement of the Prophet, but rather they rejected its ascription to him.

Fatwas of the Companions

In his early studies Malik concentrated on learning the cases of the Companions, their *fatwas,* and their judgements in respect of the questions which he concerned him. We have already seen how eager he was to learn the *fatwas* of 'Abdullah ibn 'Umar from his client Nafi'. He used to lie in wait for him when he went out so that he might ask him about the statements of 'Abdullah. He also was eager to learn the cases of 'Umar ibn al-Khattab, may Allah be pleased with him. He learned the *fiqh* of the seven *fuqaha'* of Madina. They transmitted the disagreements, perceptions, *fatwas* and decisions of the Companions as well as the *hadiths* of the Messenger of Allah, may Allah bless him and grant him peace.

After our study and investigation of the life of Malik, we can state that the knowledge which he was taught and which he mastered and on which he based himself and on the basis of which he made deduction and according to which he proceeded with the implementation of the *hadiths* of the Messenger of Allah was the decisions and *fatwas* of the Companions.

That is why the *fatwas* of the Companions occupied a major place in Malik's deduction. He took them and did not infringe them. He accepted the position of the People of Madina because the Companions had been there, as we mentioned earlier in his letter to al-Layth. Malik realised that the *Sunna* was to be found in what the Companions had. He saw that when 'Umar ibn 'Abdu'l-'Aziz wanted to spread knowledge of the *Sunna*, he commanded that the decisions and *fatwas* of the Companions in Madina be collected. Malik used to relate what this upright khalif said on this subject.

> The Messenger of Allah laid down a *sunna* and those in command after him laid down *sunan*. Accepting and acting on that is tantamount to following the Book of Allah, the completion of obedience to Allah, and firmness in the *deen* of Allah. No one after them can change the *Sunna* or is permitted to take on anything which opposes them. Whoever is guided by them is guided. Whoever seeks help by them is helped. If anyone leaves them to follow a way other than that of the believers, Allah will assign him what he has turned to and Hellfire will roast him. What an evil return!

Malik admired those words and clung to them, holding that they embodied the perfect definition of the *Sunna*. He accepted that. The *Muwatta'* contains the *fatwas* of the Companions alongside *hadiths* of the Messenger of Allah, may Allah bless him and grant him peace. So he recorded the *fatwas* and decisions of the Companions as he recorded the statements of the Prophet, may Allah bless him and grant him peace, and considered them to be part of the *Sunna*. According to ash-Shatibi, the Imam of the *Sunna* was well known in his lifetime as strongly favouring this position. He said in *al-Muwafaqat*:

> This was the way Malik viewed the *fatwas* and decisions of the Companions. He and Imam Ahmad are probably the Imams who held most strongly to the *fatwas* of the Companions and were most eager to learn them and take them as a basis for other decisions and *fatwas* and it was they who did that most often. They accepted the statements and *fatwas* of the Companions without limitation or precondition regarding their number, their attributes, their actions, or the type of opinion related from them. When they disagreed, they chose the majority position and that which was acted upon by the community as a whole.

It is clear from looking at the principles of the Malikis and the *Muwatta'* that Malik, like Ahmad ibn Hanbal, accepted the statements of the Companions as a source of *fiqh* and as having authority and constituting one of the branches of the *Sunna* of the Prophet. That is why to know them is to know the *Sunna* and to go against them is innovation. Ibn al-Qayyim clearly states in *I'lam al-Muwaqqi'in* that it is part of the *Sunna*.

> When a Companion makes a statement or gives a judgement or a *fatwa*, it may stem from discernment which he has and we do not, or from discernment in which we share. As for what is particular to him, it is likely that he heard it directly from the mouth of Prophet, may Allah bless him and grant him peace, or from another Companion narrating from the Messenger of Allah. The knowl-

97

edge they possessed and to which we do not have access is more than will ever be known. None of them related all that they heard. Where is what Abu Bakr as-Siddiq, 'Umar al-Faruq and the other great Companions, may Allah be pleased with them, heard, compared to what they relate?

There are not even a hundred *hadiths* related from the Siddiq of the Community, despite the fact that he was not absent from the Prophet, may Allah bless him and grant him peace, in any of his battles and accompanied him from the time of his prophetic mission, or indeed, even before that time, until his death. Abu Bakr was the most knowledgeable of the community about him, may Allah bless him and grant him peace, and about his words, actions, guidance and conduct. The same applies to the majority of the Companions: the amount that they transmit from the Prophet is very little indeed in comparison with what they actually heard and witnessed from him. If they had related all that they heard and witnessed, it would have been many times more than what Abu Hurayra transmitted. He was only a Companion for about four years and related a great deal from him.

The statement 'If the Companions had known anything about this matter...' can only be made by someone who does not understand the behaviour and states of people. They were in awe of transmitting from the Messenger of Allah, may Allah bless him and grant him peace, and attached great importance to it. They did not often do so, fearing to add to or subtract from his words.

Any *fatwa* which one of the Companions gave will be based on one of six foundations:

- He heard it himself directly from the Prophet, may Allah bless him and grant him peace.

- He heard it from someone else who heard it.

- He understood it from an *ayat* of the Book of Allah in a manner which is unknown to us.

- It is something which all the Companions were agreed upon but only the statement of the one who gave the *fatwa* has been transmitted to us.

- He understands it through his complete knowledge of the language and what the phrase indicates in a manner to which he has access and we do not or by direct knowledge of the actual circumstances which were being addressed; or by the sum of matters which he understood over the passage of time through seeing the Prophet, may Allah bless him and grant him peace, and witnessing his actions, states and behaviour and listening to his words, knowing his aims and witnessing the arrival of Revelation and witnessing its interpretation through action. Because of all this, the Companion was able to understand things which we cannot.

If the basis of the *fatwa* is any of the above five criteria, it is authoritative for us and must be followed.

- It was based on an individual understanding of something that the Messenger, may Allah bless him and grant him peace, about which the Prophet did not speak and the Companion was wrong in his understanding.

This sixth aspect is a theoretical one and the possibility of its occurring is remote, especially in the case of the exalted Companions who transmitted the Islamic *deen* to the next generation. This excellent directive clarifies Malik's view in considering the statement of the Companion as an authoritative source and the fact that he accepted it as being part of the *Sunna*.

On the basis of this principle, Malik sometimes used to prefer the statement of the Companions over some *hadiths,* after comparing them. In some cases there were certain aspects of opinion, the practice of the people of Madina, statements of the people or the general bases of the *Shari'a,* which made the statement of a Companion preferable to an individual *hadith.*

In so doing, Malik did not prefer the statement of the Companion over the *Sunna* but rather in that instance it was the statement of the Companion in fact which constituted the *Sunna.* Because they differed in their conclusions he carefully compared them and ended by accepting one and rejecting the other. He did not reject a statement of the Messenger of Allah, may Allah bless him and grant him peace, for a statement of a Companion. He rejected one tradition from the Messenger for another which was more reliable and had a more truthful transmission.

Fatwas of the Followers

It is clear that Malik did not consider the statements of the Followers to occupy the same position in the *Sunna* as those of the Companions; but he did take account of the positions of some of the Followers because of their knowledge of *fiqh* or their truthfulness or their exalted qualities of character. These included such people as 'Umar ibn 'Abdu'l-'Aziz, Sa'id ibn al-Musayyab, Ibn Shihab az-Zuhri, Nafi' the client of Ibn 'Umar, and others who were accurate in transmission of knowledge and had high proficiency in *fiqh.* He accepted a *fatwa* from them when its basis was a known *sunna,* or was in accordance with the practice of the people of Madina, or with the position of the majority of scholars. Sometimes he was satisfied with their *ijtihad* when he had confidence in it and did not find anything to contradict it.

Consensus (*Ijma'*)

Malik, may Allah be pleased with him, was probably the one of the four Imams who most frequently mentioned consensus and used it as evidence. If you open the *Muwatta',* you will find in many places that the ruling in the case mentions that it is "the generally agreed-on way of doing things," and that was considered to be an evidence which was sufficiently authoritative for him to give *fatwa* by it.

Let us see what Malik himself says in explanation of his use of the term 'agreed-on'. We find that he says in the *Muwatta'*:

> As for 'the agreed-upon practice', it is something that the people of *fiqh* and knowledge agree upon without dispute. This is the agreement of the people of this community who contract agreements (*ahl al-hall wa'l-'aqd*) in any matter. By agreement we mean agreement in word, action or belief.

That is the consensus which Malik took as an authoritative evidence and which you see often used in the *Muwatta'* in resolving questions about which there is no unequivocal text or when he believes that the text needs to be amplified, or when the text is an *ayat* whose meaning is of the apparent sort (*dhahir*) which admits of interpretation and specification. It is also clear that consensus in the view of Malik is the consensus of the people of Madina, and this leads us on to the practice of the people of Madina.

The Practice of the People of Madina

Malik, may Allah be pleased with him, considered the practice of the people of Madina to be a legal source on which he relied in his *fatwas*. That is why he often said, after mentioning the traditions and *hadith*, "the way of doing things generally agreed-on among us." Sometimes, when no text or other authority existed, Malik used the practice of the people of Madina as an evidence to be relied on absolutely. His previously mentioned letter to al-Layth ibn Sa'd shows the great extent to which he relied on it and his objection to those who followed anything other than the practice of the People of Madina.

It is clear that Malik was not the first person to use the practice of the people of Madina as an authoritative evidence. Malik's shaykh, Rabi'a, mentioned the method and said, "A thousand from a thousand is better than one from one." Malik said, "The learned men among the Followers quoted *hadiths* which had been conveyed to them from others and they said, 'We are not ignorant of this, but the common practice is different.'"

He also said, "I saw Muhammad ibn Abi Bakr ibn 'Amr ibn Hazm who was a *qadi*. His brother 'Abdullah knew many *hadiths* and was a truthful man. When Muhammad gave a judgement and there was a *hadith* contrary to it, I heard 'Abdullah criticise him, saying, 'Isn't there a *hadith* which says such and such? 'Yes,' he replied. 'Then what is the matter with you? Why don't you give judgement by it?' asked his brother. 'Where are the people in respect to it?' replied Muhammad, meaning 'what is the consensus of action on it in Madina?' He meant that the practice outweighs the *hadith* in that instance." (*Madarik*, p. 38)

So it can be seen that Malik, may Allah be pleased with him, did not originate that method. Rather he travelled a path which others among the Followers and the people of knowledge before him had followed. He became renowned for it, however, because of the great number of *fatwas* he was asked for and because some of his *fatwas* were contrary to *hadiths* which he also related. He became the most famous of those who accepted the practice of the people of Madina as an authoritative source and so the method was ascribed to him; but the truth is that in that respect he was a follower, not an originator.

Analogy (*Qiyas*)

Malik, may Allah be pleased with him, issued *fatwas* for more than fifty years. People came to him from the East and West to ask for *fatwa*. Since questions are endless and events occur every day, it is necessary for understanding of the texts to go beyond their immediate significance to recognition of their immediate and further aims and to perception of their indications and suggestions, so that the extent of their comprehensiveness may be correctly ascertained. Only then is it possible to understand what lies behind the judgements made by the Companions in cases where there was no well-known *sunna* and which could not be included within the meaning of the literal text, even though the text might indirectly indicate to it.

When no direct precedent was available to him Malik used to make analogies based on judgements derived directly from texts in the Qur'an and judgements derived directly from *hadiths* of the Prophet. The *Muwatta'* contains many examples of that. We find that at the beginning of the chapter he presents those *ayats* and *hadiths* which he considers to be directly relevant to the subject in hand and then after that he gives secondary rulings, connecting like to like and similar to similar.

He also drew analogies based on the consensus of the people of Madina because, as we have seen, he considered that to be the *Sunna*. In the *Muwatta'* he mentions the 'generally agreed-on way of doing things' and then gives secondary rulings in situations where there is similarity in the circumstances surrounding the questions about which he was asked for a *fatwa*.

Malik also used to utilise the *fatwas* of the Companions as a basis for analogy, as we saw in the case of the wife of the missing husband in which he followed the *fatwa* of 'Umar about the divorced woman who was not aware of having been taken back by her husband, which was confirmed by the agreement of the people of Madina on similar cases.

The *fuqaha'* of the Maliki school use analogy but always subject it to the principle of bringing about the best interests of people and averting harm from them. So even if their analogy is absolutely correct, they do not proceed with it if that would prevent benefit or entail harm. They relax the general rules and leave them for the sake of specific benefits. That is part of *istihsan*.

Istihsan (Discretion)

Ibn al-Qasim related from Malik that he said that *istihsan* was nine-tenths of knowledge. Malik used analogy but made it subject to general and partial benefit, so he only applied it when he was sure that there was no harm in its application; otherwise he left it. For Malik it was a basic rule that analogy is subject to benefit.

That is why the underlying principle of Maliki *fiqh* is benefit, as we will explain.

Judgements based on *istihsan* or which make it the deciding factor when weighing up different proofs are numerous in the Maliki school, as ash-Shatibi says in *al-Muwafaqat*. One example of this is loans. A loan might be considered to be usury because a dirham is exchanged for a dirham for a period of time but it is permissible under the principle of *istihsan* because of the way people are helped by it. If loans had remained forbidden they might have suffered great hardship.

Two things are evident from examining the questions in which judgements are based on *istihsan*.

* *Istihsan* is used for *fatwa* in questions, not on the basis of its being a rule, but rather on the basis of its being an exception to the rule or according to the Maliki definition of consideration: relaxation of the rule is a temporary principle as distinct from a universal principle. We saw an example of this in the *fatwa* about accepting witnesses who do not have good character in a land in which no witnesses of good character can be found and as mentioned above when a loan is permitted to avert distress and hardship. In these matters and those like them, *istihsan* is a relaxation of the general rule which, if followed in the particular instance in question, would lead to harm. *Istihsan* averts that harm.

* *Istihsan* is most often used when the application of strict analogy would necessarily entail distress. So *istihsan* in the Maliki school, as in the Hanafi school, is equivalent to analogy, even though the methods of the two schools in reaching it are different. Each of them proceeds according to its legal logic, and *istihsan* in the Maliki school aims to avert any distress arising from following analogy through to its logical conclusion. Asbagh, who was probably the most prolific exponent of *istihsan*, said, "People who go to extremes in making analogy are in danger of abandoning the *Sunna*. *Istihsan* is the foundation of knowledge." (ash-Shatibi, *al-Muwafaqat*, vol. 4, p. 118)

Malik further refined the principle of *istihsan* under the heading of *masalih mursala* (considerations of public interest) and gave *fatwas* based on it.

Masalih Mursala (Considerations of Public Interest)

The great majority of scholars of ethics incline to the view that the governing measure of all that is good and evil in any action is the benefit or harm which stems from it. If the action contains some advantage and does not cause harm to anyone, then it is good and performing it is an undoubted virtue. If it is an action which contains benefit for some people and harm for others, there is a conflict and clash between benefit and harm. In this case the good lies in abandoning a slight harm to obtain a greater benefit, or in abandoning a temporary benefit for a lasting benefit, or in abandoning an uncertain benefit to obtain a definite one.

Islamic *fiqh* in its entirety is based on the best interests of the community. That which contains benefit is desired and there is evidence for that, and that which is harmful is prohibited and there are numerous proofs for that as well. This is a confirmed principle which is agreed upon by the *fuqaha'* of the Muslims. None of them have ever alleged that the Islamic *Shari'a* brought anything which is not in people's best interests and none of them have ever said that there is anything harmful in any law or judgement within the *Shari'a* which has been legislated for the Muslims.

So the manifest principle governing the legality of customs and traditions in the eyes of the *Shari'a* is whether or not they are beneficial in real terms. But what is the criterion used in the *Shari'a* to ascertain whether or not a particular matter contains benefit? To discover that we have to ascertain exactly what it is that makes a particular action permitted or forbidden.

What, then, is the nature of the benefit which makes an action acceptable in the eyes the Islamic *Shari'a*? It is that which coincides with its goals, and the goal of the Islamic *Shari'a* is to preserve the five things whose preservation is agreed to be obligatory:

life, sanity, property, progeny and honour. All religions agree on the obligation to preserve these things and have that point in common. All rational people concur that society is based on protecting and preserving these things.

In taking *masalih mursala* as an independent legal principle, Malik was a follower and not an innovator. He found the Companions of the Messenger of Allah, may Allah bless him and grant him peace, doing various things after his death which had not been done while he was alive.

- They collected the Noble Qur'an into a bound book – something which had not been done during the lifetime of the Messenger – because of the inherent benefit in it, dictated by the fear that the Qur'an might be forgotten through the death of those who had memorised it. When 'Umar, may Allah be pleased with him, saw many of the memorisers of the Qur'an fall in the *Ridda* War,[1] he feared that the Qur'an might be lost through their deaths and so he suggested to Abu Bakr that it should be collected together into a book. The Companions agreed to that and were pleased with it.

- The Companions of the Messenger agreed after his death that the *hadd* for wine-drinking should be 80 lashes in view of the principle of *masalih mursala,* since they observed that one of the consequences of intoxication was the slander of chaste women.

- The Rightly-guided Khalifs agreed to make artisans responsible for any goods of other people they were working on, even though the basic position is that is the things in one's possession are a trust (under Islamic law trustees are not responsible for unintentional damage to goods in their keeping). They did so because it was found that if they were not made liable for them they would make light of guarding other people's goods

---

1. The defection of various Arab tribes after the death of the Prophet, may Allah bless him and grant him peace, brought about the *Ridda* War in which large numbers of Muslims were slain.

and property. So in this case public interest demanded that artisans should be made liable.

- 'Umar ibn al-Khattab, may Allah be pleased with him, used to confiscate half of the wealth of governors who combined their personal wealth with government assets and then used their position as governor to make a profit on it. The benefit involved in that ruling was that he thought it that would reform the governors and keep them from exploiting the office of governorship for their own ends.

- It is also reported of 'Umar ibn al-Khattab that he poured away milk which had been diluted with water, as a punishment for cheating. That was for the general benefit in order that people might be protected from being cheated.

- It is also transmitted that 'Umar ibn al-Khattab had a group of people executed for the murder of one person when they all participated in the murder, because public interest demanded that even though no text existed to support it. The benefit in this lies in the fact that it would otherwise become possible to shed inviolable blood with impunity, resulting in a loophole in the principle of retaliation. People would use assistance and partnership as a means to commit murder since it would be known that no retaliation would be demanded. If it is said that this is an innovative matter by which other parties than the killer are executed even when they were not all actually involved in the act of killing, the argument refuting this is that the killing group is a collective and so collective execution is the same as executing an individual, since killing is ascribed to the collective in the same way as it is ascribed to an individual. Therefore, individuals who join together with the aim of killing are considered as a single person. Public interest demands this since it involves the prevention of bloodshed and the protection of society.

Malik found all these things and a great fund of other legal judgements which had been left the *fuqaha'* of the Companions, may Allah be pleased with them. Since he followed their methods and adhered to their path it was impossible that he should stray from the aim and goal of the Lawgiver. His *fatwas* were given with the object of ensuring benefit in all matters, both public and private.

The Principle of *adh-Dhara'i'* (Means)

This is another of the principles on which Imam Malik often relied when deriving judgements and in that respect Imam Ahmad ibn Hanbal closely resembled him. We will begin our discussion with the meaning and categories of this term and then see how it becomes a legal principle which can be used as evidence.

The meaning of *dhari'a* is "means". *Sadd adh-dhara'i'* (blocking the means) implies preventing them, which entails making the means to what is forbidden also forbidden; and *fath adh-dhara'i'* (facilitating the means) entails making the means to what is obligatory also obligatory. Thus because adultery is unlawful, looking at the private parts of a unrelated woman is also unlawful because it is likely to lead to adultery. Because the *Jumu'a* prayer is an obligation, going to it is also an obligation, and leaving off trading to go to it is also obligatory. *Hajj* is an obligation, and going to the Sacred House and the other practices of *Hajj* are obligatory for its sake.

The principle of blocking or facilitating the means, according to al-Qarafi's definition, is considered from the aspect of consolidation of the principle of public interest which Malik adheres to. He considers general benefit to be the outcome which the Lawgiver desires, esteems, calls for and encourages, and so it is desirable to do anything that brings it about. Its opposite, which is corruption, is forbidden. So all that is known to lead to benefit, definitely or probably or mostly, even if it is not predominant, is desirable, and all that is known to lead, whether certainly or only probably, to corruption must be avoided.

The Principle of Common Usage (*'Adat*) and Custom (*'Urf*)

Custom is a matter on which a community of people agree in the course of their daily life, and common usage is an action which is repeatedly performed by individuals and communities. When a community makes a habit of doing something, it becomes its common usage. So the custom and common usage of a community share the same underlying idea even if what is understood by them differs slightly.

Maliki *fiqh*, like Hanafi *fiqh*, makes use of custom and considers it a legal principle in respect of matters about which there is no definitive text. In fact it has an even deeper respect for custom than the Hanafi school since, as we have seen, public interest and general benefit are the foundation of Maliki *fiqh* in coming to decisions and there is no doubt that respect for a custom which contains no harm is one of the types of benefit. It is not valid for any *faqih* to leave it: indeed, it is obligatory to adopt it. We find that the Malikis abandon analogy when custom opposes it. Custom makes the general specific and qualifies the unqualified, as far as the Malikis are concerned.

Making use of custom in this way is taken from an instance when the Prophet, may Allah bless him and grant him peace, said to the wife of Abu Sufyan, "Take from the property of Abu Sufyan what is adequate for you and your child in a normal manner." In this *hadith* custom is clearly made the basis of a legal decision.

Many judgements are based on *'urf* because in many cases it coincides with public interest and public interest is indisputably a fundamental principle in Malik's school. Another reason is that custom necessarily entails people's familiarity with a matter, and so any judgement based on it will receive general acceptance whereas divergence from it will be liable to cause distress, which is disliked in the judgement of Islam because Allah Almighty has not imposed any hardship on people in His *deen*.

Allah Almighty prescribes what normal people deem proper and are accustomed to, not what they dislike and hate. So when a custom is not a vice and is respected by people, honouring it will strengthen the bond which draws people together because it is connected to their traditions and social transactions whereas opposition to it will destroy that cohesion and bring about disunity.

This especially applies where patterns of speech are concerned, since natural lucidity demands that expressions be understood in accordance with customary usage. It is also desirable to apply custom where commercial contracts are concerned as long as there is nothing unlawful in doing so. If there is, however, it is of course obligatory to not adhere to custom.

Conclusion

These are the fundamental principles of Imam Malik, may Allah be pleased with him, which the scholars of his school have derived from the corpus of the secondary rulings transmitted from him. It is by means of them that his rulings were derived and upon them that they are based.

The first thing to be noticed about these principles is their flexibility. He did not make the unqualified text of the Book or the *Sunna* unequivocal. He opened the door to making its general texts specific and to qualifying what is unqualified. Just as he opened the door of specification, he showed there to be flexibility in the texts which facilitated the means of deriving judgements from them. A *faqih* should not be inflexible where the text is concerned, nor should he be excessively flexible.

The principles are all interconnected, one amplifying another, and so any unfamiliar meanings are winnowed out in favour of a meaning derived from an immediate principle. From that there emerges a mature *fiqh* that is strong, straightforward, familiar and known – one which people readily accept.

The second thing to be noticed after the flexibility of these principles is their orientation towards achieving the greatest benefit in the most direct manner. Analogy is made a way of achieving this. *Istihsan* is employed to achieve it by preferring a ruling derived by it if analogy is less apt to achieve the desired benefit. Consideration of public interest is made into a principle in order to achieve it by the easiest way. Malik also employed the method of facilitating or blocking the means which is also considered to be one of the fundamental principles used in deriving rulings. Then, finally, he considered custom, which is another means of removing distress, averting hardship, achieving benefit, and fulfilling people's needs.

Malik saw that the basic aim of the Divine Lawgiver in His *Shari'a* was to realise the greatest benefit for the maximum number of people and so he made all his *fiqh* which was not based on an unequivocal text centre on this principle. He supports it by facilitating and blocking the means and other ways which lead to it, in order to achieve it by the quickest and easiest manner.

Thirdly, the principles which Malik used in deriving judgements are interconnected with and complementary to one another. All are derived from the same source and follow the same guidance: namely, the definitive text, its spirit and meaning and the ways in which the Prophet and the Companions applied it. Hence his *fiqh* is aimed at the same goal: the welfare of people in this world and the Next and following path of the Prophet and Companions without any innovation.

We find that Malik relies on the cases and *fatwas* of the Companions in recognising the objective of the *Shari'a* and then recognises the judgements of those of the following generation with deep knowledge of the texts and goals of the *Shari'a* and of its immediate and long-term consequences. In so doing, Malik opened the same methodology for his students who came after him and their students. They understood *fiqh* as he did and followed his way. So Maliki *fiqh* spread far and wide and as a result the Way followed by the Prophet and his Companions in Madina has been preserved for all posterity.

Abu Hanifa
(d.150/767)

Preface

Praise belongs to Allah, the Lord of the Worlds, and peace and blessings be upon our master Muhammad and his family and Companions.

This is a study of Imam Abu Hanifa – his life, opinions and *fiqh.* I first address his life in order to understand his personality, psychology and thought, so that I can offer the reader a true and sound picture in which the special qualities and attributes of this Imam are revealed. Then I examine his views on dogma, *fatwas* and analogy.

Deriving a true picture of Abu Hanifa from the books of history and biographies is not easy since the adherents of his school have been excessive in their praise, going beyond acceptable bounds, and his detractors have been equally intemperate in their criticism. When faced with these two extremes, the investigator who seeks only the truth may be confused and this uncertainty can only be resolved with difficulty and great effort.

I think that I have managed to reveal a true picture of Imam Abu Hanifa, with all its shadows and shafts of light, and in the process of discovering it I have shed light on the time in which he lived and mentioned some details of the most notable contemporary sects. It is certain that he used to argue and debate with these sects and that their opinions and ideas were much discussed at that time. Mentioning them will clarify the spirit of the age and the currents of thought prevalent in it.

Then I examine his opinions on politics and dogma. This is necessary if we want to study all the intellectual aspects of any thinker. His views on politics had an effect on the course of his life. To ignore them would be to ignore an important aspect of his personality, psychology, heart and thought. His views on dogma were the clarification of all the ideas prevailing in his age and the

115

pure core of the opinions of those who were free of excess and extravagance. They were a sound expression of the views of the Muslim community. Indeed, they are the core of the *deen* and the spirit of certainty.

I then go on to look at his *fiqh*, which is the primary goal of this study. I begin by elucidating the general principles which he used in his deduction and which define its path and clarify his method in *ijtihad*. For this I rely on what the early Hanafis wrote regarding the principles on which they depended and the method employed by Abu Hanifa. Concerning that I chose to be succinct rather than comprehensive, general rather than specific, and did not go into all the principles mentioned by the Hanafis since many of them cannot be ascribed to the Imam and his companions but come from a later period.

Having identified the method of Abu Hanifa, I turn to the study of some of the secondary areas of his views derived from a detailed examination of his life, such as some of the areas of *fiqh* which are connected to human free will in respect of property and some of the areas which are connected to trade and merchants in a general fashion. Scholars also mention that Abu Hanifa was the first to speak on legal stratagems and so it is essential to clarify that area of his thought, distinguishing the reality of what he did, and balance between what is actually transmitted from him and what is said about him.

In all the methods and branches mentioned, the Imam's thought will be clarified by mentioning some of the disagreements between him and his companions. Clarification of their differences will show their ideas and orientations.

In order to reach a fruitful conclusion to this study, it was also necessary to clarify the action of the later adherents of this school in respect of the intellectual legacy left by the Imam and what subsequent generations did with it when faced with disparate customs. It was also necessary to examine the extent to which deduction played a part in the school and to look at the flexibility of its general principles of extrapolation and the role it had in preserving the path of Islam, and the Book and the *Sunna* and their guidance.

We must affirm that the need for the help of Allah Almighty in doing this is immense. If it were not for His help, we should not reach any end or achieve any goal. We beseech Him to help us and grant us success.

Muhammad Abu Zahra
Dhu'l-Qa'da 1364
November 1945

Foreword

It says in *al-Khayrat al-Hisan* by Ibn Hajar al-Haytami al-Makki: "The renown of a man in the past is indicated by the disagreement of people regarding him. Do you not see that when 'Ali died, may Allah ennoble his face, there were two parties: one of which intensely loved him and the other of which intensely hated him?"

This test is true of many people and can also be applied to Abu Hanifa. People were partisan about him to the extent that some people practically put him in the ranks of the Prophets and claimed that the Torah gave the good news of him and that Muhammad, may Allah bless him and grant him peace, had mentioned him by name and stated that he was the Lamp of his Community. They attributed to him endless virtues and qualities and exalted him above his rank. On the other hand, some people were partisan against him to a fanatical extent, accusing him of being a heretic and of leaving the path, corrupting the deen and abandoning the *Sunna*. Indeed, they accused him of contradicting it and giving *fatwas* regarding the *deen* without evidence or clear authority. Some of them went to excess in attacking him and were not content with unfounded falsification, but were so intensely hostile that they attacked his *deen*, personality and faith.

This happened even while Abu Hanifa was still alive and discussing with his students the requirements of *fatwas*: what should be taken from *hadith*, what should be derived by analogy and rules, and how to conduct *ijtihad* in a proper manner.

Why was there such disagreement about him? There are various reasons for it which shall be examined in detail in the course of this study. But it is appropriate to mention here one reason which may be the basis of the others. Abu Hanifa had a forceful personality which caused his method in *fiqh* to spread beyond his own circle and region to other regions of the Islamic world. People discussed his views in most areas of the Islamic world, some opposing them and some agreeing with them.

His views had opponents and supporters. Those who depended on texts alone regarded them as an innovation in the *deen* and strongly objected to them. Sometimes the point of objection was not even the opinion of Abu Hanifa, who was a scrupulous and godfearing man, but was merely something wrongly attributed to him. The opponent would speak of it because he saw it as an innovation without knowing its basis or who had actually said it. The sharpness of the criticism was sometimes blunted when the critic saw him or learned the evidence on which the judgement was based. Sometimes the critic would then respect the opinion and agree with him.

An illustration of such an instance is found in respect of al-Awza'i, the *faqih* of Syria, who was a contemporary of Abu Hanifa. He said to 'Abdullah ibn al-Mubarak, "Who is this innovator who has emerged in Kufa called Abu Hanifa?" Ibn al-Mubarak did not answer him, but began to mention some difficult questions and how to understand them and give *fatwa* regarding them. He asked, "Who gave these *fatwas*?" He replied, "A shaykh I met in Iraq." Al-Awza'i said, "This is a noble shaykh. Go and take a lot from him." "It is Abu Hanifa," he stated. After that al-Awza'i and Abu Hanifa met in Makka and discussed the questions which Ibn al-Mubarak had mentioned. He investigated them. When they parted, al-Awza'i said to Ibn al-Mubarak, "I envy the man his great knowledge and intelligence. I ask forgiveness of Allah. I was in clear error. Devote yourself to the man. He is not as they say about him." (*al-Khayrat al-Hisan*, p. 33)

The conflict between his supporters and opponents intensified in the fourth century AH when *madhhab* partisanship became prevalent and *fiqh* was debated by partisans. There were debates in people's houses and in mosques about these matters so that whole days were spent in debates and arguments about *madhhab*. Each was a supporter of his Imam and partisan on his behalf. It is in this time that most of the biographies of the Imams were written, usually with excessive praise of the particular Imam in question and attacking the others. The conflict was extremely severe between the Hanafis and the Shafi'is. That is why these two Imams became targets for bitter attacks, given the extreme partisanship of their supporters.

Abu Hanifa, of course, was a target because of the great number of *fatwas* he gave based on opinion which led people to attack his knowledge of *hadiths*, his scrupulousness, the quality of his *fatwas* and other things which were connected to his school regarding deduction and extrapolation. The fanatics attacked him for all those things and some exceeded the bounds to such an extent that some Shafi'is objected to it and saw such attacks as tantamount to sin and improper conduct. Some of those people were fair towards Abu Hanifa and recorded his virtues and refuted what the extreme Shafi'is said. Thus we note that as-Suyuti, a Shafi'i, wrote a treatise on the virtues of Imam Abu Hanifa. We further see that Ibn Hajar al-Haytami al-Makki, also a Shafi'i, wrote a treatise entitled *al-Khayrat al-Hisan* on the virtues of Imam Abu Hanifa. Ash-Sha'rani also mentions and defends Abu Hanifa.

A researcher does not find it easy to deal with Abu Hanifa because of the confusion of reports concerning him, which are like heaps in which jewels are mixed with mud, so that it is difficult to sift through them and find the true jewels in the midst of the muck. It requires a great deal of scrutiny and sifting.

It is the same with his opinions, where we also find the path difficult to follow because there is no book transmitted from Abu Hanifa in which he recorded his opinions or his principles. We only find opinions transmitted from him through his students, especially the books of Imam Abu Yusuf and Imam Muhammad ash-Shaybani which transmitted his opinions with those of his companions and those of some of the Iraqis contemporary with him, like Ibn Shibrama, Ibn Abi Layla and 'Uthman al-Batti. But if we rely totally on what his two main students said, we will still not have a complete picture. There are many gaps which must be filled because their books certainly do not report all of the views of Abu Hanifa and so we must examine other sources as well. All of this requires precise investigation and research.

Another drawback is that the fundamental principles and methods of deduction used by Abu Hanifa are not recorded either and we cannot know them in detail from what is transmitted from him or from his students or other people. Those principles which are recorded are deduced from the body of the secondary judgements he made and how they are connected. There are various sources which do this, among which are the treatise of Abu'l-Hasan al-Karkhi, the treatise of ad-Dabusi and the letter of al-Bazdawi. But the methods recorded are not transmitted from the Imam or his companions: they are only deduced from the Imams who formulated the Hanafi school. Thus it is not easy to uncover the sources of the school.

Another deficiency encountered when studying Abu Hanifa is that we do not find anything transmitted from him other than his legal opinions. As for his views on dogma and on the imamate, we do not find anything about them in the books of his companions. Some views on dogma are reported from him in certain books ascribed to him, including the book entitled *al-Fiqh al-Akbar*, a small treatise on which many commentaries have been written, and the *Treatise of the Scholar and Student*. There is also his letter to 'Uthman al-Batti.

But we do not, for instance, find any opinion about the imamate recorded by his pen or by dictation or transmitted by any of his companions. His life and the events and trials which occurred during it, however, do inform us about a specific political position. His biography affirms his firm connection to Imam Zayd ibn 'Ali, Zayn al-'Abidin, and other Shi'ite Imams, and the statements of his companions indicate that his inclination, as was true of the Persians as a whole, was with the descendants of 'Ali and that his trial occurred because of this leaning. Nevertheless, there is no suggestion of this in any of the books ascribed to him or in any of the reports transmitted from him. There is no doubt that his opinion about the imamate was mentioned in his circle at times and that he differed from the Abbasids.

But his companions, especially Abu Yusuf and Muhammad ash-Shaybani, were firmly attached to the Abbasids and both acted as *qadis* for them. They did not record the opinions of their shaykh regarding the Abbasid government and diminishing its authority. That is the reason why many of his opinions are lost in the past and can only be rediscovered with great difficulty.

These are gaps which the historian must strive to fill and they illustrate the difficulty involved in studying him. Moreover, the school of Abu Hanifa is found both in the East and the West and has been subject to the disparate customs of different regions. It became the official school for a long time under the Abbasids, and when the Ottomans took on the position of khalif they also made it their official *madhhab* and so it became the *madhhab* of the khalifate. It was the official school in Iraq, Egypt, Syria, and other places, and its influence extended as far as India and it also became the school of the Muslims in China. The scholars in all these different regions had their own deductions and so there are many differing opinions on questions within the Hanafi *madhhab*.

Chapter One
The Life and Times of Abu Hanifa

His birth and lineage

According to most sources, Abu Hanifa was born in Kufa in 80 AH. Although there is almost total agreement on this, there is one source which posits 61AH, but this does not tally with the facts of his life since it is agreed that he did not die until 150 AH. Most say that he died after al-Mansur instituted the Inquisition. If he had been born in 61 AH, he would have been 90 at that time.

His father was Thabit ibn Zawti al-Farisi, a Persian. His grandfather was one of the people of Kabil who was captured in the Arab conquest of the region. He was enslaved to one of the Banu Taym and then freed. His *wala'* belonged to this tribe and so he was a Taymi by clientage. This information was transmitted by the grandson of Abu Hanifa, 'Umar ibn Hammad, but 'Umar's brother Isma'il said that Abu Hanifa was an-Nu'man ibn Thabit ibn an-Nu'man ibn al-Marzban. He said, "By Allah, we were never enslaved."

So his grandsons disagreed about his lineage. One said that his grandfather was called Zawti and the other that his name was an-Nu'man. The first said that he was captured and enslaved and the second completely denied it. The author of *al-Khayrat al-Hisan* combined the two versions, maintaining that the grandfather had two names, Zayti and an-Nu'man. He denied the enslavement. This present work agrees with the names but not the fact of enslavement, because the second version totally excludes it.

It seems probable that he was captured in the conquest, but that grace was shown him, which was the custom of the Muslims towards some of the important people of conquered lands, so as to uphold their position and importance in Islam and to bring their hearts and those of their children close.

Reliable sources state that he was a Persian and not an Arab or a Babylonian. Whether his grandfather was enslaved or not, he and his father were born free men. In any case, the fact that he was a client in no way detracts from his worth. The major exponents of *fiqh* in the time of the *Tabi'un,* whom Abu Hanifa met and from whose *fiqh* he extrapolated, were clients of tribes rather than pure Arabs. Most of the *fuqaha'* in the time of the *Tabi'un* and indeed the following generation were clients.

In *al-'Aqd al-Farid*, Ibn 'Abdu Rabbih says:

Ibn Abi Layla said: 'Isa ibn Musa, a religious and very partisan man, asked me, "Who is the *faqih* of Iraq?"

I replied, "Al-Hasan ibn Abi'l-Hasan (al-Basri)."

"Then who?"

I said, "Muhammad ibn Sirin."

"Who are those two?" he asked.

"Two clients," I replied.

"Who is the *faqih* of Makka?" he asked.

"'Ata ibn Abi Rabah, Mujahid, Sa'id ibn Jubayr or Salman ibn Yasar," I replied.

"Who are they?"

"Clients."

"Who are the *fuqaha'* of Madina?"

"Zayd ibn Aslam, Muhammad ibn al-Munkadir, and Nujayh ibn Abi Nujayh," I replied.

"And who are they?" he asked.

"Clients," I said.

His face changed colour. Then he asked, "Who knows the most *fiqh* of the people of Quba'?"

"Rabi'a ar-Ra'y and Ibn Abi'z-Zinad," I responded.

"Who are they?"

"Clients."

He scowled and then asked, "Who is the *faqih* of Yemen?"

"Tawus, his son, and Ibn Munabbah," I replied.

"Who are they?" he asked.

"Also clients."

His veins bulged and he stood up. "And who is the faqih of Khorasan?"

"'Ata' ibn 'Abdullah al-Khurasani."

"Who is this 'Ata'?"

"A client," I said.

'His scowl deepened and he glared until I became quite afraid of him. Then he said, "Who is the *faqih* of Syria?"

"Makhul," I replied.

"Who is this Makhul?"

"A client," I said.

He began breathing hard and then asked, "Who is the *faqih* of Kufa?"

By Allah, were it not for fear for him, I would have said, "Al-Hakim ibn 'Utba and Hammad ibn Abi Sulayman," but seeing his violent state I replied, "Ibrahim an-Nakha'i and ash-Sha'bi."

"Who are they?" he asked.

"Two Arabs," I replied.

"Allah is greater!" he exclaimed and calmed down.

There are other transmissions to the same effect from other sources which indicate that, during the time in which Abu Hanifa grew up, knowledge was for the most part among the clients. Since they lacked the glory of lineage, Allah gave them the glory of knowledge which is purer and more lasting. This shows the truth of the prophecy of the Messenger of Allah, may Allah bless him and grant him peace, that knowledge would be found among the sons of Persia. We find the *hadith* in al-Bukhari, Muslim, ash-Shirazi, and at-Tabarani: "If knowledge were suspended in the Pleiades, some of the men of Persia would still obtain it."

Before going into Abu Hanifa's lineage, we should perhaps first discuss the reason why, in Umayyad times, knowledge was found mostly among the clients. There were several reasons for this.

- In Umayyad times, the Arabs had authority and power and they fought wars and went on expeditions. All of which distracted them from study and learning. The clients, on the other hand, were free to study, analyse and investigate. They realised that they lacked power and so they wanted to obtain honour by a means which was within their grasp: knowledge. Social deprivation can lead to excellence, high aspirations and splendid deeds, and indeed it led those clients to master the intellectual life of Islam while the Arabs were politically and economically dominant.

- The Companions spent a lot of time with the clients. keeping their company morning and evening so the clients were able to take from the Companions what they had learned from the Messenger of Allah. When the era of the Companions ended, they became the bearers of knowledge after them and thus it was that most of the great *Tabi'un* were clients.

- The clients came largely from ancient civilisations with developed cultures and science. This had an effect on the formation of their ideas and the direction of their pursuits, and indeed, at times, on their beliefs. Devotion to knowledge was part of their nature.

- The Arabs were not people of crafts and learning; and when someone devotes himself to knowledge, it becomes like a craft. A lengthy discussion about this can be found in Ibn Khaldun.

His upbringing

Abu Hanifa grew up in Kufa and was educated there and lived most of his life there as a student, debater and teacher. The sources in our possession do not mention his father's life or what his occupation and circumstances were but certain things about his circumstances can be deduced. He must have been wealthy, a merchant, and a good Muslim. In most books which recount the biography of Abu Hanifa, it states that his father met 'Ali ibn Abi Talib as a child and that his grandfather gave 'Ali some *faludhaj*[1] on the day of Nawruz. This indicates that his family were wealthy since they were able to give the khalif sweets which only the wealthy ate.

It is related that 'Ali prayed for blessing for Thabit and his descendants when he saw him. This shows that he must have been a Muslim. It explicitly states in histories that Thabit was born into Islam and Abu Hanifa grew up in a Muslim household. That is confirmed by all scholars.

We find Abu Hanifa frequenting the market before he frequented scholars. We see that throughout his life he engaged in trade and so we must deduce that his father was a merchant. It seems probable that he was a merchant in *khazz* silk and that Abu Hanifa followed his father's occupation as is the custom of people both past and present. It is also probable that, following the custom of most wealthy city dwellers, he memorised the Qur'an. That assumption tallies with what is known of Abu Hanifa being one of the people who was very frequent in his recitation of the Qur'an. It is reported that he used to recite the entire Qur'an seven times in Ramadan, and even if that is an exaggeration, it is based on the fact that he recited the Qur'an a lot. Many sources report that he learned recitation from Imam 'Asim, the source of one of the seven recitations (*qira'at*) of the Qur'an.[2]

Kufa was one of the two great Iraqi cities of the time. Iraq was home to many different religions, sects and beliefs and of various ancient civilisations. Syriac Christians were dispersed throughout it and they had schools there before Islam, in which Greek philosophy and the ancient wisdom of Persia were studied. Before Islam, Iraq was also home to several Christian sects where dogma was debated. After Islam, Iraq was a melting pot of diverse races and a place rife with confusion and disorder. There were clashes of opinion on politics and religion. The Shi'a and Mu'tazilites were there as well as the Kharijites in the desert. There were also the *Tabi'un* who strove to take knowledge from the Companions they met.

---

1. *Faludhaj* is a sweet made of ground almonds, sugar and rose-water; Nawruz is the Persian New Year.

2. A *qira'a* is a method of recitation, punctuation and localisation of the Qur'an. There are seven main readings: Abu 'Amr ibn al-'Ala', Hamza, 'Asim, Ibn 'Amir, Ibn Kathır, Nafi' and al-Kisa'i.

Knowledge of the *deen* was transmitted freely there. It was an environment of clashing sects and conflicting opinions.

Abu Hanifa observed these diverse currents and his intellect was sharpened and sifted these differing views. It appears that while still in his youth he debated and argued people from various sects. This reveals his upright natural disposition. He concentrated, however, on commerce, going mainly to the markets and rarely to scholars. This remained the state of things until one day a scholar noticed his intelligence and cleverness and thought that he should not devote himself entirely to trade. He told him to frequent the scholars as he did the markets.

It is transmitted that Abu Hanifa said, "One day I was going past ash-Sha'bi who was sitting down. He called to me, 'Where are you going?' I said, 'I am going to the market.' He said, 'I do not frequent the market. I am concerned with going to the scholars.' I told him, 'I rarely frequent them.' He told me, 'Do not be heedless. You must look into knowledge and sit with the scholars. I discern alertness and energy in you.' That affected my heart and I ceased to frequent the market and began to turn to knowledge and Allah let me benefit from what he said." (*Virtues of Abu Hanifa*, al-Makki, pt. 1, p. 59) After ash-Sha'bi's advice, Abu Hanifa turned to knowledge and frequented the circles of the scholars.

His involvement in learning

But to which group did he go? As is seen from the historical sources, there were three fields of knowledge at that time: circles which discussed the fundamentals of dogma, which was the arena of the different sects; circles which studied the *hadiths* of the Messenger of Allah, may Allah bless him and grant him peace; and circles which deduced *fiqh* from the Book and *Sunna* and gave *fatwa* about things which arose.

We have three versions of what happened. One mentions that when he devoted himself to knowledge, he turned to *fiqh* after examining all the sciences which were known at that time. Two other versions clearly state that he first selected the science of *kalam* and debated with the sects and then Allah directed him to *fiqh* to which he completely devoted himself. We will examine the three versions.

It is related by various paths, including Abu Yusuf, that Abu Hanifa was asked, "How did you happen to come to *fiqh*?" He replied, "I will tell you. Success is from Allah and praise is His as He deserves and merits. When I wanted to learn knowledge, I looked at all the forms of knowledge and read some of them and thought about the end and usefulness of each. I said, 'I will go into *kalam*.' Then I looked and found that it had a bad aim and contained little benefit. When a man is proficient in it, he cannot speak openly and cast aside every evil and is likely to be called a sectarian.

"Then I examined literature and grammar, and found that the logical end of that discipline is to sit with a child and teach him grammar and literature. I examined poetry and saw that its end was eulogy, satire, lies and tearing apart the *deen*. Then I thought about the forms of Qur'an recitation (*qira'at*) and said, 'When I reach the end of it, young people will gather to read with me and discuss the Qur'an and its meanings and that is difficult.' So I said, 'I will seek *hadith*.' But then I said, 'To amass a lot of it I will have to have a long life before I will be of any use to people, and even then only youths will gather around me who will probably accuse me of lying and poor memory and that will be a burden for me until the Day of Rising.'

"Then I turned to *fiqh* and no matter which way I looked at it, it only increased in esteem and I could not find any fault in it. I saw that it involved sitting with scholars, *fuqaha'*, shaykhs and people of insight and taking on their character. I saw that it is only by knowing it that the obligations are properly performed and the *deen* and worship established. Seeking this world and the Next World can only be done through it. If anyone desires to seek this world through it, he seeks a weighty matter and will be elevated by it. If someone wants to worship and divest himself, no one can say, 'He worships without knowledge.' Rather it will be said, 'This is *fiqh* and acting by knowledge.'"

This anedote is illustrative of the sciences which were prevalent in his time and shows that he chose between them as he was inclined.

The second transmission is reported from Yahya ibn Shayban. He reports that Abu Hanifa said: "I was a man given to debate in *kalam* and spent some time indulging in it. The people of debate and disputation were mostly located in Basra. So I went to Basra about twenty times, staying more or less a year each time. I argued with the groups of Kharijites: Ibadites, Sufrites and other Kharijite sects. I considered *kalam* to be the queen of the sciences. I used to say that *kalam* was the basis of the *deen*.

"Then I reconsidered after a considerable part of my life had been spent involved in it. I reflected and realised that the Companions of the Prophet and the *Tabi'un* knew as much as we know and had more capacity, more understanding and better knowledge of the truth of matters. But they did not have arguments about it and did not delve into it. They withheld from doing that and forbade it strenuously. I saw them dealing with laws and areas of *fiqh* and speaking about such matters. That was what they sat to learn and those were the circles they attended. That was what they used to teach people and what they invited them to learn and what they encouraged them in. They gave *fatwa* and were asked for *fatwa* concerning matters of *fiqh*.

"That was the standpoint of the Companions, and the *Tabi'un* followed them in it. When their mode of behaviour became clear to us, we left debate, argument and delving into *kalam* and confined ourselves to the basic knowledge of *fiqh* and we returned to the position of the *Salaf*, taking from what they left and legislating as they legislated. The people of knowledge sat with us for that reason and I saw that those who were involved in *kalam* and debating were people whose trait was not that of our noble predecessors and whose path was not that of the righteous. I saw them as being hard-hearted and thick-skinned. They were not worried about the fact that they were conflicting with the Book and the *Sunna* and the righteous *Salaf* and that they had neither scrupulousness nor fear of Allah."

The third transmission is reported from Zafar ibn al-Hudhayl, the student of Abu Hanifa, who stated: "I heard Abu Hanifa say, 'I used to look into *kalam* until I was advanced in it and people pointed me out. We used to sit near the circle of Hammad ibn Abi Sulayman. One day a woman came to us and said, "A man has a wife who is a slave girl whom he wants to divorce according to the *Sunna*. How many times should he pronounce the divorce?" I told her to ask Hammad and then come back and tell me. She asked him and he said, "He should divorce her once at a time when she is not menstruating and he has not had intercourse with her and then leave her until she has menstruated two more times. Then when she has purified herself she may remarry." She returned and told us what he had said. I said, "I have no further use for *kalam*," and took my sandals and sat with Hammad. I used to listen to his questions and learned what he said and then went back again day after day. I remembered while his other students erred. He said, "Only Abu Hanifa should sit opposite me at the front of the circle."'"

These three transmissions are related in various forms but all bear the same import. It is clear that he chose *fiqh* after looking into other fields of knowledge, and two say that he was skilled in *kalam* before turning to *fiqh*. It cannot be denied that his final interest was knowledge of *fiqh*.

Abu Hanifa experienced the full Islamic culture of his age. He memorised the Qur'an with the reading of 'Asim. He knew a considerable amount of *hadith*, grammar, literature and poetry. He debated with the different sects on questions of dogma and related matters. He travelled to Basra to do this and sometimes remained there for a year. But then he moved on to *fiqh*.

Abu Hanifa turned to *fiqh* and immersed himself in it as he had done with the different sects, studying the *fatwas* of the great shaykhs of his time. He devoted himself to one of them and took benefit from him. He thought that a seeker of *fiqh* should take from various different shaykhs and live in their environment but devote himself to a particular distinguished *faqih* in order to be trained by him and so be able to understand the *fiqh* of subtle questions.

During his time, Kufa was the home of the *fuqaha'* of Iraq as Basra was the home of the different sects and those who delved into the principles of dogma. Kufa was the intellectual environment which influenced him. Explaining that, he said, "I was situated in a lode of knowledge and *fiqh*. I sat with its people and devoted myself to one of their *fuqaha'*."

Abu Hanifa devoted himself to Hammad ibn Abi Sulayman, studied *fiqh* with him, and remained with him until his death. There are three questions which need answering concerning this. One is the age of Abu Hanifa when he first stayed with Hammad and devoted himself to *fiqh*? The second concerns his age when he became an independent teacher? And the third concerns whether his devotion to his teacher was so total as to preclude contact with the knowledge of others.

There is, in fact, no way that we can know the age when Abu Hanifa turned to *fiqh* or took up with Hammad. All we know is that he stayed with Hammad until he died. He did not start teaching on his own until after Hammad died when he took the latter's place in his circle which was vacated by his death. Hammad died in 120 AH when Abu Hanifa must have been in his forties. So Abu Hanifa did not teach independently until after he was forty and fully developed, physically and intellectually. He thought about becoming independent before that, but did not do so.

It is related from Zafar that Abu Hanifa said about his connection to his shaykh Hammad, "I accompanied him for ten years and then my self urged me to seek leadership and I wanted to withdraw and have my own circle. One day I went out in the evening resolved to do so that but when I entered the mosque, I saw that I would not be happy to withdraw from him and went and sat with him. That night Hammad heard that a relative of his in Basra had died leaving property and had no other heir but him. He told me to sit in his place while he was away. I replied to questions I had not heard answered by him and wrote down my replies. When he returned I showed him the questions – there were about sixty of them. He agreed with me on forty and disagreed on twenty. I decided not to leave him until he or I died and that was what I did."

It is reckoned that he was with him for eighteen years and it is related that he said, "I came to Basra and thought that I would not be asked about anything which I could not answer. Then they asked me about things which I could not answer so I decided that I would not leave Hammad until he or I died. I kept his company for eighteen years."

If we study his life, it will be seen that this was not exclusive since he often went on *hajj* to the House of Allah, and in Makka and Madina he met a number of scholars, many of whom were *Tabi'un* and his encounter with them was only for the sake of knowledge. He related *hadiths* from them, debated *fiqh* with them, and studied their methods. Thus he had many shaykhs. There were also those from whom he related regarding the different sects. It is confirmed that he studied with Zayd ibn 'Ali Zayn al-'Abidin and Ja'far as-Sadiq, who were Shi'ite Imams, and 'Abdullah ibn Hasan. He studied with some of the Kaysaniyya who believed in the return of the hidden *mahdi*.

So he met and studied with other scholars while he was with Hammad, especially the *Tabi'un* who had learned directly from the Companions and were distinguished for *fiqh* and *ijtihad*. He stated, "I learned the *fiqh* of 'Umar, the *fiqh* of 'Ali, the *fiqh* of 'Abdullah ibn Mas'ud and the *fiqh* of Ibn 'Abbas from their companions."

His replacing Hammad ibn Abi Sulayman

When Abu Hanifa was in his forties, he took the place of his shaykh, Hammad, in Kufa and began to teach his students regarding the problems they presented for *fatwa*, cases, analogies and examples with his capable, orderly intellect and direct, logical mind and thus set up that method of *fiqh* from which the Hanafi school is derived. However, before continuing to discuss the course of his life and what is connected to it, we must first consider two further important aspects of his life: his livelihood and source of income and how the events of his time affected him.

Historical deduction leads us to conclude that Abu Hanifa's father and grandfather were wealthy merchants, and it is probable that they traded in *khazz*-silk which was a very profitable business. Abu Hanifa carried on in the family business until his conversation with ash-Sha'bi after which he devoted himself to knowledge. Did he give up commerce altogether? The transmitters are agreed that he did not but remained a merchant until his death. They mention that he had a partner and it appears that this partner enabled him to continue to seek knowledge, teach *fiqh* and transmit *hadith*. This trustworthy partner must have prevented him from having to go to the markets. There were other scholars who combined trade and knowledge such as Wasil ibn 'Ata', the shaykh of the Mu'tazilites who was Abu Hanifa's contemporary. He was born in the same year and was a Persian like him. He also lived off his trade and had a partner who was a relative and dealt with business on his behalf so that he could devote himself to his studies.

Abu Hanifa, the merchant, had four qualities connected to the behaviour of people in business which made him a perfect example of the upright merchant just as he was in the first rank among scholars:

• He was wealthy and not controlled by greed which impoverishes souls. This may be due to having grown up in a wealthy home and never having tasted need.

• He was very trustworthy in all he did.

• He was generous and Allah protected him from avarice.

• He was very devout and religious. He worshipped a lot, fasting in the day and praying at night.

These qualities combined to define his business dealings so that he was unusual among merchants. Many people compared him to Abu Bakr as-Siddiq in that respect. It was as if by imitating Abu Bakr's example and proceeding on his path, he was one of the *Salaf* who are followed. Both his buying and selling were trustworthy. A woman brought a silk garment to sell and he asked, "How much is it?" She replied, "A hundred." He said "It is worth more than a hundred. How much?" She kept increasing it by hundreds until she reached four hundred and he said, "It should be more than that." She said, "You are mocking me." He said, "Bring a man to value it." She brought a man and he bought it for five hundred.

Thus we see that he was circumspect in buying as well as selling and did not see the heedlessness of the seller as something to be taken advantage of, but thought that it was necessary to guide the person correctly. When he was the seller, he would sometimes forgo profit if the buyer was weak or a friend, alternatively, he would give him some of his excess profit.

A woman once came to him and said, "I am weak and I put myself in your hands. Sell me this garment for what it cost you." He said, "Take it for four dirhams." She retorted, "Do not mock me. I am an old woman." He said, "I bought two garments and sold one of them for the cost of both less four dirhams. This garment is then worth four dirhams."

Another time a friend came to him and asked him for a silk garment of a certain description and colour. He told him, "Be patient until it comes and I will get it for you, Allah willing." That happened before a week had passed and he took the garment to his friend and said to him, "What you needed has arrived." "How much is it then?" the friend asked. "A dirham," Abu Hanifa replied. He said, "I did not think you would mock me." He said, "I am not mocking you. I brought two garments for 20 dinars and a dirham. I sold one for twenty dinars and this remains for a dirham."

There is no doubt that such behaviour involves giving or it is alms in the form of buying and selling. It is not usual commerce. Rather, it tells us about the inner character of that great merchant in himself, his trustworthiness, intelligence, *deen* and fidelity, and illustrates the generosity in his heart.

He was very distressed about anything which was tainted by the possibility of wrong action, even if such was unlikely. If he thought that there was any wrong action involved in a transaction, or suspected it in connection with any property he had, he would take it and give it as charity to the poor and needy. It is reported that he sent his partner, Hafs ibn 'Abdu'r-Rahman, with some goods and told him that there was a fault in one garment and that he must make the fault clear when he sold it. Hafs sold the goods and forgot to point out the flaw and he did not know who had bought it. When Abu Hanifa learned of that, he gave the entire value of the garment away as charity. (*History of Baghdad,* pt. 13, p. 58)

In spite of this scrupulousness and not being satisfied with anything that was not absolutely lawful, his trade was profitable and so he often spent on shaykhs and *hadith* scholars. It states in *The History of Baghdad*: "He used to accrue profit from one year to the next and he would use it to provide for the requirements of the shaykhs and scholars: their food and garments and all their needs. Then he would give the remaining dinars of profit to them and say, "Buy what you need and only praise Allah. I have not given you any money. It is simply part of Allah's bounty to you." (pt. 13, p. 360)

The profit of his trade was used to preserve the dignity of scholars and provide for their needs and to enable people of knowledge to dispense with official stipends. He was also keen about his appearance which was reported to be good. He was very concerned about his clothes and chose the best so that his cloak was worth thirty dinars. He had a good appearance and wore a lot of scent. Abu Yusuf said, "He used to take care of even his sandal straps so that he was never seen with a broken strap."

In the same way that he was concerned with his own attire and appearance, he was also concerned with that of others. For instance, it is reported that he saw one of his companions wearing a poor garment and ordered him to wait until the assembly had departed so that he alone remained. He told him, "Lift the prayer mat and take what is under it." The man lifted it and there was 1000 dirhams under it. He told him, "Take these dirhams and change your state with them." The man said, "I am wealthy and well-off. I do not need it." He told him, "Have you not heard the *hadith*, 'Allah loves the trace of his blessing to appear on His servant'? For this reason you must change your state, so that your friend is not grieved by you."

His position in respect of the revolutionary movements of his time

We know turn to something which had a strong effect on the course of Abu Hanifa's life: his position in respect to the revolutionary movements of his time, the extent of their effect on him, what assitance he gave to the instigators, and what was his relationship with those in authority. It is vital to ascertain these matters since the trial which ended his life was connected to them to the extent that one could say, it was a case of direct cause and effect. What took place was connected to something which had happened in his youth.

Abu Hanifa lived for fifty-two years under Umayyad rule and eighteen years under Abbasid rule. He experienced both Muslim dynasties. He knew the Umayyads when they were strong and when they were in their decline. He experienced the Abbasid state when it was in a missionary stage in the Persian lands, when it was emerging newly-fledged from its hidden lair, and then when it became a movement which defeated the Umayyads and wrested sovereignty from them, imposing on the people an authority which they considered to be religious because its khalifs were among the relatives of the Messenger of Allah. So the people were impelled to it by both desire and terror.

Abu Hanifa was aware of this and it had an effect on him, even if it is not known that he participated with those who rebelled. Most of the reports about his position make it clear that his heart was with the 'Alawites when they rebelled first against the Umayyads, and then later when they rebelled against the Abbasids.

It is related that when Zayd ibn 'Ali Zayn al-'Abidin rebelled against Hisham in 121 AH, Abu Hanifa said, "His going forth resembles that of the Messenger of Allah on the Day of Badr." He was asked, "Did you not stay behind?" He said, "People's trusts kept me from him. I offered them to Ibn Abi Layla but he did not accept them. So I feared that I would die without them being known." It is reported that he said about not accompanying Zayd, "If I had known that people would not disappoint him as they did his father, I would have striven with him because he is a true Imam. Nonetheless I helped him with my property and sent him 10,000 dirhams and told the messenger, 'Give him my excuse.'" (al-Manaqib, al-Bazzazi, pt. 1, p. 55)

This indicates that he considered the rebellion against the Umayyads to be legally permissible when there was a just Imam like Imam Zayd and that he wanted to bear arms with him. But the sources do not indicate that he did not anticipate a good result. The action was correct, but nothing was achieved because of lack of support. Nonetheless he supported him with money.

Imam Zayd's rebellion ended in his death in 132 AH, after which his son Yahya rebelled in Khorasan in 135 AH and was also killed. Then 'Abdullah ibn Yahya continued to pursue their cause and fought against the general whom Marwan II sent to Yemen at the end of the Umayyad era, and he too was killed as had been the fate of his fathers before him.

So this illustrates what Abu Hanifa thought of Zayd ibn 'Ali and how he compared his expedition to that of the Prophet at Badr. He considered him to be a just Imam and supported him financially so as not to be one of those who stayed behind. He saw him slain, and then his son was killed after him and then his grandson as well. It is likely that he was distressed by their deaths. When scholars are angry, their tongues can accomplish what swords cannot. Their blows are stronger and sharper. What befell him from the Umayyad governor in Iraq in 130 AH supports that. It is stated in al-Makki's *The Virtues of Abu Hanifa* and in other sources and history books that Yazid ibn 'Umar ibn Hubayra, Marwan's governor of Iraq, sought out Abu Hanifa to appoint him *qadi* or to put him in charge of the exchequer. Sedition was rife at that time in Iraq, Khorasan and Persia because of Abbasid agitators.

This is what al-Makki says about what happened:

Ibn Hubayra was the governor of Kufa for the Umayyads. There were seditions in Iraq and he gathered the *fuqaha'* of Iraq at his door, including Ibn Abi Layla, Ibn Shibrama, and Da'ud ibn Abi Hind. He appointed each of them to high post. Then he sent for Abu Hanifa and wanted to put the seal in his hand so that no document would be implemented except at the hand of Abu Hanifa. But Abu Hanifa refused and Ibn Hubayra swore that if he did not accept, he would flog him.

Those *fuqaha'* said to him, "We beseech you by Allah not to destroy yourself. We are your brothers and we all are forced to comply in this business and can find no way to avoid it."

Abu Hanifa said, "If he wanted me to restore the doors of the Wasit Mosque for him I would not undertake to do it. What should I do when he wants me to write that a man should have his head cut off and seal the document? By Allah, I will never become involved in that!"

"Let your companion alone." said Ibn Abi Layla to the others. "He is right and others are wrong."

The authorities imprisoned Abu Hanifa and he was flogged on consecutive days. The flogger came to Ibn Hubayra and told him, "The man will die."

Ibn Hubayra said, "Tell him: 'We will banish anyone who lies to us.'"

He asked Abu Hanifa to submit but he said, "If he were to ask me to restore the doors of the mosque for him, I would not do it."

Then the flogger met with Ibn Hubayra again who said, "Is there no sincere adviser of this prisoner to ask me for a reprieve which we can grant him?"

That was mentioned to Abu Hanifa who said, "Let me consult my brothers." He did so and Ibn Hubayra commanded that he be let go and he went Makka in 139 AH.

He remained in Makka until the Abbasids came and then returned to Kufa during the time of al-Mansur."

So al-Makki and others mention that Ibn Hubayra offered a post to Abu Hanifa and he refused. He thought that Ibn Hubayra wanted to appoint him to some office to confirm his loyalty or prove his suspicions against him. He offered him the seal but Abu Hanifa refused. He asked him to accept a general post but he refused even though he was severely beaten until his head was swollen and breathing became difficult for him. He did not weaken or weep until he learned that his mother was grieved by what had happened to him. Then his eyes filled with tears as he was pained by her pain and compassionate on her behalf. Such is the truly strong person; he is not concerned for himself but only concerned for others.

Abu Hanifa fled to Makka after the flogging and remained there from 130 AH until the Abbasids were in power. He was safe in the Haram while the seditions were rife throughout the khalifate. He devoted himself to the *hadith* and *fiqh* which came from the knowledge of Ibn 'Abbas. He met his students there and discussed knowledge with them. Al-Mansur came to power in 136. Abu Hanifa was in Makka from 130 AH which means he stayed at least six years in the vicinity of the Haram.

It also reports in *The Virtues* by al-Makki that Abu Hanifa was in Kufa when Abu'l-'Abbas as-Saffah entered it and asked for people to give him their allegiance.

When Abu'l-'Abbas came to Kufa, he gathered the scholars and said, "This command has come to the people of the House of your Prophet and Allah has brought you good and established the truth. You are the scholars and it is more proper for you to assist it. You will have gifts, honour and hospitality from the property of Allah as you wish. So pledge allegiance to your Imam as evidence for and against you and security for your Life to Come. Do not meet Allah without an Imam and be those who have no evidence on their behalf."

140

The people looked at Abu Hanifa and he said, "Do you want me to speak on my own and your behalf?"

"We do," they said.

"I praise Allah," he said, "Who has conveyed the right of Imamate to the kin of His Prophet and ended for us the oppression of injustice and has released our tongues with the truth. We give you homage based on the command of Allah and fidelity to you by your contract until the Hour comes. Allah has not removed this matter from the kin of His Prophet, may Allah bless him and grant him peace."

As-Saffah answered him well. "Someone like you speaks for the scholars. They did well to choose you and you conveyed well."

This would suggest that Abu Hanifa was in Kufa when as-Saffah came there and received allegiance before 136 AH. This conflicts with the report that he did not come to Kufa until al-Mansur was khalif, i.e. in 136 AH or afterwards.

I think it is possible to reconcile the two. If Abu Hanifa fled to Makka from Ibn Hubayra and stayed there until Ibn Hubayra and his dynasty were out of Iraq, he could have gone to Kufa when as-Saffah went there and pledged allegiance to him. However, the sedition continued in Iraq and matters were not completely settled so he returned to Makka. He may have gone back and forth between the two cities until things were in order in the time of al-Mansur. Then he came back to Kufa and stayed there and restored his circle in the mosque. His circle did not resume until things were more settled in Iraq and the Abbasids firmly established. That only happened during the khalifate of al-Mansur.

His relations with the Abbasids

That Abu Hanifa welcomed the arrival of the Abbasids is indicated by his behaviour with Abu'l-'Abbas as-Saffah. This is in harmony with his past experience because he had observed the oppression which 'Ali's descendants had suffered at the hands of the Umayyads. When the Abbasids first came to power they did so as a dynasty which had started as a Shi'ite movement, stating that they would hand over power to one of the descendants of 'Ali. Once in power, the dynasty was Hashimite, but from descendants of the Prophet's uncle not 'Ali. They then had to put down 'Alawite rebellions on the part of those whom they in their turn had wronged.

Abu Hanifa continued to support the Abbasids on account of his love for the entire family of the Prophet. Al-Mansur used to bring him near to him, esteem him and offer him generous gifts but he refused them with gentleness and use of stratagems. An estrangement took place between al-Mansur and his wife because he inclined away from her and she asked him to be fair. He asked her whom she would be content with as an arbiter and she chose Abu Hanifa. Al-Mansur was happy with that and Abu Hanifa was summoned.

He said to him, "Abu Hanifa, this free woman contends with me. Give me my right against her."

Abu Hanifa said, "Let the Amir al-Mu'minin speak."

"Abu Hanifa," he replied, "How many wives can a man marry at the same time?"

"Four," he replied.

"How many slavegirls is he allowed?"

"As many as he likes," was the reply.

"Is anyone permitted to say anything different?"

"No," replied the Imam.

"You have heard," said the khalif.

But Abu Hanifa continued, "Allah has allowed this to the people of fairness. If, however, anyone is not fair or fears that he will not be fair he should only have one. Allah Almighty says, *'But if you are afraid of not treating them equally, then only one.'* (4:3) So we must follow the discipline of Allah and take heed of His admonitions."

Al-Mansur was silent for a long time. Then Abu Hanifa got up and left. When he reached his house, the khalif's wife sent him a servant with money, clothes, a slavegirl and an Egyptian donkey. He refused the gift and told the servant, "Give her my greeting and

142

tell her that she endangers my *deen*. I did that for Allah, not desiring anything from anyone."

It is not known that Abu Hanifa was against Abbasid rule until punitive action was taken against the sons of 'Ali and there was a strong dispute between the Abbasids and them. It is known that he was loyal to the sons of 'Ali, partisan on their behalf, and that he preferred them, so it was natural that he should become angry when they were angry, especially when those who rebelled against al-Mansur were Muhammad an-Nafs az-Zakiya (Pure Soul) and his brother Ibrahim. Their father was one of those connected by scholarship to Abu Hanifa – *The Book of Virtues* mentions him as one of his shaykhs from whom he transmitted. When his sons rebelled, 'Abdullah was in al-Mansur's prison where he died after his sons were killed.

That is why we see words related from Abu Hanifa showing resentment against the Abbasids during the rebellion of these 'Alawites and after their deaths. It is clear that, at that time, he did not think that loyalty to the Abbasids was correct but, as had been the case with him in the past, his resentment never exceeded verbal criticism and stating his loyalty to the 'Alawites. He took no action. Such is the action of scholars who are only a little distracted from their knowledge by their devotion for those they love. Al-Mansur was aware of this and he overlooked it sometimes and sought information at other times until the tragedy occurred.

Muhammad Pure Soul rebelled against al-Mansur in Madina in 145 AH and was supported by the people of Khorasan and others but he was too far away for them to be able to help him. It is reported that in Madina, Malik issued a *fatwa,* permitting Muhammad to rebel. At-Tabari and Ibn Kathir state that he gave a *fatwa* commanding people to pledge allegiance to Muhammad ibn 'Abdullah and that when people said that they had already pledged allegiance to al-Mansur, he said that they had been forced and that a forced allegiance is not binding. So people pledged allegiance. Malik stayed in his house. The affair ended when Muhammad was slain, and the same fate befell his brother Ibrahim after he had rebelled in Iraq, takes several cities and attacked Kufa.

Some people think that this alleged *fatwa* by Malik was the reason that he was flogged and injured. Abu Hanifa held an even stronger position about the matter than Malik. He openly supported them in his classes. Things reached the point where one of the generals of al-Mansur refused to go out to fight him.

It is reported that al-Hasan ibn Qahtaba, one of al-Mansur's generals, went to Abu Hanifa and said, "My situation is not hidden from you. Can I repent?"

The Imam said, "If Allah knows that you regret what you have done. If you can choose between killing a Muslim and being killed yourself, choose your own death before his. Then you will have a contract with Allah if you do not go back on it. If you fulfil that, you have repented."

"I have done that," said Hasan. "I make a contract with Allah that I will never again kill a Muslim."

Then Ibrahim ibn 'Abdullah rebelled and al-Mansur commanded Hasan to go against him. He went to the Imam and told him what had happened and he said, "The moment of your repentance has come. If you fulfil your promise, you have repented. Otherwise, you will be punished for the first and last."

So he was serious about his repentance, prepared himself for execution, and went to al-Mansur and said, "I will not go against this man. Allah is owed obedience in everything you do as far as you are able. I will have a fuller portion with Him. If it is disobedience, I am responsible."

Al-Mansur was angry and Hamid ibn Qahtaba, his brother, said, "We have suspected his mind for a year. He seems muddled. I will go. I am more entitled to excellence than him." So he went.

Al-Mansur asked one of his confidants, "Which *faqih* does he go to?" They said, "He frequents Abu Hanifa."

If this is true, al-Mansur would regard it as a very dangerous thing for the state because Abu Hanifa had gone beyond the bounds of simple criticism and emotional loyalty into the sphere of positive action, even if his action was confined to a *fatwa*. The *faqih* must give good counsel in the *deen* of Allah and not recommend corruption.

Whatever the truth of this transmission, it is reliably confirmed that Abu Hanifa openly stated his criticism of the khalif and his behaviour towards the 'Alawites. That is in accord with his past behaviour and his links to the descendants of 'Ali. He was linked with Zayd, as we said, and also had a firm connection to Ja'far as-Sadiq. Muhammad al-Baqir was also connected to him. He was a student of 'Abdullah ibn Hasan, the father of Ibrahim and Muhammad, as we previously stated. They had his loyalty and he was pained by what befell them.

Abu Hanifa's position was not hidden from the ever-watchful al-Mansur, especially in Kufa. That is why he wanted to test his loyalty and obedience when the opportunity arose. He was in the process of building Baghdad and wanted to appoint Abu Hanifa *qadi* there but he refused. Al-Mansur insisted on him accepting some post, whatever it was. So his aim was evident. Abu Hanifa perceived his intention and wanted to avoid it. It is related that eventually he agreed to count the bricks in the construction.

At-Tabari summarised the situation in this way.

> Al-Mansur wanted Abu Hanifa to be in charge of the judges but he refused. Al-Mansur swore that he must accept a post while Abu Hanifa swore that he would not. So he put him in charge of overseeing the construction of the city; making the bricks and getting men for the work. He undertook that until they finished the city wall next to the ditch. Al-Haytham ibn Adi mentioned that al-Mansur offered Abu Hanifa the post of *qadi* but he refused. He swore that he would not leave him alone until he undertook a post for him. That was reported to Abu Hanifa and he called for a measuring rod and counted the bricks and thus fulfilled al-Mansur's oath. Al-Mansur ignored Abu Hanifa for a time, but not completely. Things were reported to him from time to time, but he deferred taking action.

Before going on to mention some of these matters which made al-Mansur do what he did without right, we can state that the tragedy which befell Abu Hanifa was not the result of the rebellion of Ibrahim ibn 'Abdullah, the brother of the Pure Soul. Abu Hanifa died in 150 AH, five years after the rebellion and death of Ibrahim.

An analytic approach forces us to reject what al-Khatib relates in *The History of Baghdad* from Zafar: "Abu Hanifa made strong public statements in the time of Ibrahim. I told him, 'By Allah, you are in his favour so spare the ropes from our necks.' It was not long before a letter came from al-Mansur to 'Isa ibn Musa ordering him to take Abu Hanifa to Baghdad. He lived for only fifteen days after that."

As Ibrahim was killed in 145 AH, he could not have been taken directly following that since five years had passed. History books often contain errors of this sort and it is necessary to exercise caution about accepting them.

After the 'Alawite opposition to al-Mansur and his persecution of them and execution of their leaders, Abu Hanifa was not pleased with his rule. He was able to avert any harm from himself and directed himself to the path of knowledge. But from time to time he would make certain statements or things were revealed about his opinion of al-Mansur and his government. We will mention two instances which aroused al-Mansur's suspicions about him.

One is when the people of Mosul rebelled against al-Mansur. Al-Mansur imposed a condition on them which stated that if they rebelled, their blood was lawful for him. So al-Mansur gathered the *fuqaha'* including Abu Hanifa and said, "Is it not true that the Messenger of Allah said, 'Believers are those who abide by their preconditions'? The people of Mosul accepted a condition that they would not rebel against me. They have rebelled against my governor and so their blood is lawful for me." A man said, "Your hand is extended over them and your word is accepted among them. If you pardon, pardon befits you. If you punish, it is according to what they deserve."

He asked Abu Hanifa, "What do you say, shaykh? Do we not have the khalifate of the Prophet and a house of security?" He said, "You imposed on them a precondition which they were incapable of fulfilling and you stipulated for them something which is not within your right. The blood of a Muslim is only lawful on account of one of three things. If you take them, you take what is not lawful. The precondition of Allah has more right to be observed." Al-Mansur commanded that the session be ended and they dispersed. Then he called him and said, "Shaykh, the position is as you stated. Go to your city but do not give people a *fatwa* which will disgrace your ruler and extend the domain of the Kharijites."

Here is what we find in *al-Kamil* by Ibn al-Athir on the events of 148 AH:

> The populace of Hamdan were Shi'ites and al-Mansur decided to send armies to Mosul and annihilate its inhabitants. He summoned Abu Hanifa, Ibn Abi Layla and Ibn Shibrama and told them, 'The people of Mosul gave me their word that they would not rebel, and that, if they were to do so, then their blood and property would be fair game. They have rebelled.' Abu Hanifa was silent. The two other men said, 'If you pardon your subjects, you are worthy of that; and if you punish, it is because they deserve it.' He said to Abu Hanifa, 'I see you are silent, shaykh.' He replied, 'Amir al-Mu'minin, they made a contract they had no right to make. Do you think that if a woman made her private parts lawful without a marriage contract or ownership, it would be permitted to have intercourse with her?' 'No,' replied the former. 'No,' Abu Hanifa continued, 'So how can it be permitted for the people of Mosul ?' Al-Mansur commanded that Abu Hanifa and his companions return to Kufa. (pt. 5, p. 217)

There are some mistakes in the details of this account – for instance, mentioning Ibn Shibrama as being with him on this occasion when the events were in 148 AH whereas Ibn Shibrama died in 144, as Ibn al-Athir himself says elsewhere.

The second incident which showed his view of al-Mansur's government is when the latter sent him a gift to test to see if he would accept and he made an excuse about it. We read in *The Virtues* by al-Makki:

Al-Mansur sent him a gift of 10,000 dirhams and a slavegirl. 'Abdu'l-Malik ibn Hamid, al-Mansur's wazir, was a noble and generous man. He told Abu Hanifa when he refused it, "I tell you by Allah, the Amir al-Mu'minin is looking for a way to get at you. If you do not accept, you will confirm his suspicions about you." He refused and so 'Abdu'l-Malik said, "As for the money, give it out in stipends. As for the slavegirl, accept her from me or make an excuse so that I can excuse you to the Amir al-Mu'minin." Abu Hanifa said, "I am too weak for women. I am old and I do not consider it lawful to accept a slave-girl with whom I cannot have relations and I would not dare to sell a slavegirl which came from the property of the Amir al-Mu'mimin."

Similar incidents took place between Abu Hanifa and al-Mansur and so he kept him under surveillance. There were those in al-Mansur's retinue who provoked him against Abu Hanifa and made him suspect his statements and *fatwas*, but he continued to make statements and *fatwas* which he believed to be true, uncon-cerned about whether people were pleased or angry as long as he was pleasing to Allah, complying to the Truth and it satisfied his own conscience.

Al-Khatib reported that Abu Yusuf said, "Al-Mansur sum-moned Abu Hanifa. Ar-Rabi', the chamberlain of al-Mansur, who was hostile to Abu Hanifa, said, 'Amir al-Mu'minin, Abu Hanifa contradicts your grandfather, 'Abdullah ibn 'Abbas. He stated that when someone swore an oath and then made an exception a day or two later, the exception was permitted. But Abu Hanifa says that the exception is not allowed unless it is simultaneous with the oath.' Abu Hanifa said, 'Amir al-Mu'minin, ar-Rabi' claims that you have no allegiance from your army.' 'How is that?' he asked. He said, 'They swear to you and then return to their homes and make an exception, and so their oaths are invalid.' Al-Mansur laughed and said, 'Rabi', do not start with Abu Hanifa!' When he left, ar-Rabi' said, 'You wanted to spill my blood!' 'No,' he replied, 'you wanted to spill mine, and I saved you and saved myself.'"

Al-Khatib also said, "Abu'l-'Abbas at-Tusi had a bad opinion of Abu Hanifa and Abu Hanifa was aware of it. Abu Hanifa went to al-Mansur at a time when there were a lot of people present. At-Tusi said, 'Today I will finish with Abu Hanifa.' So he came to him and said 'Abu Hanifa, the Amir al-Mu'minin commands one of us to strike off the head of another man without knowing who it is. Is he permitted to do that?' 'Abu'l-'Abbas,' the Imam replied, 'does the Amir al-Mu'minin command what is right or falsehood?' 'What is right,' he replied. Abu Hanifa said, 'Carry out the right wherever it is and you will not be questioned about it.' Then Abu Hanifa said to those near him, 'This one wanted to bind me so I tied him up.'"

It should be mentioned here that a position taken by Abu Hanifa may have provided al-Mansur with a means of harming him because Abu Hanifa would annul the judgements of the *qadi* of Kufa when they were contrary to his opinion and declare that they were wrong at the time they were issued and to those who had received a positive or negative judgement. That provoked the *qadi* against him and he thought ill of him and was moved to complain about him to the amir.

According to *The History of Baghdad*, Ibn Abi Layla, who was *qadi* in Kufa, examined the case of a madwoman who had said to a man, "Son of two fornicators!" He carried out the *hadd* on her while she was standing in the mosque and she received two *hadds* since she had slandered both the father and the mother. Abu Hanifa heard about that and stated, "He erred about her in six ways. He carried out the *hadd* in the mosque and *hudud* are not carried out in mosques; he flogged her while standing and women are flogged sitting; he imposed one *hadd* for the father and another for the mother but if a man were to slander a group, he would receive only one *hadd*; he combined two *hadds* and two *hadds* are not combined; a madwoman is not subject to a *hadd*; and the *hadd* was for the parents who were absent and failed to attend and claim."

After hearing about this, Ibn Abi Layla went to the amir and complained to him. The amir put Abu Hanifa under an interdiction, saying, "Do not give *fatwa*." He did not give *fatwa* for some days and then a messenger came from the authorities who had been instructed to present some questions to Abu Hanifa so that he could give *fatwa* on them. Abu Hanifa refused, saying, "I am barred." The messenger went to the amir who said, "I have given him permission." So he sat to give *fatwa*.

In his criticism, Abu Hanifa did not differentiate between a judgement of the *qadi* which was binding on the public, right or wrong, and the *fatwa* that a *faqih* made which did was not binding on anyone. Sometimes he criticised a *fatwa* that he thought was wrong more severely than an actual judgement because injustice might develop from it. Injustice pained him greatly and an incorrect *fatwa* could result in injustice to people in their lives and property.

Whatever the position of Abu Hanifa about the judgements of the *qadi*, Ibn Abi Layla did not accept the criticism of Abu Hanifa cheerfully. He was hostile to him because of that criticism and perhaps enmity led him to try to harm Abu Hanifa. Thus it is reported that Abu Hanifa said about him, "Ibn Abi Layla seeks to make lawful in regard to me what I would not make lawful for any living creature." If we blame Abu Hanifa for the severity of his criticism of the judgements of Ibn Abi Layla and his lack of restraint in making it public, we also blame the *qadi* of Kufa for allowing that criticism to provoke enmity between them.

Al-Mansur was annoyed by Abu Hanifa. Indeed, he became fed up with him when he learned of his leaning towards the 'Alawites which was confirmed by various experiences he had had with him. But he could find no way of dealing with him because he did not go beyond his teaching circle and he was not suspect in his *deen* or his outward actions. He was a firm, reliable, generous scholar to whom people travelled because of his knowledge, excellence, guidance and fear of Allah. There was no way to act against him as long as he took no action or rebelled. An opportunity eventually presented itself when he offered him the position of *qadi* and he refused to accept it.

He asked him to be *Qadi* of Baghdad which would have made him the Chief *Qadi* of the state. If he accepted, that would indicate his sincerity or his absolute obedience to al-Mansur. If he refused, that would provide al-Mansur with a means to get at him publicly without damaging his religious reputation because people thought Abu Hanifa righteous and in this case his refusal was a refusal to accept a necessary duty and he could be impelled to do that by force. Any harm inflicted was to force him to accept something which would benefit the general public, not to trick him or wrong him.

He had sometimes criticised the decisions of the *qadis* and so it was appropriate for him to sit in the highest seat of judgement in order to guide the judges to what was obligatory and impel them to what was correct. He was the *faqih* whose *fatwas* decided the correctness or error of judgements. If he refused that office, it meant that his prior criticism was merely destructive since he now had the opportunity to be constructive and had refused. Since he was the foremost *faqih* in the view of the people of Iraq, the khalif was correct in wanting to make him the Chief *Qadi*. If he refused, he could be forced to accept the post. So when he refused, al-Mansur punished him by flogging and imprisonment or simply imprisonment, according to which version of the story is correct. We will see what the sources state.

We read in *The Virtues* by al-Makki:

> When Abu Hanifa was taken to Baghdad, he came out with a shining face and said, "This man has summoned me to be *qadi* and I told him that I am not fit. I know that the claimant must provide evidence while the oath absolves the one who denies the charge. The only one fit to be *qadi* is the one whose personality is such that he can command authority over you, your children, and your leaders. I am not like that. You summon me and I experience no relief until I part from you." He said, "You do not accept my gift." I said, "I have returned whatever money the Amir al-Mu'minin sent. If that is the gift, I accept it. The Amir al-Mu'minin has connected me to the treasury of the Muslims. I have no right to their money. I am not one of

151

those who fights for them so that I should take what the fighter takes. I am not one of their children so as to take what their children take. I am not one of their poor so as to take what the poor take." He said, "You will be *qadi* in what they need from you."

Al-Bazzari said in *The Virtues*,

Al-Mansur imprisoned Abu Hanifa to force him to become Chief *Qadi* and he received 110 lashes. He was released from prison on the basis that he would stay at home and he was asked to give *fatwa* regarding the judgements presented to him. Al-Mansur used to send questions to him but he did not give *fatwa*. He ordered him to be re-imprisoned. Abu Hanifa was imprisoned again and was harsh and severe to him.

We read in the *History of Baghdad*,

Al-Mansur sent for Abu Hanifa, wanting to appoint him *qadi*, but he refused. Al-Mansur swore that he would do it and Abu Hanifa swore that he would not. Al-Mansur swore again that he would do it and Abu Hanifa swore that he would not. Ar-Rabi,' the chamberlain, said, "Do you not see that the Amir al-Mu'minin has sworn?" Abu Hanifa said, "The Amir al-Mu'minin can expiate his oaths better than I can." He refused the appointment therefore al-Mansur ordered his imprisonment.

Ar-Rabi' ibn Yunus said:

I saw the Amir al-Mu'minun clash with Abu Hanifa over the qadiship. Abu Hanifa said, "Fear Allah and do not give your trust except to the one who fears Allah. By Allah, I am safe from favouritism but how can I be safe from anger? If you threaten to drown me in the Euphrates unless I accept the appointment, I would prefer to be drowned. You have courtiers who need those who honour them for your sake. I am not fit for that." Al-Mansur said to him, "You lie, you are fit." Abu Hanifa retorted, "I have declared myself unfit so how can it be lawful for you to appoint someone who is a liar as *qadi*?"

There are a number of points to be noted in these stories. Firstly, when Abu Hanifa refused the qadiship, he refused it not only because al-Mansur appointed him, but because he saw it as a perilous post and thought that perhaps he would not be strong enough to do it, that his conscience would not be strong enough to bear its burdens and his will not strong enough to contain his feelings. He saw the post of *qadi* as a trial which made all other trials insignificant. His refusal does not necessarily have a political cause.

Secondly, al-Mansur was suspicious about the cause behind Abu Hanifa's refusal and did not believe that it was based purely the avoidance of bearing the responsibility of judgements. That is why he specifically asked for the reason he had refused the stipend, even if there was no connection between refusing to be *qadi* and refusing the stipend, as this question would indicate. Al-Mansur believed that his grounds for suspicion were confirmed. Moreover, the retinue around al-Mansur provoked him when he was undisturbed and directed his attention to Abu Hanifa.

The third point is that Abu Hanifa was not diplomatic in his replies. He did not use honeyed words and did not use devices to extricate himself. He was forthright with the truth and unconcerned about the consequences. He endured them. So he refused to be *qadi* and refused to give *fatwa* and clearly stated that he refused the stipend because it was from the Muslim treasury and that it was not lawful for him. Then the khalif took an oath and so did he without concern. Rather he thought of the ultimate end and of his reward with Allah.

Eventually the ordeal befell Abu Hanifa. The transmitters agree that he was imprisoned and that he did not sit to give *fatwa* or teach after that, since he died during or after this ordeal. Sources differ as to whether he died in prison after the flogging, which most say, or died in prison by being poisoned according to those who say that al-Mansur was not content to flog him, but poisoned

153

the shaykh to hasten his end, or was released before he died and then died at home while refusing to teach and meet people. These three versions are mentioned in his biographies and elsewhere.

It is related that he stayed in prison after the flogging until he died, and Da'ud ibn Rashid al-Wasiti said, "I was present when the Imam was tortured to force him to accept the appointment as *qadi*. He was taken out each day and given ten lashes until he had received 110 lashes. He was told, 'Accept the qadiship!' and he would reply, 'I am not fit.' The beatings continued and he said silently, 'O Allah, put their evil far from me by Your power.' When he continued to refuse, they poisoned him and so killed him."

Al-Bazzari says that after he was imprisoned for a time, al-Mansur spoke to some of his close advisors and brought him out of prison. He refused to give *fatwa*, hold audience with people or leave his house and remained so until his death.

We incline to this final version because it tallies with the course of events and what we know of al-Mansur which is that al-Mansur did not want to appear to be an oppressor of knowledge and scholars. When events forced him to punish Abu Hanifa, he produced a justification which had an adequate logical basis: to force him to act as *qadi*. He did not punish him out of simple malice. When this failed to produce a result, he did not insist on it so as to disclose his true motive. The general populace had also to be taken into account so he did not continue with the punishment. Sources agree that he ordered that he should be buried beside Abu Hanifa's grave. It is reported that al-Mansur prayed over his grave after his death and al-Mansur would not have done that if he had died in his prison.

Abu Hanifa died the death of the true men and martyrs in 150 or 153 AH. The first date is sounder. When he died, he left instructions that he should not be buried in any land which the ruler had misappropriated. When he heard this, al-Mansur said, "Who will save me from Abu Hanifa, both when he was alive and now when he is dead?"

He died in Baghdad and was buried there. Reports agree about that. But did his teaching circle also move there? No historian

154

mentions that Abu Hanifa moved his centre of teaching to Baghdad. All reports indicate that he remained teaching in Kufa until he stopped teaching and giving *fatwa*. After his ordeal, he did not resume teaching before his death. This does not mean that he did not have any teaching circle outside of Kufa. It is related that when he went on *hajj*, he gave *fatwa*, debated and studied, and at times he had a teaching circle in the *Masjid al-Haram*. We cannot deny that during the period in which he went to the Haram on account of the injustice of the Umayyad governor that he had a teaching circle in which he set forth his opinions and *fiqh*, even if the sources do not mention it, one way or the other.

He also had debates with the *fuqaha'* like those he had with al-Awza'i and there is a record of his studying some of the opinions of *fiqh* with Imam Malik and there were also many debates in Basra. Nonetheless, his principal school was in Kufa which is why he is known as 'the *Faqih* of Kufa'.

Chapter Two
The Knowledge of Abu Hanifa
and its Sources

In the history of Islamic *fiqh*, there is no man both so highly praised and so severely criticised as Abu Hanifa, may Allah be pleased with him. This dichomtomy occurred because he was an independent *faqih* who had an independent method of thought as a result of deep study. Such a person must have admirers and detractors. Most of those who criticised him were incapable of following the course of his thinking or of understanding his perception. Many were narrow-minded and considered any method which involved more than the simple statements of the *Salaf* alone as being rejected innovation.

Some of his critics were very ignorant and knew nothing of his fear of Allah, integrity, great intellect and knowledge, and were unaware of his high position with the common and elite alike. It was almost within his own lifetime that lies were forged about him and that process continued apace after his death. On the other hand, there were also those who went to excess in his praise.

His contemporary, al-Fudayl ibn 'Iyad, a man renowned for scrupulousness, said about him, "Abu Hanifa was a *faqih*, a man known for *fiqh*, reasonably wealthy and known for graciousness towards all who visited him. He was steadfast in teaching knowledge both night and day. He had a good reputation and was often silent. He was a man of few words. When a question on the lawful or unlawful would come to him, he was good at pointing out the truth and he was loath to accept the ruler's money."

Ja'far ibn ar-Rabi' said, "I sat with Abu Hanifa for five years and never saw anyone silent longer than him. When he was asked a question of *fiqh*, sweat poured from him like a river before he spoke outloud."

His contemporary, Malih ibn Waki' said about him, "Abu Hanifa was very trustworthy. By Allah, he had a noble heart and preferred the pleasure of his Lord above everything. If swords had been used on him in the Cause of Allah, he would have endured that. May Allah have mercy on him and be pleased with him as He is pleased with the pious."

His contemporary, 'Abdullah ibn al-Mubarak, described him as 'the quintessence of knowledge.'

Ibn Jurayj observed about him at the beginning of his life, "He will have amazing importance in knowledge." After Abu Hanifa was an adult, he said, "He is the *faqih*. He is the *faqih*."

When Malik was asked about 'Uthman al-Batti, he said, "He was an average man." When he was asked about Ibn Shibrama, he said, "He was an average man." When he was asked about Abu Hanifa, he said, "If he had gone to these columns and formed an analogy which showed that they were made of wood, you would have thought that they were wood."

We cannot go into all the statements in praise of Abu Hanifa. All of his contemporaries, supporters or opponents, described him as a *faqih*. Perhaps the best description is that of Ibn al-Mubarak who said that he was 'the quintessence of knowledge'. He had the heart of knowledge and took it as far as it would go. He deduced questions, reached their essence and learned their basis and then built on them. He occupied himself with thought, knowledge and debates. Thus he debated with the *mutakallimun* and refuted the erroneous views of some of them and argued against various sects.

There were several treatises ascribed to him. He also has a *musnad* in *hadith* ascribed to him. If this ascription is true, he has a position in *hadith*. So his position in *fiqh* and extrapolation, understanding of *hadiths* and derivation of the causes of judgements and building on them is of the highest calibre. One of his contemporaries said that he did not know anyone with a better understanding of *hadith* than him. That was only because he derived the reasons behind the judgements, so that it was almost as if he did not turn to the outward words but understood the meanings and derived the intention behind them and connected that to similar matters and built upon it.

From where did Abu Hanifa obtain all this knowledge? What were his sources? What was his background? What enabled him to attain the high place given to him in the history of Islamic knowledge? The necessary background for turning a person towards distinction in knowledge comprises four things.

1. Innate qualities, or quasi-innate, or those which can be acquired which become like personal talents. In general, they are qualities which characterise a person's psychological disposition and intellectual gifts.

2. The mentors with whom a person studies, their effect upon him, and who define for him the method he chooses to follow or who show him the various methods by whose light the path for him to follow becomes clear.

3. Personal life and experiences and the events which touch his life or befall him which make him proceed in certain directions. Two individuals may have the same gifts and shaykhs but one will be successful and the other not, or he will set out on a path which does not lead to success because his personal life has ordained another path for him, and so the two go different ways.

4. The era in which he lives and the intellectual environment in which he liveds and in which his gifts flourishes.

We will look at each of these factors in turn.

Abu Hanifa's Qualities

Abu Hanifa had natural qualities which set him in the highest rank of scholars and he was characterised by the qualities of the true firm, reliable scholar. He had self-control and contained his feelings. He did not indulge in unnecessary or ugly words far from the truth. He once argued about a question on which Hasan al-Basri had given a *fatwa*. He stated, "Hasan erred." A man said to him, "You say that Hasan erred, son of a whore!" He did not redden or blanch. He said, "By Allah, Hasan erred and 'Abdullah ibn

Mas'ud was correct." He used to say, "O Allah, if someone is annoyed by us, our heart is open to him."

This calmness and tolerance did not issue from a person with no feelings or stem from lack of emotion. He was a man with a sensitive heart and soul. It is related that one of those with whom he debated shouted at him, "Innovator! Heretic!" He rejoined, "May Allah forgive you. Allah knows that I am not that. I have not turned from Him since I knew Him and I only hope for His pardon and only fear His punishment." He wept when he mentioned the punishment. The man told him, "Pardon me regarding what I said." He said, "If any of the people of ignorance say something about me, I pardon them. As for the people of knowledge who say something about me, they are sinful. The slander of the scholars will cause something to remain after them."

So his calm was not an unfeeling one. It was the composure of someone who knows himself and is tranquil by his fear of Allah and is only concerned about what is connected to Allah and not what is connected to the dirt of people, like a clear unsullied sheet to which none of the harmful words of people stick. His composure was that of one who restrains himself and endures without attacking and dislikes the tempests which the self can provoke.

His independence of thought prevented him from losing himself in others' opinions. His shaykh Hammad recognised this quality in him. He used to encourage him to examine every case and not to accept any idea without examining it first. His independent thought made him see things as a free person, not subject to anything except for a text of the Book or *Sunna* or a *fatwa* of a Companion. He thought one could look into the position of the *Tabi'un* who might err or be right because their opinion did not have to be followed nor was its imitation part of scrupulousness. He lived in Kufa, which was essentially a Shi'ite milieu, and met the Shi'ite Imams in his time, like Zayd ibn 'Ali, Muhammad al-Baqir, Ja'far as-Sadiq and 'Abdullah ibn Hasan, and yet he maintained his high opinion of the great Companions in spite of his inclination to the noble family of the Prophet and his love for the People of the House.

Ibn 'Abdu'l-Barr states in *al-Intiqa'*: "Sa'id ibn Abi 'Aruba said, 'I came to Kufa and attended the gathering of Abu Hanifa. One day he mentioned 'Uthman ibn 'Affan and prayed for mercy on him. I told him, "You ask Allah to show him mercy. I have not heard anyone in this city pray for mercy on 'Uthman ibn 'Affan except you."'"

He was a profound thinker and went deeply into questions. He did not stop at the outward meaning of a text but went beyond that to its intentions. His deep philosophical intellect may have impelled him to that because at the beginning of his life he was involved in *kalam*. That profound sense of inquiry may be what led him to study *hadiths* in a deep manner, seeking the causes of the judgements they contained by examining the indications of words, aims of phrases, circumstances and related qualities. When he was satisfied about the underlying cause, he used analogy based on it and hypothesised and took that very far indeed.

He was quick-witted and ideas would come to him quickly the moment that they were needed. His thinking was not restricted or blocked when he investigated. He was never at a loss for words in debate as long as the truth was on his side and he had evidence to support it. He had ample devices to enable him to easily leave his opponent dumbfounded. There are many extraordinary examples of that in the books of biographies and histories which depict his life. We will mention some of them which reveal his excellent technique and subtle approach.

It is related that a man died and he had appointed Abu Hanifa, when he was absent, as his executor. The case was presented before Ibn Shibrama and Abu Hanifa mentioned that to him. Abu Hanifa brought the evidence that the man had died and made him executor. Ibn Shibrama said "Abu Hanifa, do you swear that your witnesses have testified truly?" He said, "I do not have to take an oath, I was absent." He said, "Your standards are in error." Abu Hanifa asked, "What do you say about a blind man with a head wound when two witnesses testify to that: does the blind man have to testify that the witnesses spoke the truth when he cannot see?" So Ibn Shibrama ordered the will to be implemented.

Ad-Dahhak ibn Qays al-Khariji, who rebelled in the Umayyad era, entered the mosque of Kufa and said to Abu Hanifa, "Repent." "Of what?" he asked. He answered, "Of your allowing arbitration." Abu Hanifa asked, "Will you kill me or debate with me?" "I will debate with you," he said. "And if we disagree on anything in the debate, who will decide between us?" He replied, "I will accept whomever you wish." Abu Hanifa said to one of ad-Dahhak's companions, "Sit and judge between us if we disagree." Then he turned and asked ad-Dahhak, "Are you content for this one to decide between us?" "Yes," he replied. Abu Hanifa said, "Then you have allowed arbitration, so desist."

It is related that there was a man in Kufa who stated, "'Uthman ibn 'Affan was a Jew," and the scholars could not quiet him or impel him to say other than what he had said. Abu Hanifa went to him and said, "I will bring you a suitor." "Who for?" asked the man. "For your daughter. It is a noble man who is wealthy, generous and who knows the Book of Allah by heart. He prays at night and weeps frequently out of fear of Allah." "One would be content with far less than this, Abu Hanifa?" "There is just one thing," said the Imam. "What is that?" asked the man. "He is a Jew," replied the Imam. The man exclaimed, "Glory be to Allah! Do you tell me to marry my daughter to a Jew!" "You will not do it?" asked the Imam. "No," replied the man. Abu Hanifa continued, "The Prophet, may Allah bless him and grant him peace, married his daughter to such a Jew," meaning 'Uthman, may Allah be pleased with him, whom the man claimed to be a Jew. He said, "I ask forgiveness of Allah. I repent to Allah Almighty."

These reports illustrate the extent of his skill in debate and the excellence of his dealing with some of the worst and most deleterious groups so that al-Mansur said to him, "You are the master of devices." It was easy for him to debate because of the strength of his insight, grasp of people's character, and his power to open the locks of their hearts and their inner selves. He would approach them from a direction which they could grasp and were familiar with so that it would be easy for them to accept the truth.

Abu Hanifa was sincere in the quest for the truth and that is the attribute of perfection which elevated him and illuminated his heart and insight into the truth. A sincere heart is the one which is free of bias, taint of the self and emotion in investigating matters and grasping problems. Allah gave him the light of recognition and lucid perception and his thoughts were directed in a straight-forward manner in seeking out the truth so that it would be under-stood and grasped.

Abu Hanifa freed himself of every appetite except the desire for sound perception and he knew that such *fiqh* is the *deen* or true understanding of the *deen*. It cannot be sought by someone domi-nated by prejudice for that is a barrier in the way of the truth. The desire for the truth was the over-riding concern which motivated him. Due to his sincerity, he did not claim that his opinion was the truth, but said, "This is our opinion. It is the best we can deter-mine. If anyone comes with a better position, he is more entitled to be correct than we are."

It was said to him, "Abu Hanifa, this *fatwa* which you give is the truth about which there can be no doubt." He said, "By Allah, I do not know. Perhaps it is falsehood about which there can be no doubt." Zafar said, "We used to go regularly to Abu Hanifa with Abu Yusuf and Muhammad ibn al-Hasan ash-Shaybani and write down what he said. One day he said to Abu Yusuf, "Woe to you, Ya'qub! Do not write down all that you hear from me. I may have an opinion today and then leave it tomorrow. I may have an opin-ion tomorrow and leave it the following day." His sincerity in seeking the truth might well lead him to retract his opinion if his opponent mentioned a *hadith* he had which was not impaired or mentioned a *fatwa* of a Companion.

Zuhayr ibn Mu'awiya said, "I asked Abu Hanifa about safe-conduct granted by a slave. He said, 'If he is not a fighter, his safe-conduct is invalid.' I said, "'Asim al-Ahwal transmitted that al-Fudayl ibn Yazid ar-Raqashi said, "We were laying siege to the enemy when an arrow was shot to them with a safe conduct attached to it." They said, "You have given us safe conduct." We replied, "It was given by a slave." They said, "By Allah, we do not know the slave from the free man among you." So we wrote that to 'Umar ibn al-Khattab and 'Umar wrote back, "Allow the safe-conduct of the slave." '" Abu Hanifa was silent. Then he was absent from Kufa for ten years. When he returned, I went to him and asked him about the safe-conduct of the slave, and he replied giving 'Asim's account. He had retracted his original statement and so I knew that he followed what he had heard." He was asked, "Do you diverge from the Prophet, may Allah bless him and grant him peace?" He replied, "May Allah curse the one who differs from the Messenger of Allah, may Allah bless him and grant him peace. Allah honoured us with him and we seek salvation by him."

All these qualities were combined with another quality through which all of these qualities were made manifest which is a gift which Allah gives to some people. That quality was strength of personality, influence, the capacity to instil awe and affect others by charisma, charm and spiritual vigour. But in spite of this he did not impose his opinion on his many students. Sometimes used to discuss with them and ascertain the opinions of the important ones among them and debate with them as an equal, not as a superior. Sometimes used to conclude with an opinion and all would be silent to listen to him but some of them would keep their own opinions. In both cases, Abu Hanifa was consistent with his position and his personality.

Abu Hanifa's circle of companions was described by his contemporary, Mis'ar ibn Kidam, who said, "They used to separate to see to their needs after the morning prayer. They would then gather to him and sit with him. Some would ask and some would debate. These was a great deal of talking because of the amount of evidence that was offered." (al-Makki, pt. 2, p. 36)

These are some of the attributes of Abu Hanifa: some are natural and some are acquired. They are the key to his personality and what enabled him to make use of all the spiritual nourishment he obtained. They are the tools which were used to process the material which he had contact with. It is through them that there occurred his interaction with the time in which he lived, his shaykhs and his experiences. These attributes were supported by a new method of thought and opinion which involved profound investigation and study and had far-reaching effects on individuals and indeed whole generations. It is by these qualities that Abu Hanifa won his supporters and provoked the spite of his envious detractors.

His Shaykhs

Abu Hanifa said of his scholarly training and his studies of *fiqh*, "I was in a lode of knowledge and *fiqh*. I sat with its people and devoted myself to one of their *fuqaha*.'"

His words clearly indicate that he lived and grew up in a scholarly environment and that he sat with scholars, studied with them, and learned their methods of investigation. Then he chose a *faqih* among them who satisfied his scholarly inclination and devoted himself to him alone. He did not shun other scholars but sometimes used to debate with them, his devotion to his own teacher not preventing him from sitting with them. All sources agree that he was the student of Hammad ibn Abi Sulayman, the shaykh of Iraqi *fiqh* in his time. But he also learned from others, related from many and debated with many, especially after Hammad's death. When he visited the *Haram* after leaving Kufa because of the Umayyad governor, Ibn Hubayra, he met many shaykhs.

Before dealing with those shaykhs, or at least those we know of, and their legal orientation in particular, we must point out three points:

- Abu Hanifa's shaykhs were from different persuasions and disparate sects. They were not all *fuqaha'* of the main *sunni* community and they were not only people of opinion. Some of them were *hadith* scholars and some taught the *fiqh* of the Qur'an and the knowledge of the great Qur'anic commentator, 'Abdullah ibn 'Abbas. When he stayed in Makka for about six years, which is understood from some of the books we have cited, he must have studied with the *Tabi'un* there who had learned the knowledge of Ibn 'Abbas from him or from his students.

  Many of those he sat with in Iraq were from among the sects of the Shi'a with all their differences. They included the Kaysanites, the Zaydites, the Twelver Imams and the Isma'ilis. Each had an effect on his thought, even if he did not follow their leanings except in respect of his love for the House of the Prophet. He took in all those disparate elements and assimilat-

164

ed them to reach his final conclusion. Abu Hanifa utilised all these elements, taking the best from them, and then produced a new way of thinking and an upright opinion.

• Abu Hanifa moved away from these different studies and learned the *fatwas* of the Companions who were famous for *ijtihad*, excellent opinion and intelligence.

We read in the *History of Baghdad*: "One day Abu Hanifa went to al-Mansur when 'Isa ibn Musa was with him. He told al-Mansur, 'This is the foremost scholar of the world today.' He asked him, 'Nu'man, from whom did you take knowledge?' He replied, 'From the companions of 'Umar from 'Umar, from the companions of 'Ali from 'Ali, and from the companions of 'Abdullah (ibn Mas'ud) from 'Abdullah, and in the time of Ibn 'Abbas none had more knowledge than him.' He said, 'You have made sure of yourself.'"

Abu Hanifa learned the *fatwas* of those majestic Companions and based himself on following their *fatwas*, or at least what he had from the *Tabi'un* from whom he learned, because he took it from their companions without intermediary.

• All the books of virtues mention that he met some Companions. Some of them state that he related *hadiths* from them. This would put him in the rank of the *Tabi'un*, and thus give him an excellence above the *fuqaha'* contemporary with him like Sufyan ath-Thawri, al-Awza'i, Malik and others.

Sources do not disagree that Abu Hanifa met some Companions who were contemporary with him and lived to the end of 100 AH or close to that or were alive in the 90s. They mention several Companions he met and saw, including Anas ibn Malik, (d. 93), 'Abdullah ibn Abi Awfa (d. 87), Wathila ibn al-Asqa' (d. 85), Abu't-Tufayl ibn Wathila, (d. in Makka in 102), the last Companion to die, and Sahl ibn Sa'id (d. 88).

There is disagreement about whether he transmitted from them or not. Some scholars said that he related from them and they mention *hadiths* which he reported, but knowledgeable *hadith* scholars consider their *isnad* to be weak.

Most scholars state that even if Abu Hanifa met some Companions, he did not relate from them. They argue that when he met them he was not at the age of someone who learns knowledge, retains it and transmits it because that could only have happened at the beginning of his life while he was going to the markets before he became involved with knowledge.

We incline to this view and accept that Abu Hanifa met some Companions, but did not relate from them. So was he a *Tabi'i* or not? Scholars disagree about the definition of a *Tabi'i*. Some say that it applies to anyone who met a Companion, even if he did not keep his company; simply having seen him is enough to make a man a *Tabi'i* according to that view. By that criterion Abu Hanifa is a *Tabi'i*. Some scholars, however, say that it is not enough to simply have seen the Companion but it is also necessary to have kept his company and learnt from him and so by that reckoning Abu Hanifa could not be said to be one of the *Tabi'un*.

Whatever the case, scholars are unanimous about the fact that he met a number of the *Tabi'un* and sat with them, studied with them, related from them and learned their *fiqh* at an age which allowed learning and transmission. Some of them were known for transmission, like ash-Sha'bi, and many were famous for opinion. He took from 'Ikrima, the transmitter of the knowledge of Ibn 'Abbas, Nafi', the bearer of the knowledge of Ibn 'Umar, and 'Ata' ibn Abi Rabah, the *faqih* of Makka, with whom he had a lengthy relationship. He used to debate with him about *tafsir* and learn from him.

We read in *al-Intiqa'*: "Abu Hanifa said, 'I asked 'Ata' ibn Rabah, "What do you say about the words of Allah Almighty, *'We restored his family to him, and the same again with them'* (21:84)?" He said, "He gave him his family and the like of his family." I answered, "Is it permitted to attribute to a man what is not from him?" He asked, "What is your position?" I replied, "Abu Muhammad, it means the reward of his family and the like of their reward." He said, "It is like that, but Allah knows best."'" If this is true, it indicates two things. One is that Abu Hanifa sat with 'Ata' ibn Abi Rabah, studied with him and took from him. 'Ata' died in 114 AH and so he must have gone on *hajj* and studied with the Makkan scholars while he was Hammad's student. The second is that 'Ata' used to teach *tafsir* of the Qur'an in Makka and that the school of Makka had inherited the Qur'anic knowledge of 'Abdullah ibn 'Abbas.

The shaykhs to whom he was connected, each of whom had a specific intellectual quality, deserve consideration, in order to ascertain the sum of the sources from which he took.

The most prominent of his shaykhs was Hammad ibn Sulayman. He was an Ash'ari by clientage since he was a client of Ibrahim ibn Abi Musa al-Ash'ari. He grew up in Kufa and learned his *fiqh* from Ibrahim an-Nakha'i, the most knowledgeable of the proponents of opinion. He died in 120 AH. He not only studied with an-Nakha'i but also studied *fiqh* with ash-Sha'bi. Both of them took from Shurayh, 'Alqama ibn Qays and Masruq ibn al-Adja'. They, in turn, had learned the *fiqh* of the two Companions, 'Abdullah ibn Mas'ud and 'Ali ibn Abi Talib.

The fact that these two Companions lived in Kufa meant that they left the people of Kufa much *fiqh*. That was the bedrock of Kufan *fiqh*. It is from their *fatwas* and those of their students who followed their path that this great legal inheritance was moulded. Hammad learned it, as said, from Ibrahim and ash-Sha'bi but it is clear that the *fiqh* of Ibrahim dominated him. Ibrahim was a proponent of the *fiqh* of the people of opinion whereas ash-Sha'bi was closer to the people of tradition even though he lived in Iraq.

As already mentioned, Abu Hanifa stayed with Hammad for eighteen years and learned the *fiqh* of the people of Iraq whose core was the *fiqh* of 'Abdullah ibn Mas'ud. He also learned the *fatwas* of Ibrahim an-Nakha'i so that Shah Waliyullah ad-Dihlawi says, "The source of Hanafi *fiqh* is found in the statements of Ibrahim an-Nakha'i." This is what he says in *Hujjatu' llah al-Baligha*: "Abu Hanifa, may Allah be pleased with him, was the strongest in holding to the school of Ibrahim and his contemporaries and only exceeded it as much as Allah willed. A very important consideration when making deduction in his school was precise analysis of the manner of extrapolation. If you wish to learn the truth of what we have said, there is a summary of the positions of Ibrahim and his contemporaries in *The Book of Traditions*, the *Jami'* of 'Abdu'r-Razzaq and the *Musannaf* of Abu Bakr ibn Shayba. The analogy used in the school of Abu Hanifa does not deviate from this procedure except in a very few places and even in those few it does not leave what the *fuqaha'* of Kufa believed." (p. 146)

When Hammad died, Abu Hanifa continued to study and research, teach and learn as do all true scholars, conforming with the tradition: "A scholar continues to seek knowledge. When he thinks that he knows, he is ignorant." We mentioned his learning in Makka from 'Ata' ibn Abi Rabah the school of Ibn 'Abbas which came through 'Ikrima. He also took the knowledge of Ibn 'Umar and the knowledge of 'Umar from Nafi', the client of Ibn 'Umar. Thus he amassed the knowledge of Ibn Mas'ud and 'Ali from the school of Kufa and the knowledge of 'Umar and Ibn 'Abbas from those *Tabi'un* with whom he studied.

We can state, therefore, that he learned the *fiqh* of the whole Muslim community with all its various methods, even though the thinking of the people of opinion was stronger in him so that he is considered the shaykh of the people of opinion. Abu Hanifa, however, did not confine himself to those *fuqaha'*. He also went to the Shi'ite Imams and studied with them and supported them. He met Zayd ibn 'Ali, Muhammad al-Baqir and 'Abdullah ibn al-Hasan, each of whom had a position in *fiqh* and knowledge.

Imam Zayd ibn 'Ali Zayn al-'Abidin died in 122 AH. He was a scholar with extensive learning in many areas of Islamic knowledge. He knew the Qur'anic readings and all the Qur'anic sciences. He knew *fiqh* and doctrine and what was said in them, to the extent that the Mu'tazilites considered him one of their shaykhs. It is reported that Abu Hanifa was his student for two years. According to *ar-Rawd an-Nadir,* Abu Hanifa said, "I saw Zayd ibn 'Ali as much as his family saw him. In his time, I did not see anyone with more *fiqh* or knowledge than him nor anyone swifter in reply or clearer in position. He was unique." He did not devote himself to him but he learned from him in some encounters.

Muhammad al-Baqir, the son of Zayn al-'Abidin, was the brother of Imam Zayd and died before him. He was one of the Shi'ite Imams on whom the Twelvers and Isma'ilis, the two most famous Shi'ite groups, agree. He was called "al-Baqir" (deep seeker of knowledge) because of the serious way he sought knowledge. Although he was one of the People of the House, he did not speak ill of the first three khalifs. It is said some of the people of Iraq spoke ill of Abu Bakr, 'Umar and 'Uthman in his presence and he became angry and said, "Are you are among the emigrants who were *'expelled from their homes and wealth'*?" (59:8) "No," they replied. He asked, "So then you must be among those *'settled in the abode and faith'*?" (59:9) "No," they replied. He said, "Nor are you among those who came after them saying, *'Our Lord, forgive us and our brothers who preceded us in belief.'* (59:10) Leave me. Allah is not near your abode. Affirm Islam. You are not among its people." He died in 114 AH.

It appears that Abu Hanifa met al-Baqir at the beginning of his development. He first met him in Madina when he was visiting it. It is reported that al-Baqir remarked to him, "Are you the one who changes the *deen* of my grandfather and his *hadiths* by analogy?" Abu Hanifa replied, "I seek refuge with Allah!" Muhammad said "You have changed it." Abu Hanifa said, "Sit in your place as is your right until I sit by my right. I respect you as your grandfather, may Allah bless him and grant him peace, was respected by his Companions when he was alive." He sat.

Then Abu Hanifa knelt before him and said, "I will present you with three things to answer. Who is weaker: a man or woman?" "A woman," he replied. Abu Hanifa then asked; "What is the share of a woman?" "A man has two shares and a woman one," he replied. Abu Hanifa said, "This is the statement of your grandfather. If I had changed the *deen* of your grandfather, by analogy a man would have one share and a woman two because the woman is weaker than the man."

Then he asked, "Which is better: the prayer or fasting?" "The prayer," al-Baqir replied. He said, "This is the statement of your grandfather. If I had changed the *deen* of your grandfather, my analogy would be that, because the prayer is better, when a woman is free of menstruation she should be commanded to make up the prayer and not make up the fast."

Then he asked, "Which is more impure: urine or sperm?" "Urine is more impure," he replied. He said, "If I had changed the *deen* of your grandfather by analogy, I would have ordered a *ghusl* for urine and *wudu'* for sperm. I seek refuge with Allah from changing the *deen* of your grandfather by analogy." Muhammad rose and embraced him and kissed his face to honour him.

Al-Makki mentions this conversation and indicates that it must have been their first encounter because al-Baqir asked a question of someone who was famous for analogy. Then Abu Hanifa showed him that he did not replace the text by analogy and he clarified his method to him. It also shows that Abu Hanifa was already known for opinion (*ra'y*) and debate regarding analogy.

As Abu Hanifa was connected to al-Baqir, he was also connected to his son, Ja'far as-Sadiq, who was the same age as Abu Hanifa. They were born in the same year, but Ja'far died about two years before Abu Hanifa, in 148 AH. Abu Hanifa said, "By Allah, I have not seen anyone with more *fiqh* than Ja'far ibn Muhammad."

We read in al-Makki, "Abu Ja'far al-Mansur said, 'Abu Hanifa, people are tempted by Ja'far ibn Muhammad, so prepare some difficult questions for him.' He prepared forty questions. Abu Hanifa said about his visit to al-Mansur in Hira, 'I went to him and entered. Ja'far was sitting on his right. When I saw him, I felt great esteem for Ja'far as-Sadiq which I did not feel for al-Mansur. I greeted him and he indicated I should sit. Then al-Mansur turned to Ja'far and asked, 'Abu 'Abdullah, this is Abu Hanifa?' 'Yes,' he replied. Then he turned to me and ordered, 'Abu Hanifa, present your problems to Abu 'Abdullah.' I began to present them and he answered them, saying, 'You say this; the people of Madina say this; and we say this. Sometimes it is the position of our Follower, sometimes that of their Follower, and sometimes we differ.' He dealt with all forty questions. Then Abu Hanifa stated, 'The most knowledgeable of people is the one with the most knowledge of people's differences.'" Scholars count Ja'far as one of Abu Hanifa's shaykhs, even though they were the same age.

Abu Hanifa was also, according to various sources, a student of 'Abdullah ibn al-Hasan ibn al-Hasan. He was a reliable and truthful *hadith* transmitter. Sufyan ath-Thawri, Malik and others related from him. He was respected by people and performed a lot of worship. He visited 'Umar ibn 'Abdu'l-'Aziz who honoured him. He also went to as-Saffah at the beginning of the Abbasid period and he showed him honour and gave him a thousand dirhams. When al-Mansur came to power, he treated him in the opposite fashion and also dealt harshly with his sons and family. They were brought in chains from Madina to al-Hashimiyya and put in prison where most of them died. 'Abdullah himself died in 145 AH at the age of about 75. He was ten years older than Abu Hanifa.

Abu Hanifa's scholarly links were not confined to the men of the Community and Imams of the People of the House. Biographies also state that he studied with some of the people of different sects and it is said that one of his shaykhs was Jabir ibn Yazid al-Ju'fi. He was an extreme Shi'ite who believed that the Prophet would return as would 'Ali and the Shi'ite Imams. Ibn al-Bazzazi said that his father Yazid was one of the followers of 'Abdullah ibn Saba' but that is unlikely. It is more likely that he was a Shi'ite but not a Saba'ite because the Saba'ites claimed that 'Ali was a god or close to a god and 'Ali disavowed them. Abu Hanifa would not take the knowledge of Islam from an unbeliever. His claim that 'Ali would return agrees with the Saba'ites, but also with the Kaysanites, and it is more likely that he was one of them.

It appears that Abu Hanifa studied some intellectual matters with him, although he believed that his creed was deviant and that he was following a sect. He used to say about him, "Jabir al-Ju'fi is corrupted by the erroneous view which he espoused. But in his subject I found no one greater than him in Kufa." He did not specify what area of knowledge Jabir was expert in: it may have been deduction or logical matters.

He used to discuss with him, but he forbade his companions to sit with him. It seems that he feared that Jabir's intellect might seduce them and lead to them into deviation and following his false views and beliefs. He stated that he was a liar. We read in *Mizan al-I'tidal*, "Abu Yahya al-Hammani claimed to have heard

Abu Hanifa remark, "Among those I have seen, I have not seen any better than 'Ata' nor a greater liar than Jabir al-Ju'fi.'""

There were two types of scholars in his time: those who confined themselves only to the *fiqh* of Islam and did not deal with anything else, even if they had more understanding of extrapolation and opinion, and those who studied creeds and philosophy which involved them in sciences outside the *deen* and sometimes led them to deviate from its aims and meanings. None of them combined profound exact legal studies and philosophical studies and proceeded in a manner neither excessive nor aberrant except Abu Hanifa. He was the only one to follow this middle path. He achieved a high level in all areas by the force of his sound intellect, firm *deen* and inquiring soul. He feared that his students would not be up to that and so he forbade them to deal with anything other than *fiqh*.

His private studies and experiences

A person's private life, circumstances and affairs, and his undirected studies in which he does not rely on a teacher, and other experiences have an effect on his knowledge and direction and the honing of his intellect or its weakness. This was, of course, also the case with Abu Hanifa.

As we said, he was from a wealthy merchant family and continued to be involved in commerce throughout his life. Therefore he knew first-hand about market transactions and commercial customs. His market experience enabled him to discuss commercial transactions, rules of behaviour and the judgements pertaining to them with familiarity and understanding. Thus custom had a place in his legal deduction when there was no elucidating example from the Book or *Sunna,* as we will explain, Allah willing.

It may be these experiences which made him prefer deduction through *istihsan,* when analogy resulted in something contrary to benefit, natural justice or custom. His student, ash-Shaybani, said, "Abu Hanifa debated with his companions about analogies and they appealed and argued with him until he said, 'I have used *istihsan.'* whereupon none of them said anything because of the great amount of *istihsan* he used in solving problems. They all submitted to it."

Abu Hanifa travelled a lot and went on *hajj* many times. His *hajj* did not keep him from studying, discussing, transmitting and giving *fatwa*. In Makka when he first met 'Ata' ibn Abi Rabah, 'Ata' asked him, "Who are you?" "One of the people of Kufa," he replied. He said, "From the people of a city who have divided their *deen* into parties?" "Yes," he replied. 'Ata' inquired, "From which are you?" He replied, "From those who do not curse the *Salaf* or hold Qadarite views and do not consider a person an unbeliever on account of a wrong action." 'Ata' said, "You are correct, so stay." He also went to Malik and discussed *fiqh* with him, and he met al-Awza'i and had discussions with him. That is how he acted when he travelled. He would present his *fatwas* and listen to criticism of them and analyse them to see where they were weak.

He was an observant man and, from the time of his youth, was fond of debate and argument in the quest of knowledge. He used to go to Basra, the home of Islamic sects, and debate with their leaders and argue with them about their views. It is reported that he debated with twenty-two sects, arguing in defence of Islam. It is related that once he debated with the Dahrites [materialist atheists] and in order to call their attention to the necessity of a Creator of the universe, he asked them, "What do you say about someone who tells you, 'I saw a laden ship full of goods and cargo which it bore across the deep seas through crashing waves and veering winds, travelling straight through them without any sailor to direct and guide it or helmsman to move it'? Would that be logically possible?" "No," they said, "this is not logically possible and cannot be imagined." Abu Hanifa said, "Glory be to Allah! If the existence of a ship on an even keel without a mariner or helmsman is not conceivable, how can it be possible for this world with all its different circumstances, changing matters and actions, and vast expanse to be without a Maker, Preserver and Originator?"

His arguments on dogma refined his thought and honed his perception. His thought was further refined by the debates he had about *fiqh* in every place he travelled – Makka, Madina and all the areas of the Hijaz where there were debates about *fiqh*. He learned *hadiths* which he did not know before, aspects of analogy which perhaps he had not thought of, and the *fatwas* of the Companions.

Abu Hanifa's method in teaching was like that of his studying; it was not simply giving lessons to students. So a question would be presented and he would give it to his students and argue with them about its ruling. Each would give his opinions and mention the analogies relevant to it, as Muhammad ash-Shaybani reports, and dispute his *ijtihad*. They might shout at one another until there was a veritable uproar, as was mentioned by Mis'ar ibn Kidam. After they had examined the matter from all sides, he would indicate the opinion arrived at by this study and its distillation and all would affirm it and be pleased with it. Studying in this fashion instructs both the teacher and student. Its benefit for the teacher does not lessen its benefit for the student. Abu Hanifa continued to teach like this which made him a seeker of knowledge until he died. His knowledge was continually growing and his thinking ever moving.

When a *hadith* was presented to him, he would point out the chief judgements which it contained and elucidate them. Then he would ramify the questions which concurred with the principles involved. That is what he considered *fiqh* to be. He said, "The like of the one who seeks *hadith* and does not learn *fiqh* is like the apothecary who has the tools but does not know what medicine to prepare. So the seeker of *hadith* does not know the value of his *hadith* until the *faqih* comes."

To summarise, he debated with his students and cared for them in three separate ways. Firstly, he supported them with his wealth, helping them in their difficulties such as when someone needed to marry but did not have the necessary funds. He would send money to each student according to his need. Sharik said about him, "He was wealthy as well as having knowledge and spent his wealth on himself and his dependants. When he taught, he stated, 'I have achieved the greatest wealth by knowing the lawful and unlawful.'"

Secondly, he paid attention to his students and carefully observed them. When he found an aptitude for knowledge mixed with delusion in one of them, he removed the delusion from him by tests which showed him that he was still in need of more knowledge which others had.

It is related that Abu Yusuf, his student and companion, felt that he should have his own place to teach. Abu Hanifa told one of those with him, "Go to the assembly of Ya'qub (Abu Yusuf) and ask him, 'What do you do about the case of a man who gives a fuller a garment to bleach for two dirhams and then asks for his garment back and the fuller says he has no knowledge of it? Then he returns again and asks for it and is given it bleached. Is the fuller paid?' If he says he is, tell him, he is wrong. If he says he is not, tell him he is wrong." The man went to him and asked him and he said, "Yes, he has a wage." He said, "You are wrong." He waited a time and then said "No, he does not." He said, "You are wrong." He went immediately to Abu Hanifa and said, "The question of the fuller must have come from you, so tell me about it." He replied, "If the bleaching took place after the misappropriation, he has no wage because he did it for himself. If it was before that he has the wage because he bleached it for its owner."

Thirdly, he always had good words for his students, especially for those of them who were about to leave or embark on something important. He used to say to them, "You are the joy of my heart and the removal of my sorrow."

Chapter Three
The Age of Abu Hanifa

Abu Hanifa was born in 80 AH when 'Abdu'l-Malik ibn Marwan was khalif. He lived until 150, thus, as we said, experienced both the strength and weakness of the Umayyads and the rise and consolidation of the Abbasids. He lived longer under the rule of the Umayyads than the Abbasids, passing fifty-two years of his life under Umayyad rule, which was the time of his education and when he reached the peak of his knowledge and full intellectual maturity. He only lived through twelve years of Abbasid rule. At such a mature age, this would not involve a reversal of his intellectual methods and customs. At that point, his output was great and input only a little. We cannot say that he absorbed nothing because the human intellect is always seeking knowledge and is constantly learning and scholars are always seeking increase in knowledge.

In fact, the difference between the end of the Umayyad era and the beginning of the Abbasid era was not great in respect of scholarly spirit, especially on the religious side, because the Abbasid period grew out of what existed under the Umayyads. In the fields of scholarship and social development, one was the result of the other, like a continuous river in which various waters clash, differing slightly in taste and colour but deviating little from the main flow. The scholarly and social spirit which dominated the Umayyads came from the larger community, not from the government.

As well as the legacy of the knowledge of the Companions, there was also the legacy of the civilisations and sciences of the conquered nations. They amplified the Arabic tradition with some of the inherited knowledge of those nations which was translated from Persian and other languages. The process of translation began in the Umayyad era. It is enough to remark that the author

176

of *Kalila wa Dimna*, and other writers lived most of their lives in the Umayyad era. We find religious knowledge growing in Abbasid times and translation spreading and being supported. That was a natural and continuing development.

We will begin our survey with the political scene. The first phenomenon can be found in the rise of the Umayyad state which was established after the governance of the first four khalifs. Until then, the khalif had been chosen from amongst prominent Qurayshi Muslims, either upon the indication of the preceding khalif, as happened with 'Umar, or without such indication, as was the case with Abu Bakr and 'Ali, or by consultation, as was the case with 'Uthman. When the Umayyads were established, the khalifate became an hereditary monarchy.

Its founder of the dynasty enjoined the support of a large group of Muslims whereas the rest of the Umayyads assumed the title through inheritance, maintaining that they alone had the right to it without the rest of the Muslims having any choice in the matter. This opinion led to disturbances and rebellions throughout the Umayyad period. Even at times when people were outwardly quiescent, their hearts were still seething with resentment.

The Ansar rebelled against Yazid I, and Madina was plundered by an army which devastated it and did not observe its sanctity. Al-Husayn ibn 'Ali refused to give allegiance, cosidering that to do so was contrary to the principles of Islamic law, and he rebelled against the Umayyad ruler. He was slain by Yazid's men, and his sisters, the daughters of Fatima, were taken as captives to Yazid. Zayd ibn 'Ali was killed as was his son Yahya. 'Abdullah ibn Yahya was also killed. That did not engender love for the Umayyads in people's hearts.

The Umayyads had a strong Arab bias. They revived a lot of the pre-Islamic Arab tradition, some of which was praiseworthy in itself, but they were excessive in doing it to the point that it became outright racism and prejudice against non-Arabs and sanctioned violation of their rights, even though, in the *Shari'a,* all Muslims are equal and Arab has no superiority over non-Arab. Muslim lands suffered waves of unrest and waves of evil because of what happened. Even when things were outwardly calm, the fire still simmered there under the surface and movements continued to operate covertly.

Abu Hanifa witnessed the harshest aspects of Umayyad rule which were epitomised by the governorship of al-Hajjaj ibn Yusuf ath-Thaqafi, who died when Abu Hanifa was about fifteen, an age at which people are capable of discernment and understanding. So he had first-hand experience of the harshest manifestation of Umayyad rule and that must have had an effect on him as a young man and coloured his appraisal of the government. His discontent could only have increased when he saw the oppression, imprisonment and torture to which the family of the Prophet was subjected.

When the Abbasid state was established, Abu Hanifa hoped that it would be more merciful because of their kinship to the family of 'Ali and because it came to power after much severity and tribulation. Therefore he offered his allegiance to as-Saffah willingly and was the spokesman for the *fuqaha'* as we have mentioned. When, however, al-Mansur came to power and began to consolidate the state with force and ruthless determination, not gentleness and clemency, and he began to persecute the family of the Prophet, throwing their old men into the dungeons and shedding the blood of the 'Alawites without the pretext of war, he saw the rule of al-Mansur as an extension of the oppression experienced under the Umayyads, even though the names had changed.

Abu Hanifa was born in Iraq, and there he grew up, lived and studied. At the end of the Umayyad and beginning of the Abbasid periods, the cities of Iraq were teeming with different races: Persians, Greeks, Indians and Arabs. Such a society is full of social upheaval since the various elements interact and each incident demands a ruling in the *Shari'a*. Thus the milieu provided many issues which expanded the mind of the *faqih* in the extrapolation of questions, theory, conception and analogy. In addition to this mixed social environment, Iraq had another intellectual characteristic: it was the home of many different religions and sects. It contained the moderate and extreme Shi'ites, the Mu'tazilites, the Jahmites, the Qadariya, the Murji'ites and others.

From ancient times, Iraq had been the locus of conflicting intellectual trends. Ibn Abi'l-Hadid said in his commentary on the

Nahj al-Balagha when discussing why the extreme Shi'ite sects appeared in Iraq: "Part of what produced such sects (the Rafidites) after the time of the Messenger of Allah was that they were from Iraq and lived in Kufa. Iraq continued to produce schismatics and people with extraordinary religions and schools ... They existed in the time of Khusrau in the form of those founded by Mani, Daysan, Mazdak and others. The Hijaz was not like this and the minds of the people of the Hijaz were not like their minds."

Added to that intellectual diversity, there was another intellectual movement which began under the Umayyads and continued and bore fruit under the Abbasids: the movement connected to Greek philosophy. Ibn Khallikan said, "Khalid ibn Yazid ibn Mu'awiya was one of the most knowledgeable men of Quraysh in the sciences and discussed chemistry and medicine and knew these two sciences well. He had treatises which indicate his knowledge and skill. He learned the craft from a monk called Maryanus the Greek and wrote three treatises on it."

This connection grew with the increase in translation of Greek, Persian and Hindi manuscripts in the Abbasid era. All of this had an effect on Islamic thought and the effect varied according to the strength of intellect and religion of the one who learned this philosophy. Some people had proper thoughts and true faith and so they controlled these ideas and benefited from them in their thinking and perceptions and intellectual discipline. Others were not strong enough for it and so their minds became confused by it and hence they deviated intellectually.

As well as that, there were *zindiqs* who openly espoused distorted views designed to corrupt the Muslim Community and destroy Islam and undermine its people. Some of them wanted to oust Muslim rule and revive ancient Persian rule as is seen in the case of al-Muqanna' who rebelled against the Abbasids in the reign of al-Mahdi.

This intellectual upheaval took place in the religious sciences as well. It was also the period when scholars began to rely more heavily on recording their knowledge in writing so that individual areas of knowledge within the *deen* and Arabic began to take on a distinct form and scholars began to specialise in particular fields.

The Shi'ite *fuqaha'* also recorded their views and, by the time of Abu Hanifa, the Shi'ites and Zaydites had known views.

It was also a time of argumentation and debate. The debates between the various groups tended to become very heated and boisterous. Scholars also travelled to take part in these debates, as we see when Abu Hanifa travelled to Basra to debate with the sects there. The people of Basra also travelled to Kufa for the same purpose. The debates which took place in the Hijaz during the *hajj* enabled scholars to meet and exchange views.

Debates also involved a sort of partisanship for one's own land. The people of Basra fanatically supported their scholars and the people of Kufa supported theirs with equal fervour. This may be a contributory factor for the intensity of argument between the people of the Hijaz and the people of Iraq. The disagreement between scholars was intense and their criticism of one another sharp at times. Even with the *Tabi'un*, when their methods differed, their criticism of each other could sometimes become bitter. There was also great disagreement regarding complicated problems which led to each person impugning his opponent's integrity. Abu Hanifa had a deep grasp of the spirit of his time and the reasoning of its scholars and he understood the direction of their thinking while maintaining his own individual thought.

One of the issues that the *fuqaha'* of the time debated and over which they had disputes about methodology was the *fatwas* of the Companions and *Tabi'un*. We will briefly mention the religious and political sects because Abu Hanifa had to deal with them throughout the course of his life.

The *Sunna* and Opinion

From the death of the Prophet, may Allah bless him and grant him peace, until the time of ash-Shafi'i there were basically two groups of *fuqaha'*, one of which was famous for opinion and the other for transmission. Among the Companions some were famous for opinion and some for *hadith* and transmission. Such was the case with the *Tabi'un* and the generation after them and then the *mujtahid* Imams: Abu Hanifa, Malik and the *fuqaha'* of the various cities. Some were famous for opinion and some for *hadith*. We will now briefly explain this.

Ash-Shahrastani said in *al-Milal wa'n-Nihal*, "The situations which arise out of acts of worship and daily life are endless and we know absolutely that there is not a text for every situation, nor is that conceivable. Because the texts are limited and situations are not, ijtihad and analogy must be considered in order that every situation may be brought within the compass of the *Shari'a*. After the death of the Prophet, may Allah bless him and grant him peace, the Companions were faced with innumerable new situations. They had the Book of Allah Almighty and the *Sunna* of the Messenger of Allah.

"So in regard to the events which befell them they had recourse to the Book, and, if they found a clear ruling, they carried it out. If there was no judgement in the Book, they resorted to the *Sunna* of the Messenger of Allah, and consulted the memories of his Companions to ascertain the ruling of the Prophet in similar cases. If there was no one who knew anything they exercised *ijtihad* in their opinions. So they proceeded to examine the case in the light of the Book, then the *Sunna*, and then opinion. 'Umar stated in a letter to Abu Musa al-Ash'ari: 'Understanding is something which reverberates in your breast which is not in the Book or *Sunna*. Learn similarities and likenesses, and form analogies on that basis.'

"The Companions used opinion but disagreed as to how much it should be used. Some used it more often than others and some hesitated if there were no text from the Book or a followed *sunna*.

"They were in agreeement about relying on the Book and a known *sunna* if one existed but if they did not find a known *sunna,* the famous *fuqaha'* used opinion. If any of them were unsure about their recollection of a *hadith* of the Messenger of Allah or of his *fatwa* about a matter, they preferred not to relate it but to give a decision by opinion, fearing that relating it might involve lies against the Messenger of Allah. It is reported that 'Imran ibn Husayn used to say, 'By Allah, I think that if I had wished, I could have related from the Messenger of Allah for two consecutive days; but I was deterred from doing so by men of the Companions of the Messenger of Allah who had heard what I heard and had seen what I saw, and who relate *hadiths* which are not exactly as they tell them. I fear that I might be confused like them.'"

Abu 'Umar ash-Shaybani said, "I sat with Ibn Mas'ud and a year would go by without him saying, 'The Messenger of Allah said.' When he did say, 'The Messenger of Allah, may Allah bless him and grant him peace, said,' he trembled and said, 'like that, or close to it.'" 'Abdullah ibn Mas'ud thus preferred to give a decision according to his own opinion and to bear the responsibility for it if he was wrong, rather than possibly lie about something the Messenger of Allah said or did. He said, after deciding a problem according to his opinion, "I say this from my own opinion. If it is right, it is from Allah. If it is wrong, it is from me and from Shaytan." He used to be elated when his opinion accorded with a *hadith* which one of the Companions transmitted. A second group criticised those who gave *fatwa* based on their opinion, saying that they gave *fatwa* in the *Deen* of Allah without authority from the Book or the *Sunna*.

The truth is that the Companions found themselves in an impossible quandary resulting from the strength of their religious feelings. On the one hand, they might memorise a lot of *hadiths* from the Messenger of Allah in order to learn the judgements from them, but then they feared that they might be inaccurate about what he said. As we read in *Hujjatullah al-Baligha* by Shah Waliyullah ad-Dihlawi: "When 'Umar sent a group to Kufa, he told them: 'You are going to a people who are confused about the Qur'an, so they will ask you about *hadith*. Do not give them too many.'" On the other hand, they could give *fatwa* by their own opinions and be in danger of making things lawful and unlawful without proper justification. Some of them preferred *hadiths* from the Messenger of Allah and some of them chose opinion when there was no clear precedent. If they subsequently learned of a clear *sunna*, they retracted their opinion. That was related of many of the Companions, including 'Umar.

After the Companions came their students, the *Tabi'un*, and two problems arose in their time. One was that the Muslims divided into parties and groups. The level of disagreement became intense and impassioned. They were severe with one another and started to accuse one another of disbelief, iniquity and rebellion, and to threaten one another and to unsheathe the sword. The Community divided into the Kharijites, Shi'ites, Umayyads and those who were quiescent in the face of the afflictions which occurred and remained far from sedition, refusing to become involved in it.

The Kharijites formed different sects: the Azraqites, Ibadites, Najdites and others. The Shi'a formed into disparate groups, some of whom had bizarre opinions which took them outside of Islam, even though they pretended to follow Islam in order to corrupt people. They were not concerned with establishing the *Deen*, but rather with destroying its basis to restore their old religion and its power and authority – or at least to shatter Muslim cohesion or to make the Muslims live with intense seditions, and to extinguish the Light of Allah.

The second problem was that Madina lost the unique authority which it enjoyed in the time of the Companions, especially in the time of 'Umar which is considered the Golden Age of legal *ijtihad*. It was the home of the scholars and *fuqaha'* of the Companions. They did not leave it without maintaining a scholarly connection with it. They corresponded regarding problems which arose, because the *sunna* of 'Umar was to ensure that the Companions of Quraysh were kept within the confines of the Hijaz. The great *Muhajirun* and *Ansar* never left the boundaries of Madina without his permission and he watched over them.

When 'Umar died, they left for outlying regions. Each group of them became the source of a legal school which was connected to them and which the people of the places to which they emigrated followed. In the time of the *Tabi'un*, there were students of those *fuqaha'* who lived in Madina or other places. Each city had its *fuqaha'* and their views grew apart as the cities were far apart, each adapting to the customs of his region and having to deal with the particular problems which troubled it. So people followed the path of those Companions who were in that region and transmitted the *hadiths* which they reported and which therefore became cur-

183

rent among them. In this way various methods of legal thought appeared in different places, all derived from the Qur'an and the *Sunna* of the Prophet.

As we have seen, in the time of the Companions there were basically two schools. In one of them, opinion dominated and transmission played a lesser role, though, if a clear *sunna* emerged, opinion would be abandoned in favour of it. The other relied almost totally on transmission and preferred not to give a *fatwa* when there was no transmission, rather than risk contravening the *Deen* of Allah by opinion. In the time of the *Tabi'un*, the gap between the two widened and those who preferred transmission increased their adherence to this path, considering it to be a protection from the seditions which had now become severe. They found safety only in holding to the *Sunna*.

The others normally had much less recourse to the *Sunna*, which had in any case become subject to falsification in outlying areas, and because of the new situations that arose and required rulings, they tended to rely far more on opinion. In addition, new ideas assailed them through contact with new cultures in lands conquered by Islam and many of the *Tabi'un* were non-Arabs, heirs to the ancient civilisations of their ancestors.

So the gap widened between the schools and they grew further apart than they had been before when it had been difficult to distinguish between them. The basis of the disagreement was not about whether the authority of the *Sunna* should be accepted or not. It lay in two matters: the extent of the use of opinion, and secondary questions deduced through its use. The adherents of tradition only used opinion when absolutely necessary, rather in the way that a Muslim may eat pork if no other possibility exists.

They did not look into secondary questions or extrapolate judgements for speculative situations which had not arisen. They only gave *fatwas* for problems which had actually occurred and did not look into hypothetical situations, whereas the people of opinion gave many *fatwas* based on opinion whenever they had no sound *hadith* on the subject. They did not confine themselves in their studies to the deduction of rulings on actual problems but also posed hypothetical questions and gave judgement on them on the basis of their opinions.

Most of the adherents of *hadith* were in the Hijaz, even though there was some *fiqh* of opinion there. This was because it was the home of the first Companions and the place of Revelation and because many of the *Tabi'un* who resided there were trained by the Companions who made little use of opinion – although a few were students of a Companion who used opinion a lot and transmitted his opinions.

Most of the adherents of opinion were in Iraq because they trained with 'Abdullah ibn Mas'ud, who refrained from transmitting from the Prophet out of fear of making a mistake but did not refrain from exercising his opinion. If there was a sound *hadith* on the subject, he referred to the *hadith*. There were a'so old philosophies and sciences in Iraq as well as the classical texts of Greece and Rome. Those who were influenced by this were comfortable with *ijtihad* by opinion, especially when there were not many *hadiths* among them to be consulted.

This process continued and in the time of the *Tabi'i't-Tabi'in* and the *mujtahids* with *madhhabs*, the gap became very wide indeed and disagreements became intense. When the two groups met, each borrowed from the other. The people of *hadith* abandoned their former hesitation and were compelled to use opinion in some cases; and when the people of opinion saw the *Sunna* and traditions, some wrote them down and began to examine them, supporting their opinions with *hadiths* or leaving opinion aside if they had a sound *hadith* which they had not known about previously. This was the period in which *fiqh* developed.

Lies about the Prophet proliferated in this period because various groups defended their positions unscrupulously with words which led to the spread of forged *hadiths* which they espoused and which then spread among the Muslims. This upsurge in lies led to two things. *Hadith* scholars started to devote themselves to the investigation of truthful transmission and to the method of distinguishing the true from the false. To this end they studied the transmitters of *hadiths*, investigated their circumstances, learned those who were truthful and ranked them according to their truthfulness.

They then studied the *hadiths* and compared them with unquestioned elements of the *Deen*. Eventually, some scholars began to record the sound *hadiths*. Among them were Malik with his *Muwatta'*, *al-Jawami‘* of Sufyan ibn ‘Uyayna, and *al-Jami‘ al-Kabir* of Sufyan ath-Thawri. The second consequence was that people gave *fatwa* more and more frequently according to opinion, out of fear of lying against the Prophet or depending on something that might well have been forged. This occurred mostly in Iraq because the *fuqaha'* there who transmitted from the *Tabi‘un* and the next generation were known for opinion and often gave *fatwa* by it.

Shah Waliyullah ad-Dihlawi says in his book, after discussing the adherents of *hadith*:

"Over and against them, in the time of Malik and Sufyan and after them, were people who did not dislike questions and were not afraid to give *fatwa*, saying that *fiqh* must be spread on the basis of the *Deen* but fearing to transmit the *hadiths* of the Prophet and attribute them to him wrongly. Ash-Sha‘bi said, 'We prefer anyone to the Prophet (as authority for *fiqh*).' Ibrahim said, 'I prefer to say "‘Abdullah said" and " ‘Alqama said".'

"They did not have the *hadiths* and traditions to deduce the *fiqh* on the principles which the people of *hadith* chose, nor were they inspired to look into the words of the scholars of other lands, collect them and investigate them. They believed that their Imams had the highest level of precision and their hearts were the closest to the Companions.

" ‘Alqama said, 'Is there anyone more solid than ‘Abdullah ibn Mas‘ud?' Abu Hanifa said, 'Ibrahim has more *fiqh* than Salim. If it had not been for the virtue of being a Companion, I would have said that ‘Alqama had more *fiqh* than Ibn ‘Umar.' They possessed intelligence and intuition, and their minds swiftly moved from one thing to another, enabling them to derive the answer to problems from statements of the Companions.

"Everyone is given ease in that for which he was created and *'every party rejoices in what it has'*. So they formulated *fiqh* on the rule of extrapolation. The people of Iraq gave *fatwa* because they felt that it was their duty and the basis of the *Deen*; but at the same time they were afraid to report from the Messenger of Allah. They did not accept the statements of the people of other lands, and were partisan towards their shaykhs."

Whatever the reasons, the Iraqis made much use of opinion but the Hijazis and Syrians used it less. As we indicated before, the adherents of opinion and those of *hadith* agreed that judgement must be by the Book and sound *Sunna* but they differed after that. The people of *hadith* were afraid of opinion but not of transmission from the Messenger, and did not adopt opinion except when forced to do so by the fact that they did not know of any *hadith*, whereas the people of opinion were afraid of relating *hadith* but not of giving *fatwa* on questions which they could later retract if they later came across a *hadith*. The people of opinion also refused to accept weak *hadiths*, whereas some of the people of *hadith* accepted them. Imam Malik, the Imam of the people of Madina, used *munqati'*, *mursal* and *mawquf hadiths*, and the transmitted practice of the people of Madina before resorting to analogy.

By the end of Abu Hanifa's life, the schools began to come closer together again because they influenced one another in their discussions and debates. Their motive was the same: to elevate the *Shari'a*. To this end, the one group had to study the knowledge of the other. Certainly, Abu Yusuf, one of the companions of Abu Hanifa and the *fuqaha'* of opinion, accepted the study and memorisation of *hadiths* and their use as evidence. If he found that an opinion he had previously held was contrary to the *Sunna*, he abandoned it for an opinion which agreed with the *hadith*.

We have briefly explained the difference between the *fuqaha'* of opinion and those of the *Sunna*. But was the 'opinion' in question merely legal analogy – which is to relate a matter on which there is no specific ruling to another prescribed matter with a ruling since the same legal reasoning applies to both – or was it more general than that? Anyone who studies the meaning of the word 'opinion' (*ra'y*) in the way it was used during the time of the Companions and the *Tabi'un* will find that it is general and did not refer to analogy alone. It included analogy and much more besides. When we deal with the formation of the schools, we also find this general use of the term. When we focus on the time of the schools, we find that each school differs in the explanation of the type of opinion which it is permitted to adopt.

Ibn al-Qayyim explains that the opinion which was transmitted from the Companions and *Tabi'un* was what the heart felt was correct after reflection, consideration, and seeking to identify what was correct when there were conflicting indications. The *fatwas* of the Companions and *Tabi'un* and those who followed their path show that the idea of 'opinion' includes everything about which a *faqih* gives a *fatwa* for which there is no text, relying in his *fatwa* on what he knows of the *deen* in a general way, what agrees with its rulings in general, or what resembles another matter for which there is a text when he connects like to like. The word 'opinion' in that context includes analogy, *istihsan*, *masalih mursala* and custom.

Abu Hanifa and his adherents used analogy, *istihsan*, and custom, and Malik used *istihsan*, *masalih mursala* (considerations of welfare) and custom. He was famous for the use of considerations of welfare. That is why there was flexibility and receptivity for all the affairs of people in different times although it was a school in which analogy was not frequent. Malik said that *istihsan* was nine-tenths of knowledge but that was only when there was no text or *fatwa* from a Companion and no precedent practice of the people of Madina.

Ash-Shafi'i came and founded a systematic method of legal reasoning which ensured that there could be reliable judgements in the event that no appropriate text was available and did not accept the previous latitude in the derivation of judgements. He thought that opinion should only be exercised in the *Shari'a* on the basis of strict analogy, only permitting a matter without a text to be connected to the ruling on another matter for which a suitable text existed. In such cases, opinion had to be traced back to a text so that there was no possibility of innovation in the *Shari'a*. As for general deduction and justification for judgements without a basis in a text, he considered that to be innovation in the *Shari'a*.

That is why ash-Shafi'i said, "Anyone who uses *istihsan* has legislated for himself." He set out rules and criteria for analogy and defended and supported it so precisely that he, in fact, went further than the Hanafis in its formulation and affirmation. Ar-Razi commented, "The extraordinary thing is that Abu Hanifa is accused of relying on analogy, and his opponents used to criticise him for over-reliance on it, when it is not transmitted from him or any of his companions that he wrote at all affirming the principle of analogy or that he responded to the proofs of his opponents in denying analogy. The first to speak on this question and report proofs in it was Imam ash-Shafi'i."

The *fatwas* of the Companions and *Tabi'un* and the practice of the people of Madina

Both the people of *hadith* and the people of opinion were inclined to accept the *fatwas* of the Companions, because following is better than innovating and because the Companions had been present with the Prophet and so their position was more likely to be correct. They are the Imams who are followed. Most of the *fuqaha'* preferred their opinions. It is reported that Abu Hanifa used to say, "When I do not find a ruling in the Book of Allah or the *Sunna* of the Messenger of Allah then I can take the statement of his Companions if I wish and leave those of other people. But I do not disregard their words for the words of anyone else. But when it is a question of Ibrahim an-Nakha'i, ash-Sha'bi, al-Hasan, Ibn Sirin, or Sa'id ibn al-Musayyab, then I can exercise *ijtihad* in the same way that they did." Since this was the position of Abu Hanifa, the Imam of the people of Iraq, on the opinions and positions of the Companions, others must have been still more inclined to accept their *fatwas* and what is reported from them.

Many *fatwas* of the Companions were transmitted at that time. The minds of the *fuqaha'* were focused on these *fatwas* and they used them as a model when exercising their *ijtihad*. They followed the same path as the Companions, respected their opinions and relied on them when there was nothing in the Book or *Sunna*. When the Companions agreed on an opinion, the *mujtahids* after them were obliged to accept it. If one of them stated an opinion not known to be opposed, the majority of the *fuqaha'* accepted it. If there was a disagreement between them, many of the *mujtahids* chose from their opinions that which agreed with their own inclination, and they did not leave the framework of those opinions for any others.

The *fuqaha'* in the time of the *Tabi'un* and *mujtahids* acted in the same way, even if they did not consider those *fatwas* to be an independent principle or a legal rule in the *Deen*. Perhaps they did so because they saw that the Companions had witnessed the descent of Revelation of the Qur'an to the Messenger and must have derived their opinions from their knowledge of the actions of the Messenger of Allah, and no one is permitted to exercise *ijtihad* about a matter ascribed to the Messenger. So they did not consider the Companions' opinion to be mere legal *ijtihad*: it was closer to the *Sunna* than to *ijtihad*. The Companions are followed because they were the first teachers who spread Islamic *fiqh* in all directions. They were stars shining with the primal light of Islam.

In this period, Abu Hanifa studied with the shaykhs of opinion and some of the people of tradition. He preferred them and put them ahead of his own opinion. Ash-Shafi'i reported that he used to say about their opinions, "Their opinions are better for us than our opinion for ourselves." We read in *I'lam al-Muwaqqi'in*, "Ash-Shafi'i said in the first version of the *Risala*, 'They are above us in every science, *ijtihad*, scrupulousness and intellect.'"

The Sects

Abu Hanifa met people from various Islamic sects and studied with some of them and examined their opinions as has been mentioned. Hence, it is appropriate to give a brief summary of the sects that existed in his time, in view of the fact that he was aware of their opinions.

The Shi'ites

The Shi'a were the oldest of the Islamic sects. They appeared with their political position at the end of the reign of 'Uthman and grew and flourished in the time of 'Ali, since, when he mixed with people, that increased their admiration for his gifts, the strength of his *deen* and knowledge. Shi'ite agents exploited that admiration and began to disseminate their sect. In the Umayyad period, when injustices were perpetrated against the descendants of 'Ali and the Umayyads injured them, people's love and compassion for them increased and they saw 'Ali and his sons as martyrs to that injustice. So the Shi'ite school expanded and its supporters increased.

The origin of the sect

The separation of the Shi'a from the body of the Muslims was political in origin and turned on the matter of how the khalif of the Muslims should have been decided upon. Their difference with the majority was based on two things. Firstly, the khalifate was a matter to be decided, not by the community as a whole, but by specific appointment. The khaliphate is the pillar of the *Deen* and the rule of Islam and, in their view, it was inconceivable that the Prophet would have ignored it and left it up to the community to decide. The *khalifa* must have been specified for them and was protected from major and minor wrong actions. Secondly, and following on from that, they maintained that 'Ali was the *khalifa* chosen by the Prophet, may Allah bless him and grant him peace, and was the best of the Companions.

Although this was the basis of their position, the Shi'a were not all the same. Some were excessive in their esteem for 'Ali and his descendants and some were more balanced. The balanced ones were content to prefer 'Ali to the other Companions without declaring anyone an unbeliever, whereas the excessive sects of the Shi'a elevated 'Ali to the rank of prophethood and some of them even went so far as to deify him. Some of them claimed that God was incarnate in the Imams, 'Ali and his sons, espousing a doctrine similar to Christian incarnation. Some of them believed that every Imam had divinity incarnate in him which then transmigrated to the next Imam.

Most of the Imami Shi'ites agree that the last Imam did not die but is still alive and will return and fill the earth with justice as it is now filled with injustice. One group, the Seveners, claimed that 'Ali ibn Abi Talib is alive and will not die and another group said that Muhammad ibn al-Hanafiyya[1] is alive and being nourished by honey and water. Various groups claimed that certain prominent people were not dead or killed but were still alive.

The Twelvers say that the twelfth Imam, Muhammad ibn al-Hasan al-'Askari, called al-Mahdi, entered the cellar of his house and disappeared when he was arrested with his mother. They believe that he is the Mahdi and will emerge at the end of time and fill the earth with justice, and they are still waiting for him. Every night they stand after the *Maghrib* prayer at the door of this cellar and they bring a mount, call his name, and call on him to come out until the stars appear. For evidence, they adduce the story of the People of the Cave in the Qur'an.

Some extreme Shi'a combined these views with social ideas in a very corruptive manner. They allowed the consumption of wine and carrion, permitted incestuous marriage, and interpreted the words of Allah, *"Those who believe and do right actions are not to blame for what they have eaten provided they are godfearing and believe and do right actions, and then are godfearing and believe, and then are godfearing and do good,"* (5:93) to mean that the prohibitions, like carrion, blood and pork, are allusions to people who must be hated, like Abu Bakr, 'Umar, 'Uthman and Mu'awiya, and that all the obligations and prohibitions of the Qur'an bear metaphorical meanings.

So we see that the Shi'ites were an amalgam of opinions and confused ideas into which a great number of false concepts from ancient religions crept wearing Islamic guise. European orientalists have posited numerous theories about their origin: Judaism (through the Yemeni Jew, 'Abdullah ibn Saba'), ancient Persia with its entrenched concept of dynastic succession, or various eastern creeds like Buddhism, Manichaeanism and others.

---

1. A son of 'Ali by a wife other than Fatima.

There is no doubt that Shi'ism, with its sanctification of the family of the House, draws from many ancient Asiatic religions, including the Hindu belief of reincarnation in which the soul moves from one person to another. The concept of divine incarnation comes from the Christians and Brahmanism. Various Messianic concepts are taken from Judaism.

After this brief glance at the basic forms of Shi'ism, we will mention some of their branches which were active at this time.

The Saba'ites

They were the followers of 'Abdullah ibn Saba', a Jew from the people of Hira who made a display of Islam. His mother was a black slave, which is why he is sometimes referred to in sources as Ibn as-Sawda'. He was one of the strongest agitators against 'Uthman. He was energetic in spreading his ideas and corruption among the Muslims, including many false things about 'Ali.

He began to circulate among people that he had found in the Torah that each Prophet has an heir and that 'Ali was the heir of Muhammad and that he was the best of heirs as Muhammad was the best of Prophets. Then he mentioned that Muhammad would return to life. He used to remark, "I marvel at those who say that 'Isa will return but do not say that Muhammad will return." Then he went further and attributed divinity to 'Ali.

The Kaysanites

They were the followers of al-Mukhtar ibn 'Ubayd ath-Thaqafi. He had been a Kharijite and then became one of the partisans of 'Ali. He came to Kufa when Muslim ibn 'Uqayl came there from al-Husayn to ascertain its position and report back to him. 'Ubaydullah ibn Ziyad had al-Mukhtar flogged and then put him in prison until al-Husayn was killed. After this, his sister's husband, 'Abdullah ibn 'Umar, interceded for him and he was released provided that he left Kufa. He went to the Hijaz.

It is reported that he stated, "By Allah, I will seek revenge for the blood of the wronged martyr, the master of the Muslims and the son of the daughter of the master of the Muslims, al-Husayn ibn 'Ali! I will kill the number of those who killed Yahya ibn Zakariya to avenge his death!" Then he joined Ibn az-Zubayr and pledged him allegiance on the condition that he should be appointed to high office if he was successful and that he would join him in the fight against the people of Syria. Then he returned to Kufa after Yazid's death and told people, "The Mahdi has sent me to you as his representative. He has commanded me to kill the heretics and revenge the blood of the people of the House and defend the weak."

He claimed that he had been sent by Muhammad ibn al-Hanafiyya, because he was the descendant most entitled to revenge al-Husayn and because Muhammad was much loved and esteemed by people owing to his great knowledge and gnosis. Muhammad proclaimed himself free of al-Mukhtar before a gathering of people when he heard about his lies, delusions and hidden aims.

The Kaysanite doctrine did not claim that the Imams were divine. It was based on the premise that the Imam was a holy person who was owed absolute obedience and was protected from error. Like the Saba'ites, they believed that the Imam would return – either that he had died and would be resurrected or that he was not dead at all. Another part of their heretical doctrines was that of *bada'*: that Allah could change His will or decree when circumstances changed. They also believed in the passing of the soul into a new body.

The Zaydites

This is the group of Shi'ites closest to the Muslim Community. They are not excessive in their dogma and most of them do not proclaim any of the Companions of the Messenger of Allah, may Allah bless him and grant him peace, to be an unbeliever nor raise any of the Imams to the rank of a deity or a Prophet.

194

Imam Zayd ibn 'Ali rebelled in Kufa against Hisham and was killed. His view was that the Imam is stipulated by description, not by name, and the qualities which the Imam must have to receive people's allegiance is that he is descended from Fatima, is scrupulous, the possessor of knowledge, generous, and that he summons people to himself. Many Shi'ites opposed him regarding the precondition of craising his banner. His brother, Muhammad al-Baqir, argued him about that and said, "According to your view, your father was not an Imam because he did not rebel or call for rebellion."

The Zaydites also held that it is permitted for the less superior to be Imam. So if a superior Imam possesses these qualities and is more entitled but those in authority choose and give allegiance to someone not as good, he is a valid Imam and must be obeyed. This, in their opinion, was the basis for the validity of the khalifate of Abu Bakr and 'Umar and not proclaiming the Companions who gave them allegiance to be unbelievers. Zayd thought that 'Ali was the best of the Companions, but the khalifate went to Abu Bakr for a benefit which the Companions perceived and in order to preserve the religious principle of suppressing seditions and heartening of the populace. People might still have resented 'Ali because the blood was not yet dry on his sword which he had wielded against them.

The Zaydis also believed that there could be two Imams in two different areas so that each was an Imam in his region. They further believed that the one who commits a major sin will be in the Fire forever if he does not sincerely repent. They derived this from the Mu'tazilites because Zayd followed the Mu'tazilite school as he was connected to their shaykh, Wasil ibn 'Ata'.

The Imamites

The Imamites are those who state that the imamate was confirmed by stipulation from the Prophet, may Allah bless him and grant him peace, by a clear text and certainty and that it was a definite and specific appointment. They cite certain traditions from the

Prophet, as well as particular events in the life of the Prophet, as evidence for the appointment of 'Ali. They agree that al-Hasan and then al-Husayn were the Imams after 'Ali. At this point, however, there is disagreement and they divide into groups, the largest of which are the Ithna 'asharites (Twelvers) and Isma'ilis.

The Ithna 'asharites (Twelvers)

They believed that after al-Husayn, the imamate went to 'Ali Zayn al-'Abidin, then Muhammad al-Baqir, followed by Ja'far as-Sadiq, then his son Musa al-Kadhim, then 'Ali ar-Rida, then Muhammad al-Jawwad, then 'Ali al-Hadi, then al-Hasan al-'Askari and then his son Muhammad, the twelfth Imam. They believe that he has gone into occultation.

The Isma'ilis

They are a branch of the Imamites who take their name from Isma'il ibn Ja'far. They are also called the Batiniya because of their view about the "concealed Imam". This group believe that Ja'far designated his son, Isma'il, as Imam. The result of this is that, even though he died before his father, the imamate continued among his descendants. So the imamate passed to his son Muhammad al-Maktum, the first of the concealed Imams, and then to his son Ja'far al-Musaddiq and then his son Muhammad al-Habib, the last of the concealed Imams, and then to his son, 'Abdullah al-Mahdi, who gained control over North Africa and from whom the Fatimid dynasty derives.

The Kharijites

The Kharijites were the most active of the Islamic sects in defending their doctrine. They showed immense zeal for their ideas, intense religiousness in general, and extreme recklessness in defence of their claims and ideas. In their position, they clung to expressions which they took literally, believing that theirs was the pure *Deen* from which no believer could be permitted to deviate. Anyone who followed a different path was someone whose soul made him incline to lies and moved him to disobedience. Their attention focused on the Qur'anic phrase, *"Judgement belongs to Allah alone"*, and they took this as their motto. They shouted it in the faces of their opponents and ended every conversation with it.

Whenever they saw 'Ali speak, they shouted these words at him and it is related that 'Ali said about them when they kept repeating it, "A true word by which something false is meant. Yes, judgement belongs to Allah alone but those people are saying, 'Amirate belongs to Allah alone.' There must be a leader for people whether pious or corrupt... Through him, booty is collected, the enemy is fought, the roads are made safe and the strong are made to provide for the weak – until the pious leader finds rest or the people find rest from the corrupt leader."

The Kharijites were carried away by the idea of being free of 'Uthman, 'Ali and unjust rulers until that notion overpowered their minds and perceptions and completely prevented them from ascertaining the truth. They sometimes acted with those who declared themselves quit of 'Uthman. Sometimes, the disagreement was so intense that it led to a split with them. Ibn az-Zubayr rebelled against the Umayyads and the Kharijites helped him and promised to fight on his side. When they learned that he had not declared himself free of his father, Talha, and of 'Ali and 'Uthman, they left him.

Although the Kharijites were sincere in their attack on 'Ali and the Umayyads after him, there were other factors which led them to rebel one of the most significant of which was their intense resentment towards Quraysh for appropriating the khalifate. Most of them were from the tribes of Rabi'a who had a long-standing enmity towards the tribes of Mudar, of which Quraysh was one. This enmity preceded Islam. Most of the Kharijites were Arabs, and very few clients were to be found among them, even though their tenets should have made the clients eligible for the khalifate. The views of the Kharijites clearly show their thinking, revealing their simplistic minds, superficial views and rancour towards Quraysh and all the tribes of Mudar.

- The first and strongest of their views was that the post of *khalifa* is to be filled by choosing any free, sane, healthy Muslim man who attends to the welfare of the Muslims. It is not for one group rather than another and someone can only remain as khalif so long as he establishes justice, supports the *Shari'a* and is far from error and deviation. If he transgresses, he should be deposed or killed.

- They did not think that any of the families or tribes of the Arabs should be singled out for the khalifate or that the khalifate should be restricted to Quraysh as others stated, or even that it should be for an Arab rather than an non-Arab. In their view all were the same. Indeed, they preferred that the khalif should not be from Quraysh so that it would be easier to depose or kill him if he opposed the *Shari'a* or deviated from truth, since then there would be no partisanship to protect him, tribe to defend him, or shelter but the shelter of Allah.

- Najdite Kharijites thought that people did not need a khalif at all. Muslims should be equitable in their mutual dealings. They thought that if that could only be achieved by means of having a khalif to encourage them to uphold the truth and establish it, then it was permitted. But in their view the existence of a khalif was not a necessary obligation but was merely permitted when needed for public welfare.

- The Kharijites thought that people who committed wrong actions were unbelievers. They did not differentiate between a sin which was done with an evil intention and an error of opinion or *ijtihad* which led to something incorrect. That is why they said that 'Ali was an unbeliever when he agreed to arbitration although it was not his choice. If, in their opinion, arbitration was not correct, then the fact that they said 'Ali was an unbeliever indicates that they considered that an error in *ijtihad* takes a person out of the deen. That was also their view of Talha, az-Zubayr, 'Uthman and other great Companions who differed from them in minor matters – they held that they were unbelievers. They had various justifications for this which were based on false interpretation of *ayats* of the Qur'an.

This is the sum of the opinions which most of the Kharijites embraced while they did not agree on other positions, opinions or views. They frequently disagreed on even the smallest of matters. Perhaps this is the secret of the great number of their defeats. They were divided into many groups.

Murji'ites

The Murji'ites began as a political group but, like the other sects, they began to mix politics with the principles of the *deen*. The basis of their difference was a negative view of a matter which preoccupied many Muslim minds at the time: the question of the status of someone who commits a major sin. This question animated the Kharijites, Shi'ites and Mu'tazilites. However, as they began politically, we consider them to be a political group.

The first seed which produced this group was sown in the time of the Companions, at the end of the rule of 'Uthman when there was unrest about his rule which ultimately culminated in his murder. A group of Companions remained silent and refused to participate in the civil war which shook the Muslims profoundly. They held to the *hadith* reported by Abu Bakr from the Prophet: "There will be civil strife in which those who sit will be better than those who walk, and those who walk will be better than those who run. When it comes, whoever has camels should stay with his camels; whoever has sheep should stay with his sheep; and whoever has land should cling to his land." A man said, "Messenger of Allah, what about someone who has neither camels, sheep or land?" He replied, "He should go to his sword and blunt its edge with a stone and then save himself if he can."

They refused to become involved in the war between the Muslims and did not concern themselves with ascertaining who was in the right. They included Sa'd ibn Abi Waqqas, Abu Bakra,

'Abdullah ibn 'Imran and many others. They refused to make a judgement about either group and left the matter to Allah while other parties were quick to apportion blame.

Then, when there was a lot of discussion about people who commit a major sin and the Kharijites claimed that such people were unbelievers and made war on all Muslims, some such people refused to take sides in the argument and withheld (*irja'*) judgement as they had withheld judgement on other occasions. Hence they were called Murji'ites ("deferrers"). This time the deferment of judgement was not a political one as the first had been but a doctrinal one, implying that belief consists of affirmation, assent, belief, and knowledge, that an act of disobedience does not impair faith, that faith is distinct from action.

So the term "Murji'ite" was applied to two groups: one who refused to take sides in the disagreement between the Companions and which continued into the Umayyad period and a second group who thought that Allah would forgive all sins except disbelief and so an act of disobedience did not harm faith just as an act of obedience was of no benefit without faith. Unfortunately, there were corrupt people within this school who used the position as an open door to evil. That is why Zayd ibn 'Ali said about this, "I am free of the Murji'ites who appease the profligate by the promise of Allah's pardon."

The Mu'tazilites used the term "Murji'ite" for all those who did not think that someone who committed a major sin would be eternally in the Fire and held the position that such people would be punished for a time and then pardoned by Allah. This is why it was applied to Abu Hanifa and his companions, may Allah be pleased with him. This is why ash-Shahrastani states in *al-Milal wa'n-Nihal*: "Abu Hanifa and his companions are called 'Murji'ites of the *Sunna*'. A number of those who wrote treatises counted him among the Murji'ites. Perhaps the reason for that was that he used to say, 'Belief is affirmation with the heart; it does not increase or decrease.'... There is another reason for this. He was an opponent of the Qadarites and Mu'tazilites who appeared early on, and the Mu'tazilites nicknamed all who opposed them in the question of Qadar 'Murji'ites.'"

200

Many others beside Abu Hanifa and his companions are considered Murji'ites by this definition, including al-Hasan ibn Muhammad ibn 'Ali, Sa'id ibn Jubayr, Talq ibn Habib, Muqatil ibn Sulayman, Hammad ibn Abi Sulayman, and others. All of them were Imams of *fiqh* and *hadith* who did not say that those who committed major sins were unbelievers or deemed that they would be in the Fire forever.

The Jabarites

During the time of the Companions, may Allah be pleased with them, the question of the Divine Decree and man's will and power in relation to the will and power of Allah Almighty was a subject discussed by the Muslims but the nature of the Arab mind and soul, close as it was to the natural state, prevented them from going too deeply into the matter and becoming obsessed by it. After their time, however, when the Muslims started to mix with the people of ancient religions and other intellectual traditions, their schools and sects multiplied and their investigations expanded and they followed the methods of the adherents of ancient religions in studying these topics.

One group claimed that man does not create his actions and that no actions whatsoever can be truly ascribed to him. The basic position of this school was to deny that the action of the slave had any reality and to ascribe it to Allah altogether. Since the creature has in reality no 'capacity' of his own, it must be that he is compelled in his actions without any power, volition or choice. Allah Almighty creates the actions in him and actions can only be ascribed to him metaphorically in the same way as they are ascribed to inanimates, just as a tree produces fruit, a stone moves, water flows, or the sun rises and sets, and other such things. Reward and punishment are predetermined and so obligation is also predetermined. It is difficult to ascertain who was the first to espouse this position, but the idea was certainly already widespread in Umayyad times so that it became a school of thought.

Although it is difficult to state with certainty who was responsible for the formation of this position as a school, it is usually attributed to al-Jahm ibn Safwan because he was the major proponent of it. He also espoused other views. He claimed that the Garden and the Fire will vanish and that nothing is eternal, and that when "eternity" is mentioned in the Qur'an, it merely means "a long time". He also stated that faith was only recognition and that disbelief was ignorance, and that the knowledge and speech of Allah are located in time. He went further and stated that Allah cannot be described with any attributes, even life, and that the Qur'an is created.

The Mu'tazilites

This group originated during the Umayyad period and dominated Islamic thought in the Abbasid era for a long time. Iraq, in the time of the Rightly Guided Khalifs and Umayyads, was home to a number of ethnic and religious groups of different origins. Some were descended from the ancient Chaldean inhabitants of Iraq; others were Persians, Christians, Jews, or Arabs. Most of them became Muslims. Some understood Islam in the light of the ancient teachings of their own traditions. Some took Islam from its pure source and imbibed it without alteration, but even so their feelings and ideas were not purely Islamic.

There was an involuntary inclination towards the past of the kind which psychologists call "unconscious". That is why, when there was much civil war at the time of 'Ali ibn Abi Talib in Iraq, the ancient sects were awakened and appeared in Iraq, gathering around the Kharijites and Shi'a. It was in the midst of this jumble of opinions and confused sects that the Mu'tazilites made their appearance.

Scholars disagree about when the Mu'tazilites first appeared. Some think that they began with the people of 'Ali who withdrew from politics and devoted themselves to the pursuit of knowledge when al-Hasan surrendered the khalifate to Mu'awiya. At-Tara'ifi states in his book, *The People of Sects and Innovations*: "They called themselves Mu'tazilites. When al-Hasan offered his allegiance to Mu'awiya, they withdrew (*i'tazala*) from al-Hasan and Mu'awiya and all people. They were among the adherents of 'Ali. They kept to their homes and mosques, saying 'We are busy with knowledge and worship.'"

Most sources state that the progenitor of the Mu'tazilites was Wasil ibn 'Ata'. He was one of those who used to attend the gathering of al-Hasan al-Basri at the time when the question arose which preoccupied the minds of so many people of the period: the question of whether committing a major wrong action makes its perpetrator an unbeliever. Wasil said in opposition to al-Hasan al-Basri, who had refused to become involved in the debate, "I say that the one who commits a major wrong action is neither a believer nor an unbeliever. He is between the two positions." Then he withdrew *(i'tazala)* from al-Hasan's assembly and set up another in the mosque. From this you see why he and his people were called Mu'tazilites.

Certain orientalists, however, believe that they were called that because they were fearful pious men who withdrew from the pleasures of life as is indicated by their name. In fact, not all the men ascribed to this group conformed to that description. Some were suspected of acts of disobedience and some were godfearing.

The doctrine of the Mu'tazilites

According to Abu'l-Hasan al-Khayyat in *al-Intisar*, "No one can properly be called a Mu'tazilite unless he holds to all five tenets of their school: *Tawhid*, Justice, the Promise and the Threat, the Position between the Two Positions, and Commanding the Right and Forbidding the Wrong. Only when a man maintains these five, is he, properly speaking, a Mu'tazilite. These are the tenets of the Mu'tazilite school." We will speak briefly about each of them.

203

Tawhid

A particular understanding of *tawhid* was at the core of their doctrine. Al-Ash'ari described their position in his book, *Maqalat al-Islamiyyin*:

> Allah is one. There is nothing like Him. He is the All-Hearing, All-Seeing. He is neither body nor spirit. He does not have corporeal form or shape, or flesh or blood. He is not substance or accident. He does not have a colour or taste, smell or tactility, heat, cold, wetness, dryness, height width, or depth. He does not have joining or separation, movement or stillness. He has no parts or components, or limbs or members. He has no directions: no right or left, front or back, above or below. He is not circumscribed by place nor is He subject to time.... He cannot be incarnate in any place. He is not described with any of the attributes of creation which involve contingency nor is He described as being finite or as being limited. He does not beget and is not begotten. No quantity can encompass Him; no veil conceal Him; no sense perceive Him. He cannot be compared to mankind nor does He resemble creation in any way... He was First before events in time and before contingent things, and existed before all creatures. He is Knowing, Powerful, Living and will always remain so. Eyes cannot see Him; sight cannot perceive Him; imagination cannot encompass Him. He is Knowing, Powerful, Living, in a way dissimilar to all others who are knowing, powerful, living. He alone is timeless and there is nothing timeless but Him, no god but Him and He has no partner in His kingdom.

On this basis, the Mu'tazilites asserted that it was impossible to see Allah on the Day of Resurrection since that would involve corporeality and direction. The Divine Attributes were nothing other than the Essence. The Qur'an was created by Allah since He does not (in their view) have the attribute of speech.

Justice

Al-Mas'udi explained this in *Muruj adh-Dhahab*:

It is that Allah does not like injustice nor does He create people's actions. They do what they are commanded or forbidden to do by the power which Allah has created for them and placed in them. He commands only what He wants and forbids only what He dislikes. He takes charge of every good action He has commanded and is free of every evil action He has forbidden. He does not oblige people to do anything they are incapable of and He does not desire of them anything they do not have the power to do. No one has power to withhold or give except by the power of Allah which He has given them and is in their possession. Had He so willed, He could have compelled creation to obey Him and prevented them from disobeying Him, but He did not do that.

The Promise and the Threat

This is that Allah repays all who do good with good and all who do evil with evil. He does not forgive anyone who does major wrong actions if he does not repent.

The "Position between the Two Positions" (concerning belief and unbelief)

Expounding the Mu'tazilites' view on the "Intermediate Position", ash-Shahrastani said, "This position was stated clearly by Wasil when he said that faith designates the qualities of good and when they are combined in a person he is called a believer, which is a name of praise. An impious man does not have all the qualities of good and does not deserve the name of praise. Hence he is not called a believer – but nor is he an unbeliever absolutely, for the *shahada* and good actions exist in him which cannot be denied. But if he leaves this world having committed a major sin without repenting for it, he is one of the people who will remain in the Fire forever, since in the Next World there are only two groups: one in Paradise and one in Hell. However, the Fire will be alleviated for him and he is above the level of the unbelievers."

Commanding the Right and Forbidding the Wrong

It is an obligation for all believers to disseminate the call of Islam, guide the misguided, and direct those in error as much as they can by means of both exposition and the sword.

The Mu'tazilites' method of deriving their doctrine

In explaining their doctrine the Mu'tazilites relied on reason and not transmission. They relied on the intellect, restricting its scope only when it was a question of the commands of the *Shari'a*. Every question was logically examined and they accepted what was logical and rejected what was not logical.

This rationalistic approach was the result of several factors: their residence in Iraq and Persia which were influenced by ancient religions and civilisations, their descent from non-Arabs, their clashes with opponents, the spread of translations of the ancient philosophers in these places, and their mixing with Jews and Christians and others who translated these ideas into Arabic.

One of the effects of their reliance on logic was that they judged that things were good or abhorrent by reason. They used to say: "All things are intelligible to the intellect and must be examined by the intellect. Beauty and ugliness are two essential qualities of good and evil." Al-Jubba'i stated, "Any act of disobedience which Allah can permit to happen is ugly because of its prohibition and any act of disobedience which He never permits is ugly in itself: like ignorance of Him and believing the opposite of that."

They based on this the idea of the existence of the best of all possible worlds. They said that only good issues from Allah.

The Mu'tazilites' defence of Islam

Groups of Magians, Sabaeans, Jews and Christians and others entered Islam, their minds still full of the teachings of those religions, and their understanding of Islam necessarily being filtered through them. Some pretended to have faith out of fear of the ruler, concealing their old belief, and began to try to corrupt the Muslims' *deen*, to make them doubt their own beliefs, and to introduce ideas and opinions for which Allah had given no authority. The fruits of their efforts appeared: there were anthropomorphists, *zindiqs* and many other groups. The Mu'tazilites tried to defend Islam, and their Five Tenets were the result of their sharp debates with their opponents. The tenet of *Tawhid* was formulated to refute the anthropomorphists; Justice was to refute the Jahmites; the Promise and Threat was to refute the Murji'ites; and the Position between the Two Positions was to refute the Kharijites who said that anyone who commits a sin was unbeliever.

The khalif's patronage of the Mu'tazilites

The Mu'tazilites appeared at the time of the Umayyads but the Umayyads did not oppose them because they did not provoke any discord or declare war. They were a group who took no action beyond thinking, countering evidence with evidence and proof with proof, and analysing matters by sound criteria. They did not involve themselves in politics – their weapons were exposition and proof, not swords. Al-Mas'udi reported that Yazid II espoused their tenets.

When the Abbasids came to power, heresy and the *zindiqs* had become a flood and the khalif found in the Mu'tazilites a sword to employ against *zindiqs* and left them to combat heresy. When al-Ma'mun came to power, he took their side and brought them near to him. He saw that there was a disagreement between them and the *fuqaha'*, and thought that debates between the two groups would result in the emergence of a single point of view, but he was completely wrong in this.

Al-Ma'mun then sought to use the power of the state to force the *fuqaha'* and *hadith* scholars to adopt the opinion of the Mu'tazilites on the Qur'an. This is not the proper role of the state. If it is forbidden to force people to embrace the *deen*, how can they be forced to accept a tenet the denial of which does not constitute disbelief? He tried to force the *fuqaha'* to declare that the Qur'an was created. Some of them complied out of *taqiyya* and fear, not true belief and adherence, while others endured violence, humiliation and long imprisonment and would not say anything other than what they believed.

That inquisition lasted after al-Ma'mun through the khalifates of al-Mu'tasim and al-Wathiq. Al-Wathiq tried to coerce people to deny that Allah will be seen – another orthodox position denied by the Mu'tazilites. When al-Mutawakkil came to power, this inquisition stopped, and things were allowed to take their course and opinions to evolve naturally, and people were left to choose their own position regarding these matters.

The position of the Mu'tazilites among their contemporaries

The *fuqaha'* and *hadith* scholars attacked the Mu'tazilites and so they were caught between strong opponents on either side: the *zindiqs* and those like them on one side, and the *fuqaha'* and *hadith* scholars on the other. One can see in the arguments and discussions of the *fuqaha'* that they pilloried the Mu'tazilites at every opportunity. One hears ash-Shafi'i, Ibn Hanbal and others criticising the science of *kalam* and those who took knowledge through the method of the *mutakallimun*. Why did the *fuqaha'* dislike the Mu'tazilites when both groups were trying to support the *deen* and did not spare any efforts in its defence? It seems that there were a number of factors which combined to produce such enmity.

The suspicions of the *fuqaha'* and *hadith* scholars

The *fuqaha'* and *hadith* scholars were strong opponents of the Mu'tazilites and suspected them of deviation. Ash-Shaybani gave a *fatwa* that anyone who prayed behind a Mu'tazilite had to repeat the prayer. Imam Abu Yusuf considered them *zindiqs*. Imam Malik would not accept the testimony of any of them. They were suspected of corruption and committing *haram* acts. In fact, the Mu'tazilite school embraced all sorts of individuals.

Disputes of the Mu'tazilites and the science of *kalam*

Kalam was used by the Mu'tazilites when debating with their opponents, whether Rafidites, Magians, dualists, people of other sects, specialists in *fiqh* and *hadith*, and others. The whole Islamic community took part in these arguments and debates for about three generations, during which assemblies of rulers, ministers and scholars flourished and opinions were exchanged. Internecine fights between the schools and sects caused reverberations that affected Islamic thought as a whole. Islamic thinking became embellished with Persian, Greek or Hindu ideas. Each faction was distinct in their argument in specific ways, while often they did not differ in their general position in the *deen*.

The methods of deduction employed by the Mu'tazilites were different from those of others among the Islamic Community and their deductive premises also differed. There were several distinct characteristics in the way they debated.

- The Mu'tazilites avoided imitation and were averse to following others without investigation, examination, comparison, proofs and proper criteria. Their respect was for opinions and not names, for the truth and not the speaker. Hence they did not imitate one another. The rule which they followed was that every responsible person is answerable for the principles of the *deen* to which his *ijtihad* has led him. Perhaps that is why they split into so many groups.

• They relied on the intellect to establish their articles of faith, finding support for their positions in the Qur'an. They did not have much knowledge of *hadiths* because they did not use them for doctrine or evidence.

• They took from classical scientific sources which were translated in their time. They borrowed from some of those sciences and used them to support their arguments in clashes with opponents in the field of *kalam*. They were joined by many Muslims educated in the foreign education and philosophical systems which were nurturing the Arab intellect in that time, which is why there were many distinguished writers and philosophers among them.

• They excelled in language, eloquence and clarity of exposition. Their men included eloquent orators and debaters who were skilled in debate, knew its rules and were experienced in its methods and how to defeat opponents. Their leading figure, Wasil ibn 'Ata', was a notable orator.

Chapter Four
The Opinions of Abu Hanifa

In the remaining part of this book we will discuss two matters: firstly, Abu Hanifa's opinions on questions of politics and dogma which exercised the minds of many of the scholars of his time, and secondly, his *fiqh*.

This first chapter will deal with his opinion regarding the khalifate and who was entitled to have it, and his view about the preconditions for being the khalif and the basis of allegiance. We will also look at his views on the articles of faith, the nature of sin and those who commit it, and man's actions and their relationship to the decree. We will also discuss the issue of "*qadar*" (decree) which was famous in his time shall also be considered. Then we will move on to his opinions on social and ethical matters.

Abu Hanifa's political views

Abu Hanifa's view on politics has not been precisely explained and analysed in the sources examined. We must, therefore, investigate scattered reports amongst the sources in order to be able to formulate from them a clear picture of his political thought.

Historical sources make two things evident about his life. One is that he was biased in favour of the descendants of 'Ali and Fatima and was almost martyred for his support of them. The second is that, in spite of this, he did not participate in any of the 'Alawite rebellions, either in the Umayyad or Abbasid periods. He confined himself to verbal support in his lessons and giving encouragement if he was asked for a *fatwa* on the matter, as he did in the case of al-Hasan ibn Qahtaba. He did not exceed the role of

211

a *mufti* who is asked for *fatwa* and answers in accordance with his conscience without paying any attention to the authorities. Thus it is certain that Abu Hanifa had Shi'ite leanings but they did not go beyond that. To which Shi'ite group was he closest? The question will now examine that question.

Abu Hanifa did not have the kind of Shi'ite perspective which blinds a person to perceiving the virtues and ranks of the Companions as a whole. He ranked Abu Bakr and 'Umar before 'Ali, and he mentioned his own esteem and veneration for the *taqwa* and generosity of Abu Bakr so that he tried to emulate him in his generosity and trading practice. He had a silk shop in Kufa as Abu Bakr had a silk shop in Makka. He placed 'Umar after Abu Bakr but he did not put 'Uthman before 'Ali. Ibn 'Abdu'l-Barr says in *al-Intiqa'*: "Abu Hanifa gave preference to Abu Bakr and 'Umar and left 'Ali and 'Uthman." His son Hammad said, "We love 'Ali more than 'Uthman." But in spite of his preference for 'Ali, he did not curse 'Uthman. He prayed for mercy on him when he was mentioned and may have been the only person in Kufa to do so.

He was not known to curse or accuse anyone, as he mentioned when he met 'Ata' ibn Abi Rabah in Makka. ' Ata' asked him, "Who are you?" "One of the people of Kufa," he replied. "From the people of a city who have divided their *deen* into parties?" "Yes," he replied. Ata' inquired, "From which are you?" He replied, "From those who do not curse the *Salaf* nor hold Qadarite views and do not consider a person an unbeliever on account of a wrong action."

Al-Makki reports in *The Virtues* that Abu Hanifa said, "I came to Madina and went to Abu Ja'far Muhammad ibn 'Ali (al-Baqir). He said, 'Brother of Iraq! Do not sit with us.' I sat down and asked, 'May Allah put you right. What do you say about Abu Bakr and 'Umar?' He replied, 'May Allah have mercy on both of them!' I said, 'In Iraq they say that you disavow both of them.' He exclaimed, 'I seek refuge with Allah! They have lied, by the Lord of the Ka'ba! Do you not know that 'Ali married his daughter, Umm Kulthum bint Fatima, to 'Umar ibn al-Khattab? Do you not know who she was, fatherless one? Her grandmother was Khadija, the mistress of the women of the Garden and her grandfather was the Messenger of Allah, may Allah bless him and grant him peace, the Seal of the Prophets, the Master of the Messengers, and the Messenger of the Lord of the worlds, and her mother was Fatima, the mistress of the women of the worlds. Her brothers were al-Hasan and al-Husayn, the lords of the young men of the Garden, and her father was 'Ali ibn Abi Talib, the master of honour in Islam. If he had not been worthy of her, fatherless one, he would not have married her to him.' I said 'If you would write to them and refute it...' He said, 'They are not up to writing. I told you directly not to sit with us and you disobeyed, so what will they do with a letter?'"

From this encounter between Abu Hanifa and Muhammad al-Baqir, one of the Imamite imams, we see that Abu Hanifa wanted to deny espousing distortionate Shi'ite views or disparaging Abu Bakr and 'Umar. Abu Hanifa believed that 'Ali was always in the right but did not attack or abuse his opponents. He stated, "No one fought 'Ali without 'Ali being in the right." He said about the conflict between 'Ali and az-Zubayr, "There is no doubt that Amir al-Mu'minin 'Ali fought Talha and az-Zubayr after they had given allegiance to him and they opposed him." When he was asked about the Battle of the Camel, he said, "'Ali was right in it. He had the best knowledge of the Muslims about the *sunna* of fighting the people of rebellion." He thought 'Ali was in the right but did not speak ill of his opponents.

In respect of his position regarding the Umayyads, we see that he helped Zayd ibn 'Ali when he rebelled against Hisham. He was asked about fighting with him and remarked that Zayd's expeditio resembled that of the Messenger of Allah, may Allah bless him and grant him peace, on the Day of the Battle of Badr. He helped him with money but did not trust his supporters.

His opinion of the Abbasids after the conflict between them and the family of 'Ali was no better than his opinion of the Umayyads. We see that he inclined to Ibrahim when he rebelled against al-Mansur. Al-Makki says in *The Virtues*: "Ibrahim ibn Suwayd stated: 'I asked Abu Hanifa, whom I respected, when Ibrahim ibn 'Abdullah ibn Hasan rebelled, "Which do you prefer

213

after the obligatory *hajj*: going forth with this man or *hajj*?" He replied, "After the obligatory *hajj*, a military expedition is better than fifty *hajj's*."' A woman came to Abu Hanifa in the time of Ibrahim and said, 'My son wanted to join this man but I forbade him.' He said, 'Do not forbid him.' Hammad ibn A'yan said, 'Abu Hanifa encouraged people to help Ibrahim and told them to follow him.'" (pt. 2, p. 84)

Political inclination was not the only sign of Abu Hanifa's ties to the family of the House of the Prophet. There was also an evident scholarly connection. That may well have been the reason for the political inclination. He studied with some of their eminent imams. It is also clear that he thought that the khalifate should go to the descendants of 'Ali and Fatima and that the khalifs contemporary with him were usurpers. So what did Abu Hanifa consider the correct means of choosing the khalif?

Reviewing Abu Hanifa's statements on this subject, we find an illustration which indicates that he thought that a general acclaim of the khalif should precede his taking power. Ar-Rabi' ibn Yunus, the *wazir* of al-Mansur, met with Malik, Ibn Dhu'ayb and Abu Hanifa and asked them about his being khalif. Malik said something mild and Ibn Dhu'ayb said something harsh. Abu Hanifa said, "The one who seeks guidance in his *deen* is slow to anger. If you are true to yourself, you will know that you have not gathered us out of desire for the pleasure of Allah. You want the populace to know that we affirm you out of fear of you. You assumed the khalifate without two of the people eligible to give *fatwa* agreeing on you. The khalifate is by the agreement of the Muslims and consultation with them." (*Virtues*, al-Bazzazi, pt. 2, p. 16)

His opinions on issues of *kalam*

As we have already mentioned, Abu Hanifa studied the positions of the sects of his time and debated with them. He used to undertake journeys for the sake of this debate. His scholarly life began with the study of these sects before he moved on to *fiqh* and became the undisputed imam of the people of opinion. He continued to argue with the various sects when that was necessary. That is why some opinions are reported from him which were dealt with by the *mutakallimun* of his time. There are, for instance, his opinions about the reality of belief, about the status of someone who commits a sin, about the decree (*qadar*), and about the relationship between man's free will and the will of Allah.

These opinions have reached us by two means: through scattered transmissions, both strong and weak, which must be scrutinised and through certain books which are ascribed to him. Abu Hanifa is listed in the *Index* of Ibn an-Nadim as having written four books: *al-Fiqh al-Akbar*, *the Scholar and the Student*, the Letter to 'Uthman ibn Muslim al-Batti (which is about belief and its connection to action) and the *Refutation of the Qadariyya*. All of them are on the science of *kalam* and dogma.

Al-Fiqh al-Akbar is a small treatise of which there are a number of versions. One is that of Hammad ibn Abi Hanifa. Another is the variant of Muti' al-Balkhi known as *al-Fiqh al-Awsat*, with a commentary by Abu'l-Layth as-Samarqandi and 'Ata' ibn 'Ali al-Jurzjani. There are others, including that ascribed to al-Maturidi, which is used for and against the argument of the Ash'arites. This indicates without a doubt that it is later than al-Ash'ari although they were contemporaries, since al-Maturidi died in 332 AH and al-Ash'ari in 334.

Scholars do not agree about the ascription of this work to Abu Hanifa. When he discusses *al-Fiqh al-Akbar*, al-Bazzazi says in *The Virtues*, "If you were to say that Abu Hanifa did not write any book, I would say, 'That is what the Mu'tazilites say. They claim that he wrote nothing on the science of *kalam*. By that they desired to deny that *al-Fiqh al-Akbar* and the *Scholar and the Student* were by him because he clearly stated in them most of the principles of the people of the *Sunna* and Community. They want to advance their claim that he was one of the Mu'tazilites and that the book was by another Abu Hanifa. This is a clear error: both books were written by Abu Hanifa.'"

We must briefly look at its contents and ascertain whether it can all be correctly ascribed to Abu Hanifa or whether there is some doubt about it. If we look at the order of the best of people after the Prophets in the Indian edition we find that it is Abu Bakr, 'Umar, 'Uthman and then 'Ali. But all transmissions in the various books of Virtues agree that Abu Hanifa did not put 'Uthman before 'Ali.

We also see that this book deals with issues which were not dealt with in his time nor the time before it. For instance, in his time and before, people did not discuss the difference between a sign (*ayat*), *karama* (miracle as a mark of honour) and temptation (*istidraj*). However, this is discussed in this book. Therefore there must be some additions to the book which do not come from Abu Hanifa.

Faith (*Iman*)

There are different transmissions about what Abu Hanifa says about faith. The one we can be most sure about is: "Faith is affirmation and confirmation." He said that Islam is submission and obedience to Allah's command. Linguistically, there is a difference between faith and Islam, but there is no faith without Islam and no Islam without faith. They are like the outward is to the inward. The *deen* is the name given to faith, Islam and the laws of the *Shari'a*. (*al-Fiqh al-Akbar*, p. 11)

So we see that Abu Hanifa did not consider faith to be pure affirmation by the heart alone. He thought that its reality was confirmation by the heart and affirmation by the tongue. He made his views on that clear in a debate between himself and Jahm ibn Safwan.

Al-Makki states in *The Virtues*:

"Jahm ibn Safwan went to Abu Hanifa to debate with him about *kalam*. When he met him, he said, 'Abu Hanifa, I have come to discuss with you some questions which I have prepared.' Abu Hanifa said, 'Speaking with you is shame and delving into what you are in is a blazing fire.' He asked, 'How can you judge me as you do when you have not heard what I say nor learned it from me?' Abu Hanifa replied, 'Words have been transmitted to me from you which the

216

people of prayer do not utter.' He said, 'Then you judge me in absentia!' He replied, 'You are well-known for that. It is known among both the common and elite and so I am permitted to assert that about you.' He said, 'Abu Hanifa, I will not ask you about anything except faith.' He asked him, 'Do you not recognise faith until the Final Hour so that you have to ask me about it?' 'Yes,' he replied, 'but I am uncertain about it in one area.' Abu Hanifa retorted, 'Doubt in faith is disbelief.' He said, 'It is only lawful for you to clarify how you attach disbelief to me.'

"He said, 'Ask.' Jahm said, 'Tell me about someone who recognises Allah in his heart and knows that He is One with no partner or like and acknowledges Allah with His attributes and that there is nothing like Him and then dies before articulating it on his tongue: does he die a believer or unbeliever?' He replied, 'An unbeliever and one of the people of the Fire unless he articulates it with his tongue along with what he knows in his heart.' Jahm asked, 'How can he not be a believer when he acknowledges Allah with His attributes?' Abu Hanifa said, 'If you believe in the Qur'an and accept it as evidence, I will speak to you using it. If you believe in it and but do not accept it as evidence, I will speak to you as one speaks to someone who opposes the religion of Islam.' He replied, 'As someone who believes in the Qur'an and accepts it as evidence.' Abu Hanifa said, 'In His Book, Allah Almighty makes belief involve two limbs: the heart and the tongue.

"The Almighty says: *'When they listen to what has been sent down to the Messenger, you see their eyes overflowing with tears because of what they recognise of the truth. They say, "Our Lord, we believe! So write us down with the witnesses. How could we not believe in Allah, and the truth that has come to us, when we long for our Lord to include us among the people of righteousness?" Allah will reward them for what they say with Gardens with rivers flowing under them, remaining in them timelessly, forever. That is the recompense of all good-doers.'* (5:83-85) So He connected the Garden to both recognition and word and made the believer someone with two limbs: the heart and tongue.

"Allah also says: *'Say, "We believe in Allah and what has been sent down to us and what was sent down to Ibrahim and Isma'il and Ishaq and Ya'qub and the Tribes, and what Musa and 'Isa were given, and what all the Prophets were given by their Lord. We do not differentiate between any of them. We are Muslims submitting to Him." If they believe the same as you believe then they are guided.'* (2:136-137)

"Abu Hanifa continued to quote *ayats* and *hadiths* to this effect. Then he stated, 'If words had not been necessary and mere recognition adequate, Allah would not have mentioned verbal articulation. Iblis would have been a believer because he recognised his Lord and knew that he disobeyed Him.'"

Al-Makki added to what Abu Hanifa said, regarding someone who dies with faith but without affirming it dying an unbeliever, that it means that when he is suspect since he has neither affirmed or openly declared his faith, then he dies an unbeliever. When there is no suspicion, as when he is on an island or in a desert, then he is not an unbeliever. So Abu Hanifa affirms that faith has two parts: firm belief and outward verbal acknowledgement of it. The verbal declaration is necessary.

Thus it is reported from Abu Hanifa that he divided faith into three, and that someone who believes with his heart, affirming it in himself, is a believer with Allah, even if he is not a believer with people. *Al-Intiqa'* clarifies what Abu Hanifa thought of faith and its categories: "Faith is recognition, affirmation and declaration of Islam. People are in three stages in respect of affirmation: some affirm Allah with heart and tongue; some affirm with the tongue and deny with the heart; and some affirm with the heart and deny wih the tongue. As for the person who affirms Allah and what has come from the Messenger of Allah with his heart and tongue, he is a believer with Allah and with people. If someone affirms with his tongue and denies with his heart, he is an unbeliever with Allah and a believer with people because people do not know what is in a person's heart and they call him a believer because of his public declaration of the *shahada*. They do not speak of the heart. The other is a believer with Allah and an unbeliever with people. This is the one who displays disbelief on his tongue through *taqiyya*." (p. 368)

As we see, the school of Abu Hanifa affirms that action is not part of faith. He was opposed in this by two groups; by the Mu'tazilites and Kharijites who considered action to be part of belief so that someone who does not act is not a believer; and by a group of the *fuqaha'* and *hadith* scholars who thought that action was an integral part of belief and affected it so that it can increase and decrease, without that affecting its basic existence. In that view someone who does not carry out the rulings of the *Shari'a* is considered a believer if the principle of affirmation exists, but his faith is not considered complete. Hence faith increases and decreases.

Abu Hanifa did not believe that faith increases and decreases. He considered the faith of the people of Heaven and the people of earth to be the same. He said, "The faith of the people of earth and the people of the heavens is the same; and the faith of the first and the last and the Prophets is the same because we all believe in Allah alone and affirm Him, even if there are many different obligations. Disbelief is one and the attributes of the unbeliever are many. All of us believe in what the Messengers believe, but they have a better reward than we do for faith and all acts of obedience; since they are better in actions, they are better in all matters: reward and otherwise. This does not wrong us because it does not diminish our due. It increases our esteem for them because they are the models for people and the trustees of Allah. No one has the same rank as they do and people only reach excellence by them; all who enter the Garden enter by their call." (al-Bazzazi, pt. 2, p. 141) Many later scholars disagreed with Abu Hanifa's view on this.

Abu Hanifa's position was that belief is confirmation and it does not increase or decrease, and so he did not consider those who disobey the *Shari'a* to be unbelievers since they have their basis of faith. The disobedient are believers who have a mixture of righteous and evil action. Perhaps Allah will turn to them.

219

These assertions of Abu Hanifa are based on sound logic in conformity with the principle of promise and threat contained by the Qur'an. Scholars and *fuqaha'* accept it. Imam Malik agreed with Abu Hanifa on this matter. 'Umar ibn Hammad ibn Abi Hanifa said, "I met Malik ibn Anas and stayed with him and listened to his knowledge. When I had got what I wanted and desired to depart, I told him, 'I fear that you will have hostile and envious people telling you things about Abu Hanifa which do not tally with his true position. I want to make his position clear to you. If you are pleased with it, that is it. If you have something better, I will learn it.' 'Go ahead,' he replied. I said, 'He does not consider a believer to be an unbeliever on account of committing a sin.' He said, 'He did well,' or 'He was correct.' I said, 'He said more than that. He used to say, "Even if he commits atrocious actions, I do not consider him an unbeliever."' He said, 'He was correct.' I went on, 'He says more.' 'What is that?' he asked, 'He said, "Even if he kills a man deliberately, I do not consider him an unbeliever."' He said, 'He was correct.' I said, 'This is his position. If someone tells you otherwise, do not believe him.'" (al-Makki, pt. 2, p. 77)

Some people misconstrued his position and he explained this in *al-Fiqh al-Akbar*: "We do not say that sins do not harm the believer nor do we say that he will not enter the Fire. We do say that he will not be in it for eternity, even if he is a deviant, provided he leaves this world a believer. We do not say that his good deeds are accepted and his evil ones forgiven as the Murji'ites say... He is subject to the will of Him who will punish him in the Fire if He wills and forgive him if He wills."

We can state that the disagreement regarding people who commit major sins has three branches. One are those groups who do not consider them believers at all – the Kharijites and Mu'tazilites. The second are those who say that disobedience is not harmful when there is belief and that Allah forgives all sins – the blameworthy Murji'ites. The third are the majority of scholars who say that a rebel is not an unbeliever and that a good action is multiplied ten times and that an evil deed is only counted as one, and that the pardon of Allah is not limited or confined. Abu Hanifa was one of these; and it is the opinion of the majority of Muslims, which would make the majority of Muslims Murji'ites by this definition. The term Murji'ites, however, is normally confined to the second group.

Qadar and a man's actions

Abu Hanifa was very perceptive and that is why he refused to become involved with the topic of *qadar* and encouraged his companions to follow the same course. When Yusuf ibn Khalid as-Samti came to him from Basra, Abu Hanifa said to him about the question of *qadar*, "This is a question which is difficult for people. How should they be capable of understanding it? It is a lock whose key is lost. If the key is found, what is in it will be known. It is only opened when someone is informed by Allah."

When the Qadarites came to argue with him about *qadar*, he said, "Do you not know that someone who looks into *qadar* is like someone who looks into the rays of the sun: the more he looks, the more his confusion increases. But you do not stop at this point. You carry on until you equate the decree and justice. How is it that Allah decrees all things and they happen according to His decree and yet people reckon that what happens is by their own actions." They said to him, "Can any of the creatures bring about in the kingdom of Allah something he did not decree?" "No," he replied, "but there are two aspects to the decree (*qada'*): command and power. He decided for them and decreed unbelievers but did not command it, and indeed forbade it. There are two commands: the existential, which is when he commands a thing to be, and the command of Relevation."

This is an excellent, precise distinction by Abu Hanifa. He separated the decree from *qadar* and made the decree what Allah had ruled which is brought by Divine Revelation and *qadar* what His power makes occur. He decreed what would be from before time. Responsibility is according to Revelation while actions occur according to the decree before time. The command has two categories: bringing into existence and imposing obligation. The second category has a reward in the Next World.

The History of Baghdad reports that Abu Yusuf said: "I heard Abu Hanifa say, 'When you speak to the Qadarite, there are two possibilities: either he is silent or he disbelieves.' He was asked, 'Did Allah know in His prior knowledge that these things would be as they are?' He said, 'Someone who responds to such a question has disbelieved. If he says, "Yes," is it that He wills that it be as He knows or did He will it to be different from what He knows?' If he says, "He wants it to be as He knows," then he avers that He desires belief from the believer and disbelief from the unbeliever. If he says, "He wants it to be different from what He knows," he makes the Lord unable to achieve what He wants because He desires the existence of that which He knows will not be. A person who affirms that is an unbeliever.'"

In summary, Abu Hanifa used to deal with this question in a restrained way. He believed in the decree of good and evil and the comprehensiveness of Allah's knowledge, will and power in created beings. None of a person's actions are independent of Allah's will even though man's acts of obedience and disobedience are ascribed to him and he has choice and will in respect of them. He will be questioned and accountable for them. He will not be wronged the weight of an atom. This is the Qur'anic dogma which is derived from Book. He debated with the Qadarites to cut them off.

Abu Hanifa did not accept the opinion of the Jahmites who espoused the theory of predetermination and said that a man's actions involve no will, even if he feels and senses will. Furthermore, we find that those who tried to attack him constantly claimed that he was a Jahmite. They forged lies and claimed that he venerated al-Jahm and followed him even though Abu Yusuf related that he said, "Two types of evil people are in Khorasan: the Jahmites and the anthropomorphists."

The Createdness of the Qur'an

In the time of Abu Hanifa, people began to spread among the Muslims the idea that the Qur'an was created. They claimed that it was created even though it was the greatest miracle of the Prophet, may Allah bless him and grant him peace. The first person to state this was al-Ja'd ibn Dirham who was executed by Khalid ibn

'Abdullah, the governor of Khorasan. This opinion was also held by al-Jahm ibn Safwan. Abu Hanifa's opponents claimed that he too held this opinion and that he was twice asked to repent of it, first by Yusuf ibn 'Umar, the Umayyad governor of Iraq, and then by Ibn Abi Layla.

It is not our habit to set aside a well-founded suspicion or an opinion based on evidence, but the transmissions which are related in support of this opinion make us hesitate to accept it because they originate with his opponents and because there are other contradictory reports related by reliable transmitters which are more likely to be correct because they are in keeping with what is known about his positions on dogma. In this respect, we will mention two sources.

We read in the *History of Baghdad*: "As for the assertion that the Qur'an was created, Abu Hanifa did not espouse it." It also states, "Neither Abu Hanifa, Abu Yusuf, Zafar, or Ahmad spoke about the Qur'an. Those who spoke about it were Bishr al-Marishi and Ibn Abi Du'ad. They vilified the followers of Abu Hanifa."

According to *al-Intiqa'*, Abu Yusuf said, "A man came to the Kufa mosque one Friday to ask them about the Qur'an while Abu Hanifa was away in Makka. People disagreed about it. By Allah, I think he must have been a shaytan in human guise who came to our circle just to ask us about it. We questioned one another and could not answer. We said, 'Our shaykh is not present and we dislike to speak out before he does so. When Abu Hanifa returned, we asked him about this question and what was the answer regarding it.... His reply about it was, 'We do not say anything about it. We fear to say anything.' He later said to us, 'Do not discuss it and do not ever ask about it.'"

The opinions of Abu Hanifa on thought, ethics and society

Abu Hanifa's intellect was remarkable for his profound thinking, analysis, and ferreting out the motives and reasons for all actions and matters which he examined. He went to markets, traded, dealt with people and studied life as he studied *fiqh* and *hadith*. He debated dogma and political methods. For that reason, he had exact views regarding thought, ethics and behaviour and on how a person should behave.

Abu Hanifa thought that righteous actions must be based on sound knowledge. In his view, a good person is not just someone who does good, but someone who can differentiate between good and evil, and who aims for good, out of knowledge, and avoids evil, understanding its evil. A just person is not someone who is just without understanding injustice; a just person must recognise injustice and its consequences and justice and its results, and act with justice because of the nobility and good consequences it entails.

He took this position in *The Scholar and Student*: "Know that action follows knowledge as the limbs follow the eyes. A little action with knowledge is far more beneficial than a lot of action with ignorance. In the desert a little provision with guidance is more useful than a lot of provision without it. That is like what Allah Almighty says, *'Say: "Are they the same – those who know and do not know?" It is only people of intelligence who pay heed.'* (39:9)"

A student asked Abu Hanifa, "What is your opinion about a man described as just who does not recognise the injustice of those who oppose him and is not capable of doing so." The answer was, "When the scholar is described as just but does not recognise the injustice of those opposed to him, he is ignorant of both injustice and justice. Know, my brother, that the most ignorant and base of all classes in my view are people like that. They are like four people who are given white garments and then are asked about their colour. One says it is red, one says it is yellow, one says it is black and the fourth says that it is white. He is asked, 'What do you say about these three: are they right or wrong?' He replies, 'I know that the garment is white, but perhaps they are speaking the truth.' That is how such people are."

Two points are evident from this. One is that righteous actions must be based on proper thought and firm knowledge. The second is that knowledge must be firm and absolute and unhesitating regarding matters of belief.

Abu Hanifa's views about people, society and the connection of the scholar to the society in which he lives are those of someone who knows the states of souls and studies them deeply, tasting both the sweet and bitter. It includes the advice which he gave to his student Yusuf ibn Khalid as-Samit:

> Know that if you harm ten people, you will have enemies, even if they are your mothers and fathers, but if you do good to ten people who are not your relatives, they will become like mothers and fathers to you. If you enter Basra and oppose its people, elevate yourself over them, vaunt your knowledge among them, and hold yourself aloof from their company, you will shun them and they will shun you; you will curse them and they will curse you; you will consider them misguided and they will think you misguided and an innovator. Ignominy will attach itself to you and us, and you will have to flee from them. This is not an option. It is not an intelligent person who is unsociable to the one who is unsociable until Allah shows him a way out.
>
> When you go to Basra, the people will receive you, visit you and acknowledge your due, so put each person in his proper position. Honour the people of honour, esteem the people of knowledge and respect the shaykhs. Be kind to the young and draw near to the common people. Be courteous to the impious but keep the company of the good. Do not disregard the authorities or demean anyone. Do not fall short in your chivalry and do not disclose your secrets to anyone or trust them until you have tested them. Do not socialise with the base or the weak. Do not accustom yourself to what you disapprove of outwardly. Beware of speaking freely with fools.
>
> You must have courtesy, patience, endurance, good character and forbearance. Renew your clothing regularly, have a good mount and use a lot of what is good. ... Offer your food to people: a miser never prevails. You should

have as your confidants those you know to be the best of people. When you discern corruption, you should immediately rectify it. When you discern righteousness, you should increase your attention to it.

Act on behalf of those who visit you and those who do not. Be good to those who are good to you and those who are bad to you. Adopt pardon and command the correct. Ignore what does not concern you. Leave all that will harm you. Hasten to establish people's rights. If any of your brethren is ill, visit him yourself and send your messengers. Inquire after those who are absent. If any of them holds back from you do not hold back from him.

Show affection to people as much as possible and greet even blameworthy people... When you meet others in a gathering or join them in a mosque and questions are discussed in a way different to your position, do not rush to disagree. If you are asked, tell the people what you know and then say, "There is another position on it which is such-and-such, and the evidence is such-and-such." If they listen to you, they will recognise your worth and the worth of what you have. If they ask, "Whose position is that?" reply, "One of the *fuqaha*"....

Give everyone who frequents you some of the knowledge they are expecting. Be friendly with them and joke with them sometimes and chat with them. Love encourages people to persevere in knowledge. Feed them sometimes and fulfil their needs. Acknowledge their worth and overlook their faults. Be kind to them and tolerant of them. Do not show them annoyance or vexation. Be like one of them. ... Do not burden people with what they cannot do.

This was Abu Hanifa's advice to one of his students who went to Basra to teach people there the *fiqh* of Kufa and the opinions of its shaykhs. It reveals three aspects of that venerable imam.

- It shows his character and his clinging to virtue and good character so that it became like second nature to him.

- It makes it clear that he was aware of the concerns of society and people's character and how to deal with them in a manner designed to bring out the best in them.

- It also shows the manner in which he instructed his students and that he knew how to disseminate his knowledge and views and make them acceptable to the learner.

Chapter Five
The *Fiqh* of Abu Hanifa

This final chapter is the core of our study since Abu Hanifa's *fiqh* is the field for which he is famous. To apply oneself to the study of his *fiqh*, however, is not an easy task because Abu Hanifa did not write a book on it, and the only surviving books ascribed to him are about dogma. There is no text written by him to examine so as to ascertain exactly what his position was.

The transmission of Hanafi *fiqh*

The fact that Abu Hanifa did not write a book on *fiqh* is in keeping with the spirit of his age. Writing books only became widespread after the death of Abu Hanifa or at the end of his life when he was old. There were *mujtahids* in the time of the Companions who forbade their *fatwas* to be recorded and even forbade the *Sunna* to be written down, so that there would be no confusion between it and the Book of Allah. As time went on, however, scholars found it necessary to record the *Sunna* in order to preserve it, and so they did so and collected *fatwas* and *fiqh* as well. The Iraqis collected the *fatwas* of the Companions and the *Tabi'un*. Abu Hanifa's son, Hammad, made such a collection.

It is clear, though, that these collections were not books organised into chapters. They were more akin to private notes to which the *mujtahid* would refer and not a book for the general public. The *mujtahid* would write them down to avoid forgetting them.

Abu Hanifa's students, however, did write down his views and record them. Sometimes that would be by his dictation but they were still in the form of individual notes. Sometimes he would ask them to read what they had written and he would confirm or alter

228

it. Most of what we have from ash-Shaybani must have come via Abu Yusuf since ash-Shaybani and other students had not been with Abu Hanifa long enough to gain such comprehensive knowledge. We read in Ibn al-Bazzazi, "From Abu 'Abdullah: I used to read Abu Hanifa's statements to him and Abu Yusuf would also insert his own statements in it. I used to try not to mention the position of Abu Yusuf along with Abu Hanifa's. One day I made a slip of the tongue and muddled them."

We read in al-Makki, "Abu Hanifa was the first to record the knowledge of this *Shari'a* which no one had done before him because the Companions and *Tabi'un* did not set down their knowledge of the *Shari'a* into topics or structured books. They relied on their strong memories and made their hearts the repositories of their knowledge. Abu Hanifa grew up after them. He saw that knowledge had become scattered and feared there would be unfortunate consequences if it were lost. The Prophet said, 'Allah Almighty will not take away knowledge by stripping it from the hearts of people. It will be taken away by the death of scholars. Ignorant leaders will remain and give *fatwas* without knowledge and be misguided and misguide.' Therefore Abu Hanifa recorded it and arranged it into topics."

By this he means the recording done by his students which may have been suggested by him. Indeed, this is probable.

The *Musnad* of Abu Hanifa

Although Abu Hanifa does not have a book on *fiqh*, scholars mention a *musnad* of *hadiths* and traditions ascribed to him. It is arranged in the order of *fiqh* and its rulings. So is this *musnad* part of what he did and did he arrange it himself or was it transmitted by his companions who received it in the way his *fiqh* was received? Did they write down what he told them in his lessons and then collect it together in chapters and publish it? It is certain that Abu Yusuf collected many of those transmissions which he called *al-Athar* and that Muhammad ash-Shaybani also collected a group which he also called *al-Athar*. Many transmissions are the same in both books.

Many scholars think that the transmissions can be correctly ascribed to Abu Hanifa. Ibn Hajar al-'Asqalani says in *Ta'jil al-Munfa'a*, "As for the *Musnad* of Abu Hanifa, he did not collect it. What is extant of the *hadiths* of Abu Hanifa is found in the *Kitab al-Athar* which Muhammad ibn al-Hasan related, and other *hadiths* of Abu Hanifa can be found in the books of Muhammad ibn al-Hasan and Abu Yusuf. Abu Muhammad al-Harithi, who lived after 300 AH, was interested in the *hadiths* of Abu Hanifa and collected them in a volume."

This would indicate that the *Musnad* ascribed to Abu Hanifa is not actually his own collection. Other scholars state the same. It seems that the traditions ascribed to Abu Hanifa are valid, but that their actual collection and ordering were done by Abu Yusuf and ash-Shaybani.

Abu Hanifa's knowledge transmitted by his students

It is clear that the only method we can use to discover the *fiqh* of Abu Hanifa is by way of his companions. We see that they wrote down the issues which they discussed with their shaykh after a specific opinion had been reached. We must, however, take note of three things:

- The writings of the companions of Abu Hanifa that have been mentioned do not preclude him having recorded his *fiqh* himself.

- The statements transmitted by his companions lack any proofs other than transmitted traditions or reports, reliance on the *fatwa* of a Companion, or the position of a *Tabi'i*. Rarely are analogy or reliance on *istihsan* mentioned, except in the books of Abu Yusuf, and he only reports them occasionally. There is no doubt that this does not take us far towards understanding the use of analogy which was so strong in Abu Hanifa's time that his opponents accused him of going too deeply into it and claimed that his analogies left the *Sunna* and exceeded the scope of the Muslim *mujtahid*.

When we read the books of ash-Shaybani, we only rarely find an analogy in which the underlying reason is clarified so that we know how it was deduced and pursued. Also, where is the *istihsan* of Abu Hanifa which his students could not dispute because of his profound perception and insight? We have no evidence that the later form of deduction was the same method of thought as that followed by Abu Hanifa.

- Abu Hanifa's companions served his school by transmitting its teachings clearly to following generations and their concern made Abu Hanifa respected. Each of those companions was an imam in his own right. Abu Yusuf was a respected and important imam. He was the Chief *Qadi* of the government for a long time. Muhammad ash-Shaybani was an imam like Abu Yusuf in both *fiqh* of opinion and *fiqh* of *hadith*. He also related the *Muwatta'* of Malik as he related the *fiqh* of Iraq and he knew both.

We have no option but to take Abu Hanifa's *fiqh* from those who accompanied him and so we should briefly mention those of them who transmitted his *fiqh*. Abu Hanifa had many students. Some travelled to him and stayed for a time and then returned home after learning his method and technique. Others remained with him. More than once, he mentioned the companions who remained with him: "They are thirty-six men: twenty-eight are fit to be *qadis*; six are able to give *fatwa*; and two – Abu Yusuf and Zafar – are fit to teach the *qadis* and those who give *fatwa*." For Abu Hanifa to make such a statement, these students must have already been mature. Because of his age, this would exclude ash-Shaybani, although he is in fact the major source for the transmission of the *fiqh* of Abu Hanifa to subsequent generations.

We will take a brief look at some of the companions who were responsible for recording the *fiqh* of Abu Hanifa, whether they were with him for a long time or whether, like Muhammad ibn al-

231

Hasan ash-Shaybani, they were not. The criterion is whether they play an important role in the transmission of his *fiqh*.

Abu Yusuf

He is Ya'qub ibn Ibrahim ibn Habib al-Ansari al-Kufi. He was an Arab and not a client. He was born in 133 AH and died in 182. He grew up poor and in need and had to work to eat. Fervour for knowledge moved him to listen to scholars until Abu Hanifa noticed him and helped him financially. After that he devoted himself to knowledge entirely. He had been with Ibn Abi Layla before joining Abu Hanifa to whom he then devoted himself. It seems that after Abu Hanifa's death, or while he was still alive, he also studied with *hadith* scholars.

He was *qadi* under three khalifs: al-Mahdi, al-Hadi and then ar-Rashid. Coupled with the fact that he was one of the *fuqaha'* of opinion, his appointment as *qadi* was one of the reasons why some *hadith* scholars have avoided his *hadiths*. The Hanafi school benefited in several ways by the appointment of Abu Yusuf as *qadi* since his selection gave the school influence. A *qadi* deals with people's problems and has to apply himself to solving them and thus the analogy and *istihsan* he used was derived from everyday life not theoretical situations. Through his appointment, the Hanafi school was put on a firm footing. Abu Yusuf may have been the first of the *fuqaha'* of opinion to base opinions on *hadith* for he combined both disciplines.

The books of Abu Yusuf

Abu Yusuf wrote many books containing his opinions and those of his shaykh. *The Index* of Ibn an-Nadim mentions a number of them, most of which have not survived. There are also a number of books which Ibn an-Nadim does not mention, one of which is the *Kitab al-Athar* and books on differences with other *fuqaha'*.

His best known book is the *Kitab al-Kharaj*, a treatise which Abu Yusuf wrote for ar-Rashid on the financial matters of the state. He clarified the sources of financial revenue for the state and the areas of taxation in great detail, basing himself on the Qur'an, transmission from the Prophet, and the *fatwas* of the Companions. He quotes *hadiths* and deduces their underlying intentions and the actions of the Companions.

This book was entirely written by Abu Yusuf, but in it he mentioned his disagreement with Abu Hanifa regarding several questions. Is it reasonable to conclude that he agrees with Abu Hanifa when he does not mention that they disagree? This would seem to be the case. When he differs, he produces the method of reasoning involved in his reaching a separate conclusion.

The *Kitab al-Athar* is transmitted by him from Abu Hanifa and contains a number of *fatwas* which Abu Hanifa selected or opposed from the positions prevalent in Kufa at that time. This book has several important scholarly implications for us:

- Its ascription to Abu Hanifa shows a group of his transmissions and the type of *hadiths* on which he relied in his deduction of rulings and *fatwas*.

- It makes it clear that Abu Hanifa accepted the *fatwas* of the Companions and how he accepted and used *mursal hadiths*.

- It includes some of what he selected of the *fatwas* of the *Tabi'un* among the *fuqaha'* of Kufa and of Iraq in general. It, therefore, provides a legal collection which was known and studied in Iraq.

Another significant book was *The Disagreement of Abu Hanifa and Ibn Abi Layla*: It contains the questions on which there was disagreement between the two. Abu Yusuf supports Abu Hanifa although both of them had been his teachers. As-Sarakhshi says about Abu Yusuf's move:

> "Abu Yusuf used at first to go to Ibn Abi Layla and studied with him for nine years. Then he moved to the gathering of Abu Hanifa. It is said that the reason for Abu

Yusuf's move was that he attended a marriage contract and sweets were distributed. Abu Yusuf had some and Ibn Abi Layla disliked that and spoke harshly to him, saying, 'Do you not know that this is not lawful?' So Abu Yusuf went to Abu Hanifa and asked him about that and he said, 'There is nothing wrong with it. We have heard that the Messenger of Allah was with his Companions at the marriage contract of an Ansari and dates were distributed and the Prophet began to pick them up and tell his Companions, "Take". We also heard that during the Farewell *Hajj* when the Messenger of Allah sacrificed a hundred camels, he ordered that a piece of each camel be kept for him.' When the disparity between them was clear, Abu Yusuf moved to Abu Hanifa."

We find this transmitted from ash-Shaybani. The book also shows how Abu Hanifa utilised analogy in Iraqi *fiqh*. Abu Yusuf's book illustrates the use of evidence and different aspects of analogy. It also shows the disagreement between the people of Madina and the people of Iraq. An example of that is the share a horse receives from the booty.

Abu Hanifa said that a man with two horses only receives a share for one horse. Al-Awza'i said that he receives the share for two horses and no further share and that this is what the people of knowledge say and the statement according to which scholars act. Abu Yusuf said, "Nothing about shares for two horses has reached us from the Prophet or any of his Companions except for one *hadith*. We consider a single *hadith* to be anomalous and do not take it as evidence. As for the statement that the Imams act by it and the people of knowledge follow it, this is like the statement of the people of the Hijaz, "And that is the past *sunna*." This is not an acceptable position to adopt. Who is the Imam who does this and who is the scholar who accepts it? We must look to see whether he is worthy to be transmitted from and certain about whether his position is based on knowledge or not. How can there be shares for two horses and not for three? How can there be a share for a horse tethered at camp which is not used in the fighting?"

Muhammad ibn al-Hasan ash-Shaybani

His *kunya* was Abu 'Abdullah. He was a client. He was born in
132 and died in 189 AH. He was only about eighteen years old
when Abu Hanifa died and had not been with him for a long time,
but nonetheless he compiled a more complete study of the *fiqh* of
Iraq than Abu Yusuf. He took from ath-Thawri and al-Awza'i, and
travelled to Malik and learned the *fiqh* of *hadith*, transmissions and
the opinions of Malik, after having learned *fiqh* of opinion from
the Iraqis. He stayed with Malik for three years. He was appointed
a *qadi* under ar-Rashid but was never Chief *Qadi*. He had great
skill in letters and so he had both linguistic training and analytic
perception. He was concerned with his appearance so that ash-
Shafi'i said about him, "Muhammad ibn al-Hasan fills both the
eye and the heart." He also mentioned his great eloquence.

Muhammad ibn al-Hasan achieved what no other companion of
Abu Hanifa did, except Abu Yusuf – he learned the *fiqh* of Iraq
completely and then was appointed *qadi*. He studied with Abu
Yusuf and then, as we have mentioned, he also learned the *fiqh* of
the Hijaz from Malik and the *fiqh* of Syria from the shaykh of
Syria, al-Awza'i. He also had skill in calculating the distribution of
inheritance. He was inclined to record things and he is truly considered to be the transmitter of the *fiqh* of the Iraqis to posterity.
As we mentioned, not only did he transmit the *fiqh* of Iraq, but he
also transmitted the *Muwatta'* of Malik.

Ash-Shaybani's position among the Iraqis came from him
being a leading *mujtahid* who had valuable legal opinions. He did
not relate *fiqh* directly from Abu Hanifa but by way of Abu Yusuf
and others. He mentions his transmission from Abu Yusuf. Indeed,
the entirety of *al-Jami' as-Saghir* is transmitted from Abu Yusuf.
The one book which he did not review with Abu Yusuf was *al-
Jami' al-Kabir*.

The books of ash-Shaybani form the primary source for Abu
Hanifa's *fiqh*, whether it be what he transmits from Abu Yusuf or
what he records of the *fiqh* known in Iraq. Not all of ash-
Shaybani's books possess the same degree of reliability. Scholars
divide them in two. Some are clear in transmission, like *al-*

Mabsut, az-Ziyadat, al-Jami' as-Saghir, as-*Siyar as-Saghir*, as-*Siyar al-Kabir* and *al-Jami' al-Kabir*. The ascription of others is not as certain. The first group are the bedrock of the transmission of Hanafi *fiqh*.

Al-Mabsut or *al-Asl,* as it is sometimes known, is the longest of his books in which he collected questions on matters which Abu Hanifa gave *fatwa*. It contains the differences between Abu Yusuf and ash-Shaybani, when there were any, and matters on which there was no disagreement. Each chapter begins with the traditions they considered sound regarding the topic concerned and then various questions and their answers. It reports Iraqi *fiqh*, but not the legal reasoning behind it.

Al-Jami' as-Saghir contains things which ash-Shaybani related from Abu Yusuf, as is mentioned at the beginning of every chapter. Some sources state that it is the only thing which he transmitted directly from Abu Yusuf. It is arranged according to legal topics.

In the case of *al-Jami' al-Kabir*, scholars agree that it did not come from Abu Yusuf, although he knew what it contained and many of the conclusions must have been transmitted from him. It, like *as-Saghir*, lacks legal deduction and there is no evidence for the conclusions reached, although a reader may discern it by reading between the lines.

He has other books as well that clarify various rulings which reflect Iraqi *fiqh* and frequently illustrate the difference between Iraqi *fiqh* and Madinan *fiqh*. His books also include transmission of *hadiths* and later traditions which were transmitted by Abu Hanifa and the people of Iraq and which were used as sources by later Hanafi scholars.

Zafar ibn Hudhayl

He was a companion of Abu Hanifa before the other two. He died in 158 at the age of 84. His father was an Arab and his mother a Persian and he had traits of both races. He was strong in using evidence and took the *fiqh* of opinion from Abu Hanifa which dominated his work. He was most acute in analogy. There is a report in *The History of Baghdad* from al-Muzani: "A man came and asked about the people of Iraq. 'What do you say about Abu Hanifa?' 'He is their master,' was the reply. 'And Abu Yusuf?' 'He is the one among them who most follows *hadith*.' 'And Muhammad ibn al-Hasan?' 'The one with the most secondary deduction.' 'And Zafar?' 'The most acute of them in using analogy.'"

No books are transmitted from him and it is not known that he recorded the school of his shaykh, and it seems that the reason for that was that he died soon after him – only eight years later – while the other two lived for more than thirty years and had time to write. He seems to have only orally transmitted Abu Hanifa's teaching.

He was *qadi* of Basra while Abu Hanifa was alive. Ibn 'Abdu'l-Barr reports in *al-Intiqa'*: "When he was appointed *qadi* of Basra Abu Hanifa said to him, 'You know the enmity, envy and rivalry which exists between us and the Basrans. I do not think that you will be safe from them.' When he went to Basra as *qadi*, the people of knowledge gathered round him and began to debate with him about *fiqh* day after day. When he saw that they accepted his arguments, he told them, 'This is the position of Abu Hanifa.' They said, 'Does Abu Hanifa find this good?' 'Yes,' he replied. He continued in this vein until they accepted Zafar completely and had transformed their hatred into love."

He took Abu Hanifa's place in his circle after he died and Abu Yusuf took it after him.

Several other *fuqaha'* of the Hanafi school are considered to have transmitted the opinions of Abu Hanifa. Among them was al-Hasan ibn Ziyad al-Lu'lu'i (d. 204) who is said to have been a student of Abu Hanifa. He became *qadi* of Kufa in 194.

The place of Abu Hanifa's *fiqh* in relation to earlier *fiqh*

We want to examine the principles on which Abu Hanifa based his deduction and which were the source of his *fiqh* and to relate it to a topic which some other writers have broached – the place of Hanafi *fiqh* in relation to the *fiqh* which preceded it. Did he innovate the method he followed? Did his *fiqh* cover an area not previously dealt with or did he simply follow a course plotted by others before him so that he did not bring anything new? Did Abu Hanifa complete a process which began in Iraq and culminated with him? These are the three possibilities and Abu Hanifa must fall into one of them.

His partisans state that he instigated a totally new way of legal thinking based on the Book, *Sunna* and sound tradition from the Companions but such claims are unsupported. Opposing them are those who claim that Abu Hanifa was merely a follower and brought nothing new, except in respect of extrapolation and speed of derivation, and that the source of the method which he followed was Ibrahim an-Nahka'i. One such person is Shah Waliyullah ad-Dihlawi who states, "Abu Hanifa, may Allah be pleased with him, was the strongest proponent of the school of Ibrahim and his contemporaries. He did not go beyond it except as Allah willed. He extrapolated according to Ibrahim's school." He concludes that Abu Hanifa did not bring any new ideas but was merely a follower and transmitter of an-Nakha'i.

There is no doubt that this is an attack on the position of Abu Hanifa in *fiqh* because it makes him an imitator, or a followed imitator, not the master of a school of *ijtihad*. If, however, Abu Hanifa had been like this, he would not have had such an effect on subsequent generations. Furthermore, we also find that Abu Hanifa transmits many traditions from other sources than Ibrahim. An illustration of this is found in the *Kitab al-Athar* by ash-Shaybani where it is reported from Ibn 'Abbas that if someone on *hajj* has intercourse after standing at 'Arafat but before his *tawaf*, he owes a camel, completes the *hajj*, and his *hajj* is complete. Then he reports from Ibrahim that if he has intercourse before or after 'Arafat and before *tawaf*, he owes a sheep, completes the *hajj* and must perform *hajj* again the following year.

Ash-Shaybani says, "The correct position is what Ibn 'Abbas said. The school of Abu Hanifa is as the books of the school state: intercourse before standing at 'Arafat invalidates the *hajj*, but it does not invalidate it after the standing, which is the opinion of Ibn 'Abbas." From this it is clear that Abu Hanifa completely abandoned Ibrahim's opinion and accepted that of Ibn 'Abbas which was related by 'Ata'. This is part of the *fiqh* of Makka, not Kufa. So he left Ibrahim and Kufa. How can this be blind imitation of Ibrahim or the people of Kufa? Such exceptions are often seen in the traditions of Abu Yusuf.

The truth is that Abu Hanifa came onto the scene when Iraqi *fiqh* was mature but he did not confine himself to what he found there. He followed a path which another had begun and went to the end of the road. We are not partisan here and take a middle course in this matter. There is no doubt that the opinions of Ibrahim an-Nakha'i had a tremendous effect on the formation of the legal reasoning of Abu Hanifa and that this was his starting point in *fiqh*, but that does not mean that Abu Hanifa did not take from anyone else or pursue any other paths. It seems that Abu Hanifa began his legal studies with what his shaykh Hammad reported of Ibrahim's *fiqh*. Then he completed his studies with others and deduced using analogy and evidence from the moment he took Hammad's place in his circle until his death, a period of about thirty years.

Whatever the position of Abu Hanifa in relation to Ibrahim, there is no doubt that Abu Hanifa and Ibrahim were the two eminent personalities in the formation of Iraqi *fiqh* and that their legal reasoning was so close that it led scholars to make that claim and make the personality of the latter vanish into the former. It is a false assertion because unity in thinking is not like unity in opinion. Abu Hanifa was not an imitator. He clearly stated that he used *ijtihad* as Ibrahim had done.

Ibrahim, as the *faqih* of Iraq, had an initial influence on Abu Hanifa who then formulated his own *fiqh*. Common factors in their manner of legal reasoning can be discerned. Both of them turned to analysis of *hadith* to extract the meaning as will become clear when we examine Abu Hanifa's reliance on *hadith*. Both interpreted *hadiths* in a legal manner to deduce the reasons for the rulings in them in order to then extend them through analogy to other matters. Ibrahim used *mursal hadiths* and Abu Hanifa also accepted *mursal hadiths* and used them as evidence.

But in spite of this agreement in legal reasoning we find that they differ in two important matters. One is that Abu Hanifa used a lot of the *fiqh* of Makka and Madina as the *musnad* of his *hadiths* indicate. The second is that Abu Hanifa used a lot of ramification and hypothetical cases and did not confine himself only to what he was asked about. He used to hypothesise problems and clarify their ruling and evidence. We will deal with Abu Hanifa's position in respect of this.

Abu Hanifa and hypothetical *fiqh*

By hypothetical *fiqh* we mean the giving of *fatwas* about situations which have not actually occurred but are only imagined. The people of analogy and opinion did this a lot. In the course of deducing the reasons behind rulings established by the Book and *Sunna*, they had to theorise situations in order to ascertain the causes for the rulings and apply them. Abu Hanifa frequently used this method since he used analogy a great deal and derived the causes from the texts and their contexts. Some claim that he devised 60,000 such hypotheses, others 30,000. The last number is more likely.

The History of Baghdad reports that when Qatada came to Kufa, Abu Hanifa went to him and asked him, "Abu'l-Khattab, what do you say about a man who is absent from his family for years so that his wife thinks that he has died and remarries but then the first husband returns: what do you say about her dowry?" He had told his companions who had gathered, "If he relates a *hadith* he will be lying. If he speaks by his own opinion he will err." Qatada exclaimed, "Bother you! Has this occurred?" "No," he replied. He said, "Why do you ask me about something that has not happened?" Abu Hanifa replied, "We prepare for affliction before it occurs. When it occurs, we will know what to do it and how to get out of it." (pt. 12, p. 348)

Abu Hanifa's leaning toward hypothesis and theorising was due to his profound grasp of the texts and his acting according to the consequences of the meaning and applying the ruling to all situations with similar root causes. Al-Hajawi claims that Abu Hanifa is the one who originated hypothetical *fiqh*. He said, "*Fiqh* in the time of the Prophet was confined to explicit rulings about what had actually occurred. After him, the Companions and great and minor *Tabi'un* used to clarify the rulings regarding what occurred in their time while preserving the rulings for what had occurred before them and thus *fiqh* increased in its branches. Abu Hanifa is the one who unleashed theoretical questions, hypothesising situations that might occur and what their rulings would be, either by analogy based on what had occurred or by extracting general principles. So *fiqh* developed and grew." (*al-Fikr as-Sami*, pt. 2, p. 107)

In fact, Abu Hanifa did not originate this method but he promoted and expanded it and added more branches and different forms of deduction. It originated before him from the circles of the *fuqaha'* of opinion. *Fuqaha'* after him continued to do the same although there was disagreement about its permissibility.

The fundamental principles on which Abu Hanifa based his *fiqh*

Abu Hanifa subjected questions to extensive ramification and close study, which inevitably led to hypothesising situations which had not occurred but which might occur, in order to clarify what their rulings would be. The books of ash-Shaybani are full of secondary questions transmitted from him. If we study them and analyse them in detail, we see that they must have been based on particular principles and that there must have been a basis for the rules of deduction used to extrapolate the rulings derived. History does not provide us with an exposition of these rules in detail connected to Abu Hanifa himself. However, there is no doubt that there are rules which Abu Hanifa used as a basis for his deductions and extrapolation.

We find such principles detailed in the books of the later people who forward them as the principles of deduction used in the Hanafi school and mention the differences between the Imams of that school on these principles and state: "This principle is the opinion of Abu Hanifa and that is the opinion of his companions and that is the opinion of all of them," and so forth.

Since the principles normally mentioned by writers are deduced by later writers and not mentioned by the Imams or their students, three points must be made.

- No detailed principles for the rulings of Abu Hanifa were related from him, although he must have had principles which he used in his reasoning, even if he did not write them down, just as he did not write down secondary rulings.

- The scholars who deduced the recorded principles, like al-Bazdawi and others, used to look for them in the statements of the Imams and the secondary rulings transmitted from them when they ascribed the principles to them. There are two categories: those ascribed to the Imam as the principles which they observed in deduction and the opinions of the *fuqaha'* of the Hanafi school.

- Although detailed rules are not transmitted from Abu Hanifa for deduction, general rules for deduction are reported.

Abu Hanifa and legal evidence

As we read in *The History of Baghdad.* Abu Hanifa said, "When I do not find the ruling in the Book of Allah or the *Sunna* of the Messenger of Allah I can then take the statement of his Companions if I wish and leave those of other people. But I do not disregard their words for the words of anyone else. But when it is a question of Ibrahim an-Nakha'i, ash-Sha'bi, al-Hasan, Ibn Sirin, or Sa'id ibn al-Musayyab, then I can exercise *ijtihad* in the same way that they did."

Al-Makki states in *The Virtues*: "Abu Hanifa took what was reliable, avoided the unseemly, and investigated people's behaviour and what was correct for them and was in their best interests. He used analogy for matters but, if analogy led to something unseemly, he used *istihsan* if it was appropriate. If it was not appropriate, he referred to what the Muslims generally did. He used to attach himself to a known *hadith* on which people were agreed and then form an analogy if that was possible. He would then use *istihsan* and take whichever of them was more correct. Sahl said, 'This knowledge of Abu Hanifa is, in fact, the knowledge of the common people.'"

He also says, "Abu Hanifa investigated which *hadiths* were abrogating and which abrogated and acted according to the *hadith* when he considered it established from the Prophet via his Companions. He knew the *hadiths* of the people of Kufa and was strong in following what he found in his land."

From these sources, we can see that the order of legal evidence used by Abu Hanifa was the Book, then the Sunna, then the statements of the Companions, then consensus, then analogy, then *istihsan* and lastly custom. We will now have a brief look at these sources.

The Book

Fuqaha' in the Hanafi school reflected on whether the Qur'an constituted text and meaning or meaning alone. Most scholars agree that the Qur'an constitutes text and meaning and it is important, at this point, to ascertain what Abu Hanifa's opinion about it was. There is no definitive text by Abu Hanifa making that clear but there are secondary sources which point to a conclusion.

One thing indicating his view is the fact that he allowed recitation of the Qur'an in the prayer in Persian and considered the person to have in that case fulfilled the obligation of recitation, whether or not he was able to recite in Arabic, even though he disliked him doing it if he was capable of reciting in Arabic. Abu Yusuf and Muhammad ash-Shaybani said, "Recitation in other than Arabic is only accepted in the case of inability to recite in Arabic." Ash-Shafi'i said, "It is not allowed in other than Arabic even if someone is unable. In such a case a person must call on Allah with what he knows and glorify Him." Al-Bazdawi reports from Nuh ibn Abi Maryam that Abu Hanifa retracted that position. It states in the *Kashf al-Asrar*, "He returned to the common position."

243

We must not forget the time in which Abu Hanifa lived, fifty years of which was under the Umayyads. He encountered Persians when they became Muslim in droves and their tongues made mistakes in Arabic and did not pronounce it well and many did not understand it well. He saw the *ayats* of the Qur'an being badly mispronounced and so he thought that as an allowance the non-Arab should be permitted to recite the meanings of *ayats* which were not subject to interpretation in a translated form. Then Abu Hanifa modified his position, only permitting the recitation of the Qur'an in translation for someone who was unable to recite it in Arabic.

The Qur'an contains the totality of the *Shari'a* and in it are defined general rules and those rulings which will not change over the course of time. Thus it contains the eternal and universal *Shari'a* for all mankind. The *Sunna* of the Prophet derives its strength from it and clarifies what needs to be clarified in it and provides necessary detail. Hence the Qur'an and the *Sunna* are inseparable as the basis of the *Shari'a*. Scholars studied its composition and expressions and clarified the rulings it indicated and the strengthen of its evidence

One area of Qur'anic evidence worth mentioning is the force of the *'amm* in the Hanafi school. *'Amm* (general) can be defined as a word which indicates various things with a shared meaning, for instance, as 'human being' indicates man, woman, black, white, Zayd, Bakr and Khalid while *khass* (particular) applies to a specific aspect of what is alluded to by a general expression, like 'white'or 'man' in relation to 'human being'. The Hanafis hold that, like the *khass*, the *'amm* is definitive in its evidence and can abrogate the *khass*, whether it occurs in the Qur'an or the *Sunna*. Al-Bazdawi mentioned that this was the view of Abu Hanifa. Accordingly, a particular solitary *hadith* will not alter the general meaning of the text.

Some *ayats* of the Qur'an connected to judgements require further clarification. They require some more details, or there is something implicit in them which requires explanation, or they are unrestricted and need to be qualified. Scholars – both *fuqaha'* of opinion and *fuqaha'* of tradition – agree that this is what the *Sunna* often does with respect to the Qur'an. Therefore the *fuqaha'* who expounded the principles of the school of Abu Hanifa and its adherents undertook to clarify the Noble Qur'an. The manner in which the *Sunna* clarifies the Qur'an is divided into three categories.

- Clarification by confirmation. This is when the *Sunna* reinforces the meaning of an *ayat*.

- Clarification by explanation. This is when the *Sunna* clarifies something implicit in an *ayat* when the text is general. This would include such things explaining details of the prayer, *zakat* and *hajj*, or defining the minimum amount of theft which entails cutting off the hand.

- Clarification by supersession, which is abrogation. Abrogation of the Qur'an by the Qur'an is permitted by the Hanafis, as is abrogation of the Qur'an by the *Sunna*, if it is confirmed by multiple transmission or well-known transmission.

The *Sunna*

This is the second source on which Abu Hanifa relied in his deduction. It is ranked after the Book because the Book is the foundation, root and primary source of the *Shari'a*, while it is clear that the *Sunna* is one of its secondary sources, coming after it in consideration. It elucidates the Book and what elucidates comes after what is elucidated and serves it. Many traditions report that the *Sunna* is the second source of deduction and we see this in the *hadith* of Mu'adh when the Prophet sent him to Yemen and asked him, "By what will you judge?" He replied, "By the Book of Allah." He asked, "And if you cannot find it?" "By the *Sunna* of the Messenger of Allah," he replied. He asked, "And if you do not find it there?" He replied, "Then I will exercise my opinion."

'Umar wrote to Shurayh the Qadi, "When a case comes before you, judge by what is in the Book. If something not in the Book of

245

Allah comes to you, then judge by what is in the *Sunna* of the Messenger of Allah." Similar things are related from other Companions.

This is confirmed in what is transmitted from Abu Hanifa. He clearly stated the same We also find that the Hanafis differentiate between a matter established by the Qur'an when the evidence is definitive and a matter established by a confirmed *sunna*. Those commands established by Qur'an are obligatory (*fard*) and what is established in the *Sunna* is mandatory (*wujub*). It is the same with prohibitions. Anything forbidden by the Qur'an is *haram,* if there is no uncertainty in the evidence, and anything forbidden by a confirmed *sunna* is *makruh* (disliked), but *makruh* in a prohibitive way, whatever the evidence. This is a slightly lesser rank.

There was conflict between the *fuqaha'* regarding the amount on which Abu Hanifa relied on the *Sunna* in his legal reasoning, so that some of them went so far as to claim that he advanced analogy before the *Sunna*. This requires some examination. Abu Hanifa was accused by his opponents, even during his lifetime, of clashing with the *Sunna*. Abu Hanifa himself denied this accusation. He stated, "By Allah, it is a lie about us if someone says that we advance analogy over a text. Is there any need for analogy when a text exists?" (*al-Mizan*, ash-Sha'rani)

So he only used analogy when there was strong need for it. He used to say, "We only use analogy when there is strong need for it. We look for evidence about the question in the Book, the *Sunna* and the decisions of the Companions. If we do not find anything then we use analogy since there is silence about the matter." (*al-Mizan*, ash-Sha'rani) He also said, "We first take the Book, then the *Sunna*, then the decisions of the Companions, and we do what they agree about. If they differ, we use analogy by comparing one ruling with another when they have the same underlying cause so that the meaning is clear." (*al-Mizan*, ash-Sha'rani, p. 52) He also said, "We act first by the Book of Allah, then by the *Sunna* of the Messenger of Allah and then by the *hadiths* of Abu Bakr, 'Umar, 'Uthman and 'Ali." (*al-Mizan*, ash-Sha'rani, p. 52)

It is reported that al-Mansur wrote to him, "I have heard that you advance analogy over *hadith*." Abu Hanifa wrote back, "The matter is not as you have heard, Amir al-Mu'minin. I act first by the Book of Allah, then by the *Sunna* of the Messenger of Allah, and then by the decisions of Abu Bakr, 'Umar, 'Uthman and 'Ali, and then by the decisions of the other Companions, and then, if they differ, I use analogy." These are clear statements from Imam Abu Hanifa in which he strenuously refutes those allegations about preferring analogy over the *hadith*.

Abu Hanifa was one of the first *fuqaha'* to accept single *hadiths* as evidence and to formulate his views according to them if he found a *hadith* which contradicted his opinion. We have mentioned how he retracted his view about the safe-conduct of the slave on the strength of the *fatwa* of 'Umar which was related to him by a single source. Since he did that with the decision of a Companion, he is far more likely to have done so with the *hadiths* of the Prophet. This can be seen in the books of Abu Yusuf and ash-Shaybani.

Although it is evident that Abu Hanifa accepted the single report, there is disagreement about his position when single reports contradicted analogy. Did he reject the single report which clashed with analogy and consider the contradiction to be a flaw in the *hadith,* or did he accept the *hadith* and ignore the analogy because there is no analogy when there is a text?

Ibn 'Abdu'l-Barr says, "Many of the people of *hadith* attack Abu Hanifa for rejecting a lot of single *hadiths* since his method of dealing with them was to compare them with what he had collected of *hadiths* and meanings of the Qur'an. If it deviated from that corpus, he rejected it." However, according to al-Bazdawi, if the tradition came from a well-known Companion, famous for his *fiqh* and insight, like the four Rashidun khalifs, it was preferred over analogy. If the source was someone not known for his *fiqh*, then it was considered in the light of analogy and accepted or ignored.

Abu Hanifa and the evidentiary status of *mursal hadiths*

A *mursal hadith* is one where the *Tabi'i* who relates it fails to mention the Companion who transmitted the *hadith* to him, saying, "The Messenger of Allah said…" without making it clear how the

247

hadith reached him. Al-Bazdawi used a wider definition of *mursal* and said that it is any *hadith* in which the *isnad* to the Prophet is not mentioned, and so it includes *hadiths* which a Companion did not hear directly from the Prophet, the *mursal* of the *Tabi'i* or of any reliable person at any time. The Hanafis say that a *mursal hadith* is accepted from the Companions, *Tabi'un* and the third generation, but not from those after them.

Examination of the sources shows that Abu Hanifa used to accept *mursal hadiths* from the first three generations, but not necessarily subsequent ones. We see that Abu Hanifa accepted *mursal hadiths* from those he knew and whose method he preferred and trusted. Ibrahim an-Nakha'i was the shaykh of his shaykh and he preferred his path, whether his *fiqh* differed or agreed with his own opinion. In both cases, he was reliable and his transmissions were not doubted. Al-Hasan al-Basri enjoyed a comparable reliability. Abu Hanifa accepted his *mursal hadiths* and those which came from anyone who had a position of equivalent reliability.

In fact, *mursal hadiths* enjoyed widespread acceptance in Abu Hanifa's time. This was before there was a great deal of forgery of *hadiths* so that scholars came to require *isnads* to ensure authenticity. We see that Imam Malik in the Hijaz also accepted *mursal hadiths*.

Fatwas of the Companions

We have mentioned that Abu Hanifa said that he acted by the decisions of the Companions in the absence of a text from the Book or *Sunna*. If there were differing opinions among the Companions, he chose from among their views, taking the position of whomever of them he wished, and he did not abandon their position for anyone else. When it came to the generation of the *Tabi'un*, like Ibrahim an-Nakha'i, Ibn Sirin, Sa'id ibn al-Musayyab and others, he exercised *ijtihad* as they had done. He did not follow the opinion of a *Tabi'i* or imitate him as he did in the case of the Companions.

Abu Hanifa used to differ from the Companions on matters in which there was scope for opinion. On matters in which there was no scope for opinion and where there was firm transmission, he followed them. That is why he took the period of menstruation to be a minimum of three and a maximum of ten days based on the position of Anas and 'Uthman ibn Abi'l-'As. He considered things such as this to be a matter of oral transmission not *ijtihad*.

In brief, Abu Hanifa put the position of the Companions before analogy and this can be seen in many of his rulings. Some later Hanafis did the reverse, preferring opinion to the statement of a Companion. Abu Hanifa did not consider that it was mandatory to follow the *fatwas* of the *Tabi'un*.

Consensus

The definition on which most scholars who accept consensus as a principle of Muslim *fiqh* agree is that it denotes the agreement of the *mujtahids* of the Muslim Community on any matter at the time of ruling. This is the soundest definition and it is that which the majority of scholars prefer. It is the one which ash-Shafi'i mentions in his *Risala* and he was the first to define its meaning and explain how it is used as evidence and to give it its weight in Islamic *fiqh*.

Did Abu Hanifa also consider consensus as one of the principles of his *fiqh* on which he based his *ijtihad*? Scholars of the Hanafi school state that it is one of his principles. They state that Abu Hanifa and his companions used to accept tacit consensus and thought that opposition to such consensus was only valid if scholars had two different opinions on a matter.

We find two instances in the sources where this principle is mentioned. One is in *The Virtues* of al-Makki when he says: "Abu Hanifa was tenacious in following what the people in his land agreed upon." (pt. 1, p. 98) The second is what Sahl ibn Muzaham said: "Abu Hanifa took what was reliable and fled from the unseemly. He examined people's behaviour and what they based themselves on and what was in their best interests." (pt. 1, p.82)

These two transmissions from his contemporaries clarify that among his principles was that he followed what the *fuqaha'* of his land agreed on. In matters about which there was no text, he proceeded in accordance with the behaviour of the people. This makes it clear, without a doubt, that he accepted the consensus of the *mujtahids* in general and was strong in following that. It appears that the consensus which counts as evidence with the *fuqaha'* has three pillars:

- The Companions sometimes exercised *ijtihad* regarding questions which were presented to them. In many cases which arose where public well-being was concerned, 'Umar would consult them and opinions would be exchanged. When they agreed, that would be his policy. If they differed, they argued until they reached something on which they agreed.

- In the era of *ijtihad*, every Imam used to strive not to have divergent positions contrary to those of the other *fuqaha'* of his land so that he would not be considered aberrant in his thinking. Abu Hanifa was firm in following that on which there was consensus between the earlier *fuqaha'* of Kufa. Malik, likewise, put the consensus of the people of Madina before single traditions.

- There are also traditions which confirm the evidentiary nature of consensus like the words of the Prophet, "My Community will never agree on misguidance," and "What the Muslims see as good is good in the sight of Allah."

Analogy

We have mentioned that if Abu Hanifa did not find a text in the Book, *Sunna* or *fatwas* of the Companions, he exercised *ijtihad* and opinion to ascertain the different aspects to be examined in the question under review. Sometimes he was guided by analogy and sometimes by *istihsan* – the best interests of people and lack of harm in the *deen*. He used analogy unless doing do would lead to something unseemly and not in keeping with people's behaviour, in which case he would use *istihsan*. People's behaviour was his guide in both *istihsan* and analogy.

The analogy which Abu Hanifa mostly used was defined by scholars after him in a general definition: to explain the ruling about a matter without a text by ruling it according to something whose ruling is known by the Book, *Sunna* or consensus since both matters share the same underlying cause.

Abu Hanifa's *ijtihad* and his method in understanding the *hadiths*, coupled with the environment in which he lived, made him use a lot of analogy and ramify secondary rulings accordingly, because in his *ijtihad*, Abu Hanifa did not stop at investigating the rulings of problems which had actually occurred but would extend his reasoning to rulings in respect of problems which had not occurred. He would theorise in order to be prepared for circumstances before they occurred so as to be ready to deal with them.

Thus Abu Hanifa's method in understanding texts led to using a lot of analogy since it is not enough to recognise simply what the rulings indicate. One must know the events which formed the context of the text and how it was intended to benefit people and the reasons behind it, as well as any peculiarities which might affect the rulings. It is only on this basis that analogy can be correct.

He used to ascertain the circumstances in which an *ayat* had been revealed. He studied those questions whose legal reasons were mentioned in *hadith* until he was considered the best of those who explain *hadiths,* because he did not confine himself to the outward sense but explained the intentions underlying the outward sense and what the *hadiths* indicated. The fact that there were not a great number of *hadiths* to be found in Iraq also compelled him to make more extensive use of analogy than he might otherwise have done.

Abu Hanifa divided texts into two categories: those dealing with worship in which case he did not investigate the reasons behind the rulings because analogy was of no use in them, and those dealing with matters of this world. In these texts he would attempt to infer the underlying reason which could then be applied to other cases.

251

Istihsan (Discretion)

Abu Hanifa used *istihsan* a lot as we have noted previously. The great amount of the use of *istihsan* by Abu Hanifa was the focus for the attack of those who criticised its worth in *fiqh*. Some fiercely attacked the use of *istihsan,* and Abu Hanifa and his followers for using it, because they regarded it as allowing a ruling to be reached that was based on personal interpretation and feeling rather than an actual text and defined judgement.

Scholars at the time of Abu Hanifa and after him disagreed about *istihsan.* Malik, Abu Hanifa's contemporary, used to say that *istihsan* was nine-tenths of knowledge, but ash-Shafi'i, who came after them, used to say, "Anyone who uses *istihsan* has legislated for himself," and he devotes a chapter in *al-Umm* to the "invalidation of *istihsan*".

But what was the *istihsan* about which some *fuqaha'* disagree but about which there was no disagreement between the *fuqaha'* of the Hijaz and Iraq, and which Malik considered nine-tenths of knowledge but which ash-Shafi'i criticised? Hanafi *fuqaha'* have explained the *istihsan* transmitted from Abu Hanifa and laid down the rules for legal reasoning in exercising *ijtihad* which involves *istihsan.* Part of their definition is that it is clear that the *istihsan* used by Abu Hanifa did not part from the text and analogy. The *istihsan* which he used was to restrain the analogy, if allowing its general application would be contrary to public interest, concern for which was the overriding consideration of the *Shari'a.*

Fuqaha' disagree regarding the *istihsan* which Abu Hanifa and his adherents used. Some of them define it as being, "Departure from what analogy entails to a ruling which is stronger than it." This is a definition which does not embrace all forms of *istihsan.* The best definition in my view is that stated by al-Karkhi: "That the *mujtahid* depart from an established precedent in favour of another ruling for a stronger reason which necessitates turning away from the precedent." This definition embraces all forms of *istihsan.*

Custom ('urf)

We recall that earlier we mentioned what Sahl ibn Muzaham said about the basic principles on which Abu Hanifa based his deduction: "Abu Hanifa took what was reliable and fled from the unseemly. He examined people's behaviour and what they based themselves on and what was in their best interests." He also mentioned that he consulted the custom of the Muslims. This shows us two things:

- Things are carried out according to analogy or *istihsan*, even if there is no text, and the Muslim uses whichever of them is most in keeping with the case and the aims of the *Shari'a*.

- When there is no analogy or *istihsan* on the question, Abu Hanifa looked to see what the behaviour of the people was. The behaviour of the people is the normative custom among them. He acted by the custom if there was no text in the Book, *Sunna* or consensus, and there had been no application of analogy based on another ruling or *istihsan* with all its methods.

Generally speaking, the sources indicate that making use of custom is one of the sources of deduction and one of the principles which can be used in the absence of any of the other principles.

Ibn 'Abidin says about the *mufti*, "The person who makes rulings must know the *fiqh* regarding the rulings of universal events and possess understanding of the actual situation and people's circumstances in order to be able to distinguish between the truthful and liar, true and false and so forth. Thus when the *mufti* gives a *fatwa* based on custom, he must know the circumstances of the time and know whether this custom is general or particular."

A note about Abu Hanifa's *fiqh*

Abu Hanifa was a free man who wished for others' freedom just as he desired it for himself. For that reason, he was very eager in his *fiqh* to show respect for man's independence in his dealings, as long as he was sane. So he did not allow anyone to become involved in the private dealings of a sane person. It was not up to the community, or the authorities who represented it, to involve themselves in people's private affairs as long as a religious injunction had not been violated or other people's rights breached. Although it is necessary for the authorities to become involved in preserving public order, a person is not to be compelled to live his private life in a particular manner nor is it stipulated how he must deal with his private property.

An example of this is seen in Abu Hanifa's view of the authority of a sane adult woman regarding her marriage. He did not accord her guardian any authority over her and he is the only one of the four imams to take that position. We also find that he forbade declaration of legal incompetence in the case fools, heedless people and debtors and he also forbade any restriction whatsoever on the way a person disposed of his property except where the *deen* was concerned.

Concluding Note

The Hanafi school, discussed by scholars, on whose principles questions are extrapolated, is not simply the position held by Abu Hanifa alone. It consists of his positions and those of his companions. If you wish, you could say that it is the position of the school of Abu Hanifa in Kufa, and then after his death it was taken by his students, Abu Yusuf and ash-Shaybani, to Baghdad.

That is why the Hanafi school was an amalgamation and did not purely reflect the positions of Abu Hanifa in the way that the positions of Malik are reflected in the Maliki school and those of ash-Shafi'i in his school. There are several reasons which resulted in the Hanafi school comprising this fusion of the opinions of Abu Hanifa, his companions and the *fuqaha'* in Iraq contemporary with him, like 'Uthman al-Batti, Ibn Shibrama and Ibn Abi Layla.

One reason for this was that Abu Hanifa's statements are not transmitted in detail as distinct from the positions of others. The

Iraqi position is transmitted as a corpus in which it is not easily possible to disentangle the various strands into the statements of each individual.

Another reason is that, in his study of various problems, Abu Hanifa relied on the debate and discussion of those issues that took place among his students. Due to his immense scrupulousness, belief in the truth and respect for freedom of thought, he asked his students to follow the direction to which the evidence led. Abu Yusuf recorded the positions of Abu Hanifa along with his own views. Thus the positions presented are a composite.

Abu Hanifa's students were in fact independent *mujtahids* in their own right. Each of them had his own opinion which might be similar or far from that of his shaykh, even if the methods they used were similar. If you read the books of the school of Abu Hanifa, you will often see a great difference in opinions because of this characteristic of his school.

It was not only the companions of Abu Hanifa whose positions were mixed together. After them the views of other *fuqaha'* were added to what had been transmitted from him and his companions. Some were Hanafis and some were not. All of this resulted in a lot of divergent views and choices, all of which was based on exact rules and clear principles. Thus what came to be Hanafi *fiqh* represents the *fiqh* of Iraq rather than simply the views of Abu Hanifa.

Imam ash-Shafi'i
(150/767 - 204/820)

Preface

Imam ash-Shafi'i's *fiqh* represents the fullest paradigm of Islamic *fiqh* at the time when it flowered and its development was complete. His *fiqh* unites the people of opinion (*ra'y*) and the people of *hadith* in a balanced manner. He is the *faqih* who systematised opinion and set out the criteria for making analogy. He was the first to attempt to formulate the *Sunna* and to lay down rules and criteria for its legal use, to specify the methods for understanding the Book and the *Sunna* and to clarify the abrogating and abrogated. Through these efforts and setting out the principles of *fiqh*, he established firm foundations for the science of deduction and the bases of extrapolation. To study him and the method of his deduction is to study Islamic *fiqh* when its growth was complete, its distinguishing features were clear and its methods were established.

An examination of ash-Shafi'i and his *fiqh* will necessarily touch on the *fiqh* of the people of the Hijaz and their methods of investigation because he trained with Malik, the Imam of the Abode of the *Hijra* and Shaykh of the Hijaz in his time. It will also touch on the *fiqh* of the people of Iraq because he studied their books, was connected to Muhammad ibn al-Hasan ash-Shaybani who wrote them down, and stayed among them and debated and argued with them. A debater is affected by the method, path and thought patterns of his opponent in the same way that a warrior is affected by the strategy, tactics and thought patterns of his enemy.

Imam ash-Shafi'i, then, studied all the areas of Islamic *fiqh* when it was at its high point of growth and perfection and was the one who laid down the principles of *fiqh*, meaning the general principles for the deduction of legal rulings from accepted sources. To study him is to study the fundamentals of *fiqh*. He began to define and isolate and to make a position for himself that was distinct from the earlier practitioners of *fiqh*. Ash-Shafi'i dictated or wrote his general books on the principles of his school and the techniques of his *ijtihad* and he developed the science of legal methodology and illuminated the way for those who wanted to study it and to know its path.

In this study we will look at his upbringing, education, shaykhs and students. All of this is the study of his life. Then we will study his time and then his *fiqh*. We will examine his works, how they were written, and how reliable they are. We will study the principles which were set out for deduction and the techniques which he used in making deduction, as well as his thought in general.

Chapter One
Lineage, Birth and Life History

Transmissions agree that Muhammad ibn Idris ash-Shafi'i was born in 150 AH which is the year in which Imam Abu Hanifa died. Some of them add that he was born on the very night that Abu Hanifa died, although there is no real evidence for this. Most historians say regarding his lineage that his father was a Qurayshi descended from al-Muttalib and that his full name and lineage is Muhammad ibn Idris ibn al-'Abbas ibn 'Uthman ibn Shafi' ibn 'Ubayd ibn 'Abu Yazid ibn 'Abdi'l-Muttalib ibn Hashim ibn 'Abd Manaf. Both he and the Prophet are descended from 'Abd Manaf through 'Abdu'l-Muttalib.

Ash-Shafi'i was descended from 'Abd Manaf whose sons were al-Muttalib, Hashim, 'Abd Shams, the ancestor of the Umayyads, and Nawfal. Al-Muttalib raised 'Abdu'l-Muttalib, the son of his brother Hashim, the grandfather of the Messenger of Allah, may Allah bless him and grant him peace. The Banu'l-Muttalib and Banu Hashim were one unit opposed by the Banu 'Abd Shams in the *Jahiliyya*. This had two consequences after the advent of Islam.

Firstly, when Quraysh ostracised the Prophet and those of the people of his clan who helped him, the Banu'l-Muttalib supported him, both Muslims and unbelievers, and accepted the injury with him. Secondly, the Prophet, may Allah bless him and grant him peace, gave them the share allotted to close relatives according to the words of Allah, *"Know that when you take any booty a fifth of it belongs to Allah, and to the Messenger, and to close relatives, orphans, the very poor and travellers,"* (8:41) and did not give it to the Banu 'Abd Shams or Banu Nawfal.

261

His mother was from Azd and was not a Qurayshite. Some partisans of ash-Shafi'i claim that she was an Qurayshite descended from Sayyiduna 'Ali, but the truth is that she was from Azd. Ar-Razi mentioned that the transmission that she was Qurayshite is rare and contrary to the general consensus. He said, "As for the lineage of ash-Shafi'i from his mother, there are two statements. The first, which is rare and is related by Abu 'Abdullah al-Hakim, is that she was Fatima bint 'Abdullah ibn al-Husayn ibn 'Ali. The second is that she was from Azd."

It is clear from this that ash-Shafi'i was Qurayshi. He grew up in a poor family who were displaced in Palestine. They lived in the Yemeni quarter there. A number of transmissions are related from ash-Shafi'i which indicate that his father died when he was young and his mother took him to Makka to live, fearing he would lose the title of being a *sharif*. Yaqut reports that ash-Shafi'i said, "I was born in Ghazza in 150 and taken to Makka when I was two." It is also related that he was ten when he arrived in Makka.

Reports agree that he lived the life of a poor orphan. So ash-Shafi'i was born with a noble lineage – the noblest of lineage in his time and one which is still the noblest – but he lived a life of poverty until he was grown-up. Growing up in poverty combined with a noble lineage gives a person strong character and noble conduct. If there are no impediments and no irregularities, that nobility from youth will cause him to direct himself to noble matters, to be averse to the base and above the lowly. He will not be content with lowliness but will strive for glory with zeal and resolve to remove the infamy of poverty and the baseness of need.

Another result of the fact that he grew up poor in spite of his proud ancestry was that it made him aware of the feelings of people when he was with them and enabled him to recognise the things hidden inside them and their society and to be aware of their emotions. That is a necessary quality for all who devote themselves to the reform of society and the regulation of its states and ties, as well as to elucidating the *Shari'a,* extracting its truths and discovering its measures and criteria.

Ash-Shafi'i grew up in a poor household as an orphan, as we have explained. His mother wanted to connect him to his relatives

out of fear of his losing touch with his lineage. The various transmissions make it clear that his intelligence and cleverness became
apparent during his primary education. For instance, when ash-
Shafi'i memorised the Qur'an, his great intellectual capacity was
evident from the speed with which he memorised it. Then after
memorising it, he proceeded to memorise the *hadiths* of the
Messenger of Allah, may Allah bless him and grant him peace,
and was eager to do so. He listened to *hadith* scholars and memorised the *hadiths* he heard, and then wrote them down sometimes
on clay tablets and sometimes on skins. All transmissions indicate
that he was devoted to knowledge of and love for the *hadiths* of
the Prophet from his earliest youth.

Along with the memorisation of Prophetic *hadiths* and the
Book of Allah, he sought to become eloquent in Arabic and to
avoid the non-Arabic words which had begun to invade Arabic
because of contact with non-Arabs in cities and towns. This was
the primary education of ash-Shafi'i, which was the most exemplary Arabic education at the time: memorisation of the Qur'an,
seeking *hadith,* clear and eloquent Arabic, and training in horse-
manship which was known by settled people and nomads.

His quest for knowledge

Ash-Shafi'i sought knowledge in Makka from *fuqaha'* and
hadith scholars who were there, becoming so eminent that Muslim
ibn Khalid al-Zanji gave him permission to give *fatwa*, saying to
him, "Give *fatwa*, Abu 'Abdullah. You may now give *fatwa*."

Ash-Shafi'i could have stopped when he reached this stage but
his zeal for knowledge did not stop at any limit, for knowledge has
no limits or borders. He heard about Malik, the Imam of Madina.
At that time the name of Malik had spread throughout the lands of
Islam and people travelled to him for knowledge from far and
wide. He was the most important source of knowledge and *hadith*.
Ash-Shafi'i was eager to emigrate to Madina to seek knowledge
but did not want to go to Madina without some knowledge of
Malik's teaching. He borrowed Malik's book *al-Muwatta'* from a

man in Makka and read it; according to the transmission, he memorised it. He read *al-Muwatta'* to increase his desire to go to the Imam of the Abode of the *Hijra*.

Ash-Shafi'i went to Malik with a letter of recommendation from the governor of Makka. It was with this emigration that the life of ash-Shafi'i began to be directed towards *fiqh* in particular. When Malik, who had great insight, saw him, he said, "O Muhammad, fear Allah and avoid acts of disobedience. You will be a man of great standing. Allah Almighty has cast light into your heart, so do not extinguish it through disobedience. Then he told him, "Come tomorrow and bring what you have read." Ash-Shafi'i said, "I went to him and began to read aloud with the book in my hand. When I wanted to stop because of my awe of Malik, he indicated that he liked my reading and inflection and said, 'Go on, boy,' until I had read it to him in a few days."

After ash-Shafi'i had related the *Muwatta'* from Malik, he remained with him to learn *fiqh* and to study the problems on which Malik gave *fatwa* until the latter's death in 179 AH. Ash-Shafi'i had now reached the prime of his youth. It seems that during the time he spent with Malik he also used to absent himself from time to time and would make journeys to other lands of Islam to learn what an intelligent traveller can learn about the circumstances of their people and the situation of their communities. He used to go to Makka to visit his mother and seek her advice. She was a lady of nobility, good behaviour and excellent understanding. Thus his remaining with Malik did not prevent him from travelling and broadening his experience.

His appointment

When Malik died, ash-Shafi'i felt that he had obtained a good portion of knowledge and since at that time he was still poor, he decided to work to earn something to satisfy his basic needs and alleviate his poverty. The governor of Yemen came to the Hijaz and a Qurayshi suggested that he allow ash-Shafi'i to accompany him. The governor took him with him as an assistant. The gifts, experience, intelligence, knowledge and noble lineage of ash-Shafi'i shone. He was known as a just and distinguished man. People mentioned his name in Makka, and the *fuqaha'* and *hadith* scholars with whom he had studied or taught discussed his situation, about which there was disagreement. Some of them censured him for accepting the post and advised him to leave it.

His post was in Najran and he was responsible for establishing justice there. The people in Najran acted as they always do, bribing and flattering governors and *qadis* to ingratiate themselves with them; but they found in ash-Shafi'i a just man who could not be corrupted. Ash-Shafi'i closed the door of bribery and flattery so that no one could reach him through it, and by doing so protected himself from every evil and injustice. He was completely devoted to justice, but dispensing justice can be difficult and only men with firm resolve are strong enough for it. They will be exposed to the harshness and evil of the time. That is what happened to ash-Shafi'i.

His trial

Najran was a district of Yemen where there was an unjust governor. Ash-Shafi'i used to restrain his power and prevent his injustices from afflicting those under him. Perhaps ash-Shafi'i injured that governor by wielding a weapon which scholars possess and think it good to use and frequently sharpen: censure. Perhaps as well as hindering him he also censured him. The governor used that as a pretext to manoeuvre against him through intrigue, slander and defamation.

The Abbasids considered their main opponents to be the descendants of 'Ali because they had a similar lineage and they also had maternal kinship to the Messenger of Allah, may Allah bless him and grant him peace, which the Abbasids did not have. When the Abbasid state was established on the basis of their lineage with the Prophet, the 'Alawites hoped for something similar, especially in view of their female kinship with the Prophet through Fatima. So whenever the Abbasids discerned any 'Alawite partisanship they put an end to it while it was still in its infancy. They executed people for it on mere suspicion without any real evidence since they believed that taking an innocent life would ensure the status quo whereas letting a suspect might disturb the peace and unsettle society.

The unjust governor raised the suspicion of ash-Shafi'i's involvement with the 'Alawites and sent word to the khalif Harun ar-Rashid that nine 'Alawites were agitating, saying in his letter: "I fear that they may rebel. There is a man here from the descendants of al-Muttalib whom I can neither command or forbid." In one transmission he said about ash-Shafi'i. "He accomplishes with his tongue what a warrior cannot accomplish with his sword." Ar-Rashid told him to send to him those nine 'Alawites, and ash-Shafi'i as well.[1]

The sources state that the nine were killed but ash-Shafi'i was saved by his strong argument and the testimony of Muhammad ibn al-Hasan. As for his argument, when he arrived as a suspect before ar-Rashid and stood between the executioner's mat and the sword, he said, "Amir al-Mu'minin, what do you say about two men, one of whom sees me as a brother and the other as his slave: which should I love?" He replied, "The one who sees you as a brother." He said, "That is you, Amir al-Mu'minin. You are the descendants of al-'Abbas and they are the descendants of 'Ali. We are the Banu'l-Muttalib while you are the descendants of al-'Abbas. You see us as brothers but the 'Alawites see us as their slaves."

As for the testimony of Muhammad ibn al-Hasan, that was because ash-Shafi'i was familiar with the way the assembly of ar-Rashid dealt with such accusations and because people of knowledge have an affinity with one another. Hence he mentioned that he had a certain amount of knowledge and *fiqh* and that Qadi Muhammad ibn al-Hasan was aware of it. When ar-Rashid asked Muhammad he told him, "He has a great portion of knowledge and the man who accused him has none." The Khalif said, "Take

---

1. Two things should be noted here: ash-Shafi'i was known for his love of the descendants of 'Ali; transmitters agree that ash-Shafi'i was suspected of being an 'Alawite and that ar-Rashid tried him for that reason. There is some disagreement whether this occurred when he was in Makka or Yemen.

266

charge of him until I have investigated him again," and by this he was saved.

Ash-Shafi'i arrived in Baghdad for this trial in 184 AH when he was 34 years old. Perhaps this trial was Allah's means of making him devote himself to knowledge and not to administration and government. From this time he directed himself to study and teaching and produced the lasting influence on and development of *fiqh* which was his legacy to the Muslims. He stayed with Muhammad ibn al-Hasan ash-Shaybani, of whom he had already heard, knowing that he was the bearer and disseminator of the *fiqh* of the Iraqis. It is even possible that he had met him previously.

Ash-Shafi'i began to study the *fiqh* of the Iraqis and to read the books of Imam Muhammad ibn al-Hasan and study with him, thus combining the *fiqh* of the Hijaz with the *fiqh* of Iraq. In this way he had both *fiqh* which was dominated by transmission and also *fiqh* which was dominated by opinion, and thus he became the master of *fiqh* in his time.

Ash-Shafi'i remained in Baghdad as a student of Imam Muhammad ash-Shaybani and debated with him and his companions on the basis that he was a Madinan *faqih* and one of the companions of Malik. After that he returned to Makka with the books of the Iraqis. He did not mention most of the transmitters he listened to in Baghdad but he must have stayed a reasonable length of time in order to be able to transmit from the people of opinion (*ra'y*) and their school. It is likely that he stayed in Iraq for about two years.

After ash-Shafi'i returned to Makka he began to teach in the *Haram* and during the *Hajj* met there the greatest scholars of the time, who heard from him. It was during this period that Ahmad ibn Hanbal met him. Ash-Shafi'i began to set forth a new *fiqh* which was neither the *fiqh* of the people of Madina nor the *fiqh* of the people of Iraq but a mixture of the two and the product of a luminous intellect which had matured in knowledge of the Book and *Sunna*, knowledge of Arabic, information about people, analogy and opinion. That is why the scholars who met him realised that he was unique in his scholarship. Ash-Shafi'i stayed in Makka at this time for about nine years, as can be deduced from the reports we have from various transmitters.

As we have seen ash-Shafi'i had been exposed to two different traditions of *fiqh*. After he had debated and argued the pros and cons and seen the ramifications of the various opinions, the divergence of views and contrast of sources, he felt that he must set out the criteria for discerning the true from the false, or at least to recognise what is closer to the truth. Having witnessed with his own eyes the differences between the views of the Hijazis and Iraqis – each of them having its own justification and evidence – it is not logical that ash-Shafi'i would judge one of the two views to be invalid without having a precise and accurate criterion for doing so. This is why he came up with his technique for extrapolating the rules of deduction.

We can understand from his long residence in Makka, far from the tumult of Iraq and the battle of opinions there, that he was able to fully devote himself to his studies and reflect on the extrapolation of these rules. He had a complete grasp of Allah's Book and knew how to evaluate its evidence and judgements, which texts abrogate and are abrogated, and the special qualities of each. He knew the place held by the *Sunna* in the science of the *Shari'a*, how to tell the sound from the weak, the methods of using it for evidence, and its position in relation to the Noble Qur'an. He knew how to extrapolate rulings when there was nothing in the Book or *Sunna* when no precise rules of *ijtihad* applied, and he set out the limits for the *mujtahid*. He himself did not exceed those limits so as to be safe from exceeding the bounds of *ijtihad*.

That is why he remained in Makka for a long time, and it must have been during this period that he laid down the principles of deduction and produced them for people. Perhaps when he reached a point where it was proper to expound it to the mass of *fuqaha'*, he travelled to Baghdad, the focal point for all the *fuqaha'* since the decline of Madina after the death of Malik. At that point Baghdad became home to both the exponents of opinion and the adherents of *hadith*.

Ash-Shafi'i visited Baghdad for the second time in 195 AH with his new system of *fiqh*. He began not by examining the details of secondary rulings and subsidiary questions but by formulating universal rules and basic principles by which the subsidiary questions could be decided. He transformed *fiqh* into a total science, not merely a matter of secondary rulings, and he derived general rules rather than *fatwas* and personal decisions. So scholars and *fiqh* students thronged to him and the *hadith* scholars and people of opinion all sought him out. It was during this visit, they say, that he first put on paper his *Risala* which set out the basis of the science of the fundamental principles of *fiqh*.

The Virtues of ash-Shafi'i by ar-Razi reports that it is related that 'Abdu'r-Rahman ibn Mahdi asked ash-Shafi'i to write a book outlining the preconditions for deducing judgements using the Qur'an, the *Sunna*, consensus and analogy, clarifying the abrogating and abrogated, and explaining the categories of the general and particular, and so ash-Shafi'i wrote the *Risala* and sent it to him. When 'Abdu'r-Rahman ibn Mahdi read it, he said, "I did not think that Allah Almighty had created such a man!" Ar-Razi continues, "Know that ash-Shafi'i wrote the *Risala* while he was in Baghdad. When he returned to Egypt, he rewrote it and there is much knowledge in both versions."

In Iraq ash-Shafi'i began to disseminate the new system he had introduced. He expounded its basic principles, and, using them, criticised the existing positions of knowledge. He wrote books, sent letters, and men of *fiqh* studied with him. He remained in Baghdad for two years during this visit. He returned again in 198 AH, stayed there for a few months and then decided to travel to Egypt which he did in 199 AH. Why did he stay for such a short time in Baghdad on this final visit when it was the cradle of so many scholars? He had students and disciples there and knowledge was widespread in all its quarters. At that time Egypt did not have anything like the position with respect to knowledge that Baghdad had. It is a puzzling question. Perhaps the answer is that in 198 AH al-Ma'mun became khalif.

During the reign of al-Ma'mun there were two problems which the personality and scholarly method of ash-Shafi'i could not endure. The first was that power in the time of al-Ma'mun was in Persian hands because the battle between al-Amin and al-Ma'mun was in reality one between the Arab army, represented by al-Amin and his generals, and the army of al-Ma'mun, the commanders of whose army were all Persian. The battle ended in the victory of the Persians, which in turn gave them substantial influence and effective power. The Qurayshite ash-Shafi'i was not content to reside in the shadow of a power which was Persian in its influence and tone.

The second was that al-Ma'mun was a theologian and philosopher and brought the Mu'tazilites close to him, appointing some of them as his scribes, chamberlains and companions. Ash-Shafi'i was averse to the Mu'tazilites and their scholastic methods. He handed down punishment to some people who delved into speculative questions as they did and spoke about matters of faith in the manner in which they did. So someone like ash-Shafi'i was not content to remain in their company under the auspices of a khalif who raised them to a position that eventually led him to impose on the *fuqaha'* and *hadith* scholars an inquisition which Islamic history describes as the Trial of the "Creation of the Qur'an".

It is reported that al-Ma'mun offered to appoint ash-Shafi'i *qadi* but he excused himself. Not being prepared to remain in Baghdad he had to move from there, but he found no suitable place to emigrate to except Egypt, whose governor was an Abbasid of Hashimi descent. Yaqut states in his *Collection*, "The reason why he went to Egypt was that al-'Abbas ibn 'Abdullah ibn al-Abbas ibn Musa, who was al-Ma'mun's governor in Egypt, invited him to go there." So ash-Shafi'i went to Egypt and obtained wealth from the share of his relatives by virtue of being a *sharif*. He gained success through the spread of his knowledge, opinion and *fiqh*. Finally he died and was buried in Fustat, dying at the end of the night on the last day of Rajab in 204 AH at the age of 54.

Before concluding the discussion on the life of ash-Shafi'i, it is important to mention one particular scholarly turning point in his life. Before ash-Shafi'i came to Baghdad in 195 AH, while he was studying in Makka, he developed a new system of *fiqh* and new opinions which were distinct from the opinions of Malik. Yet he did not criticise or Malik's opinions or say that they were wrong. He presented his opinions, whether or not they differed from those of Malik, without any criticism of him. That is because he was considered to be one of the companions of Malik, whether some of his opinions differed from his a little or much. Some of the companions of Malik differed from Malik, just as some of the companions of Abu Hanifa differed from their shaykh.

But something occurred that compelled ash-Shafi'i to criticise the views of his shaykh. He heard that in some Muslim lands Malik's relics and clothes were being sanctified and that some Muslims would hear a *hadith* of the Messenger of Allah, may Allah bless him and grant him peace, and oppose it on account of something that Malik had said. This provoked ash-Shafi'i because he thought that some people were attributing to the statements of Malik a rank which should be reserved for the *hadiths* of the Messenger of Allah. He considered this dangerous because people were contradicting *hadiths* of the Messenger of Allah with statements of people who might be either right or wrong. It was not proper for anyone to accept anyone's opinion in preference to a *hadith*. That is why ash-Shafi'i was caller "the Helper of *Hadith*" by scholars in his time: because he supported the *hadith*.

This led him to criticise some of the views of Malik and state that they were wrong, so that people would know that Malik was a mortal who could be right or wrong and that his opinion counted for nothing in the face of a sound *hadith*. He wrote a book on the subject, entitled *"The Disagreement with Malik"*. But he hesitated to make it public out of loyalty to Malik, his shaykh and teacher, for throughout his life he had called Malik "the Teacher". He hesitated to point out to people what he saw as Malik's error, but at the same time he feared for the *Sunna* because of the sanctification of Malik. So he withheld the book for a year, hesitating and then he did an *istikhara* prayer for guidance before making it public.

Ar-Razi reports: "Ash-Shafi'i wrote the book on Malik because he had heard that in Andalusia Malik's cap was used for seeking rain and that when people were told, 'The Messenger of Allah, may Allah bless him and grant him peace, said...' they would reply, 'Malik said...' Ash-Shafi'i said, 'Malik is a human being. He can err and make mistakes.' It was that which led ash-Shafi'i to write the book on Malik. He used to say, 'I was reluctant to do so and performed the *istikhara* prayer about it for a year.' Ar-Rabi' said, 'I heard ash-Shafi'i say, "I came to Egypt and did not know that Malik took a contrary position to the *hadiths* in his possession except in sixteen instances. When I examined it I saw that he spoke by the root and ignored the branch, and spoke by the branch and ignored the root."'"

Ash-Shafi'i differed from Malik, but he only did so for the sake of Allah. He endured much trouble and difficulty on that account. If Malik had been in Egypt, he would have occupied the foremost position among the *mujtahids* and so the Malikis attacked and criticised ash-Shafi'i. Some of them went to the governor to ask him to expel him. Ar-Razi says about that: "When ash-Shafi'i wrote his book on Malik, the people of Malik went to the ruler and asked him to expel ash-Shafi'i. Ash-Shafi'i had not only criticised the opinions of Malik but he had also previously criticised the opinions of the Iraqis: Abu Hanifa, his followers, and other *fuqaha'* of Iraq. He mentioned their disagreements and said that some of their opinions were wrong. He mentioned the inconsistencies of al-Awza'i and criticised his opinion about certain behaviour. Each of those had supporters among the men of *fiqh* in their time who were their partisans and defended them."

Because of his criticism of them, a flood of debate and argument burst in on ash-Shafi'i. He used to debate and argue, basing his arguments and debate on clear evidence alone without speaking ill of the person with the opinion, until this process led him to become someone with a specific legal philosophy. Ahmad ibn Hanbal said about him, "Ash-Shafi'i was a philosopher as regards four matters: language, the disagreements of people, meanings and *fiqh*."

When he set down the principles and rules of *fiqh*, he found that some of the *fuqaha'* among the Hijazis went beyond these principles and were not limited by them, including his shaykh. He found that Malik took the root and ignored the branch and took the branch and ignored the root. So he argued with the people of the Hijaz and he spent all his life in the defence of the *fiqh* of the *Shari'a* and for the path of the Truth, so that some historians thought that his death was caused by the intensity of his struggle to see the truth prevail.[1] He was truly the Imam of the *Shari'a* in his time.

---

1. One of the Malikis, Fityan, debated with ash-Shafi'i and lost. Being an intemperate individual, he resorted to abuse and was disgraced by the governor on that account. Fityan's followers resorted to violence and attacked ash-Shafi'i after one of his circles. He was taken to his home and remained unwell until he died.

Chapter Two
Ash-Shafi'i's Knowledge and Its Sources

In examining his life story we have already observed ash-Shafi'i's stages of development and his journeys and discussed their relevance to his life, but the sources of ash-Shafi'i's knowledge should be isolated and studied independently. Some of the events which happened to him were integral to the development of his *fiqh* and this *fiqh* is the core of the subject we are studying. His shaykhs, readers and the students who studied with him all agreed that he was a peerless paragon among the scholars of his time; and this testimony has been confirmed by history.

His teacher Malik praised him at a time when he was not yet fully developed and before he reached his prime. After reading the treatise on the basic principles which ash-Shafi'i wrote at his request, 'Abdu'r-Rahman ibn Mahdi said, "These are the words of a young man of great understanding." Muhammad ibn 'Abdu'l-Hakam was one of ash-Shafi'i's students in Egypt. He said, "If it had not been for ash-Shafi'i, I would not have recognised how to reply to anyone, and through him I know what I know. He is the one who taught me analogy, may Allah have mercy on him. He knew *sunna* and tradition; he had excellent character and eloquence and sound firm intelligence."

Ahmad ibn Hanbal said about him, "It is related from the Prophet, may Allah bless him and grant him peace, that Allah Almighty will send to his community every hundred years a man who will set its *deen* straight. 'Umar ibn 'Abdu'l-'Aziz was the man at the end of the first hundred years and I hope that ash-Shafi'i will be the one at the end of the next hundred." According to Da'ud ibn 'Ali az-Zahiri, "Ash-Shafi'i possessed virtues which no one else possessed: noble lineage, sound *deen* and doctrine, generosity, knowledge of sound and weak *hadith*, the abrogating and abrogated, memorisation of the Book and *Sunna,* the lives of the khalifs, and good handwriting."

These are some of the testimonies to ash-Shafi'i's position in knowledge in his time in the books on his virtues and biographies. We will leave these testimonies aside, even those that are noteworthy, because their authors may be prone to partiality and are necessarily biased against those who say the opposite. The testimony which has stronger force is what he himself left: transmitted statements, *fatwas*, treatises, books, arguments and debates. All of these contain evidence of his knowledge, his immense gifts, the breadth of his *fiqh*, the eloquence of his exposition, and the strength of his heart. He was greater than a mere writer and more than just a *faqih*.

He had knowledge of Arabic and knowledge of writing and so he understood its meaning, secrets and aims. He conveyed a taste of that in his lessons. One of his students said, "When ash-Shafi'i began *tafsir*, it was as if he were witnessing the Revelation." He had knowledge of *hadith,* memorised the *Muwatta'* of Malik, and was meticulous in the rules of the *Sunna* and understanding of its goals and stated them. He knew the abrogating and abrogated texts of the *Sunna* and knew the *fiqh* of opinion and analogy and laid out the rules for making analogy and listed the criteria needed to recognise when it is sound or faulty.

Ash-Shafi'i used to say, "Whoever learns the Qur'an has immense value. Whoever cites *hadith* strengthens his proof. Whoever studies *fiqh* has noble stature. Whoever examines language refines his nature. Whoever considers the Reckoning has sound opinion. Whoever does not protect himself does not benefit from his knowledge."

His circle of knowledge involved investigation into a number of sciences. Ar-Rabi' ibn Sulayman said, "Ash-Shafi'i used to sit in his circle when he had prayed *Subh*, and the students of the Qur'an would come to him. When the sun rose, they arose and left and the students of *hadith* came to him to ask him to explain them and their meanings. When the sun was high, they left. Then there was a circle of debate and analysis. When mid-morning came, it dispersed and the students of Arabic, poetry, prose and grammar came, and they continued until it was close to midday."

How did ash-Shafi'i acquire this huge body of knowledge and what enabled him to have this incomparable scholastic position and such a profound effect on his generation that he became the axis about which they revolved? There are four elements which affect a person's acquisition of knowledge. The first is the one on which all the other elements depend: the gifts, predisposition and aptitude of the person concerned. The second is those directors and shaykhs who establish a path for him among the various paths and methods of knowledge and prescribe lines of research which become indelibly stamped on him. The third is his own life, experiences and personal situation. The fourth is the age in which he lives and the intellectual environment which nurtures him.

We will discuss each of these elements in respect of ash-Shafi'i, for they all had an effect on his formation.

His Gifts

Allah gave ash-Shafi'i great natural gifts which put him in the first rank of the leaders of thought and opinion. He had strong mental powers and faculties. He was quick-witted and ideas came to him when he needed them. He was very good at explaining himself and was known for his clear expression, eloquent language and fine exposition, and he had a voice which had a profound effect on his listeners. The first time ash-Shafi'i met Malik, Malik asked him to read the *Muwatta'* to some of his companions and ash-Shafi'i said, "I will read a page to you." When he read the page, Malik wanted him to read on and on because of the profound effect of his voice. When he recited the Qur'an, his listeners used to weep.

Ash-Shafi'i had penetrating insight into people's characters and like his shaykh Malik he had strong *firasa* (insight into character) enabling him to recognise the states of the men and what they were capable of. That is a necessary quality for a debater who seeks to bring his opponent over to his side; it is also necessary for a teacher, to enable him to instruct his students with as much as they are capable of grasping. Ash-Shafi'i's insight, together with his clear exposition, was one reason for the great number of companions and students that gathered around him.

It is related that when ash-Shafi'i arrived in Baghdad he only had six companions but the time came when he had to go to the Great Mosque so that there would be enough room for his teaching and when he was there, there was not enough room for anyone else to hold a teaching circle in the mosque whereas before that there had been about fifty circles, as is stated in *The History of Baghdad.*

His insight into people's states led him only to impart to his listeners knowledge which they were capable of grasping. Yaqut said, "He used to recite poetry from memory with some of his contemporaries, but would tell those who recited with him: 'Do not let any of the people of *hadith* know about this. They would not be able to bear it.'"

Ash-Shafi'i had a heart free of the impurities of this world which meant that he was sincere in his quest for knowledge and his desire for the truth. He sought knowledge for the sake of Allah alone, directed himself to the Straight Path in his quest, and sincerely directed himself to seeking direct knowledge of inner realities which come into the heart by the light of gnosis and create in the soul a purity which makes the realities clear, the intellect perceptive and thought direct.

Ash-Shafi'i's absolute sincerity was necessary for all levels of his quest of knowledge. When his sincerity caused him to go against people's generally held opinions, he boldly and forcefully publicly announced his own opinion. He saw the high position of 'Ali both in history and also in the reports of the Companions and he continued to uphold this so that he was accused of being a Rafidite.[1] The more he proclaimed the truth and knowledge the more accusations he received. His judgement was that all those who rebelled against 'Ali were rebels. He also mentioned the

1. A term used for those Shi'ites who reject and display great hostility towards Abu Bakr and 'Umar as well as 'Uthman.

excellence of Abu Bakr and was accused of being a Nasibite.[1] He did not pay any attention to this, just as he had paid no attention to the first accusation. He said:

> I preferred 'Ali, so that makes me a Rafidite
>   according to those who are ignorant.

> When I mentioned the excellence of Abu Bakr,
>   I was accused of being a Nasibite on that account.

> So I continue to be both Rafidite and Nasibite,
>   holding to this until I am buried in the sands.

When ash-Shafi'i's loyalty to his shaykhs conflicted with his perception of the truth, he preferred the truth. His loyalty to Malik did not prevent him from opposing him; nor did his loyalty to Muhammad ibn al-Hasan prevent from debating with him so effectivenely that he triumphed over his followers, causing them to consider him one the people of the Hijaz and to call him the 'Helper of *Hadith*'. He was like at every stage of his quest for knowledge, seeking illumination by true sincere devotion to the truth for the sake of the truth. So he came to his debates with absolute sincerity and overcame so long as the truth was his goal.

Ash-Shafi'i believed that the basis of the Islamic *Shari'a* was the Book of Allah and the *Sunna* of His Messenger and he never believed that he had encompassed complete knowledge of the *Sunna* of the Messenger of Allah. He encouraged his companions to seek out *hadith* and, if they thought they were sound and contrary to what he stated, to reject his opinion and take the *hadith*. Yaqut reports from ar-Rabi' ibn Sulayman, "When a man asked ash-Shafi'i about something and said, 'It is related that the Messenger of Allah said such-and-such' he asked ash-Shafi'i, 'Abu 'Abdullah, do you also say this?' Ash-Shafi'i trembled, turned pale and his countenance changed. I heard him say, 'What earth will harbour me and what heaven will shade me if you relate

---

1. One of a group of people who do not like 'Ali or his family; they are the counterpart of the Rafidites.

from the Messenger of Allah, may Allah bless him and grant him peace, and I do not say, "Yes, with all my being"?'"

Ar-Rabi' also said, "I heard ash-Shafi'i state, 'There is no one who does not forget some of the *Sunna* of the Messenger of Allah. Whenever I say a word or establish a principle and what I said differs from the Messenger of Allah, the proper position is whatever the Messenger of Allah said, may Allah bless him and grant him peace, and it is my position.' He repeated these words."

There is another type of sincerity by which Allah singles out the elect of His slaves who are models and paradigms for other people. It is complete devotion to a high ideal. Sincerity of this kind is elevated and hard to attain and is a rare quality. Those who compete in debate, argue using proofs, and try to outdo each other by producing evidence, are almost always prone to arrogance and love of prominence. But ash-Shafi'i was a rare exception to this rule. That is why he did not get angry in an argument or become overbearing with a sharp tongue in an encounter. He desired only the truth when he argued and did not desire elevation. He had no concern for rank in knowledge. He simply wanted people to benefit by his knowledge without his having any concern about whether it was ascribed to him or not.

Ibn Kathir states that ash-Shafi'i used to say, "I want people to learn this knowledge and for none of it to be ascribed to me so that they may be rewarded for it and not praise me. Then by my sincerity I will have acquired intelligence, nobility and strength of self and be far from base things and above anything which does not befit a complete man." Yahya ibn Ma'in said in his description, "Even if lying were permitted, his manliness would have prevented him from doing it. This is the noblest thing that a truthful sincere person can achieve."

His shaykhs

Ash-Shafi'i learned *fiqh* and *hadith* from shaykhs who lived far apart and whose methods varied. Some of them were Mu'tazilites interested in the science of *kalam* whose study ash-Shafi'i forbade.

He obtained the good that each possessed and took from them what he thought should be taken, leaving aside what he thought should be rejected. He received knowledge from shaykhs in Makka, Madina, Yemen and Iraq.

Ar-Razi gives the names of some of them as follows, "Know that the shaykhs from whom he related were numerous. We will mention the most famous of them. There were nineteen whose discipline was *fiqh* and *fatwa*: five in Makka, six in Madina, four from Yemen and four Iraqis. Those in Makka were Sufyan ibn 'Uyayna, Muslim ibn Khalid az-Zanji, Sa'id ibn Salim al-Qaddah, Da'ud ibn 'Abdi'r-Rahman al-'Attar, and 'Abdu'l-Hamid ibn 'Abdi'l-'Aziz ibn Abi Rawwad. Those of the people of Madina were Malik ibn Anas, Ibrahim ibn Sa'd al-Ansari, 'Abdu'l-Aziz ibn Muhammad ad-Darwardi, Ibrahim ibn Abi Yahya al-Usami, Muhammad ibn Abi Sa'id ibn Abi Fudayk, and 'Abdullah ibn Nafi' as-Sa'igh, the companion of Ibn Abi Dhu'ayb. Those of Yemen were Mutarrif ibn Mazin, Hisham ibn Yusuf, the Qadi of San'a, 'Umar ibn Abi Salama, the companion of al-Awza'i, and Yahya ibn Hassan, the companion of al-Layth ibn Sa'd. Those from Iraq were Waki' ibn al-Jarrah and Abu Usama Hammad ibn Usama of Kufa, and Isma'il ibn 'Ulayya and 'Abdu'l-Wahhab ibn 'Abdi'l-Majid of Basra."

Ash-Shafi'i heard the books of Muhammad ibn al-Hasan directly from him and he related *hadiths* from him and learned the *fiqh* of the people of Iraq with him. So he was also one of his teachers. Ar-Razi refused to mention that, out of partisanship; but knowledge cannot be made subject to partisanship.

This tells us that ash-Shafi'i learned knowledge from a number of shaykhs with different schools and leanings. We may say that he learned the *fiqh* of most of the schools existing in his time. He learned Malik's *fiqh* with him and he was his Teacher and "the Luminous Star" among his shaykhs. He learned the *fiqh* of al-Awza'i from his companion, 'Umar ibn Abi Salam. He learned the *fiqh* of al-Layth ibn Sa'd, the *faqih* of Egypt, from his companion Yahya ibn Hassan. Then he learned the *fiqh* of Abu Hanifa and his students from Muhammad ibn al-Hasan.

Thus he knew the *fiqh* of Makka, Madina, Syria, Egypt and Iraq. He saw no see any harm in seeking *fiqh* from someone who was known for being a Mu'tazilite, even though he knew that in the fundamentals of doctrine he did not follow the course of the people of *hadith* and *fiqh*. This enabled him to formulate a masterly legal blend in which all the positions met in a harmonious balance in which those general ideas were fused together by ash-Shafi'i and presented to people in that splendid exposition and masterly form.

We cannot go into the details of everyone from whom he learned, but we must point out that some writers on *fiqh* have contended that in reality he took from only two schools of *fiqh*, each of which was established according to a particular method. All the *fuqaha'*, with very few exceptions, followed the path of one or the other of these two schools, not diverging from it significantly. One was the school of *hadith* in Madina and the other was the school of opinion in Iraq. We can add a third school: *tafsir* of the Qur'an. Ash-Shafi'i knew the situational exegesis of its revelation (*asbab an-nuzul*), the transmission of *tafsir* on the subject and how to understand the Qur'an in that light, the language of the Arabs, and some of their customs: that school is the school of Makka which Ibn 'Abbas founded.

In my opinion the factors which distinguish between the two schools are not opinion and *hadith*. What in fact distinguishes them is the method employed to come to a judgement, the way opinion is used, and the abundance or paucity of the *fatwas* of the Companions. It is confirmed that the seven *fuqaha'* [1] who were the teachers of Hijazi *fiqh* used opinion a great deal. Whatever the case, ash-Shafi'i took from everyone.

The school of the Hijaz was transmitted from Malik, who learned it from a group of the *Tabi'i't-Tabi'in*, who learned their fiqh from the *Tabi'un* who were renowned for their knowledge of the *fatwas* of the Companions and transmitted tradition and opin-

---

1. The seven *fuqaha'* of Madina were the early jurists among the *Tabi'un* in Madina who laid down the foundations of Madinan *fiqh*. They were Sa'id ibn al-Musayyab (d. 93 AH), 'Urwa ibn az-Zubayr (d. 94 AH), Abu Bakr 'Ubayd (d. 94 AH), al-Qasim ibn Muhammad (d. 108 AH), 'Ubaydullah ibn 'Abdullah (d. 98 AH), Sulayman ibn Yasar (d. 100 AH), and Kharija ibn Zayd (d. 100 AH).

ion as well. They had learned from the Companions who were following the transmitted method of 'Umar, Zayd ibn Thabit and Ibn 'Umar. If something happened, they derived the ruling on it from the Qur'an if there was one. If there was not, they derived it from a transmission from the Prophet. Otherwise, they made a *fatwa* according to what would serve people's best interests.

The shaykhs of the school of Iraq were the companions of Abu Hanifa who survived him. Abu Hanifa derived his knowledge from some of the *Tabi'i't-Tabi'in* who learned it from the *Tabi'un* who preferred the *fiqh* of Mu'adh ibn Jabal who used opinion after the *Sunna;* and they learned from 'Abdullah ibn Mas'ud who represented the method of 'Umar ibn al-Khattab.

Ash-Shafi'i learned the *fiqh* and *tafsir* of the Qur'an in Makka with those who still followed the method of Ibn 'Abbas which he established there. Ibn 'Abbas used to study the Qur'an to such an extent that there is a volume of *tafsir* ascribed to him. 'Abdullah ibn Mas'ud described him as the "Translator of the Qur'an." When Ibn 'Umar was asked about the meaning of an *ayat* he said, "Go to Ibn 'Abbas and ask him. He has the most knowledge of what Allah revealed to the Seal of the Prophets." 'Ata' said, "I have not seen any assembly nobler than that of Ibn 'Abbas, and he had the greatest understanding and was the greatest of them in fear of Allah. The students of *fiqh* were with him, the students of the Qur'an were with him, and the students of poetry were with him. All of them issued from one valley." Al-A'mash recalled: "Ibn 'Abbas gave the *khutba* when he was in charge of the *'Id,* and he began to recite and explain. I said, 'If the Persians and Romans had heard, they would have become Muslims.'"

Ash-Shafi'i grew up in Makka, whose scholars, or some of them, preferred the method of 'Abdullah ibn 'Abbas and his understanding of the *Deen*. Makka was where he was brought up, trained, and later taught and set out the ground-plan of his method. However, at the beginning he followed the path of Ibn 'Abbas. He raised himself on that model and followed in his footsteps. There was harmony between them and their predispositions were clearly close. The virtues of Ibn 'Abbas were much proclaimed at that time and scholars and historians related and reported them because of the position of the Hashimites.

Ash-Shafi'i was eloquent in exposition, as Ibn 'Abbas had been before him, and he was concerned with the knowledge of the Qur'an as Ibn 'Abbas had been. He was concerned with poetry as well as *fiqh*, which was also the case with Ibn 'Abbas. His lessons were attended by students of the Qur'an, students of *hadith*, students of *fiqh*, and students of poetry and Arabic, as Ibn 'Abbas's had been. So we can see that ash-Shafi'i took Ibn 'Abbas as a model.

Ash-Shafi'i, through his studies and residence in Makka, learned a body of knowledge which could not be found in either Iraq or Madina. By adopting the method of Ibn 'Abbas with his devotion to the study of the Qur'an, he developed a concern with what was *mujmal* (general) and *mufassal* (detailed), *mutlaq* (unrestricted) and *muqayyad* (qualified), *khass* (particular) and *'amm* (general), until it produced a new discipline for the *fuqaha'* of his time which they had not studied previously, even though they had all the material for it.

His private studies and experiences

A scholar does not derive his knowledge from his gifts and teachers alone: his private studies and reflection, his journeys and experiences, also have a tremendous importance in his education and a major effect on his writings and the fruits of his personal intellectual quest. While ash-Shafi'i was studying with his shaykhs in Makka and Madina, he loved to search and loved to travel. He went to the tribe of Hudhayl as a child and became eloquent in their dialect. He spent a lot of time travelling and stopped camping with them. So he had experience of the land of the Arabs, their customs and their character. It was among them that the Qur'an was revealed, and so some of their customs shed light on what is in the Noble Qur'an.

After that, he travelled to seek *hadith* and *fiqh*. He travelled to Malik and stayed with him. Then while studying with Malik, he travelled throughout the Arabian Peninsula in search of knowledge. After Malik died, ash-Shafi'i went to Yemen to occupy a post in local government. He was in Najran and studied the nature of the relationship between ruler and ruled, experiencing at first hand the relations and dealings of people with one another, and their customs and habits. All of that influenced his thinking on justice and his understanding of it and its effect on people. So his travels enabled him to formulate criteria for his deductions. He derived much benefit from travel, which is why he said:

> I will travel the length and breadth of the land
> and will obtain my desire or die in exile.

> If I perish Allah is an excellent Host!
> If I am spared I will surely return home.

There is no doubt that travel gives the *faqih* material and information whose very nature broadens the mind, increases discernment, sharpens the senses and provides food for thought through new impressions. Much experience of everyday events is necessary for any thinker who wants to set out universal principles. That is why many philosophers who dealt with effects of the human intellect travelled widely.

The journeys of ash-Shafi'i usually had a pedagogic aim, being for the most part connected to shaykhs and learning and teaching. In the course of his travels, he studied and attended various schools, some by actually listening to the one who taught them and some by reading books about them. He studied the school of al-Awza'i and recorded what was transmitted from the books of this school. It is stated in the biography of al-Awza'i that ash-Shafi'i debated the views of al-Awza'i, disagreeing with him on some of them and agreeing on others.

He studied the school of al-Layth ibn Sa'd to such an extent that it is related that he preferred him to Imam Malik in *fiqh*. He said, "Al-Layth had more *fiqh* than Malik but his colleagues did not establish it." Ash-Shafi'i could not have made this statement unless he had studied his opinions. He recognised the relative strength of opinions and what they indicated of a person's range of ability in *fiqh*. Without a doubt ash-Shafi'i studied the *fiqh* of al-Layth deeply.

Ash-Shafi'i then studied profoundly the *fiqh* of the people of Iraq. He studied the books of Muhammad ibn al-Hasan orally with him. He studied the books dealing with the disagreements of the Iraqis among themselves. Among them there was *The Disagreements of Abu Hanifa and Ibn Abi Layla,* by Abu Yusuf, setting out the conflict between the opinions of Abu Hanifa and those of Ibn Abi Layla. Ash-Shafi'i chose the opinions which he found closest to the truth.

In general, we find that ash-Shafi'i studied all the schools known in his time profoundly and sought guidance from them. His scholarly journeys prevented him from confining himself in his studies to those *fuqaha'* who obeyed the rulers. He also studied the opinions of the Shi'a and others. We find a trace of that in his praise for some of their scholars. Ibn Kathir reports that he said, "Anyone who desires *fiqh* needs Abu Hanifa. Anyone who desires *sira* needs Muhammad ibn Ishaq. Anyone who desires *hadith* needs Malik. Anyone who desires *tafsir* needs Muqatil ibn Sulayman."

Muqatil ibn Sulayman, whom ash-Shafi'i considered to be the Imam of *tafsir,* was a Zaydi Shi'ite. We find in the *Fihrist* of Ibn an-Nadim: "Muqatil ibn Sulayman was a Zaydite *hadith* scholar and reciter. He composed a large book of *tafsir*, a book on the abrogating and abrogated, a book on recitation, a book on the ambiguous expressions of the Qur'an and the answers of the Qur'an." So although Muqatil was a Shi'i ash-Shafi'i nevertheless studied his works, and as a result of his studies he encouraged people to read him and considered him an Imam in this field. This fact shows conclusively that he studied all matters relating to *fiqh* and *ijtihad* without confining himself to any one group. He was concerned only to gain knowledge, without paying attention to the particular leaning of those who possessed it.

Ash-Shafi'i studied everything that could be beneficial to a *faqih* who wanted to found a legal school based, and relying on the Book and *Sunna*. He studied Arabic language, the Qur'an, *hadith*, the transmissions of those before him, and their disagreements and

285

agreements, not confining himself to any particular sect, school or group. He undertook journeys for the sake of knowledge and to gain experience of people's natures, their states and the circumstances of their society. There are even some who maintain that he learned Greek; this is based on a report by ar-Razi of Harun ar-Rashid's questioning of ash-Shafi'i when he was brought before him. He mentioned that his knowledge of medicine included the teachings of the Greeks, Arab doctors, Indian philosophers and Persian scholars. But there is no independent confirmation of this.

Chapter Three
The Times of ash-Shafi'i

Imam ash-Shafi'i was born and lived in that part of the Abbasid era during which the rule of the dynasty was established and its power consolidated. It was an era in which Islamic life flowered. The period was distinguished by the revival of sciences, the awakening of Islamic thought and scholars borrowing from Greek philosophy, Persian culture and Indian sciences. We will discuss briefly the distinguishing intellectual and social features of this epoch.

The Muslim cities were seething with different cultural and ethnic elements: Persians, Greeks, Indians, and Aramaeans. Baghdad was the centre of power and the capital of the Muslim world. It was awash with different races and there were delegates arriving there from all areas of the Islamic world, each embodying the civilisation and feelings of his race. A society formed in such a manner is bound to have many incidents arising from the effects of the clash and interaction of the various distinct elements within it. Each incident had its ruling in the *Shari'a,* for the Islamic *Shari'a* is a universal one which deals with all matters, major or minor. The study of these incidents expanded the understanding of *fuqaha'* and opened their minds to solving problems and formulating the rules of the various branches of *fiqh.*

This was a period of active translation from ancient texts, which the Abbasid khalifs encouraged and stimulated. The Arabic language expanded with the influx of Greek ideas which came through a number of means. They came from Persian sources where people preferred Hellenism; from Syriac sources, as the Syrians were the greatest transmitters of Hellenism at that time; and directly from the Greek itself. Some of the new Muslims were proficient in both Arabic and Greek and translated some of the great Greek texts. Sometimes Greek philosophy was pure, sometimes clothed in a Persian garb, and sometimes coloured by the influences of Judaism and Christianity by way of Syriac.

All that had an effect on Islamic *fiqh*. That effect varied according to the strength of the intellect and the *Deen* of those who learned this philosophy. Some people had strong intellects and correct and true belief and so they mastered the ideas which came to them by the strength of their intellects and belief, and were encouraged and used some of these concepts to stimulate their thoughts and perceptions and to discipline their thinking. Some of them were not strong enough to cope with these influences and their intellects were unsettled by them, which resulted in intellectual confusion. Various kinds of scholars, writers and poets were overcome by those ideas and became bewildered and confused.

There were also *zindiqs* who propagated ideas designed to corrupt Muslim society, disturb the peace and undermine the Muslims. Some wanted to destroy Muslim rule and revive ancient Persian rule, as in the case of the revolt of al-Muqanna' in Khorasan against the Abbasids in the time of the Khalif al-Mahdi. The Abbasid khalifs unsheathed the sword against those *zindiqs* who rebelled – they flogged those who disrupted society and who wanted to circulate freethinking among the Muslims and to induce them to abandon the commands of the *Shari'a* and the strictures of the *Deen*. They gave rein to scholars to refute those who spread false doctrines among the Muslims with adulterated proofs.

Those scholars, who were the Mu'tazilites, countered them by making use of cogent proofs and strong evidence. The khalifs brought them close to them, joined their gatherings, and opened to them the doors of their palaces in the time of al-Mansur and al-Mahdi, and even more so in the time of al-Ma'mun, al-Mu'tasim and al-Wathiq. In the time of these latter three khalifs they acted as ministers, chamberlains and scribes. Indeed, al-Ma'mun considered himself one of them. He directed those scholars to refute the *zindiqs*, Magians and others who debated with them in order to defend Islam. This was one reason why they proceeded to formulate dogma and defend it with new means which were unknown in the manner of deduction that had been employed by the Companions and *Tabi'un*.

In doing so the Mu'tazilites borrowed ideas from philosophy to sharpen their weapons and support their arguments. Then they adopted their opponents' methods of attack and defence. Questions into which those opponents delved arose for them and consequently they became embroiled in philosophical questions which the Muslim scholars among the Companions and *Tabi'un* had never seen the need to consider. They discussed the will and actions of man and the power of Allah over them, and they spoke about the Attributes of Allah and whether they were different from the Essence or the same thing. While they considered such matters the *fuqaha'* turned aside, finding such speculative thinking distasteful.

In addition, such people differed in their deduction of doctrine from the path of the righteous *Salaf* and from the path of the *hadith* scholars and *fuqaha'*. Thus it was natural that these two groups who served the Islamic *Deen* did not meet, because their reasoning and the arenas of their thought were so different. The *fuqaha'* and *hadith* scholars learned their *Deen* from the Book and *Sunna* and their knowledge was based on understanding the texts of the Book and the *Sunna* of the Prophet. They derived their rulings from the texts or by *ijtihad* through opinion if there was no text. That is the furthest that they went. The Mu'tazilites sought to establish doctrine by purely logical criteria and to that end they used logic and philosophy.

This turn of events meant that people had to specialise in particular disciplines. Some had understanding of the texts of the Noble Qur'an and the *Sunna* of the Prophet and the deduction of Islamic law from or through them. Others undertook to clarify Islamic doctrine and to defend it by the means which their opponents used. To that end they used anything that would lead to victory in debate. However, some of the Abbasid khalifs tried to force scholars to accept the views of the Mu'tazilites regarding an issue which was known in history as "the Createdness of the Qur'an." Al-Ma'mun, al-Mu'tasim and al-Wathiq tried to force the *fuqaha'* and *hadith* scholars to accept the position of the Mu'tazilites on this and they used force against them. In this way the Mu'tazilites became the opponents of the *fuqaha'* and *hadith* scholars.

In the time of ash-Shafi'i, then, the science of *kalam* was based on the teachings and techniques of the Mu'tazilites. Ash-Shafi'i hated that science and was averse to becoming involved in it because he only knew of it in the form which he saw in the Mu'tazilites. So the effect of the Mu'tazilites on ash-Shafi'i was both negative and positive. Part of its positive effect was his method and strength in legal argument. He used to argue with some of the *fuqaha'* of opinion who were involved in Mu'tazilism, like Bishr al-Marisi, and they were very skilful in argument. Perhaps ash-Shafi'i studied their techniques of argument, how to approach the opponent, and how to produce evidence against him from his own words. That is one thing for which ash-Shafi'i was famous, and his books are full of it. In any case, the general ambience was one of argumentation and disputation.

The first Muslim groups who had resorted to force in an attempt to take power from the Umayyads – the Shi'a and the Kharijites – had dropped their swords and had lost their cohesion, and their seditions had died down. Those who followed those sects, however, moved from spears to pens and began to organise their opinions, record their arguments, and defend them with evidence and proof whenever the opportunity arose. So the schools of the Shi'a were formed: the Twelver Imamis, who had a distinct *fiqh*; the Isma'ilis, who had a philosophy and particular social customs; and the Zaydis, who had an immense body of *fiqh* which was studied at this time.

Among some Islamic works discovered in Milan are a number of lines ascribed to Imam Zayd (d. 122) which deal with *fiqh*. Whether or not their ascription to Zayd is valid, there is no doubt that the *fiqh* of the Shi'a was studied and known in the time of ash-Shafi'i. You can see in what we have already reported of the words of ash-Shafi'i that he was aware of the opinions of Muqatil ibn Sulayman, who was a Zaydi Shi'i; and there is no doubt that he had knowledge of this group, or at least of their *fiqh*, even if his name is not mentioned in his books.

One aspect of the attention that groups of people began to pay to the different sciences which they studied and debated was that scholars began to record what they learned. This is what distinguishes the Abbasid period. In the Umayyad era scholars received knowledge orally, especially where the religious sciences were concerned. In the Abbasid era knowledge began to be recorded, sciences became distinct from one another, and each science had particular scholars who were skilled in it and defined its rules. For instance, al-Khalil ibn Ahmad codified the metres of poetry and prosody, linguistic scholars produced rules for the science of grammar and morphology, and so on. The same thing happened with *fiqh* and *hadith*.

The *fuqaha'* and *hadith* scholars began to record their sciences at the end of the Umayyad period and during the period we are discussing. The *fuqaha'* of Madina collected the *fatwas* of 'Abdullah ibn 'Umar, 'A'isha, Ibn 'Abbas and the great *Tabi'un* after them in Madina, analysed them, and derived rulings from them. Similarly the Iraqis collected the *fatwas* of 'Abdullah ibn Mas'ud, the judgements and *fatwas* of 'Ali, and the judgements of Shurayh and other *qadis* of Kufa, and then deduced and extrapolated from them. In the Abbasid period, *hadith* literature expanded, with immense legal consequences. The Shi'a *fuqaha'* also began to record their opinions.

Imam Abu Yusuf wrote *The Book of Kharaj, The Book on the Disagreement between Abu Hanifa and Ibn Abi Layla*, and his refutation of the positions of al-Awza'i. Muhammad ibn al-Hasan recorded the *fiqh* of Abu Hanifa and his colleagues. In his *Fihrist*, Ibn an-Nadim mentions many books ascribed to Abu Hanifa and his people. When *fiqh* was recorded in the time of ash-Shafi'i, the *fiqh* of those before him and those contemporary with him already existed in writing. Thus the existing legal knowledge was fully recorded and he must have had extensive knowledge of it.

The Islamic empire stretched from Andalusia in the west to the kingdoms bordering China in the east. There were several Islamic centres and cities which had scholarly renown. Early on the Companions of the Messenger of Allah had dispersed to those cities, and each Companion had students and legal opinions in

291

keeping with the situation of the people of the cities in which they lived. Each city had its own social, commercial, and scholarly circumstances and sought to claim distinction through the great number of its scholars and *fuqaha'*.

There is no doubt that this situation had a great effect on *fiqh*. It also had a great effect on the education of ash-Shafi'i, especially as the *fiqh* of those cities was recorded and disseminated and scholars discussed it critically and thoroughly examined it in their debates. Ash-Shafi'i travelled to many of these regions, as he had travelled in the Arabian peninsula, including the desert, and to Yemen as an agent of one of the governors. He went to Kufa and Basra and debated with scholars there, learning from them and replying to them. His book *al-Umm* tells us that he debated with the scholars of Basra who denied that any *hadith* could be used as evidence. Thus he began to travel between Baghdad and Makka and he studied and read what the scholars wrote in every city and region until he put down roots in Egypt, where all this study and experience bore fruit.

The Abbasid khalifs had a religious position, even if they were immersed in luxury, eager for pleasure, enjoying forbidden things or some things which are not clearly lawful or unlawful if we accept the least hostile reports. So why did this corrupt dynasty still have this inclination? Because it was a dynasty founded on the basis of its connection to the Prophet, may Allah bless him and grant him peace. The authority of the Abbasids was necessarily reliant on the *Shari'a* since they were connected to the Prophet by lineage. Because of this religious disposition among the Abbasid khalifs, they brought scholars close to them, elevated them, gave them stipends, and made the scholarly way of life easy for them.

The scholars who were court favourites in the reigns of al-Mahdi, al-Hadi, al-Ma'mun, al-Mu'tasim and al-Wathiq were Mu'tazilites who were deployed to fight the *zindiqs* and the non-Muslims who attacked the principles of Islam. In the time of Harun ar-Rashid, the *fuqaha'*, *hadith* scholars and preachers were favoured at court, and it is reported that he imprisoned the Mu'tazilites and forbade them to occupy themselves with *kalam*. This may have been responsible for ash-Shafi'i's aversion to them in Baghdad under ar-Rashid. This lasted until al-Ma'mun tried to impose the Mu'tazilite position, as we already stated. Ar-Rashid's patronage of the *fuqaha'* had visible effects. He listened attentively to their advice and asked for it if they were reluctant to give it. He listened, even if the words were harsh and severe. He paid heed to Malik's advice to him and listened to others as well.

It is related that the Khalif asked ash-Shafi'i to advise him when he defended himself against the accusation of being an 'Alawite and successfully proved his innocence. Thus *fiqh* and the *fuqaha'* had standing in the time of ar-Rashid. That is one of the factors which encouraged *fiqh* and caused people of intelligence and nobility to seek it. The *fuqaha'* also had a good position in the time of al-Amin, even if he did not bring them near to them or listen to them as his father had done. They were not harmed in the beginning or middle of the reign of al-Ma'mun, but at the end of it came the whole business of the "Createdness of the Qur'an" which he innovated. At that point ash-Shafi'i was living in Egypt where *fiqh* and *hadith* had great prestige. The *fuqaha'* and *hadith* scholars there had high standing with the governor.

Scholastic debate was intense in the Abbasid era and it became the arena of scholarly rivalry, the field of competition for men of letters and an object of estimation for every masterly scholar. Every distinguished educated person wanted to use knowledge as a means to personal glory and research as a means to individual elevation. Debate was encouraged by the khalifs and they held gatherings in their palaces. Some of them participated in the debates and became involved, especially al-Ma'mun who had some knowledge of philosophy.

As well as those debates whose motive was desire for reputation and elevation, there were also purely religious debates stimulated by zeal for the *Deen* and for the school to which the debaters belonged. There were debates between *hadith* scholars and *fuqaha'* and the Mu'tazilites motivated by sincerity on the part of the *fuqaha'* and sincerity also on the part of the Mu'tazilites. Then there were debates between the *fuqaha'* themselves. During the *Hajj* to the Sacred House and in the *Haram* of the Prophet there were disputes between the *fuqaha'* and in other cities of Islam –

Baghdad, Basra, Kufa, Damascus and Fustat – there were debates between people of different orientations among the *fuqaha'*. Wherever the *faqih* went he would find someone to argue with.

The debates between them were not confined to unclear matters but sometimes involved letters and treatises. Malik heard that al-Layth ibn Sa'd in Egypt was not giving *fatwa* in accordance with the position of the people of Madina, the place to which *Hijra* had been made and where the Qur'an was revealed; and so he wrote to him on the subject. Al-Layth replied to him with sincerity and penetrating thought in *fiqh*. Al-Layth's letter reveals the legal bent of that time, and it combines the *fiqh* of opinion and *hadith*. It is quoted in *I'lam al-Muwaqq'in* by Ibn al-Qayyim.

> Peace be upon you. I praise Allah for you. There is no god but He...
>
> You have been informed that I have given *fatwas* different from those your community agrees on and that I must fear for myself because those near me rely on my *fatwas*, whereas people should follow the people of Madina, to which the *Hijra* was made and where the Qur'an was revealed. You are correct in what you wrote to that effect, Allah willing, and it came to me in a way which I do not dislike. No one is more strongly inclined than I am to prefer the knowledge of the people of Madina who have passed away and no one acknowledges their *fatwas* more readily than I do. Praise be to Allah, the Lord of the worlds, Who has no partner.
>
> As for what you mentioned about the Messenger of Allah, may Allah bless him and grant him peace, residing in Madina, the Qur'an being sent down to him among the Companions and what Allah taught them from him and that people became their followers, it is as you have stated.
>
> You mentioned the Words of the Almighty, *'The Forerunners, the first of the Muhajirun and the Ansar, and those who have followed them in doing good: Allah is pleased with them and they are pleased with Him. He has prepared Gardens for them with rivers flowing under*

them, remaining in them timelessly, forever without end. That is the great triumph.' (9:100) Many of those Forerunners went out to perform *jihad* in the Way of Allah, seeking Allah's pleasure, and they formed military garrisons and people flocked to them. They made known the Book of Allah and the *Sunna* of His Prophet and they did not conceal anything that they knew.

There were some in every group who taught the Book of Allah and the *Sunna* of the Prophet and exercised *ijtihad* in respect of anything which the Book and *Sunna* did not explain to them. They were headed by Abu Bakr, 'Umar and 'Uthman, whom the Muslims chose for themselves. These three did not neglect the armies, nor were they heedless of them. They wrote what was necessary to establish the *Deen* and warned against disagreement about the Book of Allah and the *Sunna* of His Prophet. They did not abandon any command explained by the Qur'an or carried out by the Prophet, may Allah bless him and grant him peace: they taught it and made it understood. When a command came, the Companions of the Messenger of Allah acted on it in Egypt, Syria and Iraq in the time of Abu Bakr, 'Umar and 'Uthman, and continued to do so until they died.

However, the Companions of the Messenger of Allah, may Allah bless him and grant him peace, disagreed in their *fatwas* about many things, as you well know. Then the *Tabi'un* disagreed strongly about some matters after the time of the Companions of the Messenger of Allah: Sa'id ibn al-Musayyab and people like him. Then those who came after them disagreed and they are present today in Madina. Their leaders are Ibn Shihab and Rabi'a ibn Abi 'Abdi'r-Rahman.

You are aware of this, having been present when Rabi'a disagreed with some of what happened. I heard what you said about it and what was said by some of the people of Madina – Yahya ibn Sa'id, 'Ubaydullah ibn 'Umar, Kathir ibn Farqad, and many others older than him

– until it reached the point where you were compelled to part from him because of what you disliked in what he said. Nonetheless, there is much good, intelligence, eloquence, virtue, and excellent method in Rabi'a. He also has true love for his brothers in general and for us in particular – may Allah have mercy on him, pardon him and reward him.

Ibn Shihab has made several varying statements which were sometimes contradictory. In spite of his excellent opinion and knowledge, it happened that when he wrote to us he would sometimes give three answers to one question which would contradict one another, not remembering the previous opinion he had given on it. This is what led me to abandon what you object to my abandoning.

You also know my objection to the Muslim armies combining the prayers on a rainy night. Rain in Syria is more frequent than in Madina as Allah knows. No Imam there ever joined the prayers on rainy nights, and they included Abu 'Ubayda ibn al-Jarrah, Khalid ibn al-Walid, Yazid ibn Abi Sufyan, 'Amr ibn al-'As, and Mu'adh ibn Jabal. We have heard that the Messenger of Allah said, 'Mu'adh ibn Jabal has the most knowledge of the *halal* and *haram*,' and it is said, 'Mu'adh will come on the Day of Rising one step above the scholars.' There were also Shurahbil ibn Hasan, Abu'd-Darda', and Bilal ibn Abi Rabah. Abu Dharr was in Egypt, as were az-Zubayr ibn al-'Awwam and Sa'd ibn Abi Waqqas. There were seventy of the people of Badr in Hims. In Iraq there were Ibn Mas'ud, Hudhayfa ibn al-Yaman, and 'Imran ibn Husayn. The *Amir al-Mu'minin* 'Ali settled there with an extraordinary number of Companions.

Another subject that you raised is judging with only one witness and an oath of the claimant. You know that it is still practised in Madina, but the Companions of the Muhammad in Syria, Hims, Egypt and Iraq did not do so; nor did the Rightly-Guided Khalifs, Abu Bakr, 'Umar, 'Uthman and 'Ali instruct to them to do so. Then 'Umar ibn 'Abdi'l-'Aziz came to power, and he revived the *sunan* – as you know – and strove to establish the *Deen* and find the correct position as applied by the people of the past. Zurayq ibn al-Hakam wrote to him, 'You judge in Madina by a single witness and the oath of the claimant,' and 'Umar ibn 'Abdu'l-Aziz wrote to him, 'We use that judgement in Madina but we find that the people of Syria are different and therefore we only judge by the testimony of two just men or one man and two women; and the prayers of *Maghrib* and *'Isha'* are never combined here on rainy nights.' Rain was abundant there...

I have heard something about some *fatwas* from you which are disliked and I wrote to you about some of them; but you did not did reply to my letter. I feared that it was burdensome for you and so I left off writing to you about opinions of yours of which I have heard and which I disapprove. I heard that when Zafar ibn 'Asim al-Hilali wanted to perform the rain prayer you told him to pray before giving the *khutba*. I made a strong protest against it because the *khutba* in the rain prayer is the same as in the *Jumu'a* prayer except that at the end of the *khutba* of the rain prayer the Imam switches his cloak around, descends and prays. 'Umar ibn 'Abdi'l-'Aziz, Abu Bakr Muhammad ibn 'Umar ibn Hazm and others prayed the rain prayer and all of them did the *khutba* and supplication before the prayer. That is why everyone thought that what Zafar ibn 'Asim did was weak and disapproved of it.

I have also heard that you say that two partners do not have to pay *zakat* unless both of them have the minimum amount on which *zakat* becomes obligatory. The letter of 'Umar ibn al-Khattab states that they must pay *zakat* proportionally if their combined shareholding adds up to the prescribed amount. That was done while 'Umar ibn 'Abdi'l-'Aziz was in power before you, and by others. It agrees with what Yahya ibn Sa'id says, and there were no better scholars in his time...

I have omitted many similar subjects, and I wish that Allah may give you success and long life for the sake of people's benefit...

This letter makes two things clear to us. Firstly, arguments between *fuqaha'* occurred in all branches of *fiqh* and that argument was prompted by desire to ascertain the truth, not by desire to defend a preconceived opinion. Such argument was governed by honest words, gentle speech and calmness and was far from whim, anger, acerbity and rudeness in which opinion was mixed with passion and in which truths would be hidden in the middle of storms of conflicting emotions, passions and selfishness incompatible with the truth.

Secondly, in his presentation al-Layth mentions the questions in which Malik differed from the opinion of various Companions and *Tabi'un*, and then chose among them those which he thought represented the majority opinion. This shows that study in that time included the study of opinions of the Companions, *Tabi'un* and *fuqaha'* of the cities, and that students compared them and chose from among them what was best for people and embraced by the majority.

One could refer to the time of ash-Shafi'i as the era of fruitful legal debate. It could be said that the Islamic *fiqh* which he produced owed much to these sincere debates. Questions arose which were analysed and debated and which formed the focus of the different positions of the *fuqaha'*. These debates recorded legal evidence and the principles whereby the various opinions were extended to secondary rulings. That is because when the *fuqaha'* wrote their books, with few exceptions, they recorded secondary rulings and judgements without mentioning their evidence and the principles on which they were based. When opinions clashed in legal debate, each debater brought his proof and explained his method. Debates, then, were the impetus from which the fundamental principles of the schools originated.

When ash-Shafi'i set down his school – or dictated it or it was reported from him – it had the flavour of debate because much of it was the fruit of debate. Ash-Shafi'i, eminent debater that he was, appears to have derived the maximum possible benefit from it in setting out the basic principles of *fiqh*. These different debates and comparison of different opinions influenced his thought and so he formulated the universal rules for deduction from these disparate elements.

Sunna and Opinion

From the death of the Prophet, may Allah bless him and grant him peace, until the time of ash-Shafi'i there existed a group of *fuqaha'* who were famous for opinion and a group famous for transmission. Among the Companions some were famous for opinion and some for *hadith* and transmission. It was the same with the *Tabi'un* and the generation after them and then the *mujtahid* Imams: Abu Hanifa, Malik and the *fuqaha'* of the cities. Some were famous for opinion and some for *hadith*. We will now briefly explain this.

Ash-Shahrastani says in *al-Milal wa'n-Nihal*, "Situations arising from acts of worship and daily life are endless. We know for certain that there is not a text on every situation, nor is that conceivable. Because the texts are limited and situations are not, *ijtihad* and analogy must be considered in order that every situation may be brought within the compass of the *Shari'a*. After the death of the Prophet, the Companions were faced with countless unprecedented situations. They had in their possession the Book of Allah and what was known of the *Sunna* of the Messenger of Allah. So in regard to the events which befell them they had recourse to the Book, and if they found a clear ruling, they carried it out. If there was no judgement in the Book, they resorted to the *Sunna* of the Messenger of Allah, and consulted the memories of his Companions to ascertain the ruling of the Prophet in similar cases. If there was no one who knew anything they exercised *ijtihad* in their opinions.

"So they proceeded to examine the case in the light of the Book, then the *Sunna*, and then opinion. 'Umar stated in a letter to Abu Musa al-Ash'ari: 'Understanding is something which reverberates in your breast which is not in the Book or *Sunna*. Learn similarities and likenesses, and form analogies on that basis.' The Companions used opinion, but disagreed as to how much it should be used. Some used it more often than others and some hesitated if there were no text from Book or a followed *sunna*.

"They agreed to rely on the Book and a known *sunna* if one existed, but if they did not find a known *sunna* the famous *fuqaha'* used opinion. If any of them were unsure about their memory of a *hadith* of the Messenger of Allah or of his *fatwa* about a matter, they preferred not to relate it but to give a decision by opinion, fearing that relating it might involve lies against the Messenger of Allah. They report that 'Imran ibn Husayn used to say, 'By Allah, I think that if I had wished, I could have related from the Messenger of Allah for two consecutive days; but I was deterred from doing so by men of the Companions of the Messenger of Allah who heard what I heard and saw what I saw, and who relate *hadiths* which are not exactly as they tell them. I fear that I might be confused like them.'"

Abu 'Umar ash-Shaybani said, "I sat with Ibn Mas'ud and a year would go by without him saying, 'The Messenger of Allah said.' When he did say, 'The Messenger of Allah, may Allah bless him and grant him peace, said,' he trembled and said, 'like that, or close to it.'" 'Abdullah ibn Mas'ud thus preferred to give a decision according to his own opinion and to bear the responsibility for it if he was wrong, rather than possibly lie about something the Messenger of Allah said or did. He said, after deciding a problem according to his opinion, "I say this from my own opinion. If it is right, it is from Allah. If it is wrong, it is from me and from Shaytan." He used to be elated when his opinion accorded with a *hadith* which one of the Companions transmitted.

A second group criticised those who gave *fatwa* by their opinion, saying that they gave *fatwa* in the *Deen* of Allah without authority from the Book or the *Sunna*. The truth is that the Companions found themselves in an impossible quandary resulting from the strength of their religious feelings. On the one hand they might memorise a lot of *hadiths* from the Messenger of Allah in order to learn the judgements from them, but then they feared that they might be inaccurate about what he said. As we read in ad-Dihlawi: "When 'Umar sent a group to Kufa, he told them: 'You are going to a people who are confused about the Qur'an, so they will ask you about *hadith*. Do not give them too many." And on the other hand, they could give *fatwa* by their own opinions and be in danger of making things lawful and unlawful without proper justification. Some of them preferred *hadiths* from the Messenger of Allah and some of them chose opinion when there was no clear precedent. If they subsequently learned of a clear *sunna*, they retracted their opinion. That was related of many of the Companions, including 'Umar.

After the Companions came their students, the *Tabi'un*, and two problems arose in their time. One is that the Muslims divided into parties and groups. The level of disagreement became intense and impassioned. They were severe with one another and started to accuse one another of disbelief, iniquity and rebellion, and to threaten one another and to unsheathe the sword. The Community divided into the Kharijites, Shi'ites, Umayyads and those who were quiescent in the face of the afflictions which occurred and far from sedition, not becoming involved in it.

The Kharijites formed different sects: the Azraqites, Ibadites, Najdites and others. The Shi'a formed into disparate groups, some of whom had bizarre opinions which took them outside of Islam, even though they pretended to follow Islam in order to corrupt people. They were not concerned with establishing the *Deen*, but rather with destroying its basis to restore their old religion and its power and authority – or at least to shatter Muslim cohesion or to make the Muslims live with intense seditions, and to extinguish the Light of Allah.

Madina lost the unique authority which it enjoyed in the time of the Companions, especially in the time of 'Umar which is considered the Golden Age of legal *ijtihad*. It was the home of the scholars and *fuqaha'* of the Companions. They did not leave it without maintaining a scholarly connection with it. They corresponded regarding problems which arose, because the *sunna* of 'Umar was to ensure that the Companions of Quraysh were kept within the confines of the Hijaz. The great Muhajirun and Ansar never left the boundaries of Madina without his permission and he watched over them.

When 'Umar died, they left for outlying regions. Each group of them had a legal school which was related from them, and the people of the places to which they emigrated followed their path. In the time of the *Tabi'un* there were students of those *fuqaha'* who lived in Madina or other places. Each city had its *fuqaha'* and their views grew apart as the cities were far apart: each adopted the customs of his region and had to deal with the particular problems which troubled his own region. So people followed the path of those Companions who were in that region and transmitted the *hadiths* which they reported and which therefore became current among them. Thus various methods of legal thought appeared, all derived from the Qur'an and the *Sunna* of the Pro-phet.

As we have seen, in the time of the Companions there were basically two schools. In one, opinion dominated and transmission played a lesser role, though if a clear *sunna* emerged opinion would be abandoned in favour of it. The other relied almost totally on transmission and preferred not to give a *fatwa* when there was no transmission, rather than risk contravening the *Deen* of Allah by opinion. In the time of the *Tabi'un* the gap between the two widened and those who preferred transmission increased their adherence to their path, considering that to be a protection from the seditions which had now become severe. They found safety only in holding to the *Sunna*. The others normally had much less recourse to the *Sunna*, which had in any case become subject to falsification in outlying areas, and because the new situations that arose and required rulings they tended to rely far more on opinion. In addition, new ideas assailed them through contact with new cultures in lands conquered by Islam; and many of the *Tabi'un* were non-Arabs, heirs to the ancient civilisations of their ancestors.

So the gap widened between the schools and they grew further apart than they had been before when it was difficult to distinguish between them. The basis of the disagreement was not concerned with whether accepting the authority of the *Sunna* should be accepted. It lay in two matters: the extent of the use of opinion, and secondary questions deduced through its use. The adherents of

302

tradition only used opinion when absolutely necessary, rather as a Muslim may eat pork if no other possibility exists. They did not look into secondary questions or extrapolate judgements for speculative situations which had not arisen. They only gave *fatwas* for problems which had actually occurred and did not look into hypothetical situations. As for the people of opinion, they gave many *fatwas* based on opinion whenever they had no sound *hadith* on the subject. They did not confine themselves in their studies to the deduction of rulings on actual problems but also posed hypothetical questions and gave judgement on them on the basis of their opinions.

Most of the adherents of *hadith* were in the Hijaz, even though there was some *fiqh* of opinion there. This was because it was the home of the first Companions and a place of Revelation and because many of the *Tabi'un* who resided there were trained by the Companions who made little use of opinion – although a few were students of a Companion who used opinion a lot and transmitted his opinions. Most of the adherents of opinion were in Iraq because they trained with 'Abdullah ibn Mas'ud, who refrained from transmitting from the Prophet out of fear of making a mistake but did not refrain from exercising his opinion. If there was a sound *hadith* on the subject, he referred to the *hadith*. There were also old philosophies and sciences in Iraq as well as the classical texts of Greece and Rome. Those who were influenced by this were comfortable with *ijtihad* by opinion, especially when there were not many *hadiths* among them to be consulted.

This process continued and in the time of the *Tabi'i't-Tabi'in* and the *mujtahids* with *madhhabs*, the gap became very wide indeed and disagreements became intense. When the two groups met each borrowed from the other. The people of *hadith* abandoned their former hesitation and were compelled to use opinion in some cases; and when the people of opinion saw the *Sunna* and traditions, some wrote them down and began to examine them, supporting their opinions with *hadiths* or leaving opinion aside if they had a sound *hadith*. This was the period in which ash-Shafi'i lived and studied.

Lies about the Prophet proliferated at the time of ash-Shafi'i because various groups defended their positions unscrupulously with words which led to the spread of forged *hadiths* which they espoused and spread among the Muslims. This upsurge in lies led to two things. *Hadith* scholars started to devote themselves to the investigation of truthful transmission, and to distinguishing the true from the false. To this end they studied the transmitters of *hadiths*, investigated their circumstances, learned those who were truthful and ranked them according to their truthfulness.

Then they studied the *hadiths* and compared them unquestioned elements of the *Deen*. Eventually some scholars recorded the sound *hadiths*: Malik and his *Muwatta'*, *al-Jawami'* of Sufyan ibn 'Uyayna, and *al-Jami' al-Kabir* of Sufyan ath-Thawri. The second consequence was that people gave *fatwa* more and more frequently according to opinion out of fear of lying against the Prophet or depending on something that might well have been forged.

This occurred mostly in Iraq because the *fuqaha'* there who transmitted from the Followers and the next generation were known for opinion and often gave *fatwa* by it. Ad-Dihlawi says in his book after discussing the adherents of *hadith*:

> Over and against them, in the time of Malik and Sufyan and after them, were people who did not dislike questions and were not afraid to give *fatwa*, saying that *fiqh* must be spread on the basis of the *Deen* but fearing to transmit the *hadiths* of the Prophet and attribute them to him wrongly. Ash-Sha'bi said, 'We prefer anyone to the Prophet (as authority for *fiqh*).' Ibrahim said, 'I prefer to say "'Abdullah said" and "'Alqama said".' They did not have the *hadiths* and traditions to deduce the *fiqh* on the principles which the people of *hadith* chose, nor were they inspired to look into the words of the scholars of other lands, collect them and investigate them. They believed that their Imams had the highest level of precision and their hearts were the closest to the Companions. 'Alqama said, 'Is there anyone more solid than 'Abdullah ibn Mas'ud?' Abu Hanifa said, 'Ibrahim has more *fiqh* than

Salim. If it had not been for the virtue of being a Companion, I would have said that 'Alqama had more *fiqh* than Ibn 'Umar.' They possessed intelligence and intuition, and their minds swiftly moved from one thing to another, enabling them to derive the answer to problems from statements of the Companions. Everyone is given ease in that for which he was created and 'every party rejoices in what it has'. So they formulated *fiqh* on the rule of extrapolation. The people of Iraq gave *fatwa* because they felt that it was their duty and the basis of the *deen;* at the same time they were afraid to report from the Messenger of Allah. They did not accept the statements of the people of other lands, and were partisan towards their shaykhs.

Whatever the reasons, the Iraqis made much use of opinion but the Hijazis and Syrians used it less. As we indicated before, the adherents of opinion and those of *hadith* agreed that judgement must be by the Book and sound *Sunna* but they differed. The people of *hadith* were afraid of opinion but not of transmission from the Messenger, and did not adopt opinion except when forced to do so by the fact that they did not know of a *hadith*, whereas the people of opinion were afraid of relating *hadith* but not of giving *fatwa* on questions which they could later retract if they later came across a *hadith*. The people of opinion also refused to accept weak *hadiths,* whereas some of the people of *hadith* accepted them. Imam Malik, the Imam of the people of Madina in that time, used *munqati'*, *mursal*, and *mawquf hadiths*, the practice of the people of Madina, *balaghat hadiths*, and the statements of the Companions before resorting to analogy.

In that time in which argument and dispute flourished, there was a group who denied that the *Sunna* and reports ascribed to the Prophet, may Allah bless him and grant him peace, could be used as evidence. Ash-Shafi'i mentioned them and his debates with them in *al-Umm*. There were disagreements about whether or not to use traditions as evidence because of the uncertainty about their ascription to the Prophet. In the time of ash-Shafi'i the schools began to come closer together because they influenced one another in their discussions and debates. Certainly Abu Yusuf accepted the study and memorisation of *hadiths* and their use as evidence.

We have briefly explained the difference between the *fuqaha'* of opinion and those of the *Sunna*. Was the opinion in question merely legal analogy, which is to relate a matter on which there is no specific ruling to another prescribed matter with a ruling since the same legal reasoning applies to both – or is it more general than that? Anyone who studies the meaning of the word 'opinion' (*ra'y*) in the time of the Companions and the *Tabi'un* will find that it is general and not peculiar to analogy alone. It includes analogy and much more besides. When we deal with the formation of the schools, we also find this general use of the term. When we focus on the time of the schools, we find that each school differs in the explanation of the opinion which it is permitted to adopt.

Ibn al-Qayyim explains that the opinion which was transmitted from the Companions and *Tabi'un* was what the heart saw after reflection, consideration, and seeking to identify what was correct when there were conflicting indications. The sources of the *fatwas* of the Companions and *Tabi'un* and those who followed their path show that the idea of 'opinion' includes all that about which a *faqih* gives a *fatwa* for which there is no text, relying in his *fatwa* on what he knows of the *deen* in a general way, what agrees with its rulings in general, or what resembles another matter for which there is a text when he connects like to like. That opinion includes analogy, *istihsan*, *masalih mursala* and custom.

Abu Hanifa and his adherents used analogy, *istihsan*, and custom, and Malik used *istihsan*, *masalih mursala* and custom. He was famous for the use of considerations of welfare. That is why there was flexibility and receptivity for all the affairs of people in different times although it was a school in which analogy was not frequent. Malik said that *istihsan* was nine-tenths of knowledge: but that was when there was no text or *fatwa* from a Companion and no precedent practice of the people of Madina.

Ash-Shafi'i came and founded a systematic method of deduction which allowed judgements without a text to be relied on and did not accept the previous latitude in the derivation of judgements. He thought that there should be no opinion in the *Shari'a* unless its basis was analogy permitting a matter without a text to be connected to the ruling on another matter with a text. In such cases, opinion had to be traced to a text so that there was no possibility of innovation in the *Shari'a*. As for general deduction and justification for judgements without a basis in a text with a judgement, he considered that to be innovation in the *Shari'a*.

That is why ash-Shafi'i said, "Anyone who uses *istihsan* has legislated for himself." He set out rules and criteria for analogy and defended and supported it so that he went further than the Hanafis in its formulation and affirmation. Ar-Razi commented, "The wonder is that Abu Hanifa used to rely on analogy, and his opponents used to criticise him for over-reliance on analogy, but it is not transmitted from him or any of his companions that he wrote at all affirming analogy; nor that he mentioned a judicial error let alone proof in its establishment; nor that he responded to the proofs of his opponents in denying analogy. The first to speak on this question and report proofs in it was Imam ash-Shafi'i."

The *fatwas* of the Companions and *Tabi'un* and the practice of the people of Madina

Both the people of *hadith* and the people of opinion were inclined to accept the *fatwas* of the Companions, because following is better than innovating and because the Companions had been present with the Prophet and so their position was more likely to be correct. They are the Imams who are followed. Most of the *fuqaha'* preferred their opinions. It is reported that Abu Hanifa used to say, "When I do not find the ruling in the Book of Allah or the *Sunna* of the Messenger of Allah then I can take the statement of his Companions if I wish and leave those of other people. But I do not disregard their words for the words of anyone else. But when it is a question of Ibrahim, ash-Sha'bi, al-Hasan, Ibn Sirin, or Sa'id ibn al-Musayyab, then I can exercise *ijtihad* in the same way that they did." Since that was the position of Abu Hanifa, the Imam of the people of Iraq, on the opinions and positions of the

Companions, others must have been still more inclined to accept their *fatwas* and what is reported from them.

Many *fatwas* of the Companions were transmitted at that time. The minds of the *fuqaha'* were focused on those *fatwas* and they used them as a model when exercising their *ijtihad*. They followed the same path as them, respected their opinions and relied on them when there was nothing in the Book or *Sunna*. When the Companions agreed on an opinion, the *mujtahids* after them were obliged to accept it. If one of them stated an opinion not known to be opposed, the majority of the *fuqaha'* accepted it. If there was a disagreement between them, many of the *mujtahids* chose from their opinions that which agreed with their own inclination, and they did not leave the framework of those opinions for any others.

The *fuqaha'* in the time of the *Tabi'un* and *mujtahids* acted like that, even if they did not consider those *fatwas* to be an independent principle or a legal rule in the *Deen*. Perhaps they did so because they saw that the Companions had witnessed the descent of Revelation of the Qur'an to the Messenger and must have derived their opinions from their knowledge of the actions of the Messenger of Allah, and no one is permitted to exercise *ijtihad* about a matter ascribed to the Messenger. So they did not consider the Companions' opinion to be mere legal *ijtihad*: it was closer to the *Sunna* than to *ijtihad*. The Companions are followed because they were the first teachers who spread Islamic *fiqh* in all directions. They were stars shining with the primal light of Islam.

Ash-Shafi'i came and studied with the shaykhs of the Hijaz and with Malik who thought that the opinions of the Companions must be accepted, and indeed that the opinions of some of the great *Tabi'un* should be preferred to personal opinion and, furthermore, that the practice of the people of Madina also should be preferred to personal opinion. Abu Hanifa, the Imam of the Iraqis, also preferred them and put them ahead of his own opinion. Ash-Shafi'i reported that he used to say about their opinions, "Their opinions are better for us than our opinion for ourselves." We read in *I'lam al-Muwaqqi'in*, "Ash-Shafi'i said in the first version of the *Risala*, 'They are above us in every science, *ijtihad*, scrupulousness and intellect.'"

308

Ibn al-Qayyim quoted the following from ash-Shafi'i's book *The Disagreement with Malik*: "Knowledge has stages: the first is the Book and *Sunna*; the second is consensus about what is not Book or *Sunna*; the third is the statement of the Companions which is not known to be opposed; the fourth is the disagreement of the Companions; and the fifth is analogy." The opinion of the Companions had its place in the *ijtihad* of ash-Shafi'i. We will elucidate that further when we discuss his principles. The *fuqaha'* of *hadith* used to prefer the opinion of the *Tabi'un* at times over analogy, while the *fuqaha'* of opinion took the position of their shaykh Abu Hanifa that he could use *ijtihad* as they did. Ash-Shafi'i was an upholder of the second method.

We now move on to the thing which Malik preferred and to which he held very strongly: the Practice of the People of Madina. He adhered to their practice because the Practice of the People of Madina to which *Hijra* was made and in which the Qur'an was revealed was a normative legal precedent for people, as he says in his letter to al-Layth. This issue was the focus of much debate between the *fuqaha'* of that time. Ibn al-Qayyim mentioned that Malik accepted the practice of the people of Madina, which was not binding for any of the other people of the cities and did not constitute evidence in the *Deen* that may never be opposed.

Ibn al-Qayyim said in *I'lam al-Muwaqqi'in*, "Malik himself forbade ar-Rashid to force people to act by his school when he resolved to do so. He said, 'The Companions of the Messenger of Allah dispersed in the land and each group of them had a knowledge which others did not have.'" This indicates that Malik did not consider the practice of the people of Madina to be binding upon all of the Community. It was his choice when he saw that it was the practice; but he did not say that in his land or anywhere else it was not permitted to act by something else. He mentioned reports that this was the practice of the people of his land, and he invoked the consensus of the people of Madina in about forty instances. These instances fall into three categories.

• Those in respect of which no one is known to have opposed the people of Madina.

• Those concerning which others differ from the people of Madina, even if the exact nature of their disagreement is not known.

• Those in which there was disagreement between the people of Madina themselves.

We have seen that ash-Shafi'i was a student of Malik and that for the greater part of his life he refused to oppose him publicly even though he might disagree with him. When he travelled to Baghdad for the first time in 184 AH, he was considered one of the adherents of Malik and he defended the *fiqh* of the people of Madina. On that account there were debates between him and Muhammad ibn al-Hasan. Since that was the case, he must have preferred the opinion of his shaykh regarding the practice of the people of Madina.

Several statements were transmitted from him about the people of Madina. Al-Bayhaqi related in his book *The Virtues of ash-Shafi'i* that Yunus ibn 'Abdi'l-A'la said, "In the course of a debate ash-Shafi'i said, 'By Allah, I give you only good counsel. When you find that the people of Madina have something, no doubt should enter your heart that it is truth. If anything comes to you, no matter how strong it is, for which you find no basis (in Madina), however weak, pay no attention to it.'" It is clear from this that he accepted the practice of the people of Madina. It is clear that he held this position before he had his own school in *ijtihad* and deduction. After that school was established, you will see that he did not put anything before the *hadith* except the Book of Allah. We will explain that point in its proper place, Allah willing.

The debate about consensus

As already explained, the *fuqaha'* adopted the opinions of the Companions when they agreed on an opinion and no one opposed it. All the *fuqaha'* of the Islamic community were in agreement on that – both the *fuqaha'* of opinion and *fuqaha'* of *hadith*. Then we see that Malik took the opinion of the people of Madina when they agreed on a practice and put it before a single sound *hadith* since he considered the fact that the *hadith* differed from the transmitted consensus detracted from it because of this unbroken transmission, based on the *hadith*, "My community will not agree on misguidance" and the *hadith*, "Allah has protected you from three things: from your Prophet cursing you and thus causing your destruction, from the people of lies among you overcoming the people of truth, and from your agreeing on misguidance." Thus consensus was considered to be authoritative evidence in the *Deen* and often used in debate.

Ash-Shafi'i accepted the principle of consensus. The people before him had used it constantly without defining its basis in the Book or the *Sunna*, which can in fact be found in the two *hadiths* which we indicated before. When ash-Shafi'i studied it, he said that it is clear that its basis is in the Book where the Almighty says: *"But if anyone diverges from the Messenger after the guidance has become clear to him, and follows a way other than that of the believers, We will hand him over to whatever he has turned to, and We will roast him in Hell. What an evil destination!"* (4:115) "Following the believers" means not to produce a statement different to that of the unanimous consensus of scholars.

Ash-Shafi'i found that legal facts obliged him to accept consensus as evidence. There was no way to avoid acknowledging that. But then he delimited it and formulated criteria and measures to reveal the falsity of an unfounded claim. He also found that the claim in debates that consensus existed was not founded on a scientific basis and that if the debaters were left holding to the positions they claimed, it would lead to confusion in knowledge and legal chaos.

Every partisan had his own idea and did not care for any evidence other than things which supported it. That is why ash-Shafi'i put consensus in the rank after the Book and the *Sunna*. In his view, no one could reject the Book or the *Sunna* – even a single report – in favour of consensus. He was severe towards those who argued with him using consensus to support their claims to the point that his zeal and vehemence almost led him to deny the very existence of consensus. He once said in a debate, "Claiming consensus is contrary to consensus."

Ash-Shafi'i says in *al-Umm:* "Is it not enough censure of consensus for you that no one after the Messenger of Allah has laid claim to consensus (apart from that on which no one differs) except the people of your time?" The debater stated, "Some claim it." He asked, "Do you praise what they claimed?" "No," was the reply. He said, "So how can you join in that which you censure in much of your criticism? Do you not deduce from your method that consensus consists in abandoning the claim of consensus? Do not think well of yourself when you say, 'This is consensus' and then find another of the people of knowledge who say, 'I seek refuge from Allah from this being consensus!' There is disagreement about what you claim to be consensus from all parts of the land or among most of those who relate it to us from the people of different lands." (part 7, p. 158) Ash-Shafi'i admitted the existence of some consensus, and did not deny its existence altogether. A debater once asked him in the middle of a debate, "Does consensus exist?" "Yes," he said "praise be to Allah: often in the sum of obligations of which no one is ignorant. That is consensus."

We shall now mention briefly the principles of ash-Shafi'i.

What is stated in texts

The disagreement between the *fuqaha'* was not confined to the bases, ranks and strength of secondary sources of evidence. It was more intense and deeper as regards the evidence of the basic texts themselves. That led to debates about the meaning of particular expressions and how to categorise their evidence. When the debates moved to the words themselves and what they meant, confusion vastly increased. The debate grew in intensity and reliance was placed on certain Arabic linguistic forms to define what was meant by them according to context and topic. So it was necessary to know what was meant by the "*sunna*" or the "usage (*'urf*)" of the Arabs.

For instance, the imperative in Arabic can indicate permission, direction, a command which is a recommendation, or a definitive command. When the usage comes in a Qur'anic text or Prophetic text, it can have any of those meanings, but will in every case be specified by linguistic usage, tradition, explanation of the Prophet, or the context. When Allah Almighty says, *"When you have come out of* ihram, *then hunt for game,"* (5:2), the use of the imperative in itself might imply permission, direction or command, but the context shows that before coming out of *ihram*, hunting is forbidden by the *ihram* of the *Hajj*, so what is meant in this instance is permission. That is how every 'command' must be examined.

This led to two types of dispute. One was about the weight accorded to linguistic usage and its evidence, some taking note of the context and others ignoring it. That disagreement concerned the understanding of the meaning of specific texts. The second was about the general rule concerning the imperative: does it basically constitute a binding command unless there is evidence to the contrary, or does it basically imply permissibility and direction unless there is specific evidence that it is a command which is binding or non-binding? Similarly the negative imperative (*nahy*) can denote actual prohibition, or it can merely imply dislike or even guidance. The context specifies what is meant. Hence scholars differed about specific texts and also disagreed about the basis of the evidence of prohibition.

Disagreement does not stop at the degree of prohibition but goes deeper and deals with the nature of the invalidity of a contract made in the face of a prohibition: is it null and void, or is a forbidden contract which is contracted spoiled to the extent that people commit a sin if they fulfil it? The Hanafis say that the contract is contracted but should be considered a wrong action. Others say that the contract cannot even be said to have been contracted at all. An example of that is when the Lawgiver forbade divorce in a particular state: if someone then divorces, does the divorce occur while at the same time constituting a sin – or does it simply not occur at all because the Lawgiver has forbidden it? The majority of the *fuqaha'* of the Community say it occurs but is sinful.

There were also disputes about fixing the meaning of something with more than one possible meaning. When the Companions and the *Tabi'un* and those who exercised *ijtihad* wanted to explain the meaning of *qar'* where the Almighty says: *"Divorced women should wait by themselves for three menstrual cycles (quru')"*[1] (2:228) some Companions explained *qar'* as referring to purity and some as referring to menstruation. The *Tabi'un* and *mujtahids* disagreed according to the disagreement of the Companions they followed.

There was also disagreement about the evidence of general texts which could be taken to refer to several different things, and whether it should be considered definitive or speculative. The same applied to combining texts when there were several on one subject, and to qualifying texts which were otherwise unqualified. There are many kinds of divergences of this nature. Ash-Shafi'i debated with *fuqaha'* on these subjects and then established his principles for deriving evidence from such textual sources.

A brief survey of ash-Shafi'i's time

The time of ash-Shafi'i, may Allah be pleased with him, was one in which various ancient civilisations came into contact with one another. The civilisations of India, Persia and Greece all met in one region under the auspices of the new *Deen* of Islam and a fusion occurred between those civilisations of distinctly different origins. The different strains came together in that one generation without confusion or conflict except in the case of a few people who did not feel at home and were unable to assimilate into that new situation. They wanted to unsettle and destroy it.

It was a time of much fruitful intellectual endeavour. *Hadith* scholars applied themselves to distinguishing the sound transmissions from the Messenger of Allah, may Allah bless him and grant him peace, and they set out rules and criteria by which reliable transmitters could be ascertained. In this way they removed aberrant transmissions, making it clear what could be used for evi-

---

1. *Quru'* is the plural of *qar'*.

dence in the *Deen* and what could not. Then they wrote down what they considered sound according to the criteria they had devised.

These different groups each used the tool of derived evidence to provide propaganda for their positions and each used the methodology it had devised to justify its own opinions. Every group had its legal school which it fostered and according to which it debated, and by which it established its principles using evidence from the Book and the *Sunna*. Ash-Shafi'i mixed with all the different groups, met with their representatives and debated with them to clarify their legal proofs and the evidence within their schools. He borrowed from other scholars anything he thought was sound and could be validly used for evidence.

Those *fuqaha'* and *hadith* scholars travelled far and wide in quest of *hadith*, *fiqh* and knowledge of the Qur'an. Ash-Shafi'i studied with them, especially in Makka which was a centre of learning where *'ulama'* from all parts studied, met and exchanged various scholarly views, debating in order to sift out sound opinions from weak ones. The Makkan *Haram* was where ash-Shafi'i had lived in his early youth and it was there that he began to study independently after his first visit to Baghdad when he studied with the people of opinion, debated with them, and listened to the books of Muhammad ibn al-Hasan.

So the early *fuqaha'* of opinion and of *hadith* met in one place and debated in order to ascertain the truth. Each of them took from the others while remaining convinced that they would never agree. We find that the *fuqaha'* of *hadith* used opinion and the *fuqaha'* of opinion strengthened their opinions with *hadith*, or corrected their opinions to coincide with sound *hadith* they had found – or else they turned away from some of those opinions because of *hadith* they had discovered.

All this came from the knowledge of the Companions who had dispersed throughout the cities of Islam in the time of the Rightly-Guided khalifs from whom the early *fuqaha'* learned. The *fuqaha'* of every place met and exchanged what they had inherited from the Companions, each having what he had learned and what had reached him of their knowledge. They studied those opinions and each *faqih* chose from among those opinions what was closer to

315

his predilection or stronger in evidence in his view, or what he saw was sounder for people in his area and time. Next, they debated about what each of them preferred. Then this *fiqh* was collected in books and recorded after the *Sunna* was recorded; but some *fuqaha'* had opinions other than those that had previously been recorded.

During this time there were also many debates, as we have seen. *Fiqh* began to take on a universal tone whereas previously investigation had been specific and a *mufti* or *faqih* would only give a *fatwa* about actual events. *Fuqaha'* now began to give *fatwas* about hypothetical minor cases and studies began to be directed to the principles on which those minor rulings were based. After that, they began to formulate the methodology to be followed and the ways in which different types of evidence related to each other. In debate the *fuqaha's* thought was directed to formulating the criteria of legal deduction and the principles of derivation.

They began to argue about which *hadiths* should be accepted: should a *mursal hadith* be accepted when there was a *muttasil hadith,* or only the *muttasil*? What is the position of the *Sunna* in relation to the Book and what is its strength? Does the *Sunna* merely expound the Qur'an or do its rulings actually add to Qur'anic rulings? Is it strong enough to abrogate some Qur'anic rulings? They began to speak about abrogation: "When does it happen? How does it happen?" Such were the universal themes which were debated. They disagreed about the methods to be used in approaching those themes, just as they had disagreed about the secondary rulings; but their disagreement in this case was not as frequent it had been in respect of secondary rulings. The strength of linguistic expression in evidence was examined as well as how legal texts are understood and rulings derived.

Ash-Shafi'i, as a man of that time, lived in the midst of that great scholarly turmoil. He was involved in debates and benefited the whole situation through the strength of his natural gifts and his profound studies which produced such remarkable results in scholarship.

The Sects

Ash-Shafi'i met people from various Islamic sects and he received *hadiths* from some of them and studied their opinions as we mentioned when recounting what he said about Muqatil ibn Sulayman. Hence it is appropriate to briefly indicate the sects which existed in his time, in view of the fact that he was aware of their opinions.

The Shi'a

The Shi'a were the oldest of the Islamic sects. They appeared with their political position at the end of the reign of 'Uthman and grew and flourished in the time of 'Ali, since when he mixed with people that increased their admiration for his gifts, the strength of his *deen* and knowledge. Shi'ite agents exploited that admiration and began to disseminate their sect. In the Umayyad period, when injustices were perpetrated against the descendants of Sayyiduna 'Ali and the Umayyads injured them, people's love and compassion for them increased and they saw 'Ali and his sons as martyrs to that injustice. So the Shi'ite school expanded and its supporters increased. The sect was based on two fundamental premises.

> • The khalifate is a matter to be decided not by the community but only by specific individuals. It is the pillar of the *Deen* and the rule of Islam. A Prophet would not ignore it and leave it up to the community to decide. The *khalifa* must be specified for them and is protected from major and minor wrong actions.

> • 'Ali was the *khalifa* chosen by the Prophet, may Allah bless him and grant him peace, and was the best of the Companions.

The Shi'a were not all the same. Some were excessive in their esteem for 'Ali and his descendants and some were more balanced.

The balanced ones were content to prefer 'Ali to the other Companions without declaring anyone an unbeliever.

The excessive sects of the Shi'a elevated 'Ali to the rank of prophethood and some of them even went so far as to deify 'Ali. Some of them claimed that God was incarnate in the Imams, 'Ali and his sons, in a similar doctrine to Christian incarnation. Some of them believed that every Imam has divinity incarnate in him which then transmigrates to the next Imam.

Most of the Shi'ite Rafidites agree that the last Imam did not die but is still alive and will return and fill the earth with justice as it is now filled with injustice. One group, the Seveners, claimed that 'Ali ibn Abi Talib is alive and will not die and another group said that Muhammad ibn al-Hanafiyya[1] is alive and being nourished by honey and water. Various groups claimed that certain prominent people were not dead or killed but were still alive.

The Twelvers say that the twelfth Imam, Muhammad ibn al-Hasan al-'Askari, called al-Mahdi, entered the cellar of his house and disappeared there when he was arrested with his mother. He is the Mahdi and will emerge at the end of time and fill the earth with justice, and they are still waiting for him. Every night they stand after the *Maghrib* prayer at the door of this cellar and they bring a mount, call his name, and call on him to come out until the stars appear. For evidence they adduce the story of the People of the Cave in the Qur'an.

Some extreme Shi'a combined these views with social ideas in a very corruptive manner. They allowed the consumption of wine and carrion, permitted incestuous marriage, and interpreted the words of Allah, *"Those who believe and do right actions are not to blame for what they have eaten provided they are godfearing and believe and do right actions, and then are godfearing and believe, and then are godfearing and do good,"* (5:93) to mean that the prohibitions, like carrion, blood and pork, are allusions to people who must be hated, like Abu Bakr, 'Umar, 'Uthman and Mu'awiya, and that all the obligations of the Qur'an are allegorical.

---

1. A son of 'Ali by a wife other than Fatima.

The Kharijites

The Kharijites were the most active of the Islamic sects in defending their doctrine. They showed immense zeal for their ideas, intense religiousness in general, and extreme recklessness in defence of their claims and ideas. In their position they clung to expressions which they took literally, believing that theirs was the pure *Deen* from which no believer could be permitted to deviate. Anyone who followed a different path was someone whose soul made him incline to lies and moved him to disobedience. Their attention focused on the words, "Judgement belongs to Allah alone" and they took it as their motto which they shouted in the faces of their opponents and with which they ended every conversation.

Whenever they saw 'Ali speak, they shouted these words at him and it is related that 'Ali said about them when they kept repeating it, "A true word by which something false is meant. Yes, judgement belongs to Allah alone but those people are saying, 'Amirate belongs to Allah alone.' There must be a leader for people whether pious or corrupt... Through him, booty is collected, the enemy is fought, the roads are made safe and the strong are made to provide for the weak – until the pious leader finds rest or the people find rest from the corrupt leader."

The Kharijites were carried away by the idea of being free of 'Uthman and 'Ali and unjust rulers until that notion overpowered their minds and perceptions and completely prevented them from ascertaining the truth. They sometimes acted with those who declared themselves quit of 'Uthman. Sometimes the disagreement was so intense that it led to a split with them. Ibn az-Zubayr rebelled against the Umayyads and the Kharijites helped him and promised to fight on his side. When they learned that he had not declared himself free of his father, Talha, 'Ali and 'Uthman, they left him.

They were so intense in their zeal and fanaticism that some have compared their behaviour to that of the Jacobins in the French Revolution. Sincerity for Islam characterises many people. Sometimes it is accompanied by a crazy fixation on one idea and this leads to misguidance in understanding the *Deen* and mistaking its aims. In their case the lives of any Muslim who opposed them ceased to be sacrosanct. An example of this is reported by Abu'l-'Abbas al-Mubarrad in *al-Kamil*: "A singular example of their behaviour is that when they captured a Muslim and a Christian they would kill the Muslim and spare the Christian. On one occasion they met 'Abdullah ibn Khabbab who was carrying a Qur'an and was accompanied by his pregnant wife. They said, 'That which you are carrying commands us to slay you.' After asking him several questions, they killed him."

The views of the Kharijites clearly show their thinking, and simplistic minds, superficial views and rancour towards Quraysh and all the tribes of Mudar.

• The first and strongest of their views was that the post of *khalifa* is to be filled by choosing any free, sane, healthy Muslim man who attends to the welfare of the Muslims. It is not for one group rather than another and someone can only remain as *khalifa* so as long as he establishes justice, supports the *Shari'a* and is far from error and deviation. If he transgresses, he should be deposed or killed.

• They did not think that any of the families or tribes of the Arabs should be singled out for the khalifate, that the khalifate should be restricted to Quraysh as others stated, or even that it should be for an Arab rather than an non-Arab. In their view all were the same. Indeed, they preferred that the *khalifa* should not be from Quraysh so that it would be easier to depose or kill him if he opposed the *Shari'a* or deviated from truth, since then there would be no partisanship to protect him, tribe to defend him, or shelter but the shelter of Allah.

• Najdite Kharijites thought that people did not need a *khalifa* at all. Muslims should be equitable in their mutual dealings. They thought that if that could only be achieved by means of having a *khalifa* to encourage them to uphold the truth and establish it, then it was permitted. But in their view the existence of a *khalifa* was not an necessary obligation but was merely permitted when needed for public welfare.

• The Kharijites thought that people who committed wrong actions were unbelievers. They did not differentiate between a sin which was done with an evil intention and an error of opinion or *ijtihad* which led to something incorrect. That is why they said that 'Ali was an unbeliever when he agreed to arbitration although it was not his choice. If arbitration was not correct, then the fact that they needed to say that 'Ali was an unbeliever indicates that they considered that an error in *ijtihad* brings a person out of the *deen*. That was also their view of Talha, az-Zubayr, 'Uthman and other great Companions who differed from them in minor matters: they held that they were unbelievers. They had various justifications for this which were based on false interpretation of *ayats* of the Qur'an.

This is the sum of the opinions which most of the Kharijites embraced while they did not agree on other positions, opinions or views. They frequently disagreed on the even the smallest of matters. Perhaps this is the secret of the great number of their defeats. Al-Muhallab ibn Abi Sufra, who defended the Islamic community against them during the Umayyad era, seized on their disagreements as a means of dividing them. When they were not divided, he sent someone to them to provoke disagreement between them. They were divided into several groups.

The Azraqites. These were the followers of Nafi' ibn al-Azraq al-Hanafi, from the Banu Hanifa, one of the tribes of Rabi'a. They were the most energetic of the Kharijites, the greatest in number, and those with the largest army. They fought under Nafi' ibn al-Azraq against the Umayyad generals and Ibn az-Zubayr for nineteen years. When Nafi' was killed in battle, they were led by Nafi' ibn 'Abdullah and then by Ibn al-Faja'a. They became weak in his time because of people's hatred for them, their reputation for bloodshed and their internal disagreements. They were defeated on all fronts until they disappeared. Among their extreme views were considering the children of their opponents to be idolaters who would be in the Fire forever; cancelling the *hadd* punishment for fornication since it is not mentioned in the Qur'an, cancelling the *hadd* punishment for slander of chaste men while making it obligatory on those who slander chaste women; and advocating the permissibility of major and minor sins for the Prophets.

The Najdites. These were the followers of Najda ibn 'Umaymir al-Hanafi. They opposed the Azraqites in saying that quiescent Kharijites were unbelievers and that it was lawful to kill children, and they added that that it was lawful to kill people with a treaty and *dhimma*. They were located in Yamana. They were with Abu Talut al-Khariji and then gave allegiance to Najda in 66 AH. They became powerful and conquered Bahrain, Oman, Hadramawt, Yemen, and Ta'if. They then disagreed with Najda over some matters. One was that he sent his son with the army and they captured some women and consumed some of the booty before the division had taken place and he excused them. This disagreement led them to split into three further groups. One went to Sijistan with 'Atiyya ibn al-Aswad al-Hanafi, one revolted with Abu Fudayk against Najda and killed him, and one excused Najda. They continued to be called Najdites. Abu Fudayk led them until 'Abdu'l-Malik ibn Marwan sent an army which defeated him and his head was sent to the Khalif.

The Sufrites, who followed Ziyad ibn al-Asfar. They were less severe in some of their opinions than the Azraqites but more so in others. They disagreed with the Azraqites about someone who commits a major wrong action: they did not consider him a *mushrik*. One of them was Abu Bilal Mirdas, a righteous ascetic man who rebelled in the time of Yazid I in part of Basra. He did not attack people and he took from the khalif's property only what he needed. He did not desire war. 'Ubaydullah ibn Ziyad sent an army against him which put an end to him.

The 'Ajradites. They were the adherents of 'Abdu'l-Karim ibn 'Ajrad, one of the followers of 'Atiyya ibn al-Aswad al-Hanafi. They were similar to the Najdites in their position and views.

The Ibadites. These were the followers of 'Abdullah ibn Ibad. They are the most balanced of the Kharijites and closest to the ordinary Muslims in opinion and thought and the furthest from excess. They did not consider their Muslim opponents to be either idolaters or believers. They called them ingrates (*kuffar*), saying they are ungrateful for blessings. Their property was not held to be lawful as booty in war except for horses, weapons and military equipment and they return gold and silver to their owners. They allowed the testimony of their opponents, as well as marriage with them and inheritance with them.

There are also many other extreme groups of Kharijites.

The Mu'tazilites

This group originated during the Umayyad period and dominated Islamic thought in the Abbasid era for a long time. Iraq in the time of the Rightly Guided Khalifs and Umayyads was home to a number of ethnic and religious groups of different origins. Some were descended from the ancient Chaldean inhabitants of Iraq; others were Persians, Christians, Jews, or Arabs. Most of them became Muslims. Some understood Islam in the light of the ancient teachings of their own traditions. Some took Islam from its pure source and imbibed it without alteration. But even then their feelings and whims were not purely Islamic.

There was an involuntary inclination towards the past, of the kind which psychologists call "unconscious". That is why when there was much civil war at the time of 'Ali ibn Abi Talib in Iraq, the ancient sects were awakened and appeared in Iraq, gathering around the Kharijites and Shi'a. It was in this midst of this jumble of opinions and confused sects that the Mu'tazilites made their appearance.

Scholars disagree about when the Mu'tazilites first appeared. Some think that they began with the people of 'Ali who withdrew from politics and devoted themselves to the pursuit of knowledge when al-Hasan surrendered the khalifate to Mu'awiya. Abu'l-Husayn at-Tara'ifi said in his book, *The people of Sects and Innovations*: "They called themselves Mu'tazilites. When al-Hasan offered his allegiance to Mu'awiya, they withdrew (*i'tazala*) from al-Hasan and Mu'awiya and all people. They were among the adherents of 'Ali. They kept to their homes and mosques, saying 'We are busy with knowledge and worship.'"

Most sources state that the leader of the Mu'tazilites was Wasil ibn 'Ata'. He was one of those who attended the gatherings of al-Hasan al-Basri when a question arose which preoccupied the minds of many people at that time: the question whether committing a major wrong action makes its perpetrator an unbeliever. Wasil said in opposition to al-Hasan al-Basri, who had refused to become involved in the debate, "I say that the one who commits a major wrong action is neither a believer nor an unbeliever. He is between the two positions." Then he withdrew (*i'tazala*) from al-Hasan's assembly and set up another in the mosque. From this you see why he and his people were called Mu'tazilites. Certain orientalists, however, believe that they were called that because they were fearful pious men who withdrew from the pleasures of life as is indicated by their name.

In fact, not all the men ascribed to this group conformed to that description. Some were suspected of acts of disobedience and some were godfearing.

The doctrine of the Mu'tazilites

According to Abu'l-Hasan al-Khayyat in *al-Intisar*, "No one can properly be called a Mu'tazilite unless he holds all the five tenets of their school: *Tawhid*, Justice, the Promise and the Threat, the Position between the Two Positions, and Commanding the Right and Forbidding the Wrong. When a man has these five, he is a Mu'tazilite. These are the tenets of the Mu'tazilite school." We will speak briefly about each of them.

Tawhid

This was the core of their doctrine. Al-Ash'ari described their position in his book, *Maqalat al-Islamiyyin*:

> Allah is one. There is nothing like Him. He is the All-Hearing, All-Seeing. He is neither body nor spirit. He does not have corporeal form or shape, or flesh or blood. He is not substance or accident. He does not have a colour or taste, smell or tactility, heat, cold, wetness, dryness, height width, or depth. He does not have joining or separation, movement or stillness. He has no parts or components, or limbs or members. He has no directions: no right or left, front or back, above or below. He is not circumscribed by place nor is He subject to time.... He cannot be incarnate in any place. He is not described with any of the attributes of creation which involve contingency nor is He described as being finite or as being limited. He does not beget and is not begotten. No quantity can encompass Him; no veil conceal Him; no sense perceive Him. He cannot be compared to mankind nor does He resemble creation in any way... He was First before events in time and before contingent things, and existed before all creatures. He is Knowing, Powerful, Alive and will always remain so. Eyes cannot see Him; sight cannot perceive Him; imagination cannot encompass Him. He is Knowing, Powerful, Living, in a way dissimilar to all others who are knowing, powerful, living. He alone is timeless and there is nothing timeless but Him, no god but Him and He has no partner in His kingdom.

On this basis, the Mu'tazilites asserted that it was impossible to see Allah on the Day of Resurrection since that would involve corporeality and direction. The Divine Attributes were nothing other than the Essence. The Qur'an was created by Allah since He does not (in their view) have the attribute of speech.

Justice

Al-Mas'udi explained this in *Muruj adh-Dhahab*:

It is that Allah does not like injustice nor create the actions of people. They do what they are commanded or forbidden to do by the power which Allah has created for them and placed in them. He commands only what He wants and forbids only what He dislikes. He takes charge of every good action He has commanded, and is free of every evil action He has forbidden. He does not oblige people to do anything they are incapable of and He does not desire of them what they do not have the power to do. No one has power to withhold or give except by the power of Allah which He has given them and is in their possession. Had He so willed, He could have compelled creation to obey Him and prevented them from disobeying Him, but He did not do that.

The Jabriyya[1] refuted this tenet and said, "The slave (i.e. the human being) has no choice in his action."

The Promise and the Threat

This is that Allah repays all who do good with good and all who do evil with evil. He does not forgive anyone who does major wrong actions if he does not repent.

---

1. The pre-determinist school. They claimed that everything was predestined and man had no responsibility whatsoever for his actions.

The "Position between the Two Positions" (concerning belief and unbelief)

Expounding the Mu'tazilites' view on the "Intermediate Position", ash-Shahrastani said, "This position was stated clearly by Wasil when he said that faith designates the qualities of good and when they are combined in a person he is called a believer, which is a name of praise. An impious man does not have all the qualities of good and does not deserve the name of praise. Hence he is not called a believer – but nor is he an unbeliever absolutely, for the *shahada* and good actions exist in him which cannot be denied. But if he leaves this world having committed a major sin without repenting for it he is one of the people who will remain in the Fire forever, since in the Next World there are only two groups: one in Paradise and one in Hell. However, the Fire will be alleviated for him and he is above the level of the unbelievers."

Commanding the Right and Forbidding the Wrong

It is an obligation for all believers to disseminate the call of Islam, guide the misguided, and direct those in error as much as he can through both exposition and the sword.

The Mu'tazilites' method of deriving their doctrine

In explaining their doctrine the Mu'tazilites relied on reason and not transmission. They relied on the intellect, restricting its scope only when it was a question of the commands of the *Shari'a*. Every question was logically examined and they accepted what was logical and rejected what was not logical.

This rationalistic approach was the result of several factors: their residence in Iraq and Persia which were influenced by ancient religions and civilisations, their descent from non-Arabs, their clashes with opponents, the spread of translations of the ancient philosophers there, and their mixing with Jews and Christians and others who translated these ideas into Arabic.

One of the effects of their reliance on logic was that they judged that things were good or abhorrent by reason. They used to say: "All things are intelligible to the intellect and must be examined by the intellect. Beauty and ugliness are two essential qualities of good and evil." Al-Jubba'i stated, "Any act of disobedience which Allah can permit to happen is ugly because of its prohibition and any act of disobedience which He never permits is ugly in itself: like ignorance of Him and believing the opposite of that." They based on this the idea of the existence of the best of all possible worlds. They said that only good issues from Allah.

Their defence of Islam

Groups of Magians, Sabaeans, Jews and Christians and others entered Islam, their minds still full of the teachings of those religions, and their understanding of Islam was necessarily filtered through them. Some pretended to have faith out fear of the ruler, concealing their old belief, and began to try to corrupt the Muslims' *deen*, to make them doubt their own beliefs, and to introduce ideas and opinions for which Allah had given no authority. The fruits of their efforts appeared: there were anthropomorphists, *zindiqs* and many other groups. The Mu'tazilites tried to defend Islam and their Five Tenets were the result of their sharp debates with their opponents. The tenet of *Tawhid* was formulated to refute the anthropomorphists; Justice was to refute the Jahmites;[1] the Promise and Threat was to refute the Murji'ites;[2] and the Position between the Two Positions was to refute the Kharijites who said that anyone who commits a sin was unbeliever.

In the reign of al-Mahdi, a man called al-Muqanna' appeared in Khorasan. He believed in the transmigration of souls. A group went to Transoxania and al-Mahdi had to fight to overcome him

---

1. The followers of Jahm ibn Safwan (d. 128/745) who taught that Allah has no attributes and man had no free will of any sort at all.

2. Opponents of the Kharijites who held that it is faith and not actions which are important and so suspend judgement on persons guilty of major sins.

This encouraged the *zindiqs* and he had to seek them out to eliminate them by the sword. But the sword was not always sufficient to eliminate an opinion or kill off a school. That is why he encouraged the Mu'tazilites and others to refute their errors, which is what they did.

The khalif's patronage of the Mu'tazilites

The Mu'tazilites appeared at the time of the Umayyads but the Umayyads did not oppose them because they did not provoke any discord or declare war. They were a group who took no action beyond thinking, countering evidence with evidence and proof with proof, and analysing matters by sound criteria. They did not involve themselves in politics: their weapons were exposition and proof, not swords. Al-Mas'udi reported that Yazid II espoused their tenets.

When the Abbasids came to power, heresy and the *zindiqs* had become a flood and the Khalif found in the Mu'tazilites a sword to employ against *zindiqs* and left them to combat heresy. When al-Ma'mun came to power, he took their side and brought them near to him. He saw that there was a disagreement between them and the *fuqaha'*; and thought that debates between the two groups would result in the emergence of a single point of view; but he was completely wrong in this.

Al-Ma'mun then sought to use the power of the state to force the *fuqaha'* and *hadith* scholars to adopt the opinion of the Mu'tazilites on the Qur'an. This is not the proper role of the state. If it is forbidden to force people to embrace the *Deen*, how can they be forced to accept a tenet the denial of which does not constitute disbelief? He tried to force the *fuqaha'* to declare that the Qur'an was created. Some of them complied out of *taqiyya* and fear, not credal belief and adherence, while others endured violence, humiliation and long imprisonment and would not say anything other than what they believed.

That inquisition lasted through the khalifates of al-Mu'tasim and al-Wathiq after al-Ma'mun. Al-Wathiq tried to coerce people

329

to deny that Allah will be seen – another opinion held by the Mu'tazilites. When al-Mutawakkil came to power this inquisition stopped, and things were allowed to take their course and opinions to evolve naturally and people were left to choose their own position regarding these matters.

The position of the Mu'tazilites among their contemporaries

The *fuqaha'* and *hadith* scholars attacked the Mu'tazilites and so they were caught between strong opponents on either side: the *zindiqs* and those like them on one side, and the *fuqaha'* and *hadith* scholars on the other. One can see in the arguments and discussions of the *fuqaha'* that they pilloried the Mu'tazilites at every opportunity. One hears ash-Shafi'i, Ibn Hanbal and others criticising the science of *kalam* and those who took knowledge through the method of the *mutakallimun*. Why did the *fuqaha'* dislike the Mu'tazilites? Both groups were trying to support the *Deen* and did not spare any efforts in its defence. Its seems that there were a number of factors which combined to produce such enmity.

• The Mu'tazilites differed from the method of the righteous *Salaf* in understanding the doctrine of the *Deen*. For the *Salaf* the Qur'an was the only source from which the Attributes of Allah can be known and on which all the articles of faith are based. They do not take them from anywhere else. They understood their faith from those *ayats* of the Qur'an which are clear. Whatever was unclear to them they tried to understand through linguistic means. If they were unable to understand something, they stopped without seeking danger, deviation and travelling any path other than that of the Truth.

That was sufficient for the Arabs because they were people without sciences, logic and philosophy. The Mu'tazilites opposed that method and esteemed reason above all else. They made it the basis for their analysis and

330

used their intellects to work out every question. That brought them into conflict with the *fuqaha'* who were not familiar with such an approach.

• The Mu'tazilites debated with *zindiqs*, dualists and others, and every debate has its own kind of tactics and conflict. In debate one tends to use the means and weapons of one's opponent and studies his plans, ends and goal. All of that causes a person to be affected by his opponent's views, ideas and methods. The Mu'tazilites were influenced to a certain extent by the ideas of their opponents. Some Hanbalis complained that the process of refuting heretics led them into heresy.

• The method of the Mu'tazilites lay in defining the logical position. They did not rely on a text unless the topic of discussion was a legal judgement or was connected to a legal judgement. Consequently they mostly relied on the intellect and the intellect has its own shortcomings. Sometimes the inadequacies of the logical approach led them to fallacious reasoning.

• There were many opponents of the Mu'tazilites among men who held high positions in the Community.

• One of the Abbasid khalifs was a partisan and supporter of the Mu'tazilites and embraced their position. He wanted to force people to adopt it and so harassed the *fuqaha'* and *hadith* scholars and imposed an inquisition on them, but they remained steadfast. The inquisition made people sympathetic towards the *fuqaha'* and hostile to the cause of their afflictions which rebounded against the Mu'tazilites who were responsible for it. Some, like al-Jahiz, even defended and justified this use of terror.

• Many with heretical opinions found Mu'tazilism to be a nest in which to incubate their corruptions and from which they could introduce their innovations into Islam. Ibn ar-

Rawandi,[1] was considered one of them, as were other notorious individuals who were suspected of making innovations in Islam and of reprehensible actions. This led people to suspect them.

The suspicions of the *fuqaha'* and *hadith* scholars

The *fuqaha'* and *hadith* scholars were strong opponents of the Mu'tazilites and suspected them of deviation. Ash-Shaybani gave a *fatwa* that anyone who prayed behind a Mu'tazilite had to repeat the prayer. Imam Abu Yusuf considered them *zindiqs*. Imam Malik would not accept the testimony of any of them. They were suspected of corruption and committing *haram* acts. In fact the Mu'tazilite school embraced all sorts of individuals.

Disputes of the Mu'tazilites and the science of *kalam*

Kalam was used by the Mu'tazilites when debating with their opponents, whether Rafidites, Magians, or dualists, people of other sects, specialists in *fiqh* and *hadith,* and others. The whole Islamic community took part in these arguments and debates for about three generations, during which assemblies of rulers, ministers and scholars flourished and opinions were exchanged. Internecine fights between the schools and sects caused reverberations that affected Islamic thought as a whole. Islamic thinking became embellished with Persian, Greek or Hindu ideas. Each faction was distinct in their argument in specific ways, while often they did not differ in their general position in the *Deen*.

The methods of deduction employed by the Mu'tazilites were different from those of others among the Islamic Community, and their deductive premises also differed. There were several distinct characteristics in the way they debated.

---

1. A notorious free-thinker and sceptic who espoused dualism.

• The Mu'tazilites avoided imitation and were averse to following others without investigation, examination and comparison proofs and criteria. Their respect was for opinions and not names, for the truth and not the speaker. Hence they did not imitate one another; the rule which they followed was that every responsible person is answerable for the principles of the *Deen* to which his *ijtihad* has led him. Perhaps that is why they split into so many groups, including the Wasiliyya, Hudhayliyya, Nizamiyya, Ha'itiyya, Bishriyya, Mu'ammariyya, Thumamiya, Hashimiyya, Jahiziyya, Khayyatiyya and Jubba'iyya.

• They relied on the intellect to establish their articles of faith, finding support for their positions in the Qur'an. They did not have much knowledge of *hadiths* because they did not use them for doctrine or evidence.

• They took from classical scientific sources which were translated in their time. They borrowed from some of those sciences and used them to support their arguments in clashes with opponents in the field of *kalam*. They were joined by every Muslim educated in the foreign education and philosophical systems which were nurturing the Arab intellect in that time, which is why there many distinguished writers and philosophers among them.

• They excelled in language, eloquence and clarity of exposition. Their men included eloquent orators and debaters who were skilled in debate, knew its rules and were experienced in its methods and how to defeat opponents. Their leading figure, Wasil ibn 'Ata', was a notable orator. An-Nazzam, one of their shaykhs, was intelligent, eloquent with a sharp tongue, a man of letters and a poet. Abu 'Uthman 'Amr al-Jahiz was called "the Orator of the Muslims" and "Shaykh of the *Mutakallimun*".

Chapter Four
The Opinions and *Fiqh* of ash-Shafi'i

In this section we do not intend to discuss the opinions of ash-Shafi'i about *tafsir* or language, but to study his legal opinions. So we will examine only his opinions and position in *fiqh* and the fundamental principles he adopted concerning it, even though his opinion is considered authoritative in other sciences. But there is some controversy about his position concerning the khalifate, his opinion about *kalam* and his orientation with regard to the articles of faith, since that has a connection to legal studies.

Ash-Shafi'i's opinion of *kalam*

Ash-Shafi'i abhorred the science of *kalam,* as did most of the *fuqaha'* and *hadith* scholars of his time. Ash-Shafi'i was a *muhaddith faqih.* They disliked that branch of learning because those who established its basic premises were the Mu'tazilites, whose method was contrary to the path of the righteous *Salaf* in understanding the doctrines of the noble *Deen.* Ash-Shafi'i, like every *muhaddith faqih,* preferred following to innovating, even in his method of deduction in relation to doctrine. He also disliked the fact that the Mu'tazilites studied dogma with a philosophical bias which was inimical to ash-Shafi'i and any other *muhaddith faqih.* Moreover the Mu'tazilites raised questions which were abstruse, complicated and not easy for human reason to resolve.

That is why it is reported that ash-Shafi'i discouraged people from becoming involved in the science of *kalam.* He said, "My judgement on the people of *kalam* is that they should be beaten with canes, made to ride backwards on camels and taken around to be exhibited to the tribes and clans." It is said that this is the penalty for abandoning the Book and the *Sunna* and becoming involved in *kalam*. He said, "Beware of investigation into *kalam*. If a man is asked a question in *fiqh* and makes a mistake, the worst than can happen is that he will be laughed at as, for instance, when a man kills another man and he says that his blood money is an egg. If he is asked about a question in *kalam* and errs, he is called an innovator." He said, "I see that some of the people of *kalam* call others unbelievers, while the people of *hadith* call others mistaken. Mistakes are far less grave than disbelief."

Ash-Shafi'i hated the method of the scholars of *kalam*. Ar-Razi mentioned that he first of all hated what they said and then hated them because they had encouraged the *khalifs* to injure scholars in support of this knowledge. Some say that ash-Shafi'i's prohibition of the science of *kalam* was due to his ignorance of it. According to ar-Razi, he knew it and mentioned reports which indicate that he was not ignorant of it. It is related that al-Muzani said, "We were at the door of ash-Shafi'i discussing *kalam* when ash-Shafi'i came out to us. Having listened to some of our conversation he left us and then came back again and remarked, 'I was only prevented from coming out to you because I heard you discussing *kalam*. Do you think I do not know it well? I studied it until I reached a high level but *kalam* is endless. If you debate a matter of *fiqh* people say – 'You have erred,' not 'You have committed *kufr*.'"

There is no doubt that this report shows that ash-Shafi'i knew this science and the questions which scholars discussed but disliked practising because its questions were often abstruse and complicated and could lead a believer into being accused of disbelief. So he forbade it, knowing full well what it was that he forbade.

While ash-Shafi'i hated people becoming involved in the science of *kalam* and wished they would not delve into it, he mentioned many aspects of it relating to doctrine. It is impossible that someone like ash-Shafi'i should not have had knowledge of these matters. His opinions about much of it were in keeping with the opinions of the Islamic community as a whole; he did not borrow from the philosophers and others. He sometimes used to question those with whom he debated about the proofs of *tawhid* or the proofs of prophethood. Bishr al-Marisi asked him what was the evidence that Muhammad was the Messenger of Allah. He replied, "The proof of the Prophethood of Muhammad, may Allah bless him and grant him peace, is the revealed Qur'an, the consensus of the people and the signs that cannot be attributed to any but him."

From some of ash-Shafi'i's *fatwas* one can deduce that his opinion about the Divine Attributes was that they were not different from the Essence. It is related that he said if someone swears by the knowledge of Allah or the power of Allah or the right of Allah, by the knowledge of Allah he means what Allah knows, by the power of Allah what He has decreed and by the right of Allah what He has made obligatory for His servants. This does not require *kaffara* (expiation) because it is not an oath by Allah. If by the oath he meant the Attributes of Allah, it is binding.

As all the *fuqaha'* and *hadith* scholars also stated, ash-Shafi'i held that the Qur'an was the Uncreated Word of Allah. He said that Allah Almighty says in His Book, *"Allah spoke to Musa."* (4:164) He believed in the vision of Allah on the Day of Rising and he deduced evidence in the Qur'an for that: *"No indeed! Rather that Day they will be veiled from their Lord."* (83:15) He said, "If the unbelievers are veiled by anger, that indicates that His friends will see Him with pleasure." He believed in the Decree and the Determination of good and evil. Ar-Razi deduces from the preface of the treatise which he wrote on the fundamentals of faith, that ash-Shafi'i believed that Allah created the actions of man by His will and that man acquired them. Ar-Rabi' reported ash-Shafi'i as having stated, "People do not create their actions. They are part of the creation of Allah Almighty."

Ash-Shafi'i said about faith, "Faith is both confirmation and action." Since that is the case, it increases and decreases according to actions. Ash-Shafi'i cited evidence for this view including what happened when Allah changed the *qibla* from Jerusalem. People asked, "What will happen to the prayers which we prayed to Jerusalem?" Then Allah revealed, *"Allah would not let your faith go to waste."* (2:143) He called the prayer "faith". For the increase and decrease of faith, he used as evidence the words of the

336

Almighty: *"Each time a sura is revealed, there are some among them who say, 'Which of you has this increased in belief?'"* (9:124) and His words in *Surat al-Kahf*, *"They were young men who believed in their Lord and We increased them in guidance."* (18:13)

Thus we see that ash-Shafi'i announced his articles of faith and his beliefs regarding some of the questions with which *kalam* scholars dealt, without becoming involved in it and delving into its philosophy which misled some people.

Ash-Shafi'i's opinion about the khalifate

Now we move to a question on which the scholars of *kalam* focused and which touches on an area of *fiqh:* the khalifate. Ash-Shafi'i believed that there must be a ruler under whose auspices the believer acts, enemies are fought, roads are made safe, and who takes from the strong for the weak so that the pious are relieved and there is rest from the corrupt, as 'Ali ibn Abi Talib stated. He also thought that the khalifate should be restricted to Quraysh, as the majority of Muslims thought, and the khalifate is valid without allegiance if that was necessary. This was reported from Harmala, his student, according to whom he said, "Any Qurayshite who becomes *khalifa* by the sword, and on whom the people agree, is indeed the *khalifa*." So there were two things necessary for the *khalifa*: one is that he be from Quraysh and second is that the people agree on him, whether the agreement preceded his becoming *khalifa* or not.

It is reported that he said that the Rightly Guided khalifs were five: the usual four and 'Umar ibn 'Abdu'l-'Aziz, may Allah be pleased with all of them. If being a Hashimite had been a precondition for eligibility to be the khalif, he would not have considered 'Umar ibn 'Abdi'l-Aziz to be one because he was an Umayyad and not a Hashimite. The only Hashimite among them was 'Ali.

This is what is well known from ash-Shafi'i regarding his views on the khalifate. It is also well known that he considered that Abu Bakr to have been more entitled to the khalifate than 'Ali, on the basis of two *hadiths*. One that he related was about a

337

woman who came to the Prophet, may Allah bless him and grant him peace, and asked him for something and he commanded her to come back. She said, "Messenger of Allah, and if I return and do not find you?" apparently referring to his death. He said, "Then go to Abu Bakr." This indicates that Abu Bakr was the one who would be in command after him. The second *hadith* that ash-Shafi'i related is that the Prophet said, "Follow those after me: Abu Bakr and 'Umar." He also ranked the Rashidun khalifs in virtue according to their order in time: Abu Bakr, 'Umar, 'Uthman and then 'Ali.

Such were the opinions of ash-Shafi'i on the khalifate in general; but in addition to these views, like every Muslim, he loved the family of the Messenger of Allah and was sincere in his love for them. As we saw, during his lifetime he was accused of being one of the 'Alawites who rebelled against Harun ar-Rashid. It was said that he gave allegiance to the one they chose as *khalifa*. We do not know the real source of this accusation and whether it was due to his love for the family of the Prophet or arose from actual events. He was certainly pained by the persecution to which the 'Alawites were subjected in spite of the fact that they were the family of the Messenger of Allah. That may have led him to join them from youthful exuberance. We do not know the truth of the accusation.

As for his admiration for 'Ali, there are many reports that he mentioned 'Ali ibn Abi Talib in his gatherings. Once a man remarked, "People only ran away from 'Ali because he did not care for anyone's opinion." Ash-Shafi'i said, "He had four qualities; if a man had only one of them, it would be appropriate for him not to be concerned with anyone's opinion. He was ascetic, and the ascetic is not concerned with this world or its people; he was a scholar, and the scholar is not concerned with anyone else's opinion; he was courageous, and the courageous man is not concerned with anyone else's opinion; and he was noble, and the noble man is not concerned with anyone else's opinion."

He said about 'Ali, "'Ali was given knowledge of the Qur'an and *fiqh* because the Prophet, may Allah bless him and grant him peace, summoned him and commanded him to judge between people. His judgements were examined by the Prophet and he confirmed them." So we find that ash-Shafi'i was intent on maintaining objectiveness and balance in his opinions constantly. So he loved 'Ali and admired him and considered those who rebelled against him to be rebels. But his love did not lead him to prefer him to Abu Bakr, 'Umar and 'Uthman.

The *fiqh* of ash-Shafi'i

Ash-Shafi'i did not form an independent school or independent legal opinions separate from those of Malik until after he left for Baghdad on his first journey in 184 AH. Before that he was considered one of the adherents of Malik and defended his opinions and resisted the supporters of opinion (*ra'y*) by defending the people of Madina. Hence he was called "the Helper of the *Hadith*".

After ash-Shafi'i had stayed in Baghdad for a time on this first visit, studying the books of Muhammad and debating with the supporters of opinion, he felt that he had to produce for people a fusion of the *fiqh* of the people of Iraq and the people of Madina. So he applied himself to studying the opinions of Malik in a penetrating and critical manner, not as his partisan trying to defend him.

Perhaps arguing for the opinion of Malik, even if he was moved by zeal for him, led him to see faults in it, as he saw the virtues and faults of the *fuqaha'* of Iraq when he debated with them and studied their understanding and opinions. So he thought there must be a new way of thinking and a new direction. Then the debate on the secondary branches directed him to lay out the principles of a new system and research rules and criteria to guide it. So he left Baghdad and started out on a new course.

Ash-Shafi'i went to Makka and set up a circle in the *Haram*. This marked the true beginning of his school. We can divide his action in the formation and expression of his opinions into three stages. The first stage was in Makka; the second was in Baghdad, on his second visit; and the third was in Egypt. At each of these stages he had students who studied with him, discussed with him and spread his teaching from him at those stages. We have nothing to define these three stages for us precisely but we can delineate them approximately because we see that the fruits of each stage are to some degree distinct from the fruits which came before and after it.

He stayed in Makka for nine years after leaving Baghdad the first time. It was a very productive period in his life in terms of scholarship and he reached his maturity when he was there. At the beginning of this period he was not yet forty. He was aware of the different opinions of the scholars of his generation, having studied and taken all or most of what they had. In the course of his journeys he had collected most of the *hadiths* gathered by people throughout the cities of Islam, so accumulating a store of wealth which he did not have before. When he studied them he found that sometimes they conflicted and so he preferred some to others, on the grounds of either *isnad* or abrogation of some by others. He based his deduction on those which were firm. He began to study the evidence of the Qur'an alongside the evidence of the *Sunna* he had collected, and that led him to define the position of the *Sunna* in relation to the Qur'an.

We can say that in this period his thoughts were directed to universal principles rather than secondary rulings. Perhaps most of his lessons in his circle dealt with this and with instructing his students in methods of deduction, in comparison of legal sources, and dealing with secondary rulings in the light of his theories.

It may well have been those universal studies which caught the attention of Ahmad ibn Hanbal when he saw ash-Shafi'i in his teaching circle in Makka, and which caused him to leave the circle of Ibn 'Uyayna, who was relating from az-Zuhri, for the circle of ash-Shafi'i. When someone criticised him for that, he said, "Be quiet. If you miss a *hadith* now, you will find it later and that will not harm you. But if you miss the intellect of this youth, I fear that you will not find it again until the Day of Rising. I have not seen anyone with more *fiqh* about the Book of Allah than this Qurayshi youth." He also said, "*Fiqh* was a closed book to its students until Allah opened it through ash-Shafi'i."

The first fruit of that productive stage was the *Risala* (treatise) which he wrote in Makka for 'Abdu'r-Rahman ibn Mahdi at his request. Some sources say that he wrote it in Baghdad during his second visit but even if that was the case, it was the fruit of his studies in Makka. Ash-Shafi'i brought that fruit to Baghdad and disseminated it in academic circles there, and it was something new among them. Al-Karabisi said, "We did not know the Book or the *Sunna* or consensus until we heard ash-Shafi'i say, 'The Book; the *Sunna*; and consensus.'"

Ash-Shafi'i arrived in Baghdad in 195 AH and stayed there for about three years. This was the second stage of his *ijtihad*. In it he began to examine the opinions of contemporary *fuqaha'*. He also compared the opinions of the Companions and the *Tabi'un* against the universal principles he had formulated and preferred some of them on the basis of these principles. Then he examined the opinions which he thought were in accordance with his principles.

He examined the disagreements between the Companions and the reason for them, such as the disagreements between 'Ali and Ibn Mas'ud, Ibn 'Abbas and Zayd ibn Thabit, and he examined the disagreement between Abu Hanifa and Ibn Abi Layla related by Abu Yusuf. He called that *The Disagreement of the Iraqis*. Then he examined the positions of al-Waqidi and al-Awza'i, and so on with their various opinions, and dealt with them according to his principles, choosing between them those which he thought were most consonant with his principles, or leaving them altogether for a new opinion if none of them coincided with the principles he had formulated.

Ash-Shafi'i moved to Egypt in 199 AH, remaining there for about four years until his death. In that period ash-Shafi'i completed his development, his opinions matured, and he encountered the local practice there which resulted in new ideas. He saw in Egypt what he had not seen before – new customs, an ancient civilisation and new traditions from the *Tabi'un* – and so he began to review all his prior opinions in the light of his experience, his age, and the land in which he had settled.

This resulted in his rewriting his *Risala* on the *usul* as a new book in which he added and deleted certain things while retaining the core of the old treatise. He studied his opinions on secondary rulings and jettisoned some of them for new positions, replacing the old position with the new position to which he had been guided. Sometimes he hesitated between the new and old positions and so he mentioned both without retracting the first of the two. If you wish, you could say that this stage was the stage of thorough scrutiny. In it he reviewed all his opinions and scrutinised his principles analytically. Every position was subjected to analysis and examination, to ascertain the good and bad qualities which brought it close to the *Sunna* or distanced it from it. He began to scrutinise his own opinions in this exacting and rigorous way.

Then he recorded the result of his studies and wrote his final version of the *Risala*. He himself wrote many of its questions and he dictated others. His companions related from him the sum of his opinions at that time and they transmitted his disagreements with other *fuqaha'*. So when ash-Shafi'i died he left a rich legacy of *fiqh* and deduction.

The transmission of ash-Shafi'i's *fiqh*

Ash-Shafi'i's *fiqh* was transmitted in two ways. One was by his students and the other was through the books which he wrote or dictated to his students. These should be mentioned briefly.

Ash-Shafi'i's students

Ash-Shafi'i had students who transmitted his *fiqh* in all three stages of his development. He had students who learned and transmitted from him in Makka, students who learned and transmitted from him Baghdad during his second visit, and students who learned and transmitted from him at the end of his teaching life in Egypt.

One of those who kept his company in Makka was Abu Bakr al-Hamidi, a reliable *muhaddith faqih*, who died in 219 AH in Makka. He went with ash-Shafi'i to Egypt and then returned to Makka after his death. There was Abu Ishaq Ibrahim ibn

342

Muhammad al-'Abbasi, who had a reliable memory for *hadith*, but from whom nothing about *fiqh* has been transmitted. He grew up in Makka and died in 237 AH. There was Abu Bakr Muhammad ibn Idris. Ibn 'Abdu'l-Barr said that he was the companion of ash-Shafi'i. I do not know in what year he died. He studied with him in Makka. Another was Abu'l-Walid Musa ibn Abi'l-Jarud, who stayed with ash-Shafi'i, wrote out his books and learned his *fiqh*, and adopted his position before he went to Baghdad. Those are some of the people who learned *fiqh* from ash-Shafi'i in Makka and they are mentioned among his companions.

One of his companions in Baghdad was Abu'l-Hasan as-Sabbagh az-Za'farani. There was none among the students of ash-Shafi'i more eloquent than him, or with more insight into the Arabic language and recitation. Al-Khatib al-Baghdadi reported that he said, "Ash-Shafi'i came to us and we gathered around him. He said, 'Find someone to read to you.' No was bold enough to read to him except me. I was the youngest of the people and still had no beard. Today I am amazed that I had the audacity to speak in the presence of ash-Shafi'i and I am astonished at my temerity that day." Al-Khatib also said, "When I read the *Risala* to ash-Shafi'i, he asked. 'From which Arab tribe do you come?' I replied, 'I am not an Arab. I am from a village called az-Za'faraniyya.' He told me, 'You are the master of that village.'" He died in 360 AH.

There was also Abu 'Ali al-Husayn ibn al-Karabisi, who was an exacting scholar. He was someone on whom the ruler relied for *fatwa* and he was a skilled debater. He used to follow the school of the people of Iraq. When ash-Shafi'i came he sat with him and read his books from az-Za'farani. He died in 256 AH. Another follower from this time was Abu Thawr al-Kalbi, who used to hold to the school of the people of Iraq until he accompanied ash-Shafi'i, took knowledge from him, and listened to his books from him. He died in 240 AH.

Among those who accepted ash-Shafi'i's teaching, even if they are not known as followers of his school, were Imam Ahmad ibn Hanbal and Ishaq ibn Rahawayh. Ibn 'Abdi'l-Barr said of Ibn Rahawayh: "He was one of great scholars and scholars of *hadith*. He was noble and wrote many books and works on *fiqh*. He did not meet ash-Shafi'i although he wrote out his books and used his own discretion as did Abu Thawr. He was more inclined to *hadith* and following the *Salaf*. He died in Nishapur in 277 AH."

Another of his companions in Egypt was Harmala ibn Yahya ibn Harmala. He was eminent and noble. It is said that ash-Shafi'i stayed with him. Ibn 'Abdi'l-Barr said, "He reported from ash-Shafi'i from the books which ar-Rabi' reported from him... He died in Egypt in 266, being one of the companions of ash-Shafi'i."

Another student was Abu Ya'qub Yusuf ibn Yahya al-Buwayti. Ash-Shafi'i delegated him in his circle and preferred him to Muhammad ibn 'Abdullah ibn 'Abdi'l-Hakam in spite of his great love for Ibn 'Abdi'l-Hakam. He preferred the truth over friendship as was his wont. Al-Buwayti was a scholar, an ascetic and a *faqih*. He was suspected of not accepting the Mu'tazilite position regarding the creation of the Qur'an and was imprisoned until he died in Baghdad in 231 AH. As-Subki said about him: "He had the station of the true men. The jailer said that when al-Buwayti was in prison he would perform a *ghusl* every Friday, perfume himself, wash his garments and go to the door of the prison when he heard the call. The jailer would take al-Buwayti back and he would say, 'O Allah, I have answered Your caller, but they have prevented me.'"

Another was Abu Ibrahim Isma'il ibn Yahya al-Muzani, who was a *faqih* and scholar knowledgeable in all aspects of debate and exposition. He has many books on the school of ash-Shafi'i, including the *Great Summary* and the *Small Summary*. The *Great Summary* is called *al-Mabsut* and the *Small Summary* is called *al-Mukhtasar*. Ibn Hajar said, "He wrote *al-Mabsut* and *al-Mukhtasar* on the basis of the knowledge of ash-Shafi'i. He was a paragon in evidence and argument, a man of worship and action, humble, absorbed in ideas. He died in 264 AH. Many have written commentaries on his *Summary*, including Abu Ishaq al-Marwazi and Abu'l-'Abbas ibn Surayj."

Another of ash-Shafi'i's students was Abu 'Amr Muhammad ibn 'Abdullah ibn 'Abdi'l-Hakam. Ibn Hajar said of him in *Tawali' at-Ta'sis*: "None was equal to Abu 'Amr among the people of Egypt." Al-Muzani said, "Ash-Shafi'i looked at him and followed him with his eye." He was a leading exponent of knowledge in Egypt. He died in 258 AH. He was a favourite of ash-Shafi'i and there was true brotherhood and love between them. When ash-Shafi'i became ill and felt that he was dying, his companions asked him who should succeed him in his circle, and he indicated al-Buwayti. In spite of his great love for Ibn 'Abdi'l-Hakam, he saw in al-Buwayti what he did not see in his close friend. It is said that that made Ibn 'Abdi'l-Hakam angry so that after ash-Shafi'i died, he left his school for Malik. Whatever happened after ash-Shafi'i's death, he listened to the books of ash-Shafi'i and they say that he listened to *Ahkam al-Qur'an*, *The Book of the Refutation of Muhammad ibn al-Hasan*, and *as-Sunan*.

There was also ar-Rabi' ibn Sulayman al-Jizi. As-Subki describes him as a righteous *faqih* who related from ash-Shafi'i, 'Abdullah ibn Wahb, Ishaq ibn Wahb, 'Abdullah ibn Yusuf and others. He died in 256 or 257 AH. It is not clear whether he was actually a companion who related his books from him or simply his views.

The ar-Rabi' ibn Sulayman who transmitted the books of ash-Shafi'i is Abu Muhammad ibn 'Abdi'l-Jabbar al-Muradi the *mu'adhdhin*. He used to call the *adhan* in the Great Mosque of Fustat until he died. No one had called the *adhan* from the minaret before him. Ibn 'Abdu'l-Barr says that he was ash-Shafi'i's companion for a long time, took much from him, and served him. He had travelled to him in search of his knowledge. He died in 270 AH and was the last in Egypt to relate from ash-Shafi'i. Ar-Rabi' was eminent and related all of the books of ash-Shafi'i; and people transmitted from him. According to al-Bayhaqi, if he was lacking some pages of a text he would say "ash-Shafi'i said" or report it from al-Buwayti from ash-Shafi'i. People travelled to him to listen to the books of ash-Shafi'i. Ibn Hajar al-'Asqalani says that sometimes ar-Rabi' would be absent doing something for ash-Shafi'i and would read what he missed when he returned.

There are many statements in books which throw light on the reports of ash-Shafi'i and his students and state that the transmitter of the later books of ash-Shafi'i was ar-Rabi' ibn Sulayman al-Muradi. That is why an-Nawawi said: "Know that when ar-Rabi' is mentioned in the books of the school, al-Muradi is meant. If they mean al-Jizi, they say so." Nonetheless, there were some books which ar-Rabi' did not relate.

Those are some of the companions of ash-Shafi'i who reported his school in the various stages of his *ijtihad* and disseminated his teaching to people and the generations after him.

His Books

The *mujtahids* in the time of the Companions and *Tabi'un* refused to write down their *fatwas* or *ijtihad* and they even forbade the *Sunna* to be written down, so that the written source of the *deen* would only be the Book, which is the support of this *Shari'a*, its clear light, and the rope of Allah extended until the Day of Rising. At a certain point, however, scholars decided it was necessary to record the *Sunna*, *fatwas*, and *fiqh*.

The different sects came and recorded their positions. The Shi'ites came and recorded the views of their Imams, and the Mu'tazilites recorded the views of their scholars. The *hadith* scholars, therefore, needed to record sound *hadiths* to set them apart from things falsely attributed to the Messenger of Allah, may Allah bless him and grant him peace. Then the *fuqaha'* wrote down their opinions. Some books are reported from Abu Hanifa. Abu Yusuf wrote the *Kitab al-Kharaj*[1] for ar-Rashid and other books are attributed to him. Muhammad ibn al-Hasan recorded the views of the Iraqis.

So ash-Shafi'i came at a time in which scholars were recording their views and those of their shaykhs. Some transmitters mention that his first book was a refutation of the *fuqaha'* of opinion. Al-Buwayti stated: "Ash-Shafi'i said, 'I met with the people of *hadith* and they asked me to reply to the book of Abu Hanifa. I said, 'I do not know their position until I have examined their books.' So I asked for the books of Muhammad ibn al-Hasan to be copied out for me and I examined them for a year until I had memorised them; and then I wrote the Baghdadi Book.'"

---

1. Taxes imposed on revenue from land or the work of slaves.

If that report is sound, it indicates that ash-Shafi'i first wrote about the method used by the people of Iraq to record opinions before he wrote his own independent opinions. He defended the *fiqh* of *hadith*, the *fiqh* of the people of Madina, or the *fiqh* of Malik itself, because he represented the Madinans. That was after ash-Shafi'i became aware of the books of Muhammad ibn al-Hasan. There is no doubt that this took place during his first visit to Baghdad before he had an independent opinion about *ijtihad* separate from the school of Malik.

Whatever the case, after ash-Shafi'i formulated his own method of *ijtihad*, investigation, and *fatwa*, he wrote more books. He recorded the principles he used for deduction and his opinions on various questions. He also recorded the *sunan* and the disagreements between the Companions, choosing from different opinions the one which he thought preferable and embracing it. We do not know that he wrote any book in Makka: none of the historians mention any. Nonetheless we are inclined to believe that he wrote the *Risala* to 'Abdu'r-Rahman ibn Mahdi while he was in Makka. Many works are mentioned as having been composed after he returned to Baghdad in 165 AH, and it is possible that he wrote the books in Makka, but did not transmit them until he went to Baghdad. Then in Egypt he re-examined them.

Ash-Shafi'i made his books public in Baghdad, where he issued the *Risala* and read his books to his students. As we have mentioned, az-Za'farani stated, "Ash-Shafi'i came to us and we gathered to him. He said, 'Find someone to read to you.'" This indicates that he had books which he had written and prepared and which were read and disseminated among his students. His students studied these books, and the most famous of their transmitters were az-Za'farani and al-Karabisi. The book on *fiqh* which he wrote in Iraq is called *al-Hujja*, and was a large volume.

Ibn an-Nadim calls the book which az-Za'farani related from ash-Shafi'i *Al-Mabsut*. Was it the same as *al-Hujja*? Information on the contents of *al-Mabsut* of az-Za'farani is found in the *Fihrist* of Ibn an-Nadim, who states that it is the work which ar-Rabi' related in Egypt. We find that it contains all of the opinions of ash-Shafi'i regarding secondary rulings, evidence, debate and dis-

347

agreement. So we can say *al-Hujja* is what Ibn an-Nadim called *al-Mabsut* that, and is what came to be called *al-Umm* after ash-Shafi'i had made some changes and alterations to it in Egypt.

Ash-Shafi'i went to Egypt and there he re-examined his books, his opinions and his school. He made some changes and alterations, set down his new books, and dictated many questions. His companions reported questions from him and they were reported from him in Egypt. The *Kitab as-Sunan* was reported from him. As-Suyuti said in *Husn al-Muhadara*: "In Egypt he wrote his new books like *al-Umm*, *al-Amali al-Kubra*, and *al-Imla' as-Saghir*." Ibn Hajar reported that ar-Rabi' said, "Ash-Shafi'i resided in Egypt for four years and he dictated 2500 pages to me. He produced *al-Umm*, in 2000 pages, *Kitab as-Sunan*, and many things – all in the space of four years." Al-Buwayti summarised what he heard from ash-Shafi'i in Egypt in his *Mukhtasar*. Al-Muzani wrote a similar book also called *al-Mukhtasar*. All these expounded the *fiqh* of ash-Shafi'i in Egypt and his final views.

Ar-Rabi' ibn Sulayman al-Muradi related all that ash-Shafi'i wrote and dictated in Egypt, and people travelled to him. He kept close by ash-Shafi'i throughout the course of his stay in Egypt. He related that he was with him before he came to Egypt, as is stated by Ibn Hajar. Ibn an-Nadim called what ar-Rabi' transmitted *"al-Mabsut"*, and what az-Za'farani transmitted was also entitled *"al-Mabsut"*. Az-Za'farani transmitted the books of ash-Shafi'i in Baghdad as ar-Rabi' did in Egypt.

Here we should point out something important which is connected to this in order to contrast ash-Shafi'i's old and new positions. It might be imagined from what some people have said that when ash-Shafi'i came to Egypt he produced his new books from scratch with no reference to the earlier ones. That was accepted as fact by some later writers who took it to be true and definite.

For that reason some writers say that those four years in Egypt were sufficient to write all of these books. It is not reasonable to suppose that ash-Shafi'i would start wholly afresh on the topics on which he had written about before in Baghdad. He examined what he had written and left unchanged what he thought was sound. He read it to his followers and they transmitted it from him. What he changed he wrote and dictated. It is not logical to assume that a writer would discard all that he had written and start completely afresh.

That is confirmed by the expressions used. According to Ibn Hajar, al-Bayhaqi said, "Some of his new chapters were not re-written: fasting, *hudud*, the lesser pledge, hiring and funerals. He commanded that these chapters be read to him as they were, but his *ijtihad* regarding other matters was changed." This removes many uncertainties about views on questions which ash-Shafi'i was known to have retracted but which still exist in some books.

Al-Mabsut by ar-Rabi' is the same order as that of az-Za'farani, even though there is a slight difference between them. The *Mabsut* of az-Za'farani was written in Baghdad and that of ar-Rabi' in Egypt. This indicates that the source was the same but that there were changes, alterations, additions and deletions which were included in the new book in Egypt.

The truth is that the new books are the old ones revised and augmented. The core of the old *Risala* is in the new *Risala*, but after numerous corrections, additions and deletions have been made. The same applies to all of his books. Ash-Shafi'i, as debater and analyst, scrutinised the opinions which he had debated in search of the truth which was his only objective. So he always examined his own views as he did those of others. Then he again compared them against what he extrapolated from the principles, and either left or adjusted them. So it is that different views were transmitted from him about the same questions at different times. He would report a view and then retract it because of a *hadith* he had found, a better analogy to which he was guided, or the *fatwa* of a Companion which he had not known before.

Ash-Shafi'i always had misgivings about his opinions – as do all who are sincere. He thought that there might be mistakes in his positions throughout all his *ijtihad*. As al-Buwayti related, he used to say, "I wrote these books and I did not go back to them. There must be error in them because Allah Almighty says, '*If it had been from other than Allah, they would have found many inconsistencies in it.*' (4:82) If you find anything in these books of mine which diverges from the Book and *Sunna*, I retract it."

Before we move on from the writing of his books, we must refer to a controversy which has arisen among researchers. The books which the companions of ash-Shafi'i related fall into in two categories: one which historians and transmitters ascribe to ash-Shafi'i: *al-Umm*, the *Risala*, *The Disagreement of the Iraqis*, and *The Disagreement of 'Ali and 'Abdullah*, etc.; and a group which are mentioned as ascribed to his companions although they are summaries of his writings, examples being the *Summary* of al-Buwayti and the *Summary* of al-Muzani.

There is no doubt that this latter category comprises the writing of his companions and their summary of his words, even though the opinions ascribed to ash-Shafi'i are no fewer than in the first. In the first category, ash-Shafi'i was responsible for the idea and the text, and in the second only for the idea, the text and expression being the work of his companions, like the books of Imam ash-Shaybani in the Hanafi school.

Ash-Shafi'i consulted the books of others when writing his books so that he would know the *hadiths* or legal traditions in them in order to be able to criticise and debate them. We read in *Tawali' at-Ta'sis*: "Ash-Shafi'i came and stayed in Egypt for four years and composed these books. He had with him from the Hijaz the books of Ibn 'Uyayna. He went to Yahya ibn Hassan and wrote from him. He took books with questions from Ashhab. He used to place the books in front of him and write. When a book was finished, Ibrahim came and wrote and al-Buwayti read to him. All who were present listened to the book of Ibn Hiram and then copied it afterwards. Ar-Rabi' saw to the needs of ash-Shafi'i. Sometimes he would be absent on an errand, and when he returned ar-Rabi' would read to him what he had missed."

These reports indicate that ash-Shafi'i himself wrote and composed without dictation, after which his students transmitted what he wrote and heard from him. Sometimes ash-Shafi'i dictated and the reader of the *Kitab al-Umm* often encounters the phrases, "ash-Shafi'i dictated to us" or "he reported to us".

The Kitab al-Umm

What type of book is the *Kitab al-Umm* by ash-Shafi'i? Did he write it, or did he dictate it, or is it rather an account of what he said? The answer which comes to mind immediately is that the *Kitab al-Umm* is a book which ash-Shafi'i wrote or dictated himself; and there are many reports to that effect – for example, from his companions such as al-Muzani, ar-Rabi' and al-Buwayti. They had the book itself in their possession. No one really differs from this consensus, but in the discussion on brotherhood in the *Qut al-Qulub*, a book on *tasawwuf,* Abu Talib al-Makki mentions that al-Buwayti wrote the *Kitab al-Umm* and gave it to ar-Rabi', who became known for it. We should bear in mind the topic of this chapter, which is brotherhood. According to Abu Talib:

Ash-Shafi'i, may Allah be pleased with him, formed a brotherhood with Muhammad ibn 'Abdi'l-Hakam al-Misri. He had great love for him and brought him close, saying, 'No one in Egypt gave me lodging except him.' Once Muhammad fell ill and ash-Shafi'i visited him. Ar-Rabi' said that he heard ash-Shafi'i recite when he visited Muhammad:

The beloved fell ill, so I visited him
and I fell ill out of concern for him.
The beloved came to visit me
and I was healed by the sight of him.

The people of Egypt had no doubt that ash-Shafi'i would assign his circle to Muhammad ibn 'Abdi'l-Hakam, appoint him his successor after his death, and order people to listen to him. When ash-Shafi'i was in his final illness, someone asked, 'Abu 'Abdullah, with whom should we sit after you? Who will be the master of the circle?' thinking that he would point to Muhammad. Muhammad, who was waiting for the same, was sitting by his head. Ash-Shafi'i said, 'Glory be to Allah! Is there any doubt about this? Abu Ya'qub al-Buwayti.' Muhammad was deeply disap-

351

pointed. His companions inclined to Abu Ya'qub al-Buwayti. Muhammad then proceeded to attack the knowledge and school of ash-Shafi'i and rejoin the school of Malik.

Al-Buwayti was more ascetic and scrupulous, so ash-Shafi'i was faithful to the *Deen* and the Muslims without partiality. He entrusted the task to Abu Ya'qub and preferred him because he was more worthy of it. When ash-Shafi'i died, Muhammad ibn 'Abdi'l-Hakam left his school and companions and returned to the school of Malik. He related his father's books from Malik and learned their *fiqh*. Today he is regarded as one of the great adherents of Malik.

Al-Buwayti sought to become unnoticed and withdrew from people to al-Buwayta, part of the Nile Delta, where he wrote the *Kitab al-Umm* which is now attributed to ar-Rabi' ibn Sulayman. It was compiled by al-Buwayti but he did not mention himself in it. He sent it to ar-Rabi', who added to it and made it known; and people listened to it from him. Al-Buwayti was arrested in the Inquisition, taken from Egypt to the khalif, and imprisoned for refusing to say that the Qur'an was created. Ar-Rabi' said, "Al-Buwayti wrote to me from prison encouraging me to hold assemblies, and commanding me to persevere in knowledge, gentleness to students and welcoming them, and being humble to them." He said, "I often heard ash-Shafi'i say:

'I humble myself to honour them;
and an unhumbled soul will not be honoured.'"

This is what Abu Talib al-Makki said about the story of ash-Shafi'i, al-Buwayti and Ibn 'Abdi'l-Hakam. Its aim is to show a faith in the Next World which does not allow a friend to give preference to his own affections over the *Deen* and concern for the Muslims. But can we deduce from it that Abu Talib was attacking the attribution of *al-Umm* to ash-Shafi'i by way of ar-Rabi'? Comparison of text and *isnad* does not back this up. The aim of

352

the story was to encourage people to be detached, and to prefer Allah. To this end, the Sufis sometimes report traditions which are weak and are not averse to doing so in order to achieve their desired aim. Thus there is no evidence that the story of al-Buwayti and ar-Rabi' is true in respect of the origin of *al-Umm* or should cause doubt about the generally accepted attribution.

The words which we have quoted would indicate that ash-Shafi'i did not write the *Kitab al-Umm* himself but that it was written by al-Buwayti and read by ar-Rabi' with an attribution to ash-Shafi'i. This is contrary to the consensus of scholars. It would imply that al-Buwayti was the one who collected what ash-Shafi'i wrote and dictated and then gave it to ar-Rabi' who added to it and disseminated it. That possibility is refuted by two considerations.

The first is that ar-Rabi' was one of those who clung to ash-Shafi'i when he was in Egypt, and that although he may have been absent seeing to some of ash-Shafi'i's needs, when he returned he read to ash-Shafi'i what he had missed. Hence it is unlikely that al-Buwayti would have had any of the Egyptian books of ash-Shafi'i which ar-Rabi' did not have, even if his position in *fiqh* was higher than that of ar-Rabi'. The question is one of transmission, not of knowledge or understanding.

The second is that the consensus of the scholars is that the one who transmitted the books of ash-Shafi'i was ar-Rabi'. People travelled to him for that purpose. He was reliable and did not lie, and scholars of *hadith* did not attack him but accepted his trans-mission. It would have been a kind of lie for him to transmit ash-Shafi'i's books from someone else and then ascribe them to him-self. Ibn Hajar says in *at-Tahdhib*, "Abu'l-Husayn ar-Razi reported with a chain of transmitters that Abu Yazid al-Qaratisi said, 'That ar-Rabi' ibn Sulayman listened to ash-Shafi'i is not certain. He took most of the book from the family of al-Buwayti after his death.' Abu'l-Husayn ar-Razi said, 'This is not accepted from Abu Yazid. Al-Buwayti used to say "Ar-Rabi' is firmer in ash-Shafi'i's teaching than I." Abu Zur'a ar-Razi heard all the books of ash-Shafi'i from ar-Rabi' four years before al-Buwayti died.'"

In short, there are many reports with continuous firm *isnads* that ash-Shafi'i used to write his own books. He composed books first in Iraq and later in Egypt. Then he would read what he wrote to his students, who would copy it. Sometimes he dictated, and it was ar-Rabi' ibn Sulayman who related the books of ash-Shafi'i which reached him. Scholars travelled to him for the books of ash-Shafi'i. Ar-Rabi' heard most of these books from ash-Shafi'i, even if he did not listen to some areas of *fiqh* which he mentioned in his transmission.

Ar-Rabi' was very scrupulous. He mentioned the expressions which he found in the text transmitted from ash-Shafi'i even if there were errors in it. He transmitted it and then clarified the error. If he did not hear something, he said, "I did not hear it." Sometimes he commented on the text and would sometimes quote another of ash-Shafi'i's statements before clarifying his final position. Sometimes he would state that ash-Shafi'i had retracted it.

The Legal Collection published in Egypt

There is a legal collection published in Egypt, which contains the *fiqh* of ash-Shafi'i. The commentary claims that it is from *al-Umm* but it is not. It contains the *Musnad* of ash-Shafi'i and there are various statements by ash-Shafi'i. What is in the text is not all from *al-Umm*. It contains part of the new *Risala* – unless we consider all that ar-Rabi' related to be part of *al-Umm* just as Ibn an-Nadim calls all that ar-Rabi' transmitted "*al-Mabsut*", in which case *al-Mabsut* and *al-Umm* refer to the same thing. That is all that ar-Rabi' related from ash-Shafi'i in Egypt, and so the *Risala* is part of it. According to most scholars, however, the *Risala* is not *al-Umm* because the *Risala* concerns the principles (*usul*) of *fiqh* whereas *al-Umm* is about *fiqh* itself; and ash-Shafi'i did not give his *Risala* a particular name.

Since *al-Umm* contains such expressions as "ash-Shafi'i was asked and said," can we say that ash-Shafi'i wrote it or dictated it and that it was transmitted from him with its current chapter order? There are three possible answers in this question. The first is that ash-Shafi'i wrote or dictated this book, instructing that the questions be written down and then dictating his answers to them. So all of it comes from ash-Shafi'i, with some explanations from ar-Rabi'.

The second theory is that ash-Shafi'i recorded responses to various questions with his own pen and dictated others. Then when he died, ar-Rabi' collected what ash-Shafi'i had dictated about secondary rulings himself, together with answers he had given to particular questions, in a single collection called *al-Umm*. He wrote down what he heard, and what he had not heard but others had written down, indicating in the latter case that he had not heard it himself. This is similar to the first, but in the second instance the collection, order and division into chapters were done by ar-Rabi'.

The third is that *al-Umm* was not written by ash-Shafi'i but is a collection of his statements which he wrote or dictated and his opinions on questions which he studied with his students and which they reported from him – all of that having been compiled after ash-Shafi'i's death. In this case the attribution of this book to ash-Shafi'i is like that of the books of Imam Muhammad ash-Shaybani to the *fuqaha'* of Iraq since it recounts their statements without adding to them.

The third possibility must be rejected because the consensus of scholars is that the *Kitab al-Umm* was by ash-Shafi'i and because ar-Rabi', as is clear from the written text, corrected its errors.

Finally the style of ash-Shafi'i is distinctive in its lucidity and beauty of its expression, and depth and precision of its meaning. All of the style of the *Risala* is similar and thus must be ascribed to ash-Shafi'i. There is no way to choose between the first two possibilities. And there is no disagreement that the opinions in *al-Umm* are those of ash-Shafi'i .

Our study of the *fiqh* of ash-Shafi'i

We will now turn to the *fiqh* of ash-Shafi'i. As well as elucidating its principles and general rules, we will also deal with the principles of deduction in it and how the principles are connected to distinct secondary rulings in a general manner. The area of secondary rulings, however, is a vast topic which cannot be fully dealt with in this study.

First we must turn to an particular point which people frequently bring up in relation to ash-Shafi'i's *fiqh*. The adherents of ash-Shafi'i sometimes related from him two or three positions regarding a single question. He may have retracted one or more of them; but since no definitive position was confirmed, two firm but variant statements in the school are sometimes ascribed to him about a single issue. We see in *al-Umm*, which is the *fiqh* of ash-Shafi'i in the final and definitive stage of his *ijtihad* that he related more than one statement on several questions. In his book *The Virtues of ash-Shafi'i*, ar-Razi mentions a section on the different statements of ash-Shafi'i or the positions attributed to ash-Shafi'i, whether by his tongue or pen, like those in *al-Umm* or the *Mukhtasar* of al-Muzani, or which the Shafi'ites ascribed to his school. The various positions ascribed to him are of five types.

• Questions in which there are two positions reached by transmission or extrapolation. This applies when ash-Shafi'i responded to two similar questions in two different chapters and the answer was negative in one and positive in the other. The people transmitted the answer to both questions and said, "There are two positions on it." This, in fact, is not from ash-Shafi'i, but from his adherents and companions.

• Questions regarding which ash-Shafi'i himself had two positions: the old position which he wrote in Baghdad and the new which he wrote in Egypt. The new superseded the old. Al-Bayhaqi said, "I read in the book of Zakariyya ibn Yahya as-Saji with his *isnad* from al-Buwayti that he said that he heard ash-Shafi'i say, 'I do not absolve anyone who relates my Baghdadi book from me without any change in it.'" The *mujtahid* may retract his opinion when the truth becomes clear to him, since the Companions did that in retracting some of their positions. He stated, "The Companions did so. 'Ali said, 'My opinion and that of 'Umar about *umm walads* was that they should not be

356

sold, but now I believe that they can be sold.'" 'Umar ibn al-Khattab said in his letter to 'Abdullah ibn Qays on the *adab* of *Qadis*, "If when you have already given a decision you reflect on it and are guided to something more correct, that should not prevent you from reverting to the truth. Reverting to the truth is better than remaining in error."

• Ash-Shafi'i occasionally stated two positions in places in his new books and then reported that he chose one of them, saying that it was sounder or better; or gave a secondary ruling based on one and left the other; or mentioned the evidence of one rather than the other.

• Sometimes he mentioned both denial and affirmation and hesitated between them. Ar-Razi says on that type, "The adherents say that ash-Shafi'i only did this in sixteen instances. It denotes extreme care in the *Deen* and scrupulousness."

• Occasionally ash-Shafi'i mentioned two positions regarding a question – one reached by means of analogy and the other by report and *Sunna* – and then chose the one which agreed with the *Sunna*.

From this it is clear that ar-Razi, like other partisans of ash-Shafi'i, thought that the existence of multiple opinions from ash-Shafi'i was not seemly for him and sought to refute this and reduce the number of questions on which he had more than one opinion. Those who were partisan against ash-Shafi'i thought that the great number of his variant opinions was a fault and evidence of his not reaching the truth, and was a sign of shortcomings in his knowledge. We deny their claims and affirm that knowledge obliges one to hesitate in many cases and that it is a clear sign of knowledge and certainty, not a proof of ignorance.

The truth is that the ash-Shafi'i we find in the light of his biography and scholarly life often changed his opinion regarding particular questions. The reason is that he was sincere in seeking what he believed to be the truth in the *Shari'a*. A sincere person cannot be fixed to an idea or enslaved rigidly by an opinion. If he has a specific goal it is the quest for knowledge for Allah. That makes him scrutinise and examine his opinions continually. Moreover, ash-Shafi'i had a lively mind which was constantly probing and studying. He was not content with any particular conclusion but always searched beyond it. Such a man does not have rigid opinions:. he is constantly reviewing them and measuring them against his current scholarship. Hence change is more likely than fixity.

Ash-Shafi'i always sought out new *hadiths* and it was clear to him that when his opinion was contrary to a *hadith* he should accept the *hadith*. He asked the *hadith* scholars among his companions to rely on a *hadith* if they found that his opinion was contrary to it and not to take his opinion rather than the *hadith*. Among every group there were *hadith* scholars who had *hadiths* which others did not have. So each group gave *fatwa* on the basis of what it had and used analogy when they had no option. Ash-Shafi'i would always abandon his opinion for a sound *hadith*. He travelled widely and was aware of different environments and disparate customs. Every community had its own traditions and customs. Someone who deduces laws must be affected in his thinking by a prevailing custom. Thus ash-Shafi'i had one opinion in Baghdad which reflected the situation there. When he moved to Egypt, he changed his opinion and was influenced by the environment there.

The numerous debates that ash-Shafi'i had with opponents made him examine and review his opinions constantly. If he was shown their faults and saw shortcomings in them or compared them before he entered into debate, he would revise them. In short, the abundance of the opinions of ash-Shafi'i is consistent with his method in *ijtihad* and his intellectual life. It does not indicate a failing but rather his devotion to seeking the truth.

Chapter Five
The Principles of ash-Shafi'i

In his principles ash-Shafi'i formulated the methods to be followed in deducing secondary rulings. He would clarify a principle of deduction and then follow it with some of the secondary rulings stemming from it and explain the method of extrapolating these rulings from that principle. The study of the fundamental principles involves study of the principles themselves, discerning some of the rulings of the school, and above all the legal methodology of ash-Shafi'i. The study of the intellectual methodology of a scholar is also a sound and direct study of the consequences of his methodology.

The study of a scholar is a study of what is peculiar to him, and ash-Shafi'i was singled out among the *mujtahids* before him and contemporary with him since he is one who defined the principles of deduction and formulated them as general rules.

Ash-Shafi'i set out the principles of *fiqh* because the *fuqaha'* before him had exercised *ijtihad* without having defined limits to the way they deduced their rulings. Before him they relied on their understanding of the meanings of the *Shari'a*, the goals and aims of its rulings, and what its source texts indicated. They were like people who assess proofs by instinct without having recourse to any logical procedure.

Ash-Shafi'i mixed and debated with the *fuqaha'*. Their methods of deduction found expression in the course of argument and debate. Accordingly, he laid down limits and rules and formulated criteria. Ar-Razi said about the achievements of ash-Shafi'i in this area: "Know that the ascription to ash-Shafi'i of the knowledge of the fundamental principles is like that of logic to Aristotle and that of prosody to al-Khalil ibn Ahmad."

The first book which ash-Shafi'i wrote on *usul* was the *Risala* which he wrote to 'Abdu'r-Rahman ibn Mahdi before he went to Egypt and then later rewrote in Egypt. It is famous, and contains most of ash-Shafi'i's opinions about *usul* but not all of them. Ash-Shafi'i has other studies about *usul*: *The Book of the Invalidity of Istihsan* and the *Kitab Jima' al-'Ilm*. Many of the rules arose in the course of his debates with his opponents.

Knowledge of the *Shari'a*

Ash-Shafi'i divided knowledge of the *Shari'a* into two parts. One was the science of the common people – the knowledge of which no Muslim may be ignorant and which every Muslim must know. This refers to essentials of the *Shari'a*, such as the five obligatory prayers, the fast of Ramadan, the *Hajj* for whoever can perform it, the obligation of *zakat*, and the prohibitions against fornication, murder, theft and drinking wine. This is in the Qur'an in clear texts which do not admit interpretation and in the *mutawatir sunna* from the Messenger.

The second part concerns the secondary rulings which people see in the *Shari'a* about which either there is no text from the Qur'an, or there is a text which needs interpretation and there is no *mutawatir* text from the Messenger; or if there is a *hadith*, it is a single tradition, or a *hadith* whose text can be interpreted in different ways. That is the knowledge of the elite.

The two types of knowledge are divided in respect of responsibility and acquisition. As far as responsibility is concerned, the common knowledge is required of every Muslim while the knowledge of the elite is only demanded of the elite, like the *fard al-kifaya* which is demanded of those capable of it, the performance of which by some removes the sin of non-participation from others. Any sane person can understand the first part and it does not require special capacities. The second is only undertaken by the elite who inherit the knowledge of the Book and the *Sunna*, the reports of the Companions, and matters of disagreements. Those have the right of deduction and it is a duty for them.

Ash-Shafi'i explained the difference between the knowledge of the common people and the knowledge of the elite as follows: "There are two types of knowledge: the knowledge of the common people of which no sane adult is ignorant, like the five prayers, the fact that Allah has obliged people to fast the month of Ramadan, to make *Hajj* to the House if they are able, and to pay *zakat* on their property, and that they are forbidden fornication, murder, theft, and wine, and similar things which people must know, learn, give from their property or refrain from. All of this knowledge exists by a text in the Book of Allah and is universally recognised by all the people of Islam. It is transmitted by ordinary people. They relate it from the Messenger of Allah and cannot argue about it. This is common knowledge in respect of which error is not possible from a tradition or interpretation and which cannot be disputed."

The second type is the knowledge of the elite, which he describes as: "Secondary rulings which arise for people and other matters which have no text in the Book or the *Sunna* in most cases. If there is a *sunna* about something, it is one of the reports of the elite [single reports], not the common, and is susceptible to interpretation and analogy."

The knowledge of the elite is the subject of the investigation of the *fuqaha'*, and it is that which the *mujtahid* strives to deduce. It is that about which there is dispute. It is that for which rules are formulated so that deduction can be sound and so that those rules become the criteria by which the difference between an error and a correct judgement are ascertained and a decision is reached between two opponents who disagree.

There is no doubt that common principles of deduction are those rules which specify the knowledge of the elite and it is not obligatory for all Muslims to obtain it. Indeed not every Muslim is capable of obtaining it since there are precise criteria to evaluate opinion and which guide the *mujtahid* to deduction.

The evidence for judgements according to ash-Shafi'i

Ash-Shafi'i classes knowledge in five categories, ranked as follows in descending order.

First rank: The Book and the firm *Sunna*. The *Sunna* and the Book occupy the same rank because the *Sunna* expounds the Book in many cases. If a *hadith* is sound, it is put alongside it. If the reports are single ones, they do not have the same rank as the Qur'an since the Qur'an is related by multiple transmission. The Qur'an cannot be contradicted by the *Sunna*.

Second rank: Consensus on what is in the Book or the *Sunna*. What is meant by consensus is the agreement of those *fuqaha'* who were given knowledge of the elite and who are not confined to the knowledge of the common people. Their consensus is evidence for those after them regarding the questions on which they all agree.

Third rank: The statement of one of the Companions of the Prophet. This is when one of the Companions of the Prophet voiced an opinion about a matter and when it is known that no other Companion opposed him in it. The opinion of a Companion is better for us than our own opinion.

Fourth rank: A question on which the Companions of the Messenger of Allah had differing opinions. In that case a *faqih* should adopt whichever opinion he considers closest to the Book and *Sunna*. Their opinions should not be overridden in favour of those of any other people.

Fifth rank: Analogy made on the basis of what is known from the other categories: the Book, *Sunna*, and consensus. An analogy should be made on the basis of a textual matter which has a ruling in the Book or *Sunna* or whose judgement is known by consensus; or by following the unopposed position of one of the Companions or a statement of his which another Companion opposes.

These are the categories of knowledge which ash-Shafi'i formulated and we will deal with each in turn.

The Qur'an

Ash-Shafi'i considers the Book and *Sunna* to have equal rank in the *Shari'a*. Indeed, he considers them to constitute a single source of this *Shari'a* because all other sources of deduction are based on them, and derived from their spirit if they are not taken from their text. So all sources of deduction, however numerous and varied, derive from one source which has two branches: the Book and *Sunna*. However, we see the Book preferred in some sources after ash-Shafi'i and in the expressions of the *fuqaha'* before him. Indeed, in some of ash-Shafi'i's writings, he himself does not put the *Sunna* in the same rank as the Book, but makes it subsidiary to it. So why does ash-Shafi'i consider them as having one rank? Ash-Shafi'i replies that the Book and *Sunna* are both from Allah since the Prophet *"did not speak from passion. It is only a revelation revealed."* (53:3-4) Thus both of them are from Allah even if their means and causes vary. It is also because the *Sunna* is knowledge taken from the Book of Allah and so is inextricably connected with it.

The *Sunna* accompanies the Qur'an, clarifies all the general questions which arise in it, and provides details of matters which are unqualified. It can only clarify it if it enjoys the same rank. Many of the Companions took the same line as ash-Shafi'i in that. It is related that 'Abdullah ibn Mas'ud quoted the sound *hadith*, "Allah curses women who tattoo and are tattooed, women who pluck their eyebrows, and women who file their teeth to make gaps for beauty, altering Allah's creation." A woman of Banu Asad who used to recite the Qur'an heard about that and asked 'Abdullah, "What is the *hadith* that I heard from you, that you curse such and such?" 'Abdullah replied, "Why should I not curse those whom the Messenger of Allah cursed when it is in the Book of Allah?" The woman said "I have listened to the Book and never heard that." He said, "If you listened carefully, you would have heard it. Allah says, *'Take whatever the Messenger gives you take and leave anything He forbids you.'* (59:7)"

In order not to misconstrue ash-Shafi'i's aim in this matter, three things should be noted of which many people may not be aware.

- Ash-Shafi'i elevated knowledge of the *Sunna* as a whole to the rank of the Qur'an. That does not mean that everything related from the Messenger, whatever its path of transmission, had the same rank as the definitive *ayats*. Single *hadiths* do not have the same rank as the *mutawatir*, famous and widespread *hadiths*, let alone that of the *ayats* of the Qur'an. Ash-Shafi'i noted this since he limited the *Sunna* which was in the rank of the Qur'an to the established *Sunna*.

- He gave the *Sunna* the same rank as the Book in the deduction of rulings in secondary areas. This does not mean that they have the same position in the formulation of the articles of faith. Denying something found in the *Sunna* is not like denying something which is clearly stated in the Qur'an and in which there is no scope for interpretation. Anyone who denies something stated in the Qur'an is an apostate; but anyone who denies what is found in single *hadiths* is not outside Islam, since matters of faith must be confirmed with definitive *isnads* and the reports of single *hadiths* are not definitive.

- Ash-Shafi'i placed the *Sunna* at the same rank as the Qur'an in the extrapolation of derivative rulings. That is not to deny that the Qur'an is at the same time the root of this *Deen,* its support, its proof and the miracle of the Prophet, and that the *Sunna* is a branch from this root. That is why its strength stems from it. The *Sunna* simply complements the Book by expounding the rulings it contains, and supports it by making clear the laws that the *Shari'a* has brought which are good for people in this life and the Next, and by which the virtuous society will be formed.

'Amm and *khass* in the Qur'an

'Amm (general) can be defined as a word which indicates various things with a shared meaning, as "human being" indicates man, woman, black, white, Zayd, Bakr and Khalid. These individuals are different but all have the quality of humanity and so the same general word can be applied to them.

Khass (particular) applies to part of what is alluded to by a general expression, like "white" or "man" in relation to "human being". It is also possible for something particular to be general in itself, like "man", since that is applicable to many separate individuals who share the quality of manhood. Nonetheless, it is particular in relation to "human being".

Ash-Shafi'i divided general expressions in the Qur'an into three categories: apparent general expressions by which the general is meant; apparent general expressions by which the general is meant but the particular is included; and apparent general expressions by which the particular is meant. He formulated these three categories of the general, and gave examples of these three categories.

For instance, as an example of general expressions with general meanings, he quoted the words of Allah: *"Allah is the Creator of everything and He is Guardian over everything"* (39:63); *"He created the heavens and the earth"* (14:37); and *"There is no creature on the earth which is not dependent upon Allah for its provision."* (11:8) Ash-Shafi'i states in the *Risala*, "All of the heavens and the earth, everything with a spirit, trees and other things are all the creation of Allah and He provides for them and knows their lodging place and repository."

Next, he gives examples of general expressions by which the general is meant but in which the particular is included, and quotes the words of Allah, *"The people of Madina and the desert Arabs around them should not remain behind the Messenger of Allah, nor should they prefer themselves to him"* (9:121) and *"When they reached the inhabitants of a town, they asked them for food but they refused them hospitality."* (18:76) The form here is general, but there is a particular aspect (i.e. not all of the inhabitants were asked for food).

The third category is apparently general expressions by which the particular is meant and which are not intended to be general at all. This is understood either from the circumstances of the Revelation, by other *ayats* of the Qur'an, or by clarification from the *Sunna*. An example of this is found in Allah's words: *"Those to whom people said, 'People have gathered together against you, so fear them.' But it increased them in belief and they said, 'Allah is enough for us and the best of guardians.'"* (3:173) This only refers to certain people, namely the idolaters. Another example is *"The woman and man who commit fornication: flog both of them with one hundred lashes and do not let compassion for either of them possess you where Allah's* deen *is concerned,"* (24:2) where only free people are meant and not slaves, who receive half of the punishment.

How the Qur'an sheds light on the *Shari'a* and the position of the *Sunna* in respect of it

The Qur'an is the ultimate source of the *Shari'a* and the fount from which its roots and branches are derived and evidence is taken. It is related that 'Abdullah ibn 'Umar said, "If anyone knows all the Qur'an he has taken on something immense and prophethood is lodged between his shoulders although he is not given Revelation." Ibn Hazm the Zahirite said, "None of the areas of *fiqh* is without a basis in the Book, and the *Sunna* and the Book is the basis and support of the *Sunna,* as we shall explain. Allah Almighty says, *'This Qur'an guides to the most upright Way'* (17:9) and He says, *'What We send down in the Qur'an is a healing and a mercy to the believers, but increases the wrongdoers in nothing but loss.'* (17:82) 'A'isha observed, 'If anyone recites the Qur'an, there is no one above him.'"

So the Qur'an is the universal source of the *Shari'a,* as is clear from these texts and others. So there must be a comprehensive exposition of it since something universal must be made clear. That is why it must be supplemented by the *Sunna* in order that rulings may be deduced from it and laws extrapolated. The Almighty says, *"And We have sent down the Reminder to you so that you may make clear to mankind what has been revealed to them."* (16:44) Ash-Shafi'i regarded the Qur'an in this light and mentioned that it was the universal source of the *Shari'a* and he who is ignorant of it knows nothing and he who knows it is not ignorant of anything.

The Qur'an contains all of the *Shari'a;* by explicit text, deduction, or inference. According to ash-Shafi'i, "All that is revealed in the Book is a mercy and a proof. Whoever knows it knows it and whoever is ignorant of it is ignorant of it. He who is ignorant of it has no knowledge and he who knows it is not ignorant. People are in different classes in knowledge. Their position in knowledge depends upon their ranks in knowledge of the Qur'an. Those who seek knowledge must strive as much as possible to increase their knowledge of it, to be steadfast in the face of every obstacle to seeking it, have a sincere intention for Allah to grasp its knowledge in text and by deduction, and ask for Allah's help in it, for good is only obtained with His help. Whoever gains knowledge of the rulings of Allah in His Book in text and deduction if Allah grants him the success to speak and act according to what he knows, he has obtained virtue in his *Deen* and in this world. Doubt is expelled from him and his heart is illuminated with wisdom, and he merits leadership in the *Deen*."

If you read the *Risala* of ash-Shafi'i from beginning to the end you will be aware that the Qur'an is the axis about which its knowledge revolves because it connects the roots to knowledge of the *Shari'a.* Since, however, the Qur'an needs explanation, it must be the *Sunna* which does that. The *Sunna* clarifies the details of the *Shari'a* while the Qur'an clarifies its universal principles. So the prayer, *zakat, hajj, jihad* and fasting are all in the Qur'an and the *Sunna* elucidates them. It is the same with family and social matters, and punishments which are designed to deter corruption in society. The principles of all this are in the Qur'an and its details are in the *Sunna*.

The *Sunna*

We have mentioned ash-Shafi'i's method of deduction from the Qur'an and seen that he explained his method and did not oppose the evidentiary quality of the Qur'an in the *Shari'a* because that requires no other evidence for Muslims. Anyone who denies the authority of the Qur'an as evidence in establishing the *Shari'a* has left the *Deen* and must be required to repent. If he does not repent he is killed. In the case of the *Sunna*, ash-Shafi'i met some who denied that the *Sunna* was evidence. He met people who said worse things than that: some people denied that the *Sunna* established rulings other than those of the Qur'an, on the grounds that it it clarifies but cannot add to it. There were people who denied the evidence of single reports. Therefore he had to present evidence to confirm that the *Sunna* had the authority to establish rulings – even single reports, as long as the report was reliable. The *Risala* is the book in which these proofs are set out and *al-Umm* is the book which contains the discussions between him and his opponents who denied that the *Sunna* had authority or could add to the Qur'an, or who denied the legislative force of single reports.

Let us now explain the opinions of these groups as ash-Shafi'i discusses them. Ash-Shafi'i mentions in the *Kitab Jima' al-'Ilm* of *al-Umm* that those who opposed consensus followed three different schools. One denied the authority of the *Sunna* altogether. The second denied its authority unless the Qur'an upheld it. The third school are those who deny the authority of single *hadiths* and only consider *mutawatir* or well-known reports.

Obviously, followers of the first school are those who relied on the Qur'an alone. Their argument was transmitted from one of them in *al-Umm*: "Someone who is considered a scholar by his adherents said to me, 'You are an Arab and the Qur'an was revealed in the language of your people. You know it by heart and in it Allah has placed the obligations which He revealed. If any doubts one letter of the Qur'an, you ask him to repent. If he does not repent, you kill him. Allah describes the Qur'an as *'making all things clear.'* (16:89) How is it permitted among you or anyone to say about anything that it deems obligatory that "Sometimes the obligation in it is general and sometimes particular, and sometimes the command in it is evidence of obligation and sometimes merely of permissibility?"

'You have a *hadith* which you relate from one man or from another man or from two or three back to the Prophet, while you and those of your school do not place total reliance in anyone you have met or consider him to be entirely accurate in memory. No one is absolutely immune from erring, forgetting or making a mistakes in his transmission of a *hadith*. I find when a man says on the basis of a *hadith* that something is lawful or unlawful, or part of the knowledge of the particular issue, you sometimes say, "The Messenger of Allah did not say this. You or whoever reported it to you erred. You or the one who reported to you lied." Yet you do not ask him to repent: do no more than tell him, "What you have said is bad." So how can it be permitted to differentiate between any of the judgements of Qur'an when their apparent texts are the same, on the basis of a tradition from someone who fits the description you have given – and to accord their reports the same rank as the Book of Allah?"'

In general, such people argued that the Book contained the clarification of every matter. The language of the Book was Arabic and required no other explanation for those with knowledge of Arabic and the Arabic style of the Qur'an, no further exposition being required. *Hadiths* are reported by men who cannot be completely exonerated from lying, erring or forgetting. The transmission of such things cannot be linked with the Definitive Book in affirmation and evidence in any way.

It is clear that such an opinion would demolish the authority of the *Sunna* so that it could be considered one of the bases of Islamic *fiqh* at all. Ash-Shafi'i elucidated the results of this school which, if taken to their logical conclusion, lead to something very terrible. Acceptance of it leads to not understanding the prayer, *zakat, hajj* and other general obligations in the Qur'an which the *Sunna* elucidates. So the minimum obligation of the prayer is that to which the name "prayer" is applied and that of *zakat* the minimum of what is called "*zakat*". This would enable someone to pray two *rak'ats* a day and say, "There is nothing more in the Book of Allah and so it is not an obligation." That would be to eliminate prayers and *zakat* which are all transmitted as obligatory so that knowledge of them is one of the essential elements of knowledge of the *Deen*. Anyone who says that is not a Muslim in any sense of the word.

The second of the three schools of thought does not accept the *Sunna* unless it refers to something contained in the Qur'an. Ash-Shafi'i expressed their position thus: "Another group say that the *Sunna* can only further explain what is already in the Qur'an." This school accepts the *Sunna* when it provides further support for what is in the Qur'an, but holds that the *Sunna* cannot add any legislation which is not in the Qur'an.

The third school, which is also contrary to the position of the Community, reject the use of any single traditions as authoritative evidence. They only take note of *mutawatir* traditions or well-known (*mashhur*) ones. As a rule, therefore, they accept only very general and unspecific traditions.

Ash-Shafi'i presents various proofs that these positions are not acceptable. First of all, Allah Almighty has connected belief in Himself to belief in His Messenger Muhammad. Belief in the Messenger entails following his words and actions. Therefore it is mandatory to consider the *Sunna* of the Prophet as a source of the *Shari'a*. This is confirmed by the words of Allah: *"So believe in Allah and His Messenger, the Unlettered Prophet, who believes in Allah and His Words; and follow him, so that you may be guided"* (7:158) and *"The believers are those who believe in Allah and His Messenger and who, when they are with him on a matter of common concern, do not leave until they have asked him for permission."* (24:62) These two *ayats* clearly state that belief in the Messenger is a part of Islam. So it is obligatory to follow him, since that is a necessary consequence of faith.

A second proof is that Allah mentions in His Book that the Messenger teaches people the Book and Wisdom. He says: *"Our Lord, raise up among them a Messenger from them to recite Your*

Signs to them and teach them the Book and Wisdom and purify them. You are the Almighty, the All-Wise." (2:129) There are many *ayats* which convey this. "Wisdom" in this context can only mean the *Sunna* of the Messenger of Allah, may Allah bless him and grant him peace.

A third proof is that Allah has obliged the believers to obey and follow the Prophet. If it is obligatory to obey someone, then his words must be obeyed and anyone who opposes them is a rebel. Thus the *Sunna* of the Prophet has authority in the *Shari'a* because Allah explicitly states in the Qur'an that it is mandatory to obey him and juxtaposed obedience to the Prophet with obedience to Him in various passages, as where He says: *"When Allah and His Messenger have decided a thing, it is not for any believing man or believing woman to have a choice about it. Anyone who disobeys Allah and His Messenger is clearly misguided."* (33:36) Again He says: *"O you who believe! Obey Allah and obey the Messenger and those in command among you. If you have a dispute about anything, refer it to Allah and the Messenger, if you believe in Allah and the Last Day."* (4:59)

A fourth proof is that Allah Almighty did not make the calling of the Messenger to judge between people the same as their calling of themselves; nor is opposing him like opposing other people. Anyone who opposes his judgement is not a Muslim. This is confirmed by the words of Allah: *"Do not make the Messen-ger's summoning of you the same as your summoning of one another. Allah knows those of you who sneak away. Those who oppose his command should beware of a testing trial coming to them or a painful punishment striking them."* (24:63) He also says: *"When they are summoned to Allah and His Messenger so that he may judge between them, a group of them turn away."* (24:46) Thus Allah informs us that being summoned to the Messenger so that he may judge between us is like being summoned to the judgement of Allah, because the one rendering the judgement is the Messenger. When we submit to the judgement of Allah's Messenger, we submit to the judgement of Allah.

A fifth proof is that Allah Almighty commanded the Prophet to convey His Message, to elucidate His *Shari'a* and to follow His

Revelation. This is achieved by reciting and expounding the Qur'an.

Thus the *Shari'a* consists of the Qur'an and the words of the Prophet since it is based upon conveying and following the Revelation. As Allah says: *"Then We placed you on the Right Road of Our Command, so follow it. Do not follow the whims and desires of those who do not know."* (45:18) Allah further points out that He protects the Prophet in this respect. He says: *"Were it not for Allah's favour to you and His mercy, a group of them would almost have managed to mislead you. But they mislead no one but themselves and do not harm you at all. Allah has revealed the Book and Wisdom to you and taught you what you did not know. Allah's favour to you is indeed immense."* (4:113)

The position of the *Sunna* in relation to the Book

As we have seen, ash-Shafi'i spent much time defining the position of the *Sunna* of the Messenger of Allah, may Allah bless him and grant him peace, in relation to His Book. He designated five aspects of their relationship.

- The *Sunna* elucidates what is undefined in the Qur'an such as the obligations which are unspecified in the Qur'an for which it provides the details and times.

- The *Sunna* shows when the general is meant to be general in the Qur'an and when Allah means a particular category by a general expression.

- The *Sunna* adds, by Divine inspiration, rulings to obligations confirmed by texts in the Qur'an which are a consequence of them or connected to them.

- The *Sunna* conveys rulings which are not in the Qur'an and are not additions to Qur'anic texts.

- The *Sunna* further explains what is abrogating and abrogated in the Qur'an.

The *Sunna* elucidating the Qur'an

Scholars agree that the Book is elucidated and its goals and rules defined by the *Sunna* of the Prophet. No one claims to be able to understand the Qur'an and know all its rulings without the help of the *Sunna*, even though there are some people who reject some of the *Sunna*. One of them said to Mutarrif ibn 'Abdullah, "Only relate the Qur'an to me." Mutarrif said, "We do not mean to replace the Qur'an. Our intention is to follow him who knows the Qur'an better than us. Al-Awza'i related that Hassan ibn 'Atiyya said, 'The Revelation came down to the Messenger of Allah and Jibril supplied him with the *Sunna* which explains it. Nonetheless a man claimed that the Qur'an contains the clarification and details of everything so that there is no need for the *Sunna*. 'Imran ibn Husayn told him, "You are a stupid man! Do you find in the Book of Allah that *Dhuhr* is four *rak'ats* and recitation is not aloud in it, or the number of prayers or the amount of *zakat*? Do you find this explained in the Qur'an?""

Since the Qur'an needs the explanation of the *Sunna* in this way, the question arises: How can it be said that the Qur'an is clear when it needs to be elucidated by the *Sunna*? The answer is that the clarity of the Qur'an is universal and not partial, general and not detailed, and the *Sunna* fleshes out the details of the generality of the Qur'an. The knowledge of the particular is only achieved through the Messenger. Allah says, *"It is We who have sent down the Reminder and We who shall preserve it."* (15:9)

Consensus

Ash-Shafi'i confirmed that consensus furnishes an authoritative proof and confirms that its rank comes after the Qur'an and *Sunna* and before analogy. We already mentioned that. Ash-Shafi'i states at the end of the *Risala*, "Judgement is made by the Book and *Sunna* and what is agreed upon about which there is no dispute. So we say that we judge by the truth in the apparent and implicit and we judge by a *sunna* which is reported by a single chain and on which not everyone agrees. So we say that we judge by the truth and the apparent because there might be error in the one who relates the *hadith*. We judge by consensus and then by analogy, which is weaker because analogy is not lawful where a sound tradition exists."

From here we see that ash-Shafi'i considered that consensus came before analogy, he deems it weaker as evidence than the Book and the *Sunna* and that it is only resorted to when there is no text from the *Sunna* or the Book.

For ash-Shafi'i consensus is that the scholars of the time all agree on a matter, in which case their consensus is evidence for that about which they agree. He says in the chapter on the invalidity of *istihsan*: "Neither I nor any of the people of knowledge would say 'this is agreed on' except on a matter about which you would never find any scholar who would not repeat it to you and relate it from a predecessor, such as the *Dhuhr* prayer being four *rak'ats*, wine being unlawful, and the like."

The first consensus which ash-Shafi'i considers is that of the Companions. This did not refer to their having heard a *sunna* from the Messenger of Allah which they all agreed on, in which case it is the *sunna* which constitutes the proof and not their agreement, but when it was a question of their own *ijtihad*. The very existence of a *sunna* means there is no need for *ijtihad*. They used their *ijtihad* only on subjects about which there was no text from the *Sunna* contrary to their consensus.

As the *Risala* indicates, ash-Shafi'i accepted consensus as authoritative and considered it as evidence in itself for two reasons. The first is shown in the *Risala* where he reports a *hadith* related by Sulayman ibn Yasar that 'Umar ibn al-Khattab gave a speech at al-Jabiya in Syria in which he said: "The Messenger of Allah, may Allah bless him and grant him peace, stood among us as I am standing among you and said, 'Honour my companions, then those after them and those after them. Then lying will spread among them to such an extent that a man will swear an oath without being asked to swear. Those who seek the joy of Paradise should cling to the Community. Shaytan is with the isolated person but further from two people. A man should not be alone with woman, for Shaytan is the third of them. Whoever is happy at his good actions and distressed at his bad action is a believer.'"

Clearly in this *hadith*, we are urged to cling to the Community and this is not merely a physical matter and it cannot happen if hearts are divided. Holding fast to the Community results in the cohesion which the Community must have in respect to what is lawful and unlawful and acting accordingly. Ash-Shafi'i gave the clearest exposition of his understanding of consensus in stating: "Since the Community is dispersed through different lands, no one will be able to cling to a physical community which consists of bodies which are separated. Furthermore, these physical bodies comprise both Muslims and unbelievers, godfearing and impious. So there is no sense in clinging to physical bodies. But the Community forms a cohesive single unity in forbidding certain things and considering others lawful and acting accordingly. Those who say what the Community of Muslims says cling to their Community. Whoever opposes what the Community of Muslims says has diverged from the Community to which he must hold. There is heedlessness in separation. The Community cannot be heedless of the meaning of the Book, *Sunna* or analogy."

The second proof is the words of Allah: *"But if anyone splits with the Messenger after the guidance has become clear to him, and follows other than the path of the believers, We will hand him over to whatever he has turned to, and We will roast him in Hellfire."* (4:115) This is confirmation of the fact that Allah Almighty made following any way other than that of the believers equivalent to splitting from Allah and His Messenger and the punishment is also the same. Splitting from Allah and His Messenger is forbidden and so following a way other than that of the believers is forbidden. Thus it is obligatory to follow their way. This is evidence that consensus is an authority which cannot be opposed, in the same way that it is not permitted to oppose the Book and the *Sunna*, because Allah juxtaposed following other ways than that of the believers with splitting with the Messenger and He made a terrible threat about the consequences of doing so.

This is evidence for its authority. But exactly whose consensus is being referred to? That of the people of *fiqh* and *mujtahids* alone, or both theirs and others? The answer is clear in what ash-Shafi'i said about consensus: "Neither I nor any of the people of knowledge would say that 'this is agreed upon' unless it were a matter about which you would never find any scholar who would not repeat it to you and relate it from a predecessor, such as the *Dhuhr* prayer being four *rak'ats,* wine being unlawful and the like." This shows us that he only considers the consensus of scholars, because only they know the lawful and unlawful in respect of matters about which there is no text in the Book or *Sunna.*

Then another question arises: who are the scholars who form this consensus? There were many discussions about this. The consensus referred to, according to ash-Shafi'i, is that of the Muslim scholars in all the cities and regions of Islam. Thus ash-Shafi'i refuted the position of his shaykh Malik who considered it to mean the consensus of the people of Madina and therefore rejected many *hadiths* on account of that consensus. Ash-Shafi'i discussed in the *Risala* those who contend that an opinion agreed upon in Madina is stronger than a single *hadith*. He himself rejected that position for two reasons. One was that he believed that "the agreed-upon opinion" means not agreement in a single region but the agreement of the scholars of all lands. The second was that in the case of questions in which the consensus of the people of Madina is claimed, some of the people of Madina opposed it and some of the people of other regions opposed it.

Ash-Shafi'i put single *hadiths* before consensus or opinion, whatever the reason for the consensus, unless it was clear that that consensus was based on transmission and a group of people related it from a group of people back to the Messenger. This is what is called the 'tradition of the general public' and so it is put ahead of single traditions.

Before we move on, two further points should be mentioned about consensus. One is that ash-Shafi'i did not take note of tacit consensus, which is when one of the people of *ijtihad* takes an opinion which is known in his time and to which no one objects. Ash-Shafi'i did not consider that to be consensus and stipulated that for consensus to exist, every scholar must transmit an opinion and then the opinions of all must agree on the matter.

The second point is that in his debates ash-Shafi'i did not concede to his opponents when they claimed there was consensus. Then he restricted the definition of consensus until it was almost impossible to reach. He ended by basically confining it to the obligations which are part of indispensable knowledge of the *Shari'a*. Allah knows best.

Analogy

Ash-Shafi'i was the first to formulate the rules cf analogy and explain its basis. The *fuqaha'* before him and in his time made use of opinion without explaining its limits and its basis: in other words, they did not have a set of criteria by which to distinguish between sound and unsound opinions. They did not lay down limits or set out rules and establish principles until ash-Shafi'i laid out the rules for deducing which rulings he considered to be sound and which he considered not to be sound. He defined the limits of analogy, classifying it into several grades, and the strength of *fiqh* based on analogy in relation to *fiqh* based on texts. Furthermore, he elucidated the preconditions which a *faqih* must have when making analogy. Then he distinguished analogy from other types of deduction by opinion since he thought that they were all unsound, with the exception of analogy.

Ash-Shafi'i did not actually define analogy but in the examples he gave and the categories and preconditions he formulated he made it clear what he meant by it when used as a technical term by the scholars of *usul* as an independent objective. It is evident that in his time logical methods were not prevalent in sciences. That is why he did not try to explain analogy in terms of a logical definition as was done later when things were systematised. Scholars have defined analogy as relating a question for which there is no ruling to another matter whose ruling is based on a text, on the grounds that they have the same underlying cause. He used many examples to illustrate this.

One of the major premises of ash-Shafi'i in his discussion of analogy is that all events and occurrences must be subject to a ruling in Islam. Since the *Shari'a* embraces all things, there must be a ruling on every occurrence, either from a text or from an indication or evidence which the seeker can find. What must be explained is the methodology of evidence and indications which Allah has prepared to guide thinking minds to find these rulings. This is what the *mujtahid* must strive to discover. For ash-Shafi'i *ijtihad* on points for which there is no text or consensus can only be made through analogy. One could say that for him, *ijtihad* means analogy.

The invalidation of *istihsan*

Ash-Shafi'i says in *The Invalidation of Istihsan*: "All that is described as I have mentioned regarding the ruling of Allah, then the ruling of the Messenger of Allah, and then the judgement of the community of Muslims, is evidence. No judge or *mufti* is permitted to judge or give *fatwa* unless it is based on a binding report: that is, the Book, then the *Sunna*, or what the people of knowledge said and is not disputed, or an analogy based on one or more of these. There is no *fatwa* by *istihsan* since *istihsan* is not mandatory nor does it fall into one of these categories."

This sentence is representative of his position on *istihsan* in all his books and shows two things. One is that any *ijtihad* in which the *mujtahid* does not rely on the Book, *Sunna*, tradition, consensus, or analogy based on one of them, is *istihsan* because the *mujtahid* takes what he prefers in it, not being based on the evidence or indication of a text. The second is that *ijtihad* by way of *istihsan* without relying on a firm text and proper evidence is, in his opinion, false and has no connection to the *Shari'a*.

Statements of the Companions

We mentioned earlier that ash-Shafi'i put the statements of the Companions in the fourth rank after the Book, *Sunna* and consensus and before analogy; and that he accepted the statement of a Companion if it was not opposed, and chose between them when there were conflicting statements. So we say here that he accepted the statements of Companions and used them in deriving judgements. You might think that he did this in his old school but not in the new – but this is not what we find in the Egyptian *Risala* from ar-Rabi' and in *al-Umm*, which articulates the new school. He did the same in both the old and new schools, as Ibn al-Qayyim states in *I'lam al-Muwaqqi'in*. However, it appears that he did not consider that the statements of *Tabi'un* constituted evidence in themselves.

Ash-Shafi'i's reliance on outward rather than inward meaning

We can say that in his explanation of the *Shari'a*, his extrapolation of its rulings, and his deduction of its principles, ash-Shafi'i relied on the outward and apparent indication of the texts. That is why he rejected *istihsan:* because it was based on the state of the *faqih* or the spirit of the *Shari'a* and depended on the perception of the *faqih* who was trained and skilled in the practice of the *Shari'a* and had a firm grasp of its roots, branches, and sources. Ash-Shafi'i rejected this approach because it was not based on a text in its expressions, indications, or evidence. He took a more literal and objective approach to texts. In his view the legal rulings and judgements of the *Shari'a* concerned outward matters only. The function of the *qadi* is not to delve into people's inner secrets – that is between them and their Creator.

The work of ash-Shafi'i on the fundamental principles

There is no doubt that the science of *fiqh* preceded the science of the principles of *fiqh* and *fiqh* developed by deduction, *fatwa* and *ijtihad*. *Ijtihad* occurred even while the Messenger was alive. The Companions used to exercise *ijtihad* when they were away from him and later submit the matter to him to learn whether their decision was correct or not. Then *ijtihad* continued after him and *ijtihad* was at its peak in the time of the Rightly Guided Khalifs.

Along with the *hadiths* of the Messenger of Allah, they bequeathed to people a wealth of cases, *fatwas* and actual rulings made in the course of running the state and keeping order and dealing with others. Then came the *Tabi'un*, some of whom were skilled in *fatwa* and gave *fatwas* in connection with situations that occurred or might occur. Then the time of the *mujtahids* who founded the schools of law arrived, bringing a wealth of *fatwas*, cases and judgements in Muslim lands which had various and disparate forms. Malik had a legal collection; the *hadith* scholars of Makka had a collection of *hadiths* and traditions relating to *fiqh*; and the people of Iraq had their *fiqh*, much of which was collected from Muhammad ibn al-Hasan ash-Shaybani. There were various legal collections which were a very rich source of knowledge and deduction.

Ash-Shafi'i came upon this wealth and the vigorous debates over it between people of different orientations. He became involved in it in an intelligent manner. The debating led him to reflect on the criteria which underpinned people's positions in debate: how to distinguish the correct from the false, and the bases of investigation, deduction and *ijtihad*. One aspect of that was to examine the principles of the methodology of *fiqh* so as to formulate a firm basis for deduction, systematic rules and criteria by which to analyse opinions and ascertain the sound from the weak.

When ash-Shafi'i arrived on the scene, because of his knowledge of language he was able to deduce rules for the understanding of the rulings of the Qur'an. He was helped in that by the studies the Companions had made of the Qur'an, especially 'Abdullah ibn 'Abbas who was the first teacher of the Makkan school and the Companion with the greatest knowledge of the Qur'an and its abrogating and abrogated verses. At the same time, because of his knowledge of *hadiths* and the agreement and disagreement about them, he was able to define the position of the *Sunna* in relation to the Qur'an. It is clear from ash-Shafi'i's books that he was interested in studying the disagreements of the Companions and analysing them. He was familiar with the *fiqh* of the adherents of opinion who were concerned with analogy even though they had not formulated its rules.

Ash-Shafi'i took upon himself the task of setting out the principles for the methodology of deduction to provide guidance for the *mujtahid* and formulate its criteria. He set out a universal system founded on firm principles other than a mere collection of *fatwas* and precedents or resolving hypothetical questions, thus providing a system for all subsequent *mujtahids* to follow. His influence on the subsequent development of Islam cannot be overstated and it is fair to say that the Islam we have inherited today is in no small part due to the system which ash-Shafi'i formulated twelve centuries ago.

Ahmad ibn Hanbal
(164/780 - 241/855)

Preface

Abu Thawr said about Ahmad ibn Hanbal, "If anyone were to say that Ahmad ibn Hanbal was one of the people of the Garden, he would not be rebuked for that. For if you went to Khurasan, you would hear people say, 'Ahmad ibn Hanbal is a righteous man.' The same is true if you went to Syria: they too would say, 'Ahmad ibn Hanbal is a righteous man.' The same would apply if you went to Iraq: they would say, 'Ahmad ibn Hanbal is a righteous man.' That is the consensus, so if he were to be rebuked for his opinion it would be like saying that the consensus was invalid."

This is the statement of a *hadith* scholar contemporary with Imam Ahmad. He shows his opinion of the Imam by demonstrating how he was seen by all his contemporaries. The people of all regions of the Muslim *Umma* agreed that he was a righteous man and his righteousness, fear of Allah, scrupulousness, strength of faith and asceticism were well-known and doubted by none.

In fact Ahmad was tested and passed the test, and he purified himself by undergoing some difficult and unpleasant trials. He emerged from them like gold which has been refined by the bellows – purified of every impurity. Ahmad was tested by this world and its pleasures and turned from it. Although his self desired the good things of life, he abandoned its appetites, weaned himself from all luxury, and left what gave him doubt for what gave him no doubt. He rejected comforts and was not attracted to any of the luxuries of life, in the same way that dirt will not adhere to a polished surface. Ahmad was tested with both good and bad, and persecution did not bow his neck nor did joy disturb his composure.

Four khalifs tried him in various ways but he emerged from all these trials a righteous man. Al-Ma'mun tested him through injury. He was brought to him shackled in heavy iron chains and subjected to great hardship. Al-Mu'tasim tested him with imprisonment and flogging. Al-Wathiq tested him with a ban and constriction. They did not deflect him from his convictions. Then after those afflictions, he was tested by a different sort of trial. Al-Mutawakkil sent him good things but he rejected them, making himself go hungry and not taking anything whose lawfulness was uncertain. He was scrupulous about that.

Finally Ahmad was tested after all this with the greatest trial which the human soul can undergo: the excessive admiration of other people, which can so easily delude people and beguile them into pride. But he humbled himself before the majesty of Allah, and Shaytan failed to misguide him. He said, "If I could find a way to avoid being mentioned, I would take it." He also said, "Would that I were in a ravine at Makka so that I might be unknown! I have been tested by fame to such an extent that I wish for death morning and evening."

Imam Ahmad was the *faqih* who was dominated by righteousness to the point that his very righteousness prevented him from following through his *fiqh* to the furthest extent. He hesitated when others went ahead and wavered when others resolved. He paused over the meaning when others spoke. He was silent about *fatwas* when others rushed to give them. That is why his inclination to *hadiths* predominated over his *fiqh*, leading some scholars to reckon him a *hadith* scholar rather than a *faqih*.

Thus at-Tabari did not mention Imam Ahmad's school when discussing the disagreements of the *fuqaha'*. He said about him, "He was a man of *hadith*, not a man of *fiqh*, and he was tried on that account." Some *fuqaha'* who used to study disagreements, like at-Tahawi, ad-Dabusi, an-Nasafi, al-Asili al-Maliki and al-Ghazali, did not mention him among the *fuqaha'* whose disagreements are taken into account. In *al-Ma'arif* Ibn Qutayba did not mention him among the *fuqaha'*. Al-Maqdisi mentioned him in the best category of the people of *hadiths*.

Qadi 'Iyad states in *al-Madarik*: "He was less than an Imam in *fiqh* although he had excellence in investigation of its sources." The view of those who denied that Imam Ahmad was a *faqih* is supported by the fact that no book on *fiqh* is reported from him, whereas the *Musnad* is. During his time a great deal was written about *fiqh*. Muhammad ash-Shaybani collected the *fiqh* of Iraq. Abu Yusuf wrote books on *fiqh*, and ash-Shafi'i dictated or wrote down his school. Ahmad, on the other hand, as historians agree, did not do so at all.

That shows that he was a *muhaddith* and not a *faqih*, or at least that *hadiths* dominated his *fiqh*. There is no doubt that some *hadith* scholars held opinions regarding matters of *fiqh*: al-Bukhari falls into that category, as does Muslim. That does not change them from being *hadith* scholars to being *fuqaha'*. If someone is absorbed in the study of *hadiths* and specialises in it, he is a *muhaddith*. If someone gives many *fatwas* and is absorbed in that, he is a *faqih*. We do not find anyone who combines them both equally except Imam Malik ibn Anas, who was unique in that respect.

Ahmad ibn Hanbal was a *faqih* as well as a *hadith* scholar, even though we admit that his inclination to *hadiths* was stronger. He did not leave any writing on *fiqh* but left the great *Musnad* on *hadiths*. He became an Imam in *fiqh* after his death, and that was because his students collected together his statements, *fatwas* and opinions, forming a legal collection which was ascribed to him. Sometimes the transmissions from him varied, as was the case on several occasions, and sometimes they agreed.

That was the view of Ibn al-Qayyim, who states in *I'lam al-Muwaqq'in:* "The reason why Ahmad did not write a book was that he strongly disliked writing books on any other subject than *hadiths*, but Allah knows best what his intention was. It was his students who concerned themselves with recording his books and *fatwas*." Ibn al-Qayyim also says in the same book: "Al-Khallal collected Imam Ahmad's texts in the *Great Collection*, which comprised twenty or more volumes. His *fatwas* and questions were related, and people reported them generation after generation. He became an Imam and model for people of the *Sunna* in subsequent generations, to the point that even those who opposed his school by *ijtihad* and imitated others esteemed his texts and *fatwas*. They gave them their due and acknowledged their closeness to the texts and *fatwas* of the Companions. Anyone who considers his *fatwas* and those of the Companions will see a correspondence between them. All can see that it seems as if they came from the same niche."

Since Ahmad declined to write a book of *fiqh* and forbade his companions to read books of *fiqh* out of fear that doing so would make them dispense with *hadiths*, he relied on his companions' transmission from him for the transmission of his *fiqh*. They transmitted his *fatwas* and statements in simple books. Transmission varies to the extent that it is based on verbal transmission. The Imam himself was not concerned with recording his *fiqh*, and so one must choose among the various transmissions.

We find that those who composed biographical collections speak about the transmission of some of his companions. In his *Tabaqat* Ibn al-Farra' transmitted from Abu Bakr al-Marwazi, al-Athram, Musaddad, Harb and others. There were many reliable men who transmitted Hanbali *fiqh* and ascribed it to the Imam. But we also find some of the writers of reports saying, "Two righteous men were tested by inconsistent colleagues: Ja'far ibn Muhammad and Ahmad ibn Hanbal."

Ja'far ibn Muhammad, known as Ja'far as-Sadiq, was one of the Shi'ite Imams and many words are ascribed to him which are recorded in Imami *fiqh*. Some of the Hanbalis ascribe views on dogma to Ibn Hanbal which cast doubt on the ascription to Ahmad of Hanbali *fiqh*, or at least some of this *fiqh;* for when there is doubt about the truthfulness of the transmitter, the soundness of what is transmitted is also impeached. So there is controversy surrounding the ascription of Hanbali *fiqh* to Imam Ahmad.

If we wanted to study the schools of law in a systematic way it would be sufficient to examine the collection of *fiqh* which forms the Hanbali school inasmuch as it comprises a legal corpus with a unified method, reasoning and direction. One would be justified in studying the corpus without investigating its origins. However, since we are studying the Imam and his *fiqh*, we must study the extent to which this legal collection can truly be ascribed to him and what doubts there are about it.

We must, therefore, study these matters without jumping to conclusions. Our method in this study is based on what scholars of different times have accepted, including evidence of false ascription. This is because scholars accept a text when it appears to be the truth on the basis of its having been transmitted and accepted by subsequent generations. When there is multiple transmission close to the actual time, it is not rejected unless there is evidence against it. If every ascription of doubt were to invalidate received facts, there would be no history at all. So we accept the ascription of *fiqh* to Imam Ahmad as a valid fact and will examine the controversy concerning it.

When we study Hanbali *fiqh* we find a mature strong living *fiqh* in which two elements can be seen, both of which were strengthened and their scope extended in the area of behaviour more than other areas of *fiqh*: tradition and latitude.

• Ahmad's *fiqh* is one in which tradition is manifested in its strongest and clearest form. He preferred the opinions of the Companions. When there were two opinions among the Companions he chose between them. Sometimes he opted for one, but sometimes he had two opinions on the same question, when he did not consider that he had the right to choose between the opinions of those noble people without a justifying text since that would involve contradicting one of them. When there was no text or tradition on a matter from the Companions, he exercised *ijtihad*.

• In the area of social transactions, when there was no text or tradition or possible analogy, he let the matter rest on its basic permissibility. That is why in the field of contracts and preconditions, his is the Islamic *fiqh* with the widest and most extensive scope because it considers contracts and preconditions to be basically sound unless there is clear evidence that they are invalid. No evidence of validity is necessary. Evidence is only required to demonstrate invalidity.

Studying this great school, two main subjects must be dealt with: the basis of legal reasoning in this school and how its sub-branches and secondary rulings are deduced from its main premises, and the precise rules for the branches of investigation of diverse problems on which its *ijtihad* is based. The rules and fundamentals are not all from Imam Ahmad, nor are they transmitted in detail from him. The details were developed after him, being deduced from secondary rulings and extrapolation.

Chapter One
The Life of Ahmad ibn Hanbal
164-241 AH

Birth and lineage

Ahmad was born in Rabi' al-Awwal 164 AH, according to his sons Salih and 'Abdullah. There is no disagreement about the date of his birth as there is about those of Abu Hanifa and Imam Malik. The date of his death also known: sources agree that he died on the 12th of Rabi' al-Awwal 241 AH. His funeral took place on a Friday and his bier was brought out after the people left the *Jumu'a* prayer. There were no fewer than 300,000 present at his funeral in Baghdad. He was very famous at the time of his death.

It was in Baghdad, too, that Ahmad was born. His mother was pregnant when she arrived from Marw where his father had been stationed. It is also said that she gave birth to him in Marw, but the sound version is that he was born in Baghdad. He was a Shaybani Arab on both his mother's and father's side. He was not Persian or non-Arab, but of pure Arab descent.

Shayban was a clan of an Arab tribe known for its pride and zealotry. Al-Muthanna ibn Haritha, who led the Muslim armies against Persia in the time of Abu Bakr, was a Shaybani. The tribe was renowned for zeal and steadfastness. Their dwellings were at Basra and in the surrounding desert. In *Jahiliyya* times they had been located elsewhere in Iraq but when 'Umar ibn al-Khattab built Basra as a settlement for the Arabs who needed the desert air, Shayban settled there. That was where Ahmad's family settled. His grandfather, 'Abdul-Malik ibn Sawda, was one of their notable men.

391

His father was Muhammad ibn Hanbal and his grandfather was Hanbal ibn Hilal. Ahmad's grandfather travelled to Khurasan and he was governor of Sarakhs in the Umayyad period. When the Abbasid uprising came, he assisted them and joined their ranks and was injured in the fighting. Ahmad's father Muhammad was also a soldier. Ibn al-Jawzi described him as a general. Whether he was a general, as Ibn al-Jawzi said, or merely one of the ranks, he was definitely a soldier as was the custom of Arabs of that time. They were rarely farmers or artisans: they were warriors and fighters.

It appears that after the move to Baghdad the family worked for the Abbasids and maintained their connection with them, even if they were not governors. It is known that Ahmad's uncles used to send information about Baghdad to one of the governors when he was absent. From an early age, Ahmad was too scrupulous to involve himself in that activity. It is reported that one of the governors said, "On one occasion news of Baghdad was slow in arriving and so I sent to Ahmad's uncle saying, 'You have not conveyed today's news. I wanted to review it and send it to the khalif.' He said, 'I sent it with Ahmad.' Ahmad, who was then a boy, was summoned and asked, 'Were you not sent with news?' 'Yes,' he said. He asked, 'Why did you not convey it?' He said, 'Would I be likely to forward such information? I threw in it in the river.' The governor said 'We belong to Allah and to Him we return! This lad is scrupulous, so what about us?'" (Ibn al-Jawzi, *al-Manaqib*, p. 22)

Ahmad's father died while he was still a child. It has been said that he never saw him or his grandfather but it is known that his father died after he was born, so he probably saw him as an infant but did not remember him. It is mentioned that he died a young man in his thirties. Ahmad's mother continued to bring him up in his father's family. His father did not leave them totally bereft: they had some property in Baghdad to live in and another estate with a small income which was more or less sufficient to cover their necessities.

Ahmad possessed five qualities which endow the person who possesses them all with distinction and innate nobility. They are:

noble lineage, orphanhood from an early age, self-reliance, self-control and experience of adversity. In addition, he was also in a state of continual, although not overwhelming, poverty which prevented him from becoming arrogant through indulgence or being abased by indigence. He was also endowed with contentment and had a natural bent for intellectual advancement inspired by his fear of Allah and his awareness that nothing else in existence has any real power.

His lineage and poverty combined had their effect. When this world was placed before him, he cast it aside and avoided it with abstemiousness and a fearful heart. Al-Mutawakkil offered him wealth and he returned it with humility. He was aware of people's feelings and his biography reports that "No poor person has been given such honour in an mighty assembly as was Ahmad."

Upbringing and education

Imam Ahmad grew up in Baghdad and received his preliminary education there. He used to mix with all sorts of people of different backgrounds and all types of backgrounds and sciences. There were reciters, *hadith* scholars, Sufis, linguists, philosophers and doctors. Baghdad was the capital of the Muslim world and contained what every capital city contains: many schools, cultural activities, educational resources and varied forms of knowledge. Ahmad's family had chosen for him from his youth that he would be a man of the *deen* and he devoted himself to it, studying all those subjects which were preparation for it: Arabic language, Qur'an, *hadith*, traditions of the Companions and Followers, the life of the Prophet, and the *fiqh* of the *deen*. This education, coupled with his innate capacity, bore great fruit. He memorised the Qur'an at an early age and from his earliest childhood showed himself to be trustworthy and godfearing, qualities which remained with him throughout his life.

When he finished his early studies of the Qur'an and Arabic language, he went to the government offices to study editing and writing. He said about that period, "When I was a lad, I frequented the scribes and then I went to the government offices when I was fourteen."

His trustworthiness as a youth was recognised by both men and women. It is related that while ar-Rashid was at Raqqa with his army, men in the army used to write to their wives, and the women did not trust anyone but Ahmad to read what had been written to them and to write their replies for them. He never wrote anything which he considered objectionable. His qualities were known and remarked on so that fathers saw him as a model for their sons. One father said, "I have spent a great deal employing tutors to teach my son but I find that they do not succeed in doing so. Yet Ahmad ibn Hanbal is a poor orphan and see how he is! His learning and his excellent conduct are both admired." The child is the secret of the man and that was true of the orphan, Ahmad ibn Hanbal. His scrupulousness was in order to please Allah, not to please his uncle or the ruler. Al-Haytham ibn Jamil remarked about him, "If this lad lives, he will be evidence against the people of his time."

From an early age, Imam Ahmad directed himself to learning, with his family's backing. Such knowledge was abundant in Baghdad: the sciences of the *deen*, language, mathematics, philosophy, Sufism. Every field of knowledge was available. He opted for the sciences of the *Shari'a*, from which he could choose either the path of the *fuqaha'* or that of the transmitters of *hadith*. The two sciences had begun to be distinct in his time, one being devoted to *fiqh* and the derivation of *fatwas*, and the other to all the branches of transmission and producing the sources on which the deductions of the *fuqaha'* were based. He was in Baghdad where the *fiqh* of Iraq had been recorded by Abu Yusuf, ash-Shaybani, al-Hasan ibn Ziyad al-Lu'lu'i and others; but there were also many *hadith* scholars in Baghdad.

Ahmad chose the men of *hadith* and their method at the beginning of his life, and devoted himself to it. It appeared that he had accepted the path of *hadith* scholars, not that of the *fuqaha'* who combined *fiqh* and *hadith*. It is related that the first teacher he studied with was Qadi Abu Yusuf, a colleague of Abu Hanifa, but then he inclined to *hadith* scholars. He said, "The first thing I wrote was the *hadiths* of Abu Yusuf." He continued to study with him at the same time that he was going to the *hadith* scholars.

We can say that he devoted himself to *hadiths*, but not in such a way as to cut himself off from examining the findings of the Iraqi *fuqaha'* in respect of *fatwas*, questions and extrapolation. He was knowledgeable on the subject, but it was not his prime interest. His concern with it was a by-product of the science of *hadiths*. Al-Khallal said, "Ahmad used to write books of opinion and memorise them, and then pay no attention to them." One can accept this, for it would be odd for him not to have had this information or to have rejected it without first examining it.

Hence the position of Ahmad regarding the *fiqh* of opinion was that he rejected this course at the beginning of his life. We can infer this from the fact that he first learned *hadiths* from Abu Yusuf who was one of the principal *fuqaha'* of opinion but who nonetheless supported his legal opinion with *hadiths*. But when he completed his basic scholarly education, Ahmad turned to *hadiths*. So he studied the *fiqh* of opinion in a penetrating manner, weighing all the science of *hadiths* which had reached him against the legal decisions which the *fuqaha'* of opinion had arrived at, and then chose the path of the Companions and *Tabi'un* or Followers. That is why he memorised the books of the people of opinion.

Once Ahmad resolved to seek *hadiths*, he had to go to the *hadith* scholars in Iraq, Syria, and the Hijaz. He may have been the first *muhaddith* to collect the *hadiths* of every region of the Muslim world and record them. His *Musnad* is testimony to the fact that he collected *hadiths* in many places.

Logic demands that he must first have learned and memorised the *hadiths* of Baghdad. He took up the study of *hadiths* from the year 179 and continued to reside in Baghdad taking from the shaykhs of *hadith* there and writing down what he heard until 186. In that year he went to Basra and in the following year to the Hijaz. Then he continued travelling, visiting Basra, the Hijaz, Yemen and elsewhere in his quest for *hadiths*. Since he started his search for *hadiths* in 179 and did not travel before 186, he must have continued to collect the *hadiths* of Baghdad for seven years or more, during which he made no journeys of any great distance.

So for those seven years he devoted himself to the study of the *hadiths* of the scholars of Baghdad and their transmission of the *fatwas* as well as the decisions of the Companions and Followers in all areas of *fiqh*.

It is normal that beginners do not pick and choose but rather devote themselves to one scholar for a longer or shorter period until they have drunk deeply from the reservoir of their knowledge. That was the case with Ahmad. He started studying *hadith* and the *fiqh* of Traditions at the age of sixteen in 179 AH, but did not try to negotiate the scholarly minefield without a guide. He devoted himself to an Imam of *hadith* and the science of Traditions in Baghdad and remained with him constantly for four years until he was 20. That man was Imam Hushaym ibn Bashir ibn Abi Khazim al-Wasiti (d. 182). According to Imam Ahmad: "We wrote from Hushaym in 179 and remained with him until 182 when he died. We wrote from him about a thousand *hadiths* on *hajj*, some *tafsir*, and the chapter on judgement, and some other small chapters."

He also studied with others at times and attended some of the gatherings of other shaykhs. It is related that he listened to 'Umayr ibn 'Abdullah in 182 before Hushaym died. He also listened to 'Abdullah ibn Mahdi and it is related that he said, "''Abdu'r-Rahman ibn Mahdi came to us in 180 when he was middle-aged and I used to go and see him in the General Mosque." He also listened to Abu Bakr ibn 'Abbas and related from him.

After Hushaym's death, Ahmad began to take *hadiths* wherever he found them. He stayed in Baghdad for a further three years, diligently taking from its shaykhs without singling out any of them more than another in the way he had with Hushaym. He was about 20 when Hushaym died. He became very serious about seeking *hadiths* and his mother encouraged him in it.

In 186 he began his journeys to learn *hadiths* from men in other lands, in which he travelled to Basra, Hijaz, Yemen and Kufa. He wanted to go to Rayy to listen to Jarir ibn 'Abdu'l-Hamid, as he had not seen him before in Baghdad, but he could not do so because of the great expense involved, so he took his *hadiths* directly from the mouths of those who knew them.

Ahmad went to Basra five times, sometimes staying there for as long as six months at a time. He also travelled to the Hijaz five times, the first time in 187 when he met ash-Shafi'i. As well as taking *hadiths* from Ibn 'Uyayna whom he visited, he also learned the *fiqh* of ash-Shafi'i, his principles and his explanation of the abrogating and abrogated *ayats* of the Qur'an. He met ash-Shafi'i later in Baghdad, when he came there and his *fiqh* and proofs were being refined, even though they were to reach their full maturity in Egypt. Ash-Shafi'i relied on Ahmad to ascertain the validity of some *hadiths*. Ash-Shafi'i used to say to him, "If you consider the *hadith* sound, then tell me and I will take it, be it Hijazi, Syrian, Iraqi or Yemeni."

Ibn Kathir gives us the details of these journeys to the Hijaz: he first made *hajj* in 187 and then in 191, then in 196. He was also there in 197, then went on *hajj* again in 198 and stayed until 199. Imam Ahmad said, "I performed five *hajjs*, three of them on foot. I spent 30 dirhams on one of them. I got lost on the way on one of them while I was on foot. I began to say, 'O slaves of Allah, show me the way,' until I found it." He expected a reward for walking to *hajj* because the greater the hardship which can be borne, the greater the reward. Lack of money was another reason why he went on *hajj* on foot. He stayed near the Ka'ba to seek the *hadiths* of the Messenger of Allah and to discover the *fatwas* of his Companions and their Followers.

Ahmad travelled to Kufa and encountered hardships on that journey even though it was not far from Baghdad. He slept in a house with a brick for a pillow. He said, "If I had had 70 dirhams, I would have travelled to Jarir ibn 'Abdu'l-Hamid in Rayy. Some of my companions went but I was unable to go because I did not have the means." It is clear that he welcomed hardship in his quest of *hadiths* because that which comes easily may soon be forgotten.

After completing his *hajj* in 198, he had the intention to visit 'Abdu'r-Razzaq ibn Himam in San'a. He mentioned this to his companion on *hajj*, Yahya ibn Ma'in. While they were performing *tawaf*, 'Abdu'r-Razzaq also came to do *tawaf* and Ibn Ma'in saw and recognised him. He greeted him and said, "This is Ahmad ibn Hanbal." 'Abdu'r-Razzaq said, "May Allah give him life and make him thrive. I have heard good things about him." Yahya said, "Tomorrow, Allah willing, we will come to listen to you and record your *hadiths*." When he left, Ahmad said, "Why did you make an appointment with the shaykh?" "So that we could listen to him," he replied, "Allah has spared you a month's journey each way and the expense involved." Ahmad said, "Allah would not show me him when I have made an intention, making me invalidate my original intention. We will go and listen to him." But he also went to San'a to listen to him after *hajj*.

His journey to San'a proved to be a difficult and arduous one. His money ran out on the way and he had to hire himself out as a porter until he reached San'a. His companions tried to help him but he refused, praising Allah that he had the strength to earn his livelihood. When he reached San'a, 'Abdu'r-Razzaq tried to help him, saying to him, "Abu 'Abdullah, take this and use it. We are not in a land where trade or earning are easy," and he offered him some dinars. Ahmad said, "I am all right." He remained in that state of hardship for two years, listening from az-Zuhri and Ibn al-Musayyab to *hadiths* which he already knew.

Ahmad continued to travel in search of knowledge. In his last meeting with ash-Shafi'i, he promised to visit him in Egypt, but he did not succeed in doing that. Harmala reported that ash-Shafi'i said, "Ahmad ibn Hanbal promised to come and visit me in Egypt, but he did to come."

He continued in this way until he became an Imam and was seen as such by his contemporaries who wrote from him and listened to him. He was told, "Abu 'Abdullah, you have obtained this level and you are an Imam of the Muslims." He said, "I will need my inkwell until the grave," and "I will seek knowledge until I enter the grave." He based himself on the saying, "A man is a scholar as long as he seeks knowledge. When he thinks that he knows, he is ignorant." This is how he behaved.

Before we move from his constant travel in search of knowledge, we will mention two matters which are connected to his scholarly life and later position. One is that Ahmad was concerned with writing down all the *hadiths* of the Messenger of Allah and the traditions of his Companions that he heard and did not rely on memory alone. That is because it was a time of recording knowledge: *fiqh*, grammar, and *hadiths*. When he related a *hadith*, he did so from a book out of the fear that his memory might err. There are many reports about the prodigious memory of Ahmad and sometimes he did not record an *isnad* because he had memorised it. So he only read the *hadiths* out of scrupulousness and in order to check them.

The second question concerns the sort of knowledge Ahmad sought. There is no doubt that he was concerned with *hadiths* of the Prophet and the *fatwas* and Traditions of the Companions. Does that mean that his knowledge was restricted to Tradition, meaning that he did not look any further than it and used that and nothing else in his *fiqh*? His early association with Abu Yusuf must have called his attention to the derivation of rulings from texts, and, as we have seen, in Makka he learned the principles and method of legal deduction adopted by ash-Shafi'i.

Yaqut reports in the *Collection* that al-Aburri said, "Ishaq ibn Rahawayh said 'We were with Sufyan ibn 'Uyayna writing the *hadiths* of 'Amr ibn Dinar. Ahmad ibn Hanbal came up to me and told me, "Get up, Abu Ya'qub, and I will show you a man whose like you have never seen." I got up and he took me to the courtyard of Zamzam, where there was a man (ash-Shafi'i) wearing a white garment, with a radiant face, good comportment and manifest intelligence. He made me sit beside him. He said, "Abu 'Abdullah, this is Ishaq ibn Rahawayh al-Hanzali." Ash-Shafi'i greeted me and welcomed me and we discussed many things. His knowledge was amazing. After some time I said, "Let us return to the shaykh." He replied, "This is the shaykh." I said, "Glory be to Allah! You left a man who says, 'Az-Zuhri related to me.' I could only imagine that we were going to a man like az-Zuhri or close to him and you bring us to this youth!" He said to me, "Abu Ya'qub, learn from this man. My eyes have not seen anyone to compare with him.""

This indicates Ahmad's esteem for the knowledge of ash-Shafi'i. He said, "It is related that the Prophet, may Allah bless him and grant him peace, said, "Every hundred years Allah Almighty will send to his Community a man who will put the *deen* to rights. 'Umar ibn 'Abdi'l-'Aziz came at the end of the first hundred and I hope that ash-Shafi'i is the one at the end of this hundred." What then was it that Ahmad so admired about ash-Shafi'i? It was not his transmission, since he was not in the same league as Sufyan ibn 'Uyayna or himself in that respect. What he learned from him was legal reasoning, the principles of deduction, and the method of deduction; that was what he so admired. One must acknowledge, therefore, that Ahmad learnt the science of *fiqh* and deduction as well as transmission, since that is what he valued in ash-Shafi'i and in ash-Shaybani and others before them. He was concerned with the study of *fiqh*, opinion, analogy and deduction, even if he was not satisfied with what he found in the books of the Iraqi *fuqaha'* of opinion.

So although he was primarily concerned with *hadiths* and the transmission of Traditions Ahmad also studied *fiqh*. His study of *hadiths* involved investigating their aims, ends and legal significance, and he used to seek out the *fatwas* of the Companions. In his *Musnad* a large section on each Companion is devoted to his *fiqh* and *fatwas*. The section on 'Umar contains the *fatwas* which he gave and he also reports those given by 'Ali, 'Uthman, and 'Abdullah ibn Mas'ud. The transmission of those collections shows a concern for the *fiqh* which they contain.

From all this we see that Ahmad knew both *fiqh* and *hadiths* and so was both a *hadith* scholar and a *faqih*. Abu Hanifa said, "One who learns *hadiths* but does not have *fiqh* can be likened to a chemist who makes up remedies but does not know what they can cure until the doctor comes and tells him. Anyone who learns *hadiths* but does not know the import of the *hadith* until the *faqih* comes is just like that." So in respect of having both *hadiths* and *fiqh*, Ahmad was like Imam Malik, although Malik is better known for *fiqh*.

Did Ahmad study anything other than *fiqh*, *hadiths* and the Arabic language? It seems likely that he did not. He did not study *kalam* or philosophy, as was common in his time, because he did not consider them worthy of consideration. We must not imagine, however, that Ahmad was unaware of the opinions of the various factions, like the Kharijites, Shi'ites, Jahmites, Mu'tazilites and others. He was familiar with them because they were so prevalent at that time. He went five times to Basra, spending long periods there and Basra was the home of the Mu'tazilites, the Kharijites raided from its deserts, and the Jahmites and Murji'ites had groups there and in Kufa. He must have had some experience of them because of their proximity. We also know that he used to accuse the people who held those opinions of innovation and stated that they were far from the path of the *Salaf,* which he could not have done if he had not known their various positions.

Ahmad also forbade the men to whom he related to delve into those positions which he saw as innovations in the *deen,* and so he must have been aware of them. The presumption that he was aware of the views of the sects is further strengthened by the fact that Ahmad knew Persian and sometimes spoke it when the person he was speaking to did not speak Arabic well. This is known by sound reports. Ash-Shaybani mentioned that Ahmad knew Persian and when visitors came from Khurasan, he spoke Persian with them.

Imam Ahmad's sitting to teach *hadiths* and give *fatwa*

Ahmad learnt *hadiths* from those who knew them by listening to them, writing down what he heard and memorising it, and visiting all possible locations where he might learn more of them. He regretted not meeting those great scholars who came before him but Allah compensated him for this. He used to say, "I missed Malik and so Allah gave me Sufyan ibn 'Uyayna in his stead. I missed Hammad ibn Yazid and Allah gave me Isma'il ibn 'Ulayya instead." He sought out *hadiths* from all possible sources and learned the various areas of knowledge connected to the *deen.*

Finally he sat to pass on his knowledge. Ibn al-Jawzi said, "Ahmad did not set himself up to transmit *hadiths* and give *fatwa* until he was forty years old. It is reported that some people came to seek *hadiths* from him in 203 but he refused to relate to them. Then he went to 'Abdu'r-Razzaq ibn Himam in Yemen and returned to Baghdad. Not until 204 was Ahmad found giving *hadiths* and people sitting with him. Until then he did not allow himself to hold assemblies. Why was that? Other *fuqaha'* had gatherings before that age: Malik, for instance, sat for teaching and *fatwa* before that. The reason was that Ahmad did not consider his knowledge of *hadiths* exhaustive and also because some of his shaykhs were still alive. One of his contemporaries mentioned that Ahmad was asked to dictate a *hadith* which he had learnt from 'Abdu'r-Razzaq, but refused because 'Abdu'r-Razzaq was still alive.

I believe that Ahmad acted as he did out of his scrupulousness in following the *Sunna*, from which he tried never to deviate. He attempted to do what the Prophet did in every instance and tried not do what the Prophet, may Allah bless him and grant him peace, had not done. So when he was cupped, he gave the cupper a dinar because it is related that the Messenger of Allah was cupped and gave Abu Tayyiba a dinar, and he travelled by night because that was what the Prophet used to do.

As Ahmad was assiduous about following the *Sunna* in these small actions, he was even more diligent in doing so where major actions were concerned, and there was no action more important in the view of Ahmad than teaching others, one of the core actions of all the Prophets, may Allah bless them and grant them peace. The Prophet was appointed by Allah at the age of forty, first received the Qur'an at that age, and was only sent as a teacher to mankind at that age. So Ahmad felt that he should follow him in that and was too modest to sit to give *fatwa* and *hadiths* before he reached the age of forty.

We cannot claim that Ahmad was never asked for a *fatwa* about something regarding which he knew a tradition and refused to give it before that age, or was asked about a *hadith* and refused to recount it. In fact the opposite is probably true, since to have refused would have meant withholding knowledge and the *deen* requires that the *hadiths* of the Messenger of Allah be disseminated. Indeed there are reports which testify that he was seen giving *fatwa* in the Khayf Mosque in 198 when he was 34.

Since Ahmad was quite renowned in the Islamic world before he sat to teach and give *fatwa*, his classes were very crowded. Some transmitters mention that the number of those who attended them was 5000 of whom about 500 wrote down what he related. The place must have been very large to have been able to accommodate that number, and since only the Great Mosque in Baghdad was big enough that is where he must have taught. It also indicates that the standing of Ahmad among the people of Baghdad must have been very high. The magnitude of the number attending also means that there were a great many people who transmitted his *fiqh* and *hadiths*.

Not everyone who attended was necessarily seeking knowledge. Some were seeking blessing, some desired admonition, and some came to learn about the man and observe his character and *adab*. Ibn al-Jawzi mentions in *al-Manaqib* that one of his contemporaries said, "I went to Abu 'Abdullah Ahmad ibn Hanbal twelve times. He was reading the *Musnad* to his sons. I did not write a single *hadith*. I was just interested in his character and *adab*." (p. 210)

It appears that Imam Ahmad had two assemblies for study and *hadiths*. One was at his home where he taught his students and children privately and the second was in the mosque which the public and large numbers of students attended. But only 500 wrote – in other words, about a tenth of those present.

In the mosque he taught after *'Asr*, as is stated in the *History* of adh-Dhahabi. Perhaps he chose that time because it was before nightfall and after the heat of the day and a time of inactivity for most people so it was easy for them to attend. To hear *hadiths* or *fatwas* at that time coincided with a time of natural receptivity of the soul. Three characteristics could be observed in Ahmad's classes which had a profound effect on the souls of those present.

• His gatherings were dominated by gravity, tranquillity, humility and calm. There were no jokes or jesting, because jocularity on the whole is unfruitful and because jests tend to be the chattering of the mind. His companions were aware of his attitude and they never joked in his presence in a gathering of knowledge or elsewhere. His shaykhs knew of that and they

403

too did not jest in his presence. Ibn Nu'aym related that Khalaf ibn Salim said, "We were in the gathering of Yazid ibn Harun and Yazid joked with those to whom he was dictating. Ahmad ibn Hanbal cleared his throat. He struck his brow with his hand and asked, "Why didn't you tell me Ahmad was here! I would not have joked."

• The second characteristic is that he did not give lessons unless asked. He would be asked for the *hadiths* on a certain subject and then call for the books written on those *hadiths*. He would first discuss what had been asked about, and if it was a *hadith* of the Prophet he would only relate it from a book out of the desire to have accurate transmission and as little suspicion of error as possible. So rarely did he not consult a book that they could count the times he transmitted without it.

Ibn al-Jawzi reported that Abu Hatim ar-Razi said, "I went to Ahmad ibn Hanbal for the first time when I met him in 213. He brought with him the Book of Drinks and the Book of Faith to the prayer. He prayed and no one asked him about anything, so he returned to his house. I went to him another day and he brought out two books. I thought that he expected Allah to reward him or that he had brought them because the Book of Faith is the basis of the *deen* and the Book of Drinks keeps people from evil: the root of every evil comes from intoxication."

So we see that Ahmad took books with him to the mosque in case people should ask about the *hadiths* in them. It also shows that he transmitted from the text. His son 'Abdullah said, "I only saw my father relate *hadiths* from his memory without a book less than a hundred times."

• The third characteristic of the lessons of Ahmad ibn Hanbal was that there were two categories of subject matter. One was the transmission of *hadiths*. This was dictated to his students from a book, as we said. The second was the legal *fatwas* which he had to deduce. He did not allow his students to record them nor did he give them leave to transmit them from him, since he would not permit anything to be recorded apart

404

from the *hadiths* of the Messenger of Allah, may Allah bless him and grant him peace. He considered the knowledge of the *deen* to consist of knowledge of the Book and the *Sunna* and that it was an innovation to record people's opinions alongside the Book of Allah and the *Sunna* of His Messenger. The most detestable thing in his view was to see a book in which his *fatwas* were recorded. He detested his adherents transmitting his *fatwas* and attributing them to him.

He heard that one of his students had related *fatwas* from him and disseminated them in Khurasan. He said, "Bear witness that I retract all of them." A Khurasani man brought him books, and when he looked in the books and found his views and words he was so angry that he threw the book to the ground. That applied not only to his own opinions but also to those of others. A man asked him whether he wrote books of opinion and he said, "No." The man said, "Ibn al-Mubarak writes them." Ahmad said, "Ibn al-Mubarak did not descend from heaven. We are commanded to take knowledge from above." He forbade *hadith* scholars to write the books of ash-Shafi'i and Abu Thawr even though ash-Shafi'i was his shaykh and he had a high regard for him.

Before moving on, we should mention Ahmad's lifestyle during the time that he was seeking *hadiths* and *fiqh* and while he was teaching. He led a pure *Salafi* life, in which he kept himself above the intellectual controversies of the time as well as its political, social and military quarrels. He chose to confine himself to the ambience of the Companions, the elite *Tabi'un* and those after them, and to follow their path. So his knowledge and *fiqh* were the *Sunna* and its *fiqh*. He did not investigate anything unless he knew that the Companions had investigated it and even then he followed their opinion and rejected that of others. If he did not know that the Companions had delved into it, he refused to do so. He protected himself by exercising extreme caution. Why did he follow that course? For the answer to this question we must touch on his times to shed some light on the environment in which he lived.

405

Ahmad's time was one in which Persian elements dominated the Arab elements and Persian civilisation was in ascendance in general in Muslim society. The Muslim cities were awash with differing nations and races, and philosophical treatises were being translated from Syriac, Greek and other languages so that cultures were mixed together. The nature of the time was that there were many conflicts as different religions clashed with one another and deviant views appeared. There was a great deal of intellectual deviation so that the odd was frequent and the strange familiar.

These things appeared in the Abbasid era from the time that matters were settled by Persian swords. Al-Mansur's reign had been energetic but not firm and when al-Mahdi succeeded, there were armed insurrections but he was able to curb them. Ar-Rashid wanted to suppress these conflicts and move to an Islamic society. He brought *fuqaha'* and *hadith* scholars close to him and gave them a prominent position in his government. Then when al-Ma'mun came to power, his supremacy over his brother al-Amin could only be consolidated by means of Persian arms and so the non-Arab elements became strong again. Philosophy and new sciences found a great proponent in al-Ma'mun.

Villains and corrupters multiplied and there were many concealed saboteurs in Islamic society as well as many strange views. Scholars took divergent paths. Some followed the path of opposition and conflict, but Ahmad chose to be far from disputes although he was in their milieu. He turned to the spirit of the righteous *Salaf* so that some of his contemporaries described him as a great Follower outside his proper time.

Ahmad cut himself off from those who delved into anything other than what was transmitted from the *Salaf* and did not allow himself to waste time in responding to such people. Such was his way until his death. A man wrote to him to ask about debating with the people of *kalam* and Ahmad wrote back to him, "May Allah make your end good. What we have heard is that our forebears used to dislike *kalam* and sitting with members of deviant sects. What is required of us is submission and stopping with what is in the Book of Allah and not going beyond that. People dislike any innovator who writes a book, and sitting with such people to reply to them may confuse us about our *deen*."

Ahmad forbade people to study *kalam*, the science which discusses dogma using philosophical means. He criticised those who involved themselves in *kalam*, even if they were correct, and forbade detailed investigation of the Names and Attributes of Allah. That was because it was not something which the *Salaf* had done. It might be correct or might lead to misguidance because the mind may become confused about such matters.

The Inquisition (*Mihna*): its causes and stages

The cause of the Inquisition, which was to play such a painful part in the life of Imam Ahmad, was that al-Ma'mun called on the *fuqaha'* and *hadith* scholars to adopt the Mu'tazili position and declare that the Qur'an was created. They were to state that the Qur'an was created and originated within time, as the Mu'tazilites said. Al-Ma'mun chose the Mu'tazilite view and supported its adherents. People disagree about Ahmad's position on this question and we will deal with it in detail when we examine his opinions; but scholars confirm that Ahmad did not agree with al-Ma'mun's opinion and refused to make that statement and endured severe persecution on that account. The Inquisition began in the time of al-Ma'mun but continued through the reign of al-Mu'tasim and al-Wathiq on al-Ma'mun's instructions.

Al-Ma'mun wanted to compel Ahmad to state that the Qur'an was created. The first to make this statement was al-Ja'd ibn Dirham in Umayyad times. Khalid ibn 'Abdullah al-Qasri executed him on the *'Id al-Adha* in Kufa. He was brought in chains and Khalid said to the people, "Go and make your sacrifices. They will be accepted, Allah willing. I want to slaughter al-Ja'd ibn Dirham. He claims that Allah did not speak directly to Musa and that Allah did not take Ibrahim as a Friend. Exalted is Allah above what He says!" Something similar is also said about al-Jahm ibn Safwan who denied that Allah had speech and stated that the Qur'an was created and not timeless.

Then the Mu'tazilites came on the scene and denied the reality of Allah's Attributes. They denied that Allah Almighty speaks, saying that what is related in the Qur'an about Allah speaking to Musa does not mean direct speech but rather that the words were created in the Bush before Musa heard them. They do not accept that Allah can be described as speaking but hold that He creates all speech as He creates everything else. In the same way they believe that the Qur'an is created. The Mu'tazilites went very deeply into the concept of the createdness of the Qur'an in Abbasid times. A few *fuqaha'* joined them in that, such as Bishr al-Marisi whom Abu Yusuf expelled from his assembly when he refused to retract.

Their efforts began to intensify in the reign of ar-Rashid and they began to call people to their position. Ar-Rashid was not so bold as to delve into theological details and argue about them in philosophical terms, so the Mu'tazilites were not endorsed by him and it is even related that he jailed a group of them. But when al-Ma'mun came to power his entourage and the men closest to him were Mu'tazilites; he honoured them to such an extent that it is reported that when Abu Hisham al-Qawti, one of the Mu'tazilite leaders, came to him, he rose to honour him – something which he did not do for anyone else. The reason for this inclination was that al-Ma'mun had been a student of Abu'l-Hudhayl al-'Allaf who was a leader of the Mu'tazilites.

When al-Ma'mun convened gatherings for the purpose of debating about religious positions, the Mu'tazilites proved to be the most proficient in that arena against their opponents owing to their extensive study of philosophy. That had such a great influence on al-Ma'mun that he chose some of them as his companions and officials, especially Ahmad ibn Abi Du'ad. When the Mu'tazilites became aware of this preference, they started to propagate openly their view that the Qur'an was created. Al-Ma'mun agreed with it and proclaimed it in 212 AH as his own position, having examined the evidence and proofs presented for it. However, he left people free in respect of their beliefs and did not impose it on those who did not believe it or, indeed, had not even considered the matter.

But in 218 AH, the year he died, al-Ma'mun decided to use the power of the authorities to force people to embrace the createdness of the Qur'an. While he was in Raqqa, he sent letters to Ishaq ibn Ibrahim, his viceroy in Baghdad, ordering him to question the *fuqaha'* and *hadith* scholars and compel them to say that the Qur'an was created. It appears that he began to force those in positions of authority, and all who were connected to the government, to accept the Mu'tazili position by any means, even witnesses in the courts. The first letter he sent to Baghdad ends as follows:

> Assemble the *qadis* and read to them the letter of the *Amir al-Mu'minin*. Begin by examining what they say and investigate their beliefs regarding the creation and origination of the Qur'an. Inform them that with respect to governmental posts the *Amir al-Mu'minin* will not seek the help of or rely on or entrust his flock to anyone whose deen is not secure and whose *tawhid* and certainty is not pure. If they affirm that and concur with the *Amir al-Mu'minin* and follow the path of guidance and salvation, then command them to provide a list of witnesses and to ask them about their view regarding the Qur'an. Refuse the testimony of those who do not affirm that it is created and forbid them from being registered. Write to the *Amir al-Mu'minin* listing the *qadis* in your district who come to you regarding this question. Order them to do the same, and then oversee them so that the judgements of Allah are only carried out by the testimony of those with insight into the *deen* and sincerity in *tawhid*." (at-Tabari)

We can see from this that at first the only punishment was removal from government positions and the non-acceptance of testimony. The khalif's governor, Ishaq ibn Ibrahim, carried out these instructions in respect of the *qadis*; he then summoned the *hadith* scholars and all of those who gave *fatwas* and questioned them and sent their answers to al-Ma'mun. Al-Ma'mun then sent his governor a second, much harsher, letter stating his opinion of the foolishness of the answers, outlining the penalties for those who did not accept his position and ordering him to send to him in chains those who refused. He said, "Mention those whom you have named who have denied idolatry (*shirk*) or refused to answer and did not state that the Qur'an was created. Send them all, under guard and in chains, to the army of the *Amir al-Mu'minin*. If they do not retract and repent, he will compel them all at sword-point, Allah willing."

Ishaq hastened to fulfil his instructions and summoned the *hadith* scholars, *fuqaha'* and *muftis*, including Ahmad ibn Hanbal, threatening them with dire punishment if they did not affirm what was asked of them and take the position that al-Ma'mun demanded of them. All but four did so. The hearts of those four remained firm, content with the decree of Allah, preferring the everlasting to the ephemeral. They were Ahmad ibn Hanbal, Muhammad ibn Nuh, al-Qawariri and Sajjada. They were chained and fettered and spent the night in chains. In the morning, Sajjada submitted and they let him go but the rest remained.

The following day, they were questioned again and al-Qawariri faltered and told them what they wanted and they let him go, so that now only two remained. They were taken in chains to al-Ma'mun in Tartus. Ibn Nuh was martyred on the way. Those who had done what was wanted of them went unfettered to al-Ma'mun and were well-treated. On the way, news of the death of al-Ma'mun arrived, but he had ordered his brother al-Mu'tasim to hold to his position about the Qur'an and to compel all people to accept it by force. He felt he had to do so. The Inquisition reached its apex in the reign of al-Mu'tasim and that of al-Wathiq. Let us look briefly at the letters sent by al-Ma'mun to investigate their tone.

The first letter of al-Ma'mun

"The right due to Allah from the Imams and Khalifs of the Muslims is to strive to establish the *deen* of Allah, which they must preserve, and to safeguard the legacy of the Prophet, which they have inherited. They must prefer the knowledge which he entrusted to them, act by the Truth in respect of their subjects, and obey Allah regarding them. Allah requires the *Amir al-Mu'minin* to resolve on guidance and to be just in respect of what Allah has entrusted to him by His mercy and grace.

"The *Amir al-Mu'minin* knows that the common people do not investigate or deduce by the evidence and guidance of Allah or seek illumination by the light of Allah and its proof in all areas. They are ignorant and blind to the reality of His *deen* and *tawhid* ... They are unable to value Allah as He should be valued; to recognise Him as He should be recognised, or to distinguish between Him and His creation, because of their deficient intelligence and inability to think logically. That is why they set forth an equivalence between Allah and the Qur'an He has revealed, maintaining that it is outside time, not created and originated by Allah.

"Allah Almighty says in His Book, which He has made a healing for the breasts and a mercy and guidance for the believers, *"We made it an Arabic Qur'an."* (43:3) 'Made' means created. He says, *"Praise belongs to Allah who created the heavens and the earth and appointed darkness and light."* (6:1) He says, *"Thus do We give you news of what has gone before."* (20:99) So He reports the stories of things after they have happened. He says, *"Alif Lam Ra. A Book whose verses are perfectly constructed, and then demarcated, coming directly from One who is All-Wise, All-Aware."* (11:1) Every 'constructed' and 'demarcated' thing must be created and originated.

"Then people presented a false argument, called people to their position and claimed to be the upholders of the *Sunna* while in every part of the Book of Allah are stories whose very words invalidate their position and refute their claim and position and their creed..."

The rest of the letter, as already mentioned, orders to examine the position of the *qadis* and witnesses and to inform the Khalif of their positions. The letter is dated Rabi' al-Awwal, 218 AH.

411

The second letter

In the previous letter al-Ma'mun was writing to Ishaq ibn Ibrahim about seven particular individuals, including Muhammad ibn Sa'd al-Waqidi and others, instructing him to examine them and question them about the createdness of the Qur'an. They all agreed that the Qur'an was created and so he sent them to Madinat as-Salam (i.e. Baghdad) and Ishaq ibn Ibrahim brought them to his house. They were famous among the *fuqaha'* and shaykhs of *hadith*. They confirmed their previous reply and so were released by Ishaq at the command of al-Ma'mun. Then al-Ma'mun wrote to Ishaq ibn Ibrahim a second time:

> "One of the rights due to Allah from His khalifs on the earth, and those entrusted with authority over His slaves, whom He has been pleased to appoint to establish His *deen*, preserve His creation, carry out His judgements and *sunnas*, and to lead with justice, is that they themselves should strive for the sake of Allah to be faithful to Him in what they preserve and guide to Him with the best knowledge with which He has entrusted them and the recognition which He has placed in them..."

(Then after citing people's views regarding the createdness of the Qur'an and citing the reasons for his own position, he goes on:)

> "Read to Ja'far ibn 'Isa and 'Abdu'r-Rahman ibn Ishaq, the Qadi, the letter of the *Amir al-Mu'minin* which I have written to you and examine their knowledge concerning the Qur'an. Inform them that the *Amir al-Mu'minin* will not seek help in the affairs of the Muslims from any except those whose sincerity and *tawhid* he trusts, and that no one has true *tawhid* except those who affirm that the Qur'an is created. If they take the position of the *Amir al-Mu'minin*, then have them test those who attend their gatherings to bear witness and ascertain their position about

412

the Qur'an. Whoever does not say that it is created, his testimony is invalid and judgement may not be given on the strength of it. Do the same with all those you appoint to be *qadis*. Investigate them so that Allah may increase your insight. Write to the *Amir al-Mu'minin* about what transpires."

These are the two official letters which began the Inquisition. Ishaq began to examine people receiving after the first letter and completed his examination after the second. He transcribed the replies he received and then informed al-Ma'mun or, more precisely, Ahmad ibn Abi Du'ad. He summoned a group of the *fuqaha'*, judges and *hadith* scholars, including Bishr ibn al-Walid, Sajjada, al-Qawariri, Ahmad ibn Hanbal, Qutayba, Sa'dawayh al-Wasiti, 'Ali ibn Abi Muqatil and others. He began by reading out al-Ma'mun's letter twice so that they understood and then he began to ask questions.

He said to Bishr ibn al-Walid, "What do you say about the Qur'an?"

"You know my earlier statement to the *Amir al-Mu'minin*."

"Reiterate for the *Amir al-Mu'minin* what you think."

"I say that the Qur'an is the Word of Allah."

"I am not asking about that. Is it created?"

"Allah creates everything," responded Bishr.

"Is the Qur'an a thing?" asked Ishaq.

"It is a thing," he replied.

"Then it is created."

"It is not a creator," replied Bishr.

"I am not asking you about that. Is it created?"

"Nothing good can be said on the subject beyond what I have said to you. I made a contract with the *Amir al-Mu'minin* that I would not speak about it. I have nothing further to add to what I have told you."

Ishaq took the paper before him and read it to him. Then Bishr said, "I testify that there is no god but Allah, alone, unique. There was nothing before Him and there is nothing after Him. He does not resemble any of His creation in any way."

413

The governor told the scribe, "Record what he said."

Then he said to 'Ali ibn Abi Muqatil, "What do you say, 'Ali?"

"You have heard my reply to the *Amir al-Mu'minin* more than once. I have nothing to add to what he heard from me."

He read what was in the document and then Ishaq asked him, "Is the Qur'an created?"

"The Qur'an is the Word of Allah," answered 'Ali.

"I am not asking about that," responded Ishaq.

"It is the Word of Allah and the *Amir al-Mu'minin* has commanded something and we obey."

He told the scribe, "Record what he said."

He had a similar exchange with adh-Dhayyal. Then he asked Abu Hasan az-Ziyadi, "What do you say?"

"Ask what you like," said Abu Hasan.

Ishaq read him the document. Abu Hasan agreed with its contents and then said, "Whoever does not say this is an unbeliever," adding, "The Qur'an is the Word of Allah and Allah created everything and what is other than Allah is created. The *Amir al-Mu'minin...* We obey his command."

Then Ishaq turned to Ahmad ibn Hanbal and asked, "What do you say about the Qur'an?"

"It is the Word of Allah."

"Is it created?"

"It is the Word of Allah. I add nothing to that."

He read to him what was in the letter and when he came to the words "He does not resemble any of His creation in any way," Ahmad said, "I say, *'There is nothing like Him and He is the Hearing, the Seeing.'*"

Ibn al-Bakka' turned to him and said, "May Allah put you right. He means hearing with an ear, seeing with an eye."

"What is the meaning of "Hearing, Seeing'?" Ishaq asked Ahmad.

"He is as He describes Himself," replied Ahmad.

"What does it mean?" He repeated.

"I do not know. He is as He describes Himself."

Then he called all of them man by man and took down their replies which he sent to al-Ma'mun. Nine days later, after the letter of al-Ma'mun in reply to that of Ishaq had arrived, he summoned them again.

The third letter

The *Amir al-Mu'minin*, replying to Ishaq's letter, said that he had reflected on the replies of those named in the letter. He declared that Bishr al-Walid, who had denied the resemblance of anything with Allah and said that what kept him from saying that the Qur'an was created was that he had a contract with him, lied and disbelieved. There had been no conversation with him on the subject and no agreement: Bishr must actually state that the Qur'an is created. Al-Ma'mun said about Ibn Hanbal, "As for Ahmad ibn Hanbal and what you wrote about him, inform him that the *Amir al-Mu'minin* knows the import of those words and his method in them and they are evidence of his ignorance."

So much for the letters. Before moving on to the persecution and humiliation involved in the Inquisition and the transportation of scholars in abasement and chains and iron fetters so that one died a martyr on the road owing to the weakness of his body, we should see what moved al-Ma'mun to undertake that course of action which lifted Ahmad ibn Hanbal to the ranks of the heroes so that it has been said, "If he had been one of the tribe of Israel, he would have been a Prophet." We find that the reason for al-Ma'mun's action is quite evident; history records it and these letters and style of writing clearly indicate the perpetrator.

Al-Ma'mun appointed Ahmad ibn Abi Du'ad al-Mu'tazili as his minister and made him his scribe and agent in his government. He thought well of him and so ordered his brother, who succeeded him, to maintain him in his position. The letters which were written are clearly in the language of Ibn Abi Du'ad. No khalif would have written at such length and in such detail. Furthermore the expression is almost always in the third person, only occasionally slipping into the first person. It descends to attacking the *fatwas* of an individual and accuses another of allowing usury. Al-Ma'mun would never have sunk to that level. So we can only suppose that these letters were written while al-Ma'mun was ill in bed. If he had been strong and healthy, he would not have allowed a letter to be sent in his name which contains attacks on specific individuals and descends to trivialities.

We know that al-Ma'mun believed in the createdness of the Qur'an from the time he came to power and even before that. He used to argue about it and invite people to debate with him about it without ever investigating their hearts, examining their intellects, or imposing any punishment. Why should he suddenly change at the very end of his life? Why should he suddenly make the issue a matter of violent persecution? There is no doubt that Ahmad ibn Abi Du'ad wrote these letters and instigated the Inquisition, taking advantage of al-Ma'mun's weakness to do so.

If that were not the case, why did al-Ma'mun not summon these scholars for examination while he was in Baghdad and they were all there around him? Why did he wait until he was absent from Baghdad to send these letters when he was on the point of death? There is no doubt that it was Ahmad ibn Abi Du'ad, using the authority of al-Ma'mun's name, who was responsible for this.

Leaving aside the rights and wrongs of such a course of action, al-Ma'mun died as Ahmad was being brought to him in chains, but his death did not stop the Inquisition. Indeed, it began to move into a harsher and more wide-ranging phase. The reason is that it was claimed that al-Ma'mun left two instructions to his brother al-Mu'tasim on the subject: one was to continue to question people about the createdness of the Qur'an, and the second was to keep Ahmad ibn Abi Du'ad in power. It was his idea that people should be forced by using the power of the state to adopt the Mu'tazili position and that punishment and imprisonment should be employed to that end.

Al-Mu'tasim was not a man of knowledge. He was a man of the sword, which he never put down. He left the business of the createdness of the Qur'an to Ibn Abi Du'ad to carry out. When al-Ma'mun died, Ibn Hanbal was returned to prison in Baghdad until his case could be presented. Then he was sent to al-Mu'tasim and subjected to threat and promise. When neither enticement nor menace worked, they carried out the threat and began to flog him

416

time after time. Each time it continued until he lost consciousness and was insensible to the prick of a sword. The torment was repeated throughout Imam Ahmad's imprisonment, over a period of about twenty-eight months. When they despaired of him they began to show some compassion and released him, sending him home exhausted from wounds, continual flogging, and imprisonment in dark dungeons.

Ahmad remained in his house after he returned to it, too weak to move. Helped by his fear of Allah, he defeated others even though they were strong. He remained unable to teach, perhaps owing to weakness resulting from his injuries, but was able to go to the mosque. When Allah restored his health and his body recovered, even though he was left with chronic effects and pains in some parts, he continued to relate *hadiths* and teach in the mosque until al-Mu'tasim died. When al-Wathiq came to power, he renewed the Inquisition on Ahmad; but he did not flog him as al-Mu'tasim had done, because he saw that that would increase Ahmad's reputation in the eyes of the people and anger the masses. He forbade him to mix with people. Al-Wathiq told him, "Do not meet with anyone and do not live in any city where I am." So Imam Ahmad remained in hiding and did not go to the prayer or anywhere else until al-Wathiq died.

The Inquisition was not confined to Ahmad, although he was the most famous for his steadfastness under it. Others endured it as *fuqaha'* were brought from all cities to Baghdad to be examined about their faith; amongst them was al-Buwayti, ash-Shafi'i's student, who died in chains.

Imam Ahmad's livelihood and environment

We have mentioned Imam Ahmad's scholarly life and that he sought knowledge and *hadiths* in all parts of the Muslim world and became an Imam to be followed. We have mentioned the hardships to which he was exposed in his life. We have not as yet examined the sources of Ahmad's income and whether it was ample or merely adequate. Did he accept the gifts of the khalifs, as Malik, Abu

Yusuf, and ash-Shaybani had done; or did he abstain like Abu Hanifa; or was he in the middle like ash-Shafi'i? These questions should be examined and we will briefly do that. We will mention his situation and income and then his relations with the khalifs before and after the Inquisition.

Ahmad was poor and his means were very limited. He preferred poverty to wealth unless he could be certain that it was completely lawful and that it would not incur obligation. He was often compelled to work with his hands to earn or to hire himself out to work when he had no money. He preferred that to accepting gifts in spite of his hardship. He lived off the income of an estate which he inherited from his father. According to Ibn al-Jawzi, "Ahmad inherited a weaving shop from his father and used to take the income from that place which he rented out to people." It also appears that he had other shops which he let out.

We read in *Hilya al-Awliya'*: "Ahmad ibn Muhammad ibn Hanbal dropped some scissors into a well and the resident came and got them out for him. When he got them out, Abu 'Abdullah gave him half a dirham. The man said, "The scissors are worth a *qirat*. I will not take anything." He then left. After some days Ahmad asked him, "How much do you owe for the shop rent?" He replied, "The rent for three months," and its rent was three dirhams a month. So he put it on his account and told him, 'You owe nothing.'"

This indicates that Ahmad did not bear a grudge and that he repaid acts of kindness many times over. He had shops and income from them, but they did not did provide him with an income adequate for his needs. There are conflicting reports about its size. Ibn Kathir said, "The income from his property was seventeen dirhams a month, which he spent on his family and remained steadfast and patient." This is a small estate indeed and would certainly not have been enough to support him. If anyone asked him for something he gave it. Ibn al-Jawzi says, "A man asked Ahmad ibn Hanbal about the estate which was the source of his income and the house in which he lived. He said, 'This is something I inherited from my father. If a man came to me and proved it was his, I would leave it and give it to him.'"

He would not accept a gift or help from anyone. Sometimes he was in very straitened circumstances because his income was not enough for his family's expenses, and he experienced great hardship. But he was patient and endured that as he had on his journeys when his provisions ran out. He refused gifts, considering that being beholden to people was worse than hardship. He had three ways of supplementing his income and making sure that his family's needs were met.

The first means was collecting the gleanings of the crops after harvest, which it is permitted. That great scholar carried his tools on his shoulder and went and gathered the gleanings left on the ground. He was careful not to go onto anyone's land without first asking permission and not to ruin anyone's crops. It is reported that he said, "I went to the outlying fields on foot and collected gleanings. I saw some people ruining people's crops. No one should enter a person's field without their permission." (Ibn al-Jawzi, *al-Manaqib*, p. 224)

The second way he used was to hire himself out, for instance as a porter on the road, when he could not find other income except wages. He also used to act as a scribe for a wage if he needed money. Adh-Dhahabi says in his *History*: "'Ali ibn al-Jahm said, "We had a neighbour who sent a book to us. He asked, 'Do you recognise this handwriting?' We replied, 'It is that of Ahmad ibn Hanbal. How did he come to write this for you?' He replied, 'We were staying in Makka with Sufyan ibn 'Uyayna and we missed Ahmad for some days. So we went to ask after him and his door was shut. "What's up?" I inquired. He replied, "My clothes have been stolen." I said, "I have some dinars. If you wish, they are a gift. If you wish, a loan." He refused to accept my offer so I said, "Then write something for me for a wage." He agreed, so I paid him a dinar and he told me, "Buy me some cloth and cut it into two pieces so I can use one as a waist-wrapper and the other as a cloak, then bring me some paper. I did that and brought him paper and he wrote this for me."'"

Adh-Dhahabi reported that Ishaq ibn Rahawayh said, "Ahmad and I were in Yemen with 'Abdu'r-Razzaq. I was in the top room and he was below. Once when I was going out to buy something I discovered that his funds were exhausted and I offered him money, but he refused. I said, 'It can be a loan or a gift.' He refused. He wove waistbands and then sold them."

The third way he solved the problem was by resorting to loans. It is clear that he did not do that in all cases. He sometimes did it when his own income was due and about to come and when he was certain that the lender did not intend to turn his loan into a gift. Sometimes he took a loan and resolved to repay it even when the lender did not want him to, for Ahmad would always insist on repayment. He once borrowed 200 or 300 dirhams from a godfearing man, knowing that his property was purely lawful. When he went to repay him the man said, "Abu 'Abdullah, I did not give it intending to take it back from you." He replied, "I took it only intending to repay it to you."

Ahmad's refusal of appointments and stipends from the khalifs

You have seen how Ahmad refused to accept gifts and how scrupulous he was about his *deen*. He only took good and lawful money about which there was no doubt. In *zakat* he went to extremes in imposing it on himself, choosing the most rigorous positions, so that he paid *zakat* on the estate which provided his livelihood following the *fatwa* of 'Umar at the conquest of the Sawad[1] of Iraq.

Such were Ahmad's abstinence and spending where the people of knowledge and *hadith* were concerned; and he behaved in the same way where the money of the khalifs was involved, it being wealth collected from the *zakat* of the people. One of the duties imposed on them is to spend it for public benefit, and there is no doubt that assisting scholars is one of the ways in which it can lawfully be spent. Had he taken it, he would not have been taking from the property of the khalifs but from the wealth of the

1. lit "the Black", the fertile agricultural area of southern Iraq. When it was conquered, 'Umar decided to levy the *kharaj* tax on it.

Community. But Ahmad shunned the khalifs and avoided them completely, refusing to take money or appointments from them in any manner whatsoever.

When ash-Shafi'i came to Baghdad for the second time and his school spread there, Ahmad stayed in his assembly and did not leave it except to seek *hadiths* on a journey or at home. Ash-Shafi'i found out that Ahmad had gone to Yemen to learn the *hadiths* of 'Abdu'r-Razzaq ibn Himam and was experiencing great hardship because of his lack of money. He was asked to choose a *qadi* for Yemen and thought it would be a good idea to appoint Ahmad so that he could listen to 'Abdu'r-Razzaq without hardship. The position was offered to Ahmad but he refused. The offer was repeated and Ahmad told his shaykh, ash-Shafi'i, for whom he had great esteem, "Abu 'Abdullah, if I hear this from you again you will not see me with you again." He refused the generous offer because he wanted to be independent and to have money that was free of any doubt. Besides, he believed that hardship undergone for the sake of knowledge increased steadfastness.

What is very clear is when he had no funds he refused to have any recourse to the money of the khalifs. The Imams fall into three groups in that regard. One group firmly refused any money from rulers. Along with Ahmad, Abu Hanifa and ath-Thawri were among them. Abu Hanifa knew that he was exposing himself to punishment by his refusal because al-Mansur was testing him through his offer, but he still refused.

The second group accepted stipends from the khalifs and used the money to see to the needs of the poor among the people of knowledge, enabling them to live in a manner befitting people of knowledge without extravagance. At the head of this group are al-Hasan al-Basri and Malik. Malik did not refuse to take from khalifs because it was the wealth of the Muslims and it was acceptable that the people of knowledge who were teaching people their *deen* and commanding them the correct and forbidding the wrong should share in it. Their task was similar to that of the army in defending the frontiers of Islam against the enemy so that they would not find a way to get at the Community. What the army do outwardly the scholars do inwardly, preventing misguidance and inroads being made into the hearts of the Muslims. So Malik thought it proper to accept that help and to strive to influence the ruler through admonition.

The third category is in the middle between the two. They agreed to work for the khalifs and take stipends but to give them away as *sadaqa*. If there was an allotted portion which was not a gift, they took it, as ash-Shafi'i did: he was appointed to an official position by ar-Rashid and accepted payment.

There is no doubt that Ahmad chose the course of Abu Hanifa even though his situation exposed him to more hardship because he was poor. He had to work for a wage and copy out books for a fee, whereas Abu Hanifa was a wealthy man and had more than adequate provision, which enabled him to satisfy his own needs and those of the *fuqaha'* and *hadith* scholars connected to him. Ahmad refused to take anything at all from the khalifs. Al-Ma'mun thought that money should be paid to all the shaykhs of *hadith*, who could then dispense it to those who were needy. All took it except Ahmad.

When the Inquisition was over and there was peace and tranquillity in the reign of al-Mutawakkil, Ahmad underwent another test which is hard on the self, when al-Mutawakkil offered him lot of money and wealth and wanted to honour him. Ahmad sternly refused and did not take it or give it as *sadaqa*; he would not have anything whatever to do with it.

Chapter Two
The Erudition of Ahmad ibn Hanbal

Ahmad's great learning was well-known and people spoke about it while he was still alive. In fact his knowledge of *hadiths* and tradition was already celebrated while he was still young and studying with his shaykhs, so that Ahmad ibn Sa'id ar-Razi said about him when he was young, "I have never seen anyone with black hair who had memorised more *hadiths* of the Messenger of Allah, may Allah bless him and grant him peace, or had more knowledge of *fiqh* than Ahmad ibn Hanbal." His shaykh ash-Shafi'i told him, "You have better knowledge of sound reports than we do. If it is a sound report, inform me so that I can take it, be it Kufan, Egyptian or Syrian."

Al-Muzani reported that ash-Shafi'i observed, "Three of the wonders of the time are Abu Thawr, an Arab who cannot decline a single word; al-Hasan az-Za'farani, a Persian who does not err in a single word; and Ahmad ibn Hanbal, a young person who is such that whenever he says anything, old people accept what he says." Harmala ibn Yahya, the student of ash-Shafi'i, reported that he said, "When I left Baghdad I did not leave behind anyone more scrupulous or godfearing, or with more *fiqh,* than Ahmad ibn Hanbal." Given what ash-Shafi'i, the great scholar, said about Ahmad as a young man, there can be no doubt that as he grew older, with his constant search for *fiqh* and *hadiths*, his knowledge and intellect increased and his name and fame spread, especially after he endured affliction with steadfastness.

Many of his contemporaries mentioned his knowledge. 'Ali ibn al-Madini said, "There is no one among us who has a greater memory than Abu 'Abdullah ibn Hanbal." He said, "I have known Abu 'Abdullah for fifty years and he is still increasing in good."

Al-Qasim ibn Sallam said, "Knowledge has reached four men: Ahmad ibn Hanbal, 'Ali ibn al-Madini, Yahya ibn Ma'in and Abu Bakr ibn Shayba. Ahmad has the most *fiqh* among them." He said, "I have not seen a man with more knowledge of the *Sunna* than he has." Yahya ibn Ma'in said, "By Allah we were not strong in the way Ahmad was strong nor could we follow the path of Ahmad." 'Abdu'r-Rahman ibn Mahdi said, "This is the man with the most knowledge of the *hadiths* of Sufyan ath-Thawri." He said, "I have never looked at Ahmad ibn Hanbal without being reminded of Sufyan ath-Thawri." Sufyan was an ascetic *faqih*.

That is a small selection of what has been transmitted about the knowledge of this Imam showing the esteem he enjoyed among his contemporaries. Now we want to look briefly at his intellectual development. There are four factors which govern a person's development. The first are a person's qualities of character, whether innate or acquired; the second are the teachers who directed him and influenced him; the third is the actual life of the individual and his personal studies; and the fourth is the time in which he lives. We will examine these factors one by one.

Qualities of character

Imam Ahmad possessed outstanding qualities of character, and this is one of the reasons for the fame he acquired. One of them was the extensive knowledge for which he was known. Some of them were gifts from Allah, the Exalted and All-Powerful, who gives to whoever of His creatures He wills. Some were acquired. We will now discuss these characteristics and the effect they had on the formation of his knowledge.

The first quality was a strong retentive memory, which is an essential attribute in any *hadith* scholar and particularly the leaders among them – and one that was shared by Malik and ash-Shafi'i, who were among the *fuqaha'* who left a legacy of *fiqh*, investigation and deduction. A good memory is the basis for any kind of knowledge and investigation, and scholars must have it in order to retain what they learn. One aspect of intelligence is the ability to memorise information and then access it once it is stored in the memory.

Ahmad was gifted with a prodigious memory and we know that because he said so himself. He recalled, "Once I was discussing the *hadiths* of ath-Thawri with Waki'. After he prayed *'Isha'*, he would walk home from the mosque and I used to talk with him then. Sometimes he gave nine or ten *hadiths*, and I would memorise them. When he entered, the students of *hadith* would say to me, 'Dictate to us,' so I dictated them to them and they wrote." His contemporaries also noted his excellent memory. Abu Zur'a was asked, "Who has the best memory among the shaykhs and *hadith* scholars?" "Ahmad ibn Hanbal," he replied.

Imam Ahmad did not merely have a good memory. He transmitted what he received and not only memorised the *hadiths* of the Messenger of Allah and the *fatwas* of the Companions and *fatwas* of the *Tabi'un* who were famous for scrupulousness, *fiqh* and *fatwa*, but also understood what a knowledgeable deducer would understand. He was remarkable among the *hadith* scholars of the time in that respect. They confined themselves to transmission without *fiqh* and understanding, as if they were leaving deduction to the *fuqaha'* whose speciality it was. To quote Abu Hanifa's comparison, they were like the chemists who had the medicines while the *fuqaha'* were the doctors who knew how to use them. Ahmad, on the other hand, was both pharmacist and doctor, being concerned with grasping the *fiqh* contained in the Traditions as well as simply memorising them and passing them on.

Ishaq ibn Rahawayh said, "In Iraq I used to sit with Ahmad ibn Hanbal, Yahya ibn Ma'in and their companions. We would discuss a *hadith* by one, two and three paths of transmission. I would ask, "What does it mean? What is its explanation? What is its *fiqh*?" They would all pause, except Ahmad ibn Hanbal. He had knowledge of *hadith*, *Sunna*, the *fatwas* of the Companions and derivation of judgements from them, which made him an imam in *hadiths* and an imam in *fiqh*."

Ibrahim al-Harbi said of him: "I have met three men whose like I have not seen and never will see. I saw Abu 'Ubayd al-Qasim ibn Sallam. He was a rope into which a spirit had been breathed. I saw

Bishr ibn al-Harith. He was like a man who was intelligence personified from head to toe. I saw Ahmad ibn Hanbal and it was as if Allah had gathered in him the knowledge of the first and the last: that is the memory of *hadiths,* the traditions of the *Salaf* and a grasp of their *fiqh.*"

The second quality, the foremost of Ahmad's qualities and the one for which he is most renowned, was his steadfastness, endurance, and patience. They form the sum of noble qualities and their basis is strength of will, true resolve and far-reaching aspiration, no matter how weary the body becomes. Ahmad possessed such a temperament and through it had nobility in spite of poverty, chasteness, self-reserve, and an immense capacity to endure injury. This enabled him to bear all the hardships he had to face in his quest of knowledge and prevented him from being content with little knowledge, enabling him to travel extensively and cross wastelands and deserts, on foot if necessary, to gain it.

We should mention the quality of steadfastness, for which Ahmad was famous, which is mentioned by Allah in Qur'an where the Prophet Ya'qub says, *"but steadfast patience, that is beautiful."* (12:18) This sort of patience is without any moaning, complainting, or lamentation. That is was the kind of patience Ahmad had. He did not complain but endured, as was amply demonstrated during the Inquisition.

The reader may wonder about the secret of this strength which gave Imam Ahmad the capacity to endure and overcome hardship. I believe that the secret lay in the fact that great men are supported by Allah alone and rely on Allah alone: they do not feel the power of anything but Him, their hearts being filled with an overwhelming awareness of the Divine presence before which everything else fades into insignificance. It is reported that a man slandered him in the most appalling way and then said to him, "Abu 'Abdullah, I have slandered you. Return me to a lawful state." He said, "You are in the lawful provided you do not repeat it."

The third quality for which he was distinguished was integrity in every sense of the word, and integrity takes many forms and has many manifestations. He was honourable and did not take either a little or a lot from other people's property. He was scrupulous in his beliefs and said only what he believed, not flattering or dissimulating, even when facing the sword. He was honest in his intelligence and never delved into any topic which the *Salaf* had not delved into. Such was his approach in *fiqh*. He used to say that asceticism made hearts yielding and souls tender.

At-Tartusi reported on the same subject, "I went to Abu 'Abdullah and asked him, 'What makes the heart tender?' He looked at his companions and was silent for a time. Then he lifted his head and said, 'My son, consumption of the lawful.' I went to Bishr ibn al-Harith and asked him, 'Abu Nasr, what makes the heart tender?' He replied, 'Is it not by remembrance of Allah that the hearts are made tranquil?' I said, 'I have come from Abu 'Abdullah.' He asked, 'What did Abu 'Abdullah say to you?' 'Consumption of the lawful,' I replied. He said, 'He came up with the heart of the matter.' I went to 'Abdu'l-Wahhab ibn Abi'l-Hasan and asked him the same question. He said, 'Is it not by remembrance of Allah that the hearts are made tranquil?' I stated, 'I have come from Abu 'Abdullah.' His cheeks were rosy with joy and he asked, 'What did Abu 'Abdullah say?' 'Consumption of the lawful,' I replied. He said, 'He has come up with the essence of the matter. The basic truth is as he said. The basic truth is as he said.'"

Imam Ahmad loved friendship and friends and knew that a life without friends was a harsh, abased life. He used to say, "When friends die, a man is brought low." He was generous with the little lawful wealth he obtained, and used to say about it, "If a Muslim man has only a little of this world, even if the amount be no more than a morsel, and then takes it and puts it in the mouth of his brother Muslim, he is not being prodigal. This is the furthest extent of generosity."

The integrity of his intellect and faith are clearly illustrated by what is reported about the Inquisition and how he was steadfast in the face of it, refusing to consider a matter that had not been considered by the *Salaf* and to become involved in questions which might lead to misguidance. This same integrity kept him from arguing with the people of sects and innovations because the clash of ideas between debaters made things confused for others. So he forbade his companions to debate with such people in order to preserve their faith from doubt.

One of Ahmad's companions asked him what he thought about those who debated with the Jahmites, explaining their errors and showing them and others where they went wrong. He replied, "I do not think that the ideas of any of these sects should be discussed and I do not think that anyone should debate with them. Did not Mu'awiya ibn Qurra say, 'Disputes wipe out good deeds and corrupt words cannot call people to good. Avoid the people of argumentation and *kalam* and hold to the *sunan* and what was done by the people of knowledge before you. They used to dislike theological discussion and becoming involved with the people of innovation. Safety lies in avoiding this. We do not command debate and disputation.' He also said, 'When you see that someone likes *kalam*, admonish him.'" (*Tarikh adh-Dhahabi*, p. 22)

Someone wrote to Ahmad to ask him about debating with the people of *kalam* and sitting with them, and he dictated this letter in reply to the question: "May Allah grant you a good end. What we used to hear and receive from those we met is that they disliked *kalam* and sitting with the people of deviation. We are commanded to submit to and stop at what is in the Book of Allah and not to exceed that. People continue to dislike any innovator who writes a book, or sitting with an innovator, since that might being about something which will cause confusion in a person's *deen*."

The line Imam Ahmad took was also the line of Imam Malik ibn Anas, may Allah be pleased with him. He too disliked argumentation and considered that argumentation was far from the core and reality of the *deen*, and that the people who were involved in disputation were those who corrupted matters of the *deen* for other people. This was the course followed by Ahmad ibn Hanbal.

Abu Hanifa and ash-Shafi'i followed a different course. Abu Hanifa debated with the Jahmites and others and argued with them and confounded them. Ash-Shafi'i debated forcefully with his opponents, but in order to arrive at the truth, not win an argument. His books all take the form of excellent direct debate, using all manner of methods and techniques to make their points.

As regards the integrity of his *fiqh*, Ahmad was keen to deduce directly from the *Sunna* and to follow the Messenger and Companions in all his *fiqh* and opinions. The basis of his *fiqh* was what was related from the Prophet, the Companions and the *Tabi'un*. He was very eager in his *fiqh* not to reject a *hadith* of the Messenger of Allah unless it was countered by something stronger. He used to say, "Anyone who rejects the *hadith* of the Messenger of Allah is on the verge of destruction." He also used to say, "I have never written down a *hadith* of the Prophet without acting by it."

Where there was no *sunna* from the Companions, he exercised *ijtihad* to resolve the question following the method of those before without inventing a method other than the one they had followed. He forbade *ijtihad* concerning any question about which there was no previous discussion or method. He told his students, "Beware of speaking about a question in which you have no imam." Thus we see that he was eager to ensure that his *fiqh* did not digress from the *Sunna*.

The fourth of the qualities for which Ahmad was known was sincerity. Sincerity in the quest of the truth purifies the soul of base desires, illuminates insight, makes perception correct, and illuminates the heart with the light of gnosis and true guidance. We find that the three Imams who preceded Ahmad in legal *ijtihad* all had this quality and were distinguished by it. For guidance can only be possessed by someone into whose heart Allah has cast the light of sincerity, since sincerity towards Allah is to love something for Allah's sake alone. He does not seek knowledge for the sake of debate or dispute, or in order to have a following, or to gain the esteem of the ruler. Whoever rises to this rank with his knowledge is not attached to argumentation and sects, but to the reality which is straight with no crookedness. He reaches that by the light of Allah and speaking wisdom by the guidance of Allah.

Allah gave Ahmad a large portion of sincerity in seeking knowledge of the Book and *Sunna*, and his quest was not made out of any desire for position or fame. Indeed, he was averse to that and hoped to go unnoticed by people. He was so keen on avoiding reputation that he kept his inkwell hidden so that people would not think that he was eager to write. He said, "Displaying an inkwell is part of showing off." He preferred no one to listen to him and said, "I would like to settle in Makka where I could lose myself in one of the ravines and so escape being recognised."

The fifth quality he possessed – the one which enabled his lessons and words to have an effect on the souls of his listeners – was natural authority. He was awe-inspiring without causing fear and greatly venerated and esteemed. His students had great reverence for him and would not jest in his presence. The police were in awe of him, even when they passed by his house. It is related that a policeman was appointed to call him at night for prayer, but was too in awe of him to knock on his door, preferring to knock on his uncle's door. The respect his students had for him was even greater. One of his contemporaries who was his student said, "I visited Ishaq ibn Ibrahim and other rulers, but I did not see anyone who inspired more awe than Ahmad ibn Hanbal. I went to speak to him about something and I began to tremble from awe when I saw him." Al-Qasim ibn Sallam said something similar. What was the secret of the awe that this great man inspired? It is a gift of Allah Almighty which He bestows on whomever He wishes among His slaves. There are people to whom Allah gives strength of soul, strength of will and spiritual radiance which has an effect on others. Ahmad possessed this.

In spite of this majestic presence he was good company. He was not harsh and rude. He had a cheerful disposition and expression as well as noble character. He was very modest with true self-effacement before Allah. He was also modest before people and not averse to them or arrogant towards them. Someone who described him said, "I did not see anyone in the time of Ahmad who more combined religiousness, chastity, self-control, good manners and noble character, a firm heart, generous and noble companionship, and lack of laziness." Another said, "Ahmad was the most modest and the noblest of people. He had the best manners. He often bowed his head and lowered his eyes. He avoided ugliness and levity. Only discussion of *hadith* was heard from him. He mentioned the righteous and ascetics with gravity, tranquillity and fine words. When he met anyone he smiled at him and welcomed him. He was very humble towards shaykhs and honoured and respected them." (*al-Manaqib*, p. 214)

Such was the character of Ahmad. It was based on the guidance of the Prophet, may Allah bless him and grant him peace, and taking him as a model as commanded by Allah in His Noble Book.

Imam Ahmad's shaykhs

The shaykhs of Ahmad all taught him *fiqh* or a *sunna* or related a *hadith* to him, whether that had been transmitted to them elsewhere or they had learned it in Baghdad. The number of his shaykhs, as enumerated by Ibn al-Jawzi in the *Virtues of Ahmad*, exceeds a hundred, so his shaykhs were very numerous indeed; and all of them had some effect on him, even if some of them only reported one or two *hadiths* to him or he only met them a few times. We will concentrate on the most notable ones, confining ourselves to one or two in the life of the Imam. We recognise in studying Ahmad two kinds of shaykhs: those who increased his inclination towards the *Sunna* and those who directed him to *fiqh* as well as the *Sunna*. There are two important personalities who stand out in this respect, both of whom had a profound effect on him.

The first person who influenced him and caused him to seek the *Sunna* constantly was Hushaym ibn Bashir ibn Abi Khazim. We know that when Ahmad turned to the study of *hadiths* at the age of sixteen, he went to Hushaym and stayed with him for four or five years. He directed himself completely towards the *Sunna* and related from Hushaym and all the *hadith* scholars of Baghdad, but it was Hushaym who had the greatest effect on him.

Hushaym was born in 104 AH and died in 183 AH. He met *Tabi'un* such as 'Amr ibn Dinar, az-Zuhri and others. He was concerned with learning the traditions of Ibn 'Amr and Ibn 'Abbas. He had a *hadith* circle in Baghdad, and when Ahmad turned to *hadith* he found that he was the shaykh of this circle. He had great renown in Islam and had a great effect on Ahmad so that he hardly questioned him because of his awe of him and his esteem for his knowledge. Throughout the entire time he was with Hushaym, he only asked him one or two questions. He used to praise and glorify Allah between the transmission of *hadiths*. Hushaym's life was entirely devoted to knowledge and he strove for it and made things difficult for himself.

His roots were in Bukhara but his father lived in Wasit. It is related that he was the baker of al-Hajjaj ibn Yusuf. When the family moved to Baghdad, he practised that profession and he was famous for preparing certain types of fish dishes. When his son inclined to knowledge, that was not customary in his family and it seemed odd to them. He used to forbid his son to study and criticise him for it, but he endured the criticism and continued to learn *hadiths*. He used to attend the gatherings of Qadi Abu Shayba and debate with him about *fiqh*. Once he was ill and Abu Shayba missed him. He was told he was ill and he said, "Let us go and visit him." So the people of the gathering all went to visit him, following the *Qadi*. They went to the house of Bashir the Baker. When the *Qadi* and his companions left, Bashir said to his son, "My son, I used to forbid you to seek knowledge. Today I do not. Fancy the *Qadi* coming to my door! How could I ever have imagined that!" (*Tarikh Baghdad*, pt. 14, p. 92)

So Imam Ahmad continued to seek *hadith* and made various journeys to Makka, where he met az-Zuhri and learnt a large number of *hadiths*. He also travelled to Basra, Kufa, and elsewhere. He took from the scholars in all these places and continued to do so until he was a leading light in the knowledge of *hadiths* in Baghdad and had his own circle, although there were rival circles, like that of Waki'. Enough proof of his position is that men like Malik ibn Anas were among those who transmitted from him. His position and knowledge had a great effect on Ahmad. He said, "I memorised everything from Hushaym while he was alive, before his death."

It appears that Ahmad learned many *hadiths* from Hushaym, but little *fiqh*. This other aspect was satisfied by another personality – Imam ash-Shafi'i, to whom Ahmad attached himself after Hushaym's death. When he went on *hajj*, Ahmad met ash-Shafi'i and admired his legal intellect and effective deduction and the

432

rules and criteria which he made the basis of deduction. That was while ash-Shafi'i was teaching in the Masjid al-Haram and reflecting about the rules of deduction, after he had returned to Makka having studied the *fiqh* of opinion in Baghdad with ash-Shaybani. Ahmad listened to him for his *fiqh*, not his transmission of *hadiths*, as he told Ishaq ibn Rahawayh, "Abu Ya'qub, learn from this man. I have never seen anyone comparable to him!"

Since it was legal thought, logical deduction and the setting out of the principles of deduction which Ahmad admired in ash-Shafi'i, it is clear that this formed a second aspect of Ahmad's knowledge, the first being the direction he took at the beginning of his life with Hushaym in studying *hadiths* and the *Sunna* and deducing *fiqh* from that source. Thus Ahmad had two sources, even though that of the *Sunna* predominated over the other. As we said earlier, he had many other shaykhs whom we have not mentioned and we have selected these two in order to point out the two main sides of his development – his *hadiths* and his *fiqh*.

Ahmad's private studies

Ahmad also studied a great deal on his own according to his own inclinations. He sought out *hadiths* with great eagerness like someone who tastes and enjoys food and finds it delectable. He never had his fill of them and hence constantly travelled in search of them. He said, "I will continue to seek knowledge until the grave."

One question which arises is: in this scholarly effort and these qualities did Ahmad not have a prior model to follow? There is no doubt that the desire of Ahmad at the beginning of his life and with the direction of his shaykhs Hushaym and ash-Shafi'i was like that of Sufyan ibn 'Uyayna, the Imam of *hadith* in Makka, and 'Abdu'r-Razzaq, the Imam of *hadith* in Yemen. There is no doubt that all of this, coupled with his taste for the *Sunna* and its *fiqh*, was the strongest of his motivations. But there must have been a model for him to have based himself on in this great effort. It is not difficult to discover some of these Muslim personalities in whose footsteps Ahmad followed.

'Abdu'r-Rahman ibn Mahdi said about Ahmad, "He is the most knowledgeable of people of the *hadiths* of Sufyan ath-Thawri." Ibrahim ibn Ishaq al-Harbi mentioned those who preserved the *Sunna* and said, "Sa'id ibn al-Musayyab in his time; Sufyan ath-Thawri in his time; and Ahmad ibn Hanbal in his time." Sufyan was in the middle of the chain and Ahmad at the end of it. Even if Ahmad did not meet Sufyan himself, he took from him via his students and knew his transmissions.

There are other personalities who resemble Ahmad, such as 'Abdullah ibn al-Mubarak. Ahmad at-Tirmidhi said, "Ahmad resembles no one more than 'Abdullah ibn al-Mubarak in both method and presence." The contemporaries of these three men observed the link between Ahmad and these two Imams. When Ahmad began to study he wanted to meet the second of them, but he died before that could happen. Ahmad said, "I sought knowledge when I was sixteen and the first person I listened to was Hushaym, in 179. Ibn al-Mubarak came in that year, which was the last time he came. I went to his gathering and was told that he had left for Tarsus. He died in 181." (*al-Manaqib*, p. 25)

Sufyan ibn Sa'id ath-Thawri was a *faqih* and *hadith* scholar in Kufa contemporary with Abu Hanifa. Abu Hanifa's *fiqh* was dominated by analogy and *istihsan*, while *hadiths* and *Sunna* were predominant in Sufyan's so that he was reluctant to go beyond what was transmitted. Both of them avoided the ruler and refused to accept appointment as *qadis*. Sufyan had absolutely no Shi'ite leanings, while Abu Hanifa did. When Sufyan was in Syria he extolled the virtues of 'Ali, since he had no partisans there; and when he was in Iraq he extolled the virtues of 'Uthman because he had no supporters there. He mentioned the virtues of Abu Bakr and 'Umar in Kufa, where support for 'Ali was strong, and mentioned the virtues of 'Ali when he was with those who attacked him.

Sufyan lived off the income of his inheritance from his family and refused to humble himself by asking for money or accepting gifts from the Khalifs. Ahmad did the same, although his income was less. Sufyan frequently angered the khalif of the time by his forthright statements and several times he was forced to flee. Sufyan also travelled a great deal in search of *hadiths*. He too, like Ahmad, was very serious.

The second personality is 'Abdullah ibn al-Mubarak, whom Ahmad tried to meet but who died in 181 before he was able to do so. He also followed the way of Sufyan ath-Thawri in his method and was one of the strongest men and most scrupulous to do that. He also kept himself far from the ruler and official positions. However, Ibn al-Mubarak was very rich and had enough means to prevent him having to work. He gave a great deal away. As well as having abundant knowledge, Ibn al-Mubarak was a warrior and *mujahid*. Thus he combined *fiqh*, *hadith*, *jihad*, and spreading Islam. He often went on *hajj*.

He was very concerned with the knowledge of Traditions and *sunan* and used to spend the night studying them. He was asked, "When you have prayed, why do you not sit with us?" He replied, "I go and spend time with the Companions and *Tabi'un*." He was asked, "How do you spend time with the Companions and *Tabi'un*?" He replied, "I go and look into my knowledge and learn their traditions and actions. Why should I sit with you? You slander people."

These men were models for Ahmad's behaviour and his course of action in scrupulousness, asceticism and concern for the *Sunna* and steering well clear of innovations.

Chapter Three
Ahmad's Time and its Effect on Him

Ahmad lived at the time when all the elements of the Abbasid era reached their high point. Everything brought its fruits in his time, be they sweet or bitter, pleasant or unpleasant. On the political front, the Abbasid state was established and stabilised and there was no powerful contender against it. The Kharijites were broken and played no further role. After ar-Rashid, the 'Alawites had no power with which to launch an attack. So there was no rebellion against the Abbasids.

The government was severe with those who came out against them, whether they were relatives or others, and conflict and rivalry between its members occurred. A civil war broke out between al-Amin and al-Ma'mun which ended in the killing of al-Amin and the victory of al-Ma'mun. But the end was not praiseworthy because victory was only achieved with the help of Persian arms, the battle of between al-Amin and al-Ma'mun being basically between the Persian and Arab armies.

Then al-Ma'mun turned to *jihad* as did al-Mu'tasim and al-Wathiq after him, and the state became a feared power. But, at the same time, the factors were already present which were to bring about its eventual downfall. There was the fact that the khalifs relied on non-Arabs for their power. Al-Ma'mun based his on the Persians and al-Mu'tasim based his on the Turks. They drew their strength and their armies from them. Later these forces were to kill the khalifs and appropriate power for themselves, and on this account the Abbasid state eventually broke up into smaller states.

Such were the political circumstances of the time and the end that they would lead to, some of which Ahmad lived to see. He was a Shaybani Arab and his grandfather had been one of those who fought to establish the Abbasid state but did not live to see the abasement of the Arabs. That situation did not please Ahmad. It angered him. But he was not a man of the sword and did not form a party and would not encourage sedition. He did not criticise the rulers: what he did was to devote himself to knowledge and turn away from politics.

Ahmad proceeded on a middle path, between those of the two Imams before him, Malik and Abu Hanifa. Abu Hanifa criticised the Abbasids in his lessons and encouraged people against them by some expressions he used in his *fatwas,* openly encouraging the 'Alawites. Malik did not think that it was permitted to rebel. He discouraged people from doing so, and involved himself with rulers with the aim of rectifying them and encouraging them to remove injustices and behave correctly. Ahmad was between the two. He neither called for sedition nor encouraged it; he did not direct himself against the rulers but neither did he befriend them or accept their stipends or gifts.

That Persian domination or, to be more precise, the reign of al-Ma'mun, was accompanied by the influence of a group of Mu'tazilites in respect of both knowledge and governance. Ahmad considered their method of deduction of dogma to be deviation from the path of the *Salaf* and the *Sunna.* That increased his desire to avoid rulers, because he could not remain silent in the face of what he saw as Mu'tazilite innovations. He forbade people to sit or debate with them, and thereby open the gate to innovations. At this point we need to speak briefly about the Mu'tazilites.

The existence of the Mu'tazilites was needed in the Abbasid era because at that time there were *zindiqs* who proclaimed views which corrupted the Muslim community, concocted plots to destroy Islam and schemed against the Muslims. There were those who wanted to destroy Islamic rule and revive Persian rule, as was the case with al-Muqanna' in Khurasan, who rebelled in the time of al-Mahdi. Therefore the Khalifs drew the sword against the *zindiqs* and encouraged scholars to counter them on the intellectual front. The Mu'tazilites were at the forefront of this offensive and so the khalifs brought them close to them and opened their palaces to them in the time of al-Mansur, al-Mahdi, al-Ma'mun, al-Mu'tasim and al-Wathiq.

The Mu'tazilites effectively refuted the *zindiqs*, Magians and others who engaged in debate with them and fought hard in the defence of Islam. They used deduction as their means of deriving dogma, using new techniques different from those used by the Companions and Followers. They used the same means as their opponents in attack and defence, and dealt with the same issues they dealt with. Hence they dealt with philosophical questions which the *Salaf* had never been concerned with. They spoke about man's will and actions and Allah's power in them, and the Attributes of Allah and whether they are other than the Essence or part of the Essence.

The *fuqaha'* and *hadith* scholars saw all this, and that it was a different course from that followed by the Companions and Followers in the deduction of dogma. They deduced their doctrines from the texts of the Book and the *Sunna*, exercising *ijtihad* when there was no text, whereas the Mu'tazilites sought to affirm creeds by logical criteria and employed the method of philosophical analysis for the *deen* as a whole.

Both groups continued along these separate tracks. But from the reign of al-Ma'mun until the time when al-Mutawakkil came to power, the khalifs tried to force scholars to embrace some of the Mu'tazilites' views, particularly that of the createdness of the Qur'an. There was strong antagonism between the two groups, so that the Mu'tazilites became the opponents of the *fuqaha'* and *hadith* scholars. That is why Ahmad was averse to them.

Leaving *kalam* aside for the moment, we will turn to the science of *fiqh* and *hadith* in that time. As we said, it was an era in which things came to fruition, *fiqh* reached its maturity, and its methods were established. Scholars met and travelled to different regions and knowledge from each locality spread throughout other regions. The books of ash-Shafi'i display an amalgamation of the efforts of scholars of various regions. Each juristic school was recorded by a group of *mujtahids*. Malik wrote the *Muwatta'* and his students after him set out Maliki *fiqh*. Abu Yusuf wrote books containing some of Abu Hanifa's *fiqh* and Muhammad ash-Shaybani wrote a comprehensive collection of Iraqi *fiqh*. Then

438

ash-Shafi'i produced *al-Mabsut* which reflected all the *fiqh* of the time and became known as *al-Umm*.

Ahmad inherited that immense legal legacy, read much of it, and studied with some of those scholars. He studied with ash-Shafi'i during his second stay in Baghdad and wrote down his *Risala* and *Mabsut* as related by az-Za'farani. He had already met the *fuqaha'* of Iraq and the sources state that he departed from their *fiqh* after having studied it because he decided to follow a different course. Nonetheless his intellect and thinking were nourished by these legal fruits, of which he was aware, in addition to his knowledge of the *Sunna*.

The study of *hadiths* also became mature in Ahmad's time. The study of *Sunna* and Traditions was not yet complete. Much was transmitted as coming from the Messenger of Allah, but there were no rules for distinguishing what was sound or weak, what was truthful and what was not. 'Umar ibn 'Abdi'l-'Aziz had wanted to collect the sound *hadiths* but died before that could be accomplished. Scholars recorded the *Sunna*, Malik compiled his *Muwatta'*, ash-Shafi'i his *Musnad*, and Abu Yusuf and ash-Shaybani also had their collections of Traditions. These collections, however, were regionally based.

The *Muwatta'* contains the Traditions in Madina which Malik considered to be sound and the same applies analogously other collections of the time. In Ahmad's time, the *hadiths* of different regions were brought together, which led to a more comprehensive collection, and *hadiths* began to be arranged under legal headings. This was accompanied by comparison of *isnads*, weighing the relative strengths of the transmissions, and a comprehensive knowledge of abrogated and abrogating texts.

Not only was the collection of *hadiths* well-developed at that point: their study was as well. Malik began to examine the men from whom he related as one might examine a coin to see if it was genuine, then he analysed *hadiths* in the light of the Book and well-known *Sunna* texts. Ash-Shafi'i came and studied *muttasil*, *mursal* and *muntaqi'* *hadiths*, and the weight of each in terms of legal deduction, how they were ranked, and which should be accepted when there was a contradiction. Then the study of *isnads*

439

was perfected, going through each chain of transmitters back to the Messenger of Allah, upon whom be Allah's blessings and peace. In the time of Abu Hanifa and Malik, who were near to the *Tabi'un*, people were only concerned with those from whom they took and transmitted, because there were still many *Tabi'un* who had had close contact with the Companions. They accepted *mursal hadiths* because they trusted those who transmitted to them and the time was close to that of the *Tabi'un*. By ash-Shafi'i's time and thereafter the *isnads* had already become much longer, and thus became an object of concern and study.

It was a time of frequent debates, sometimes verbal and sometimes in letters, like Malik's letter to al-Layth ibn Sa'd about not judging according to the normative practice of Madina and al-Layth's reply to him. These debates took place everywhere – in Makka during the *hajj* and in other Muslim cities, as well as at gatherings held by the khalifs and governors for the purpose. Such debates were held not between *fuqaha'* alone but also between them and the scholars of *kalam* among the Mu'tazilites, Jahmites, Murji'ites and others. Likewise the scholars of *kalam* also debated among themselves, as happened between the Mu'tazilites and Jabarites; and there were debates between the scholars of *kalam* and others who attacked Islam, or between them and non-Muslim philosophers who lived in Muslim lands, such as the Socratics, Cynics, free-thinkers, Manichaeans and others.

All in all, this was a time of intellectual intercourse between different religions, different theological opinions and different legal schools. Part of the nature of intellectual differences is that they produce debates and arguments, of which some are aimed at reaching the truth and some arise out of a desire for intellectual domination. There were both types in this time.

Perhaps the clearest illustration of the spirit of knowledge in that age, and the intellectual ferment and its fruits, was Imam ash-Shafi'i. He embodied the spirit of the age in relating its intellectual conclusions about *fiqh* and the *Sunna*. There were those among the Basran scholars who refused to accept the evidence of the *Sunna*, and those who would not use single *hadiths* as evidence or accept the *Sunna* unless it was *mutawatir*, i.e. reported by the Community

440

as a whole. His reply to them was strong and severe and he refuted their approach. There were also those who put analogy before single Traditions. In general, there is no book which deals with the legal forms of the age of *ijtihad*, which was the time in which Ahmad ibn Hanbal grew up, like *Kitab al-Umm* by ash-Shafi'i. It records all the various opinions, distinguishing those supported by strong evidence from those that are weak. It is probably the most representative example of the spirit of the time in these fields.

But what was the effect on Ahmad of this time of argument and intellectual ferment and maturing of the Islamic sciences? The time and environment in which they live inevitably affect thinkers according to their different orientations and their exposure to these factors. An intellectual milieu like that of the Abbasids in which Ahmad lived might have had many different effects since there were various streams of thought. There were scholars who accepted isolated Traditions, those who rejected them and preferred analogy, those who considered the *fatwas* of the Companions part of the *Sunna*, and those who insisted on considering only the *Sunna* of the Prophet himself.

Ahmad took from this mixed provender those elments which accorded with his own inclination and nature. From the outset, his method consisted of turning to the *Sunna* and learning the *fatwas* of the Companions and great Followers and transmitting them, so that he was always keenly concerned with the narrations of the Companions and Followers. In spite of the great amount of debate at that time, there were also those who were averse to it because of its inbuilt tendency to generate uncertainty and corrupt thought. Malik, Sufyan ath-Thawri, Ibn al-Mubarak and others hated debate concerning matters of the *deen* and Ahmad preferred to follow their course and avoid debate.

Islamic Sects

Ahmad himself mentions the names of various Islamic groups and proceeds to refute them, and so we should briefly mention

441

them in order that the reader will know what the names mean in this context. At that time there were people who joined these sects and spread them among the Muslims, using a different method from that employed by the *hadith* scholars and *fuqaha'*. In some instances they even used the power of the state, as we saw with the Mu'tazilites in connection with their view about the createdness of the Qur'an and their denial of the vision of Allah on the Day of Rising which they attempted to impose on scholars by force. The other prominent sects were the Shi'ites, Kharijites, Qadarites, Jahmites and Murji'ites.

Shi'ites

The Shi'ites were the oldest of the Islamic sects. They appeared with their political position at the end of the reign of 'Uthman and grew and flourished in the time of 'Ali, when the injustices perpetrated against members of the Hashimite family increased the number of their supporters.

Shi'ites held that 'Ali had been the man most entitled to the khalifate, but they formed into various groups. Some were excessive in their esteem for 'Ali and his descendants and some were more balanced. The moderate ones were content to prefer 'Ali to the other Companions without declaring any of them unbelievers.

The most moderate group were the Zaydites, who followed Zayd ibn 'Ali, Zayd al-'Abidin. They believed that the leadership of Abu Bakr and 'Umar was valid, even if they were not the best, and that it was permitted to have two leaders at the same time. They thought that anyone who commits a major wrong action would be forever in the Fire because he is between belief and unbelief: a view similar to that of the Mu'tazilites. Zayd was killed during the reign of Hisham, in 122 A.H.

Some Shi'ites held extreme views, including the Kaysaniyya, followers of al-Mukhtar ibn 'Ubayd ath-Thaqafi who rebelled in Marwanid times. They believed that the khalif must be from the sons of 'Ali: al-Hasan, al-Husayn and then Muhammad ibn al-Hanafiyya. They also believed in metempsychosis; that everything has an inward and outward truth; and that the Imam alone has inward knowledge.

There are also the Twelver Shi'ites who believe that the twelfth Imam went into occultation and are still waiting for him to return. They believe that the Imam is designated by name without description, which is the same as the Zaydites say. There is a branch of the Imamites who take their name from Isma'il ibn Ja'far. They are also called the Batiniyya because of their view about the "Concealed Imam". This group believe that Ja'far's son Isma'il was designated as Imam by him.

They were other extreme Shi'ite groups who ceased to have any link with Islam, such as the Saba'ites, who deified 'Ali, and the Ghurabiyya who claimed that 'Ali should have been the Prophet and Jibril made a mistake.

Kharijites

Another political sect was the Kharijites. They arose in 'Ali's army after he agreed to arbitration when they had forced him to do so, but after he accepted they began to shout, "Judgement belongs to Allah alone", and claimed that 'Ali had committed disbelief by accepting arbitration. Then they attacked him, saying that he had to repent, and so he was forced to fight them. They continued to cause trouble in the Umayyad era. One of their views was that anyone could be khalif if he was a free man, and that he could be deposed. Anyone who committed a major sin was an unbeliever.

They had numerous splinter groups, each with its own views and leadership. Some left Islam because of certain views which they held, like the Yazidites who claimed that Allah would send a Persian Prophet who would abrogate the *Shari'a*, and the Maymunites who allowed certain forbidden marriages and claimed that *Surat Yusuf* (12) was not part of the Qur'an.

These two were the main political groups. The other sects were largely concerned with matters of dogma.

Murji'ites

The Murji'ites' view was counter to that of the Kharijites concerning the question of the status of those who commit a major sin and whether they are forever in the Fire or not. The Murji'ites held that disobedience does not harm belief, just as obedience does not benefit disbelief. The Mu'tazilites used this term for those who did not hold that those who committed major sins would be in the Fire forever. That is why Abu Hanifa was accused of being a Murji'ite. Ash-Shahrastani counted him among the Murji'ites of the *Sunna* who hoped that Allah would forgive sinners.

Jabarites or Jahmites

There were also the Jabarites or Jahmites who contended that man has no will in anything he does; that Allah is the Doer of all that takes place by his hands, good or evil; and that his actions are like a feather moving in the wind. The Jabarite position was well-known in Umayyad times. It is said that the first to articulate it was al-Jahm ibn Safwan, which is why they are sometimes called Jahmites. Al-Jahm was also the first to state that the Qur'an was created. That is why Ahmad sometimes called those who espouse that position "Jahmites", even though the Mu'tazilites, who were its main exponents, disagreed with the Jahmites about man's actions.

Qadarites

There were also the Qadarites, who took the opposite view to that of the Jabarites, saying that man creates his own actions himself by choice. They became indistinguishable from the Mu'tazilites. The Mu'tazilites had great importance in Islamic thought in the Abbasid era since they refuted the *zindiqs*. They had five tenets: *tawhid* – that Allah is One in His Essence and His Attributes and does not have the same attributes as any of His creatures (and so they denied the Vision of Allah); Allah's justice in repayment of actions; the threat of Hell and promise of Paradise; that someone who commits a major sin is between two positions, being neither a believer or unbeliever; and commanding the right and objecting to the wrong, even by the sword if necessary.

Chapter Four
Ibn Hanbal's Views

Ahmad ibn Hanbal was not one of those who devoted themselves to the study of different religions and sects and their arguments, nor was he was one of those who devoted themselves to the
rational sciences without basing themselves on the principle of the
Book or *Sunna*. He did not permit himself to debate any of its precepts, for the truth is not revealed by argument or exposition. True
knowledge consists in seeking out the truths of Revelation and
studying what is commanded. It is not a matter of victory or defeat
in debate or a contest of words. Furthermore anyone who seeks
religious knowledge by argumentation makes his *deen* a target for
disputes – and this is not something which the Imam of the *Sunna*
would descend to.

While Ahmad devoted himself to studying only the *Sunna* and
the knowledge of the *deen* and its *fiqh* through transmission from
the Messenger of Allah, may Allah bless him and grant him peace,
the battles of *kalam* were raging nearby and heated debates concerning the khalifate and the previous khalifs and the disparity
between the Companions were being carried on incessantly.
Ahmad did not involve himself any of that. But the time he lived
in and his contacts did not allow Ahmad's religious knowledge to
remain completely aloof from dispute and the conflict between
sects and ideas. Various factors moved him to make certain statements, particularly when al-Ma'mun attempted to force the *fuqaha'* and *hadith* scholars to accept his position, willingly or unwill-
ingly. Ahmad refused to accede to this demand of the khalifs.

Certain statements regarding dogma have been transmitted
from him which are as true to the true *Salafi* position as his *fiqh*
was. He did not seek to interpret but took the position of the

Qur'an and *Sunna*, as the Qur'an says, *"We believe in it. All of it is from our Lord."* (3:7) Ahmad respected all the Companions and did not attack any of them. He avoided saying anything negative about any Companion. He preferred to follow the course of the *Salaf* in that respect. He did not get involved in politics or openly disdain authority or encourage rebellion. He devoted himself to knowledge while others were debating the relative value of the Companions. He did, however, express some opinions on politics and dogma which we will mention briefly.

Imam Ahmad's views on certain doctrines

At this time there were questions connected to Islamic dogma which were raised by the Muslim sects and were disseminated among the majority of Muslims. The latter relied on the knowledge of *fuqaha'* and *hadith* scholars and did not ask anyone else about them, because they were the only ones who were able to remove the uncertainty these questions provoked. As we have already seen, these questions included the following: the reality of faith, the question of Qadar and man's actions and his will in relation to the Will of Allah, sins and their effect on faith, the position of Muslims who commit major sins and whether or not they will be forever in the Fire, the issue of the Divine Attributes, and other matters of controversy, like the createdness of the Qur'an and the possibility of seeing Allah.

Faith

The reality of faith is one of the issues about which there was dispute and different groups provoked discussion. The Jahmites thought that faith was affirmation, even if not accompanied by action, and did not state that it was obligatory to proclaim it out loud. The Mu'tazilites held that actions were integral to faith. To them, a person who committed major sins was not a believer, even if he believed in Allah's unity and testified that Muhammad was the Messenger of Allah, but he was not an unbeliever either: he

447

was between the two. The Kharijites said that action is integral to faith and that anyone who commits major sins is not a believer, but an unbeliever.

The *fuqaha'* and *hadith* scholars discussed these ideas using their method, which was to rely on the Book and the *Sunna* and not the faculty of reason. They had various views about these matters which were not far apart. Abu Hanifa thought that faith was definite belief and its verbal affirmation. The physical token of it was the articulation of the two *shahadas*. No other action was necessary for it. Faith is a reality which does not increase or decrease. So in his view the faith of Abu Bakr was exactly the same as that of other people, but he was better in respect of his actions and because the Prophet testified that he would enter the Garden.

According to Malik, faith is affirmation and confirmation, but it increases through right action because the Noble Qur'an clearly states that some of those who believe are increased in faith. He also said that faith decreases, but noted that the Qur'an only mentions increase and not decrease.

Ahmad affirmed in a number of places that faith is both articulation and action and that it increases and decreases. Ibn al-Jawzi reports that Ahmad used to say, "Faith is word and action. It increases and decreases. All piety is from faith and acts of disobedience decrease faith." He said, "The description of the believer among the people of the *Sunna* and the Community is that he is someone who testifies that there is no god but Allah alone with no partner and that Muhammad is His slave and Messenger, and who affirms all that the Prophets and Messengers brought, and who binds his heart to what appears on his tongue and does not doubt his faith." (*al-Manaqib*, p. 165)

In another place he said, "Faith is word and deed. It increases and decreases. It increases when you do good, and decreases when you do evil. A man can leave faith but remain within the fold of Islam. If he repents, he returns to faith. He is only removed from Islam by associating things with Allah or by rejecting one of the obligations imposed by Allah. If he abandons them through neglect and laziness, he is subject to His will and He may punish or may pardon him." (Ibn al-Jawzi, p. 168)

448

This indicates that someone who disobeys Allah is a Muslim but should not be called a believer. That is close to the view of the Mu'tazilites, but he was swift to distance himself from them because they thought that whoever died disobedient would be in the Fire forever. He left their fate to their Lord. In this Ahmad only relied on texts for his position.

The judgement on those who commit a major sin

This was a disputed question among the scholars. The Kharijites considered such a person an unbeliever and al-Hasan al-Basri considered him a hypocrite. The Mu'tazilites put him between the two positions and called him a Muslim although he would be forever in the Fire. Abu Hanifa, Malik and ash-Shafi'i considered him a believer and left him to the judgement of Allah.

Ahmad was like the earlier *fuqaha'* in this respect, and did not deviate from their path. There are many texts transmitted from him on the subject. He said about the believer that he left his destiny to Allah, as everything was subject to Allah's decision and decree. He said, "We do not testify that the people of the *qibla* can perform any action which necessarily incurs the Garden or the Fire. We are optimistic in the case of the righteous and pessimistic in the case of the sinner and evildoer, although we hope for Allah's mercy for him. If anyone meets Allah with a sin which he repented of and did not persist in, Allah will turn to him. He accepts the repentance of His servants and pardons evil deeds. Whoever meets Him having had a *hadd* carried out on him in this world for sins which deserve that punishment, his destiny is up to Allah as to whether He punishes him or forgives him." (*al-Manaqib*, p. 174)

Imam Ahmad declared, "We do not declare any of the adherents of *tawhid* to be unbelievers, even if they commit major sins." He criticised the Mu'tazilites for claiming that someone who sins is an unbeliever and the consequences of that position. But we do find it transmitted from him that anyone who abandons the prayer is an unbeliever. He singled out that particular sin above all others, saying, "The only practice whose non-performance constitutes dis-

449

belief is the ritual prayer. Whoever abandons it is an unbeliever and Allah has allowed that he be killed." (*al-Manaqib*, p. 173)

This text is somewhat strange in that the prayer is singled out and the *isnad* is not clear. Perhaps Imam Ahmad meant someone who persists in not praying in such a way that it is tantamount to denial of one of the pillars of the *deen*. If he denies one of the pillars, the Muslims agree that he is an unbeliever because that which he denies what has come from the Messenger of Allah.

Qadar and human actions

One of the most evident qualities that characterised Ahmad's life was his absolute self-surrender to the judgement of Allah and his full submission to the Decree of Allah. He entrusted his affairs to Allah in respect of what was absent and what was present. But he was not one of those who are passive and do not act. He acted but put his trust in his Lord, believing in His decree of good and evil. The statements transmitted from him which show his absolute belief in the decree of good and evil are numerous. It was a deep and firm belief he held without that making him cease to act.

We read in *al-Manaqib* that "Seventy men of the *Tabi'un*, Muslim Imams and *fuqaha'* of the cities agreed that the *Sunna* to which the Messenger of Allah held until he died was first of all contentment with the Decree of Allah, submission to His command, steadfastness under His decree, taking what Allah commanded and being far from what He prohibited, sincerity in acting for Allah, belief in Destiny for good or evil, and abandoning argument, debate and quarrels about the *Deen*." (*al-Manaqib*, p. 186)

This quotation indicates that Ahmad believed in Destiny for good or evil, and in surrendering all affairs to Allah. It also shows that he did not consider it proper to debate and argue this question. He particularly detested argument on this matter because it was an endless conundrum. The more it was debated the most abstruse it became. As Abu Hanifa observed, "This is a question which is difficult for people. How should they be capable of understanding it? It is a lock whose key is lost. If the key is found, what is in it will

450

be known. It can only be opened when someone is informed by Allah."

So Ahmad believed that all that a man does is by the Decree and Will of Allah. That is contrary to the Qadarite view that man creates his own actions. Ahmad and the Orthodox Muslim Community believe that nothing occurs in existence except by the Will of Allah. Nonetheless Ahmad refused to debate this matter. He wrote to a friend of his, "I am not someone who deals with *kalam* and I do not think that there should be discussion about any of this except what is in the Book, or the *hadiths* of the Messenger of Allah, may Allah bless him and grant him peace, or what the Companions said. Anything other than that is not praiseworthy." (*al-Manaqib*, p. 156)

The Divine Attributes and the createdness of the Qur'an

Ahmad affirmed all the Attributes by which Allah describes Himself in His Book and those by which Allah is described in *hadiths*. The Attributes are as the texts state and no one should go further than that. So Allah is Hearing, Seeing, Speaking, Powerful, Knowing, Willing, and so forth, and "He is not like anything". The *hadiths* are taken as related. Ahmad did not investigate what they meant, as he considered excessive interpretation to be outside the *Sunna* and that delving into the simile or metaphor would lead to discord and innovation. He described the believer among the people of the *Sunna* as someone who "leaves things which are beyond his ken to Allah," as when the *hadith* from the Prophet reports that the people of the Garden will see their Lord and affirm him.

One of the Attributes of Allah is speech and this pertains to the issue of the createdness of the Qur'an. As we saw in the Inquisition, Ahmad would not affirm that the Qur'an is created, as the Abbasid authorities demanded. Was his view that the Qur'an was uncreated, and did that also apply to the Qur'an which is recited, written in copies and spoken by the reciters and whose letters are present in copies of the Qur'an? Or did he simply not say that the Qur'an was created because to say so would be innovation?

Transmissions from Ahmad vary, and before we explain his opinion we say that the Qur'an, meaning its recitation, is in time, not timeless. If someone says that the Qur'an as recitation is created and in time, his words are sound. That is because recitation is a description applying to the reader, not to Allah. This usage of "Qur'an" is found in the Qur'an where Allah says, *"The dawn recitation (qur'an) is certainly witnessed."* (17:78) This requires no analysis. Nonetheless, Ibn Qutayba reports that some people said that the actual recitation was timeless – which would entail the actions of the human being who performed it being uncreated.

In the time of Ahmad there was great confusion on this topic. There was disagreement about actual recitation and there was also disagreement about the Qur'an itself. There were two views. One considered its source: Allah has speech, and His speech is timeless as His Essence is timeless. The second view considered the letters, words and the meanings indicated by them. One group said that Ahmad preferred not to delve into the details because he thought that to do so was innovation.

Although some hold that he refused to discuss it, Ibn Qutayba reports that Ahmad was not silent on this matter. He said about those who were silent, 'I cannot see in these sects anyone with less excuse than him who demands silence and claims ignorance after this sedition. ... It is not in human nature to refrain from a matter concerning the *deen* which has spread like this and become public in this way. If intelligent men were to refrain, the ignorant would not refrain. If tongues are restrained, hearts are not. People have a model in earlier scholars, since Jahm and Abu Hanifa spoke about the Qur'an. This had not happened before and was unprecedented, since people had not previously spoken about it. When people resorted to their scholars, they did not tell them it was innovation to discuss it, but they removed doubt with certainty, dispelled confusion and removed distress. They agreed that the Qur'an is not created and gave a *fatwa* to that effect. They used evidence and proofs, investigated and compared, and deduced evidence for their *fatwa* from the Book of Allah..."

Ahmad is reported as saying, "Whoever claims that the Qur'an is created is a Jahmite. The Jahmites are unbelievers. Whoever

452

claims that it is not created is an innovator." Ibn Qutayba rejected this transmission and said it was rare and was unlikely to be authentic.

After looking into all the sources, it seems that at first Ahmad hesitated to discuss the matter at first. Eventually, he did express himself on it as we see in a letter which he wrote to al-Mutawakkil and which is recorded in the *History of Islam* by adh-Dhahabi. In this letter he pointed out that discussion on the subject leads to the inculcation of doubts in people's hearts, and he shows that in the view of the *Salaf* the Qur'an is not created. The Qur'an is the Word of Allah and the Word of Allah cannot be considered Allah's creation. The Qur'an is part of Allah's knowledge and Allah's knowledge is not created. This is all derived from the texts of the Book and *Sunna* and reports of the Companions and Followers, not just from logic. So after studying the texts of the Book and *Sunna*, Ahmad concluded that the Qur'an is not created. He relied on the Qur'an and Traditions and followed the Path of the *Salaf* without employing reasoning – something he did not consider his business as he was not one of the people of *kalam* and debate.

Seeing Allah on the Day of Rising

This is a question which was discussed in the time of Ahmad. The Mu'tazilites denied that Allah would be seen on the Day of Rising because vision entails corporeality and corporeality resembles temporal things, and "there is nothing like Allah". They interpret in other ways the verses about vision which appear in the Qur'an such as *"Faces that Day will be radiant, gazing at their Lord"* (75:22-23), and other such verses which suggest actual vision.

At the end of his life, al-Ma'mun tried to compel people to say that the Qur'an is created, but did not insist on their believing in the negation of vision of Allah even though, as a Mu'tazilite, he took that position. But al-Wathiq went on to force people to deny the vision of Allah and that continued until al-Mutawakkil's reign.

Ahmad accepted the texts without interpreting them. He believed fully in the Vision. One of his letters expounded the doc-

453

trine of the people of the *Sunna* and Community that belief in the vision on the Day of Rising was part of belief. He said, "Belief in the Vision on the Day of Rising is as it is related by the Prophet, may Allah bless him and grant him peace, and confirmed in sound *hadiths*. The Prophet saw his Lord. That is reported in sound *hadiths*. Qatada reported it from 'Ikrima from 'Abdullah ibn 'Abbas... Discussion about it is innovation. We take it at face value and do not debate with anyone about it." (*al-Manaqib*, Ibn al-Jawzi, p. 173)

Ahmad believed in the Vision of Allah on the Day of Rising because the texts mention it and the Prophet, may Allah bless him and grant him peace, saw his Lord; but he also thought that one should not debate how that would come about and how it does or does not relate to or reflect the idea of corporeality. *"There is nothing like Him,"* (42:11) and so the true nature of Vision in this context is unknown. Thus he took a middle course between those who totally rejected the possibility of seeing Allah and those who anthropomorphised. We also see that in his method Ahmad relied on the *Sunna* and not the Qur'an, since the *Sunna* explains the Qur'an.

This is a general summary of the views of Ahmad regarding the subjects into which the proponents of *kalam* delved and which were problematical in his time. You can see that in his studies he followed the same method as he did in the study of *fiqh* and kept himself from exceeding the limit by two means. One is that he did not go beyond the texts or try to interpret them or explain them at any level beyond face value, even if they required understanding, and he did not use pure reason to help. He sought help in the *Sunna* and used it to explain the Book. The second is that in respect of the Attributes which Allah affirms in the Book or which are in the *Sunna* of the Prophet he was eager to negate any resemblance between Allah and His creation and cling to the words of the Almighty, *"There is nothing like Him."* (42:11) In affirming the Attributes and the Vision, he was eager to deny any resemblance between Allah and creation.

Imam Ahmad's political views

In his studies of political matters, Imam Ahmad followed sound tradition and did not deviate from that course. As regards his opinions about the Companions, he followed what was transmitted and the position of the great majority of the Companions and *Tab'iun*, may Allah be pleased with all of them. He was a traditionist in this as in the rest of his studies.

In respect of the khalif and khalifate and who should be chosen and how he should be chosen, he was a pragmatic man who avoided sedition and strove for the unity of the Muslims and preferred to obey the ruler, even if he was unjust, to rebellion against the Community. His views in this respect resembled those of Imam Malik. They both agreed on the order of the relative positions of the Companions, the choice of the khalif, and that rebelling against the khalif, even if he was unjust, was not permitted because of the possible consequences.

If there are differences between the two Imams, it is because Malik witnessed and lived through rebellions and civil war. Ahmad did not witness civil unrest and only saw the civil war between al-Amin and al-Ma'mun, observing how it led to evil rather than good and to the ascendancy of Persian influence, and the appearance of different religions and innovations in the *deen* and opened the way to unjust rule. He endured flogging, imprisonment and constriction and experienced the consequences of such injustice.

Regarding the Companions, he doubted whether anyone who curses one of the Companions of the Messenger of Allah was or indeed could really be considered a Muslim believer. He said, "I saw a man speak ill of one of the Companions of the Messenger of Allah, may Allah bless him and grant him peace, and so I suspected his Islam."

He defined a Companion as "Anyone who kept the company of the Prophet for a year, a month, a day or an hour is one of his Companions. He was a Companion if he was with him, listened to him, or looked at him, even once. The least of them is better than all of the generations which did not see him, even if they meet

455

Allah with every good action, so those who were Companions are better than the *Tabi'un* by virtue of their companionship of the Prophet, even if the latter were to perform all possible good actions. Anyone who deprecates any of the Companions of he Messenger of Allah, may Allah bless him and grant him peace, or hates one of them for something he did, or mentions his bad qualities is an innovator. One should pray for mercy for all of them." (*al-Manaqib*, p. 161)

In ranking the Companions, Imam Ahmad followed the *Salaf* and *Tabi'un*. He said, "The best of this Community after its Prophet are Abu Bakr as-Siddiq, 'Umar ibn al-Khattab, and 'Uthman ibn 'Affan without dispute, and after them the five members of the *Shura*: 'Ali, az-Zubayr, Talha, 'Abdu'r-Rahman ibn 'Awf and Sa'd, all of whom were fit to be khalif." After those of the *Shura,* he mentioned the *Muhajirun* present at the Battle of Badr and then the *Ansar* who were at Badr. He took a middle position, based on the sources. Abu Hanifa preferred 'Ali to 'Uthman; Malik mentioned the first three and then said that the others were equal.

Ahmad was also strong in defending 'Ali against anyone who attacked his khalifate, for in the reign of al-Mutawakkil there were many people who attacked that just Imam and Sword of Islam since al-Mutawwakil was a Nasibite, i.e. one of those who were hostile towards 'Ali and attacked him. Ahmad refuted their statements and mentioned the khalifate and virtues of 'Ali. He said, "The khalifate did not adorn 'Ali: 'Ali adorned it." He stressed 'Ali's virtues but he did not attack 'Ali's opponents. When asked about the conflict between 'Ali and Mu'awiya, he said, "I have only the best to say about them. May Allah have mercy on all of them. Mu'awiya, 'Amr ibn al-'As and Abu Musa al-Ash'ari were all described by Allah Almighty in His Book when He says *'Their mark is on their faces, the traces of prostration.'*" (48:29)

But we do not find that Ahmad proposed any clear method for the selection of the khalif; nor did he clearly state whether he preferred any particular house for the khalifate, except that he seemed to consider that the khalif's designation of his successor was valid. He related a Tradition about this, in which the Prophet indicated his choice of Abu Bakr by selecting him to lead the prayer when he was ill. Then Abu Bakr chose 'Umar, and 'Umar chose one of six and left the decision to them. Ahmad, who, followed the method of the Companions, must have thought this correct because that is what the Companions did.

Chapter Five
The *Hadiths* and *Fiqh* of Ahmad

This subject is in fact the object of our studies. We passed by way of Ahmad's political views and views on dogma because they were occasioned by the intellectual environment and circumstances of his time, the debates which were taking place with the Mu'tazilites, and the khalifs who espoused their views. He avoided dealing with the adherents of sects. He called people to what he thought contained true guidance, avoided disputation, and was steadfast in the face of affliction. So it was to *fiqh* and *hadiths* that he directed his efforts and gifts by learning *hadiths* and the traditions and decisions of the Companions. When he met ash-Shafi'i, he learned the rules for sound understanding of the Book, comparison of textual sources, and knowledge of the abrogating and abrogated, and in general how to deduce and extrapolate secondary rulings from the basic sources of the *Shari'a*.

What Imam Ahmad learned from ash-Shafi'i and saw him through his own intellect was that he was a genius, not to be ignored by anyone seeking knowledge of the Book and *Sunna*. A scholar is nourished by various sources and it is a righteous nourishment whose fruit is sincere knowledge. By learning the *fiqh* and deductive methods of ash-Shafi'i, he was able to study the *Sunna* and traditions in a correct manner and proceed with his *fiqh* even if he did not know the decision of a Companion or Follower in a particular case.

Thus we can say that Ahmad was an Imam in *hadiths* and that through this leadership in *hadiths* and traditions, he became an Imam in *fiqh*. His *fiqh*, in its reality, logic, criteria, rules, tone and appearance, was based on Tradition. That is why at-Tabari denied that he was a *faqih* and Ibn Qutayba counted him among the *hadith* scholars and not among the *fuqaha'*. Several people took this view, but a close analysis of Ahmad's studies and the positions and *fatwas* transmitted from him on different questions makes it clear to us that he was a *faqih* absorbed in Tradition and its methodology.

Whatever the verdict of the scholars as to whether Ahmad was a *faqih* or not, we possess a legal collection attributed to him and different transmissions with an *isnad* on which scholars disagree. The reason for the controversy over the soundness of its ascription to him is that Ahmad used to forbid his adherents and those who listened to him to write down anything except *hadiths*. In the beginning he thought that recording anything other than *hadiths* was an innovation: how could pages containing the words of the Messenger be combined with the words of other people? He also feared that people would abandon the knowledge of *hadiths* and traditions when they recorded the opinions of *fuqaha'*; and that they would concentrate on studying what was said about secondary rulings and their extrapolations about questions and so would dispense with *hadiths* and the study of transmission and Tradition. He was worried and fearful about what might happen to people.

He used to say, "Do not look into what Ishaq, Sufyan, ash-Shafi'i or Malik wrote; you have the source." When asked about some of the people of *hadith* who wrote out the books of ash-Shafi'i he said, "I do not think they should do so." He was asked about the books of Abu Thawr and said, "A book that is innovated is an innovation. It is *hadiths* which are essential." It appears that first he did not allow the transmission of any book except the *Muwatta'* of Imam Malik, and that only because it contained many *hadiths*.

But along with these traditions relating to us Ahmad's prohibition of the transmission of his *fatwas* and his instructions to his followers to confine themselves to *hadiths*, we find other traditions which indicate that he later permitted such transmission both orally and in writing. Indeed he sometimes consulted books and referred to them. To reconcile the two positions, we may say that at the beginning of his career he forbade transmission of anything other than *hadiths*, and did not allow his *fatwas* to be disseminated because he thought that giving a *fatwa* was a kind of disaster into which a *faqih* fell when forced to give a ruling on a matter about which there was no explicit text from the Prophet or *fatwa* from the Companions. Ahmad thought that personal *fatwas* were something which should only be resorted to as a last resort. As such, they should not be transmitted since they were in fact an affliction which it was not good to disseminate although they were acceptable provided they were soundly based on *hadith* or valid tradition.

At the end of his life, however, Ahmad had to permit his *fatwas* to be written down and disseminated. He disliked his personal opinions being transmitted but was too diffident to forbid them being written down completely. Furthermore, his companions kept insisting on it until he became reconciled to it and his dislike more or less ended. It is reported in *Kitab al-Minhaj* by Ishaq ibn Mansur al-Marwazi (d. 251 AH) that Imam Ahmad retracted some rulings which had been transmitted from him. Ishaq collected those rulings in a book, took them to Baghdad and presented to Ahmad every question on which he had issued a *fatwa*; and he confirmed them a second time, approving of what he had done. He was the fittest of people to have his *fatwas* accepted since they were derived from *hadiths* and he was clear in following the *Salaf* in them rather than adopting legal reasoning which did not have as strong a connection to *hadiths* and tradition as his *fatwas* did.

In brief, Ahmad the *hadith* scholar transmitted to us his *Musnad*, which he collected and passed on to posterity in the form of a book as to whose transmission from him there is no doubt. As for Ahmad the *faqih*, he did not write a book on *fiqh* or dictate anything to his companions about it. At first he refused to allow anything to be recorded from him on the subject of *fiqh* but eventually his companions had him agree to the transmission of his *fatwas* and opinions.

The *Musnad*

The *Musnad* is the collection of *hadiths* which Ahmad transmitted and which he travelled to many places to collect. The

Musnad contains those *hadiths* which Ahmad learned and recorded together with their *isnads*. He began to compile it when he started to learn *hadiths* at the age of sixteen. Scholars of the *Sunna* agree that he began compiling it in 180 AH at the beginning of his quest for knowledge.

Although Ahmad disliked writing in general, he liked writing *hadiths* and began to write down the *Musnad* early on. The reason is evident in his answer to a question posed to him by his son 'Abdullah, who said, "I asked my father, 'Why do you dislike writing books when you have compiled the *Musnad*?' He replied, 'I created this book as a model for people to consult when they disagree about a *sunna* from the Messenger of Allah, may Allah bless him and grant him peace.'"

Ahmad set himself the task of collecting *hadiths* from reliable men, meeting them and relating from them, and he exerted himself to that end, no matter how much difficulty might be involved. He continued doing this throughout his entire life. He did not concern himself with organising it and dividing it into chapters, but only with compiling it and recording *hadiths*. It appears that he continued to collect and write on separate pages until he felt his end approaching. Then he gathered his sons and elite students and dictated to them what he had written and collected. Ibn al-Jazari states: "Imam Ahmad began to compile the *Musnad*, wrote it down on separate sheets, and divided it into separate parts in instalments in a rough copy. But he died before being able to complete it properly. He had given it orally to his sons and the people of his house, but died before reviewing and editing it. It remained as it was until his son 'Abdullah supplemented it and added to it what he had heard."

This would indicate that Imam Ahmad only read the *Musnad* to his sons and the people of his house. That would appear to contradict what is known about him dictating the *hadiths* which he had compiled to all who asked him about them. In fact there is no contradiction because in his lessons he only read to his students from his books things which they specifically asked him about. This is not the same as letting them hear the complete collection from all the different shaykhs in different regions. He transmitted what he thought the enquirer needed. What Ibn al-Jazari is referring to is the actual transmission of the *Musnad* itself.

Ahmad's son 'Abdullah was his greatest transmitter: Ahmad had remarked on his memory. We read in the *Tabaqat* of Abu Ya'la, "Salih (Ahmad's other son) wrote little from his father. As for 'Abdullah, there is no one in the world who transmitted more from his father than him. He learnt the *Musnad* and the *Tafsir* and also many other works." 'Abdullah transmitted the *Musnad* from his father and disseminated his knowledge among people. It seems that it was he who put the *Musnad* in its present order. The *hadiths* are arranged according to the Companions from whom they are transmitted and, if they are *mursal*, from the *Tabi'i* from whom they are transmitted.

The transmission of Ahmad's *fiqh*

We have already mentioned that Ahmad did not write a book on *fiqh* which could be considered as the foundation on which his school is based and therefore as its source. He wrote only *hadiths*. Scholars, however, have mentioned some books on legal subjects attributed to him, including one about the rites of *Hajj* and a small treatise on ritual prayer which he wrote to an imam behind whom he had prayed and who had prayed incorrectly. They take the form of treatises in sections which contain many Traditions and in which there is no opinion, analogy, or legal deduction; so they are really books of *hadiths*, even though they do pertain to *fiqh* by explanation and clarification.

Since Ahmad did not write on *fiqh*, one must rely on the words of his students for the transmission of his *fiqh*. We find, as has been noted, that there is considerable confusion concerning that transmission, which stems from several factors.

• As we know, Ahmad disliked his *fatwas* being transmitted or written down or published in his name. In that connection it is related that Ahmad ibn al-Husayn said, "A man told Abu

'Abdullah, 'I want to write these rulings: I am afraid that I will forget.' Ahmad said, 'Do not write them down. I dislike my opinions being written down.' Once he was aware of someone writing secretly and said, 'Do not write down my opinion. I might say something today and retract it tomorrow.'" Because of his dislike of rulings being transmitted from him, if anything was written it was despite his objection or done secretly, and so there is a greater possibility of error in the transmission. Many opinions were transmitted from him, no less than were transmitted from Abu Hanifa and Malik, and so there must be numerous errors in many of them.

• Some of Ahmad's companions, who transmitted many statements from him and were a major source of the *fiqh* attributed to him, use expressions which indicate that his opinions had become public knowledge before they met him. Thus Harb al-Harmani, who transmitted much from him, mentioned that he published 4000 rulings of Ahmad which he had heard before he saw him.

• It is known that Imam Ahmad did not resort to opinion except in dire necessity; and yet a great number of statements were related from him, many of which are contradictory. That is not in keeping with what is known about him. Moreover he was not known to give *fatwa* except on cases that had actually arisen. He did not resort to theoretical cases in order to derive secondary rulings by the use of legal reasoning. He often said, "I do not know," and in that respect he imitated Malik and Ibn 'Uyayna. This abundance of opinions is, therefore, not consonant with the known fact that he often said, "I do not know" and, as that is well-known, he did not issue *fatwa* by opinion except in the utmost necessity.

• Ahmad was famous for having disowned many of the opinions attributed to him in Khurasan, saying that they were not his. So how can so much be ascribed to him which he himself repudiated and said were not his views?

463

• Much of the *fiqh* transmitted from Ahmad is contradictory, and it is logically difficult to accept that all the positions ascribed to him are his. Open any of the books of the Hanbalis and go to any chapter and you will find that a number of questions have different transmissions, some affirming a position and others negating it.

These points raise some uncertainty about Hanbali *fiqh*. Furthermore some early authorities, like at-Tabari and Ibn Qutayba, considered Ahmad to be a *hadith* scholar rather than a *faqih*. If his legal rulings had been well-known, there is no doubt that Ahmad would then have been considered a *faqih* by those sources. Thus there is controversy surrounding the legal collection ascribed to him, despite which generations of scholars have accepted the ascription of that *fiqh* to Ahmad. Our approach regarding the soundness of historical questions is that we do not reject or deny what generations of scholars have accepted unless there is substantive evidence to invalidate their conclusions.

If those scholars did not consider Ahmad a *faqih*, that is because his first and primary concern was for *hadiths*, and his *fatwas* and the questions he answered were closer to transmission than to legal deduction. He was not like Malik, who had a particular legal method in the light of which he studied *hadiths*, or like Abu Hanifa who viewed transmission as a *faqih*, as a source from which to deduce a ruling in cases with no precedent, or like ash-Shafi'i who developed the principles of *fiqh* and facilitated the study of its techniques, even though he based his work on the transmitted texts.

Ahmad was a *hadith* scholar before he was a *faqih*, and he did not study *hadiths* with a view to extrapolation. For him the study of the *hadiths* was the goal in itself and not a means to something else. His *fiqh* came about when he became an imam for people who asked him for *fatwas* and so he was forced to provide them. If there was a text on the question, even from a Companion or one of the great *Tabi'un*, he would mention it. If there was no *fatwa* by any of them, he derived from what he had without resorting to analogy except when that was absolutely unavoidable. Hence his *fiqh* was tradition-based.

The two points which cast doubt on the body of Hanbali *fiqh* are its abundance, in spite of the Imam's known reluctance to transmit it, and the fact that some of his companions transmitted a large number of his *fatwas* before actually meeting him. The truth is that after the Inquisition and what he endured during it, Imam Ahmad became famous in all Muslim regions for knowledge of all branches of religious knowledge, whether it be dogma, *hadith* or *fiqh*. He lived for more than 20 years after the Inquisition, and many people considered him to be their Imam and consulted him about any matters which troubled them and whose rulings they wanted to learn. He could not leave the giving of *fatwas* to Bishr al-Marisi and his like whom he considered to be deviants, so he must have given many *fatwas* based on the knowledge which he had.

As for the differences in position attributed to him, the same applies to all the Imams. There are disagreements in a general sense within all the schools and they are transmitted from all the Imams. That is a consequence of their sincerity in seeking the truth. One of them would make a statement based on opinion and then something else would become clear to him and so, out of desire for the truth, he would voice another opinion. Since Ahmad's *fiqh* was transmitted orally, differences are very likely: Ahmad may have given an opinion on a question and then later retracted it while those who heard the first position did not know that it had been retracted, and so two positions were transmitted.

Ash-Shafi'i either wrote or dictated his *fiqh*, and yet there are different positions related from him so that ar-Rabi' ibn Sulayman, the transmitter of the books of ash-Shafi'i in his final stage, transmits two opinions from him about a particular question. That should not occasion any suspicion about their soundness. Sometimes ash-Shafi'i would mention two possibilities and not prefer either. This was a result of scrupulousness.

The transmitters of Ahmad's *fiqh*

Ahmad had many companions, including some who transmitted only *hadiths* from him, some who transmitted *hadiths* and *fiqh*, and some who were known especially for transmission of *fiqh*. The author of *al-Minhaj al-Ahmad* mentioned a number of them and categorised them: "Some of them transmitted a lot and some a little. They also varied in their position with Imam Ahmad, the amount they heard from him, and their precision and memory. Among those who transmitted a great deal were Ibrahim al-Harbi, Ibrahim ibn Hani' and his son Ishaq, Abu Talib al-Mishkati, Abu Bakr al-Marwazi, Abu Bakr al-Athram, Abu'l-Harith Ahmad, Ishaq ibn Mansur al-Kawsanj, Isma'il ash-Shalikhi, Ahmad ibn Muhammad al-Kahhali, Abu'l-Muzaffar Isma'il, Bishr ibn Musa, Bakr ibn Muhammad, Harb al-Kirmani, al-Hasan ibn Thawab, al-Hasan ibn Ziyad, Abu Dawud as-Sijistani, 'Abdullah, Salih, and many others."

Imam Ahmad mentioned those in his book, and they are only the men who transmitted much of his *fiqh* or, according to the definition of the historians of Hanbali *fiqh*, who transmitted legal questions rather than *hadiths* only. We find that the person who collated all this material was one of the scholars of the second generation, Abu Bakr al-Khallal. In Hanbali *fiqh* he occupies a position equivalent to that of Muhammad ash-Shaybani in Hanafi *fiqh*, Sahnun in Maliki *fiqh*, and ar-Rabi' ibn Sulayman in Shafi'i *fiqh*, although ash-Shaybani saw Abu Hanifa and transmitted from him and ar-Rabi' was a student of ash-Shafi'i. We will now mention some of the men from whom al-Khallal learned Ahmad's *fiqh*, confining ourselves to those who transmitted a lot.

Some of the transmitters among Ahmad's companions

As we have seen, many listened to Ahmad, and the Hanbalis became very numerous. We have therefore singled out a few of those who played a prominent part in disseminating his teaching.

Salih ibn Ahmad ibn Hanbal

Salih was the eldest son of Imam Ahmad. Ahmad was concerned with his upbringing, glad that he was ascetic like him. He brought him up in an exemplary manner and he became a very scrupulous and upright man. Salih had many children and was very generous. Because of the size of his family he had to accept the office of *Qadi* of Tartus. He wept at to do so. He learned *fiqh* and *hadiths* from his father and other contemporaries. He transmitted many rulings on *fiqh* which his father had decided. Abu Bakr al-Khallal says: "He listened to many questions and people used to write to him from Khurasan to ask his father about certain questions to which he would send them replies. Thus he was a means of disseminating the *fiqh* of his father. He died in 266 AH.

'Abdullah ibn Ahmad ibn Ahmad

Imam Ahmad's son 'Abdullah was born in 213. Ahmad took care over his upbringing as well as that of his brother Salih. He was very concerned with *hadiths*, being more interested in them whereas his brother was interested in *fiqh*. He died in 290 AH.

Ahmad ibn Muhammad ibn Hani' al-Athram

Al-Athram was one of the companions of Ahmad ibn Hanbal who studied with him when he was mature. He was interested in *fiqh*, deduction and legal disagreements. Once he had met Ahmad, he restricted himself to Tradition. He devoted himself to Ahmad because of his scrupulousness and righteousness. He related questions of *fiqh* from Ahmad as well as many *hadiths*. Al-Athram died in either 260 or 261 AH.

'Abdu'l-Malik ibn 'Abdi'l-Hamid Mahran al-Maymuni

'Abdu'l-Malik listened to Ahmad and other contemporary scholars. Al-Khallal admired his transmission from Ahmad and often relied on him for his transmission. He wrote down the rulings of Ahmad; because of his knowledge, Ahmad was too diffident to forbid him to record them. He had recommended that Ahmad should have his rulings recorded because they were derived from the *Sunna* and did not oppose it or add to it. He kept his company for more than twenty years until 227 AH. He died in 274.

Abu Bakr al-Khallal says about him: "He was the highly esteemed Imam among the companions of Ahmad, and Ahmad honoured him. He behaved with him as he did not behave with others. He told me, 'I accompanied Abu 'Abdullah devotedly from 205 to 227 AH, and after that I used to come and go from time to time. Abu 'Abdullah used to compare me to Ibn Jurayh ibn 'Ata' because of the great amount I asked him. He said to me, "I do not behave with anyone as I do with you."' He had many rulings from Ahmad in a collection of about twenty sections and two large sections taking up 100 pages. I have not heard of that in the case of anyone but him."

Ahmad ibn Muhammad ibn al-Hajjaj al-Marwazi

Al-Marwazi was the closest of Ahmad's companions and it was who washed him when he died. He was esteemed by Ahmad and transmitted the *Book of Scrupulousness* from him. He was reliable and Ahmad trusted him completely. He related many rulings from Ahmad which al-Khallal transmitted. He died in 275 AH.

Harb ibn Isma'il al-Hanzali al-Kirmani

Harb began as a Sufi, as was common at that time. He met Ahmad late in life. It is reported that al-Khallal asked him why he met him so late and he replied, "I was a Sufi before and I did not study." He was friends with al-Marwazi and stayed in his house when he came to Ahmad. It was al-Marwazi who encouraged al-Khallal, his student, to travel to Harb and listen to him and transmit rulings from him, and who assisted him in doing so. Harb transmitted a lot from Ahmad, but did not hear from him directly all that he disseminated from him. He mentioned that Ahmad said, "People need knowledge as much as they need bread and water." He probably died in 280 AH.

Ibrahim ibn Ishaq al-Harbi

Abu Ya'la describes al-Harbi thus: "He was an imam in knowledge, a leader in asceticism, with knowledge of *fiqh* and insight into rulings and memory of *hadiths*. He wrote many books." Ibrahim, who transmitted the *fiqh* and *hadiths* of Ahmad, died in 285 AH.

Ahmad ibn Muhammad Abu Bakr al-Khallal

We have mentioned here some of the most notable students of Ahmad who transmitted his *fiqh*. They were his closest companions and some recorded his *fiqh* with his permission. Some memorised his rulings, even before meeting him. But, as we mentioned earlier, there was one *faqih* who collated all this material, travelling great distances to do so: Abu Bakr al-Khallal. He is considered to be the great compiler and transmitter of Hanbali *fiqh* and so we must single him out for mention.

Al-Khallal kept the company of al-Marwazi until he died. It seems that he preferred to transmit the *fiqh* of Ahmad and put all his energy into that. He travelled extemsively in search of it, deriving much from the sons and uncle of Imam Ahmad, Harb al-Kirmani, al-Maymuni and others. Al-'Alimi said, "He collected from so many sources that it is impossible to name them all. He heard the rulings of Ahmad from them and travelled to remote parts of the earth to collect them and hear them."

After he had collected Ahmad's transmissions, al-Khallal taught them to his students at the Mahdi Mosque in Baghdad, which became the circle from which the Hanbali school spread out. He transmitted it as a legal collection in about twenty volumes.

The *fuqaha'* agree that he compiled all the various legal rulings ascribed to Ahmad and there is no doubt about that. But is the transmission so accurate that there is no room for uncertainty? In our view, many accepted his transmission of *hadiths*, and so his transmission of *fiqh* should also be accepted. The scholars of al-Khallal's generation accepted his transmission. There is a great deal of testimony to the soundness of his transmission, including that of the major figures of this school.

What are the books which al-Khallal wrote to record the school of Ahmad ibn Hanbal? Ibn al-Jawzi says, "He wrote several books, including *The Great Collection* in about 200 parts." It is clear that this collection constitutes the basis of all Hanbali *fiqh*. He also has books on other subjects. That is why Ibn al-Qayyim said, "Al-Khallal collected his texts in *The Great Collection*, which contains 20 volumes or more." This indicates that *The Great Collection* is the compendium of the *fiqh* of Ahmad by all its paths and transmissions. To reconcile the numbers given by Ibn al-Jawzi and Ibn al-Qayyim, Ibn Qayyim refers to volumes, which are large, and Ibn al-Jawzi to fascicules, which are smaller. Al-Khallal died in 311AH.

Chapter Six
Description of Hanbali *Fiqh*

Al-'Alimi reports, regarding the knowledge of Imam Ahmad and the position of his *fiqh,* that 'Abdu'l-Wahhab al-Warraq said, "I have not seen anyone to compare with Ahmad ibn Hanbal." He was asked, "How was his excellence made apparent to you?" He replied, "What can you say about a man who was asked 60,000 questions and replied to all of them, 'It was reported to us' and 'It was related to us'?"

This illustrates two points. One is that Imam Ahmad answered as many as 60,000 legal questions, which is a huge number. He was the most trusted person in respect of giving *fatwa* in his time throughout the Islamic world. The second point is that it shows that Ahmad's *fatwas* were based on *hadiths*, traditions, and reports from the *Salaf*, of which his knowledge was vast. He supported his *fatwas* with statements and decisions of the Prophet and undisputed positions of the Companions. When there was a disagreement between the Companions he would choose the position of one of them. He would also accept the position of a Follower or that of a *faqih* famous for knowledge of tradition, like Malik, al-Awza'i and others. Ahmad made great efforts not to be an innovator and to remain firm in following the path of the Companions. He resorted to use of opinion (*ra'y*) only when absolutely necessary.

Hanbali *fiqh* avoids hypothetical rulings about matters which have not happened or are unlikely to happen. Ibn al-Qayyim said on this point, "When one is asked for a *fatwa* about something which has not occurred, is a reply recommended or disliked, or can one choose? There are three positions. It is reported of many of the *Salaf* that they did not discuss things that had never arisen. When one of the *Salaf* was asked a question, he would say, 'Has it happened?' If the answer was affirmative, he would give an answer.

471

Otherwise, he would say, 'Leave us as we are.' Imam Ahmad said to one of his students, 'Beware of speaking about matters for which you have no precedent. If there is a text from the Book of Allah and the *Sunna* of the Messenger of Allah, may Allah bless him and grant him peace, or a tradition from the Companions, it is all right to discuss it. If there is no text or tradition, and it is unlikely to occur and therefore hypothetical, it is not recommended to discuss it. If its occurrence is not rare or it appears likely to happen, and the questioner wants to know so that he will have a correct view of it if it occurs, then it is recommended to give an answer according to what one knows, especially when the enquirer will thereby learn something.'" (*I'lam al-Muwaqqi'in,* pt. 4, p. 193)

The reader should not suppose that Ahmad's reliance on traditions in his *fiqh,* and his only leaving them when he was sure of being illuminated by their light, made his *fiqh* rigid or distant from the needs of everyday life. He found adequate and complete texts for all acts of worship, so that no analogy was ever needed in that realm whereas it was sometimes required where human transactions were concerned. In worldly matters he held strongly to texts about what is unlawful or a sin so as to avoid calling unlawful something Allah had made lawful. If there was no text stating that something was unlawful, he proceeded on the assumption that it was permitted. He only declared unlawful what Allah had declared unlawful. As Ibn al-Qayyim says, "The basic position in respect of all transactions is that they are sound unless there is definite evidence that they are invalid or unlawful."

Since its basic position is broad and transactions are basically allowed unless there is evidence from the Lawgiver that they are unlawful, the Hanbali school is the most permissive of the schools regarding freedom of contract and the preconditions which can be stipulated in a contract. The school presumes validity unless there is definite evidence to the contrary. We also find that Ahmad ibn Hanbal gave *fatwas* on the basis of the public interest (*masalih*) in the absence of relevant texts because the general good is the basic intention behind most legal judgements. In this he resembled

472

Malik ibn Anas, even though he did not accord that principle as much force as Malik did.

Hanbali *fiqh* also admits the principle of judgement of the means (*dhara'i'*) so that the means incur the judgement of the end: in other words, the things which lead to a particular result bear the same ruling as the result which comes from them. That also expands the scope of Hanbali *fiqh* and makes it fruitful and vibrant. It is not rigid, but rules according to motives and ends. In this respect, it is very clearly distinct from the Shafi'i school which takes a more inflexible view of transactions. The Hanbali school is a psychological and pragmatic one which judges actions and statements according to clear intentions and actual results.

The foundations of deduction in Hanbali *fiqh*

Ibn al-Qayyim indicated that the principles on which Imam Ahmad based his *fatwas* are five. The first is firm texts. If there was a firm text, he gave a *fatwa* accordingly, and did not pay any attention to what was contrary to it. That is why he put the text before the *fatwas* of the Companions. Ibn al-Qayyim gives examples of his disregarding *fatwas* of the Companions in favour of a text. One example was his preferring the *hadith* of the Aslamite woman and so considering the *'idda* of a pregnant widow to end when she gives birth and not the longer of the two terms,[1] which was the *fatwa* given by 'Abdullah ibn 'Abbas and 'Ali in one of two transmissions. Nor did he pay any attention to the position of Mu'adh and Mu'awiya about Muslims inheriting from non-Muslims, because of the *hadith* which prohibits it.

The second basis is the undisputed *fatwas* of the Companions. If one of them had given a *fatwa* and there was no known opposition to it, he did not follow anything else, but he did not call that consensus. He said out of scrupulousness, "I do not know of anything to refute it." An example was accepting the testimony of a

---

1. Ahmad did not consider that she had to wait to the end of the full term of a normal *'idda* or waiting period of four months and ten days. Her *'idda* ended when she gave birth, even if that was only a day after the death of her husband.

473

slave. It is related that Anas said, "I do not know of anyone who rejects the testimony of a slave." Ibn al-Qayyim said, "If Imam Ahmad found this type of statement from a Companion, he did not prefer opinion or analogy to it."

The third of the five bases mentioned by Ibn al-Qayyim is that in the case of a disagreement between the Companions, he would choose the statement which was closest to the Book and *Sunna* but would not leave their statements for anything else. If it was not clear which of the statements was most in accord, he related the disagreement and did not take a definite position. Ishaq ibn Ibrahim said in his *Questions*, "Abu 'Abdullah was asked, 'What about when a man is among his people and is asked about something about which there is disagreement?' He said, 'He gives *fatwa* according to what agrees with the Book and *Sunna* and avoids what disagrees with the Book and *Sunna*."

The fourth basis is accepting *mursal* and weak *hadiths* if there was nothing better on the subject. He preferred that to analogy. What is meant by weak is not the false or *munkar*, or that about which there is something suspect in the transmission, since that is not allowed. Ibn al-Qayyim mentioned that that principle was accepted by many of the *fuqaha'*. It is also ascribed to Abu Hanifa, Malik, and ash-Shafi'i.

The fifth basis which Ibn al-Qayyim mentioned is analogy. If Imam Ahmad did not have text on a question, or a statement of one or more of the Companions or a *mursal* or weak Tradition, he resorted to analogy, using it as a last resort as Ibn al-Qayyim observed. Al-Khallal transmitted that Ahmad said, "I asked ash-Shafi'i about analogy and he said, 'Resort to it if need be.'"

These principles are mentioned by Ibn al-Qayyim in his book, *I'lam al-Muwaqqi'in*. But anyone who studies the books of principles which the Hanbalis have written, or indeed studies what was written by Ibn al-Qayyim in any of his books, must add to these five and note that they are not in fact totally distinct from one another.

Regarding the first principle, the fact is that the texts in reality contain two bases: the Book and the *Sunna*, since any text is either from the Book or the *Sunna*; but Ahmad did as ash-Shafi'i had

474

done before him and put them together because the role of the *Sunna* is to clarify and expound the Book and so they are considered as having the same rank.

The second principle, the *fatwas* of the Companions, overlaps with third, which is the *fatwa* of a Companion when he disagreed with another Companion. So the two can in fact be considered as one: the *fatwas* of the Companions whether they agree or disagree.

The fourth is his acceptance of *mursal* or weak *hadiths*, which is in reality part of the science of knowing which texts are fit to be used for derivation, even though Ibn al-Qayyim mentioned it as a distinct and separate principle. It is an implicit judgement of its rank in deduction that he does not give a *mursal* or weak *hadith* precedence over the *fatwa* of one of the Companions. *Mutawatir* and sound texts come over a *fatwa* of a Companion. The fact is that Ahmad considers the word "*Sunna*" to include *mutawatir hadiths*, *sahih hadiths*, *fatwas* of the Companions, and *mursal* and weak *hadiths*.

So we consider the principles which Ibn al-Qayyim mentioned to be in reality four: the Book, *Sunna*, *fatwas* of the Companions and analogy. When we add what the legists have also mentioned as among the principles of Ahmad being – presumption of continuity (*istishab*), public interest (*masalih*) – and judgement of the means (*dhara'i'*), the number increases.

The books of the Hanbalis also contain discussion about consensus which resembles what ash-Shafi'i said about considering consensus to be evidence when it occurred. However, if it was suggested to Ahmad that consensus was evidence with respect to a specific question, he made it clear that there was no consensus in it. This view was expressed by ash-Shafi'i, Abu Yusuf and Ahmad himself, so we must mention it and discuss Ahmad's position and whether he denied consensus or permitted it in some matters.

We will now explain the foundations of Ahmad's *fiqh*. They are: the Book and the *Sunna*, consensus, *fatwas* of the Companions, analogy (*qiyas*), *istishab*, *masalih mursala*, and *dhara'i'*.

The Book

The Noble Qur'an is the foundation and basis of the *Shari'a* and is its primary source. It contains the basic premises and rulings which do not change with time and place and which are universally applicable to all people and not specific to one group rather than another. In it are universal rules, exposition of the sound Islamic creed and definitive proof of the firm *deen*.

Because it is the primary source of the Muslim *Shari'a*, scholars have always been concerned with studying it and finding the best means of deriving rulings from its expressions, indications and texts, just as they have striven to interpret what is unclear, define the general, clarify what needs to be clarified, explain its general and specific terms, and discover the abrogating and abrogated *ayats* and the reason for the abrogation and how it occurs. Scholars differ about these details although they all agree that the Qur'an is the first source of all the laws of Islam. They do not differ on that point, but they disagree about the relationship of the *Sunna* to it and whether it is an additional factor or simply an extension of it.

We do not intend to delve deeply into this subject, since Ahmad did not dwell on it, but there is one matter which we must discuss and clarify, which is Ahmad's position regarding the rank of the *Sunna* in relation to the Qur'an: is it second or equal to it in respect of the derivation of rulings? No scholars consider the *Sunna* to have exactly the same status as the Qur'an. Scholars agree that it is less because the Qur'an is the primary proof of Islam and its first source. But the fact that the *Sunna* is primary evidence is established by the words of the Almighty: *"When Allah and His Messenger have decided a thing it is not for any believing man or believing woman to have a choice about it"* (33:36); *"Whatever the Messenger gives you you must accept and whatever He forbids you you must forgo"* (59:7); and *"Whoever obeys the Messenger has obeyed Allah."* (4:80). There are other *ayats* which indicate the evidentiary nature of the *Sunna*, but there is no doubt that it has a lesser position than the Qur'an.

The fact that the *Sunna* ranks below the Qur'an with respect to deduction is not questioned. The question is whether rulings from the Qur'an can only be extrapolated by way of the *Sunna*, which serves to explain it. The Hanafis and Malikis extrapolated rulings from the Book and compared single *hadiths* against the Book. They accepted those which agreed with the Book and rejected those which did not. The Hanafis did the same regularly and the Malikis on occasion, as when they rejected the *hadith* about having to wash seven times any vessel licked by a dog because it contradicts the Qur'an.

The Shafi'is apply the *Sunna* to clarify the Qur'an when the literal sense of the Qur'an contradicts the *Sunna*. The *Sunna* sometimes makes literal texts of the Qur'an specific and the Qur'an is understood in that way. It acts as clarification and explanation of the Book, so that one of the *fuqaha'* stated that the *Sunna* governs the Qur'an since it is the means of explaining it, detailing it, clarifying what is abrogated of the Qur'an and defining what is undefined. This is why ash-Shafi'i put them on the same level: because the second clarifies the first. Ahmad held the same view and Ibn al-Qayyim rightly states that Ahmad put Qur'anic texts above *Sunna* texts in clarification of rulings.

Ahmad was adamant in considering the *Sunna* of the Prophet a sound explanation of the Noble Qur'an. He did not believe that there could be any conflict between the literal text of the Qur'an and the *Sunna*, because the *Sunna* clarifies it and explains the *fiqh* and rulings the Qur'an contains. He wrote a letter in which he refuted anyone who took the literal meaning of the Qur'an and abandoned the *Sunna*. He begins by saying:

> Allah Almighty sent Muhammad *"with the Guidance and the* Deen *of Truth to give it victory over all other* deens, *even if the idolaters dislike it."* He revealed His Book to him as guidance and a light for those who follow it, and taught the Messenger of Allah what He willed of its inward and outward, specific and general, abrogating and abrogated and what the Book intended. The Messenger of Allah interpreted the Book of Allah and pointed out its

477

meanings. His Companions, with whom Allah was pleased and whom He selected for His Prophet, bore witness to that and transmitted it from him. They were the most knowledgeable of people about the Messenger of Allah, may Allah bless him and grant him peace, and about what Allah meant by His Book, being witnesses to the event. After the Messenger of Allah, may Allah bless him and grant him peace, died they interpreted what was meant by the Book.

This passage shows three things: Firstly, the apparent text of the Qur'an does not have precedence over the *Sunna:* that is clearly stated. Secondly, the Messenger of Allah, may Allah bless him and grant him peace, explained the Qur'an and after him no one can interpret it or explain it because that is the role of the *Sunna* alone and it may not be expounded by any other means. Thirdly, the Companions explained the Qur'an since they transmitted from the Messenger of Allah; they witnessed the Revelation and heard its interpretation and knew the *Sunna* of Muhammad, may Allah bless him and grant him peace, and so their explanation is part of the *Sunna*. Thus Ahmad clearly states that there is no *tafsir* except through tradition. Ibn Taymiyya stated in his treatise which he wrote on *tafsir* that if there was no *tafsir* on an *ayat* from the Companions he took that of the *Tabi'un* in some cases. He disliked explaining the Qur'an by opinion in the way az-Zamakhshari did.

This takes us to the position of Ahmad ibn Hanbal regarding the understanding of the Qur'an in the texts transmitted from the *Salaf* where there was no teaching from the Prophet. He stated that he did not think that the literal text of the Qur'an could refute the *Sunna*. The *Sunna* is what made its evidence specific and so it was not possible for the *Sunna* to relate anything contradictory to the general meaning of the Qur'an.

In relation to the Qur'an, Ibn al-Qayyim divided the *Sunna* into three categories and stated: "The *Sunna* has three aspects in respect of the Qur'an. First, it agrees with it from every aspect and so the Qur'an and *Sunna* provide multiple transmissions of the same ruling and hence it is multiple evidence. Second, it clarifies and explains what the Qur'an means. Third, it provides a ruling on something about which the Qur'an is silent or prohibits something about which the Qur'an is silent. The Qur'an lays down the principle that the Prophet should be obeyed and that one is not allowed to disobey him. That is not putting the *Sunna* over the Book of Allah, but rather affirming the obedience to His Messenger which Allah has commanded in it."

The position that the school of Ahmad holds is that the apparent text of the Qur'an can only be explained by the *Sunna*; and that is also the course followed by ash-Shafi'i, as he affirms in his *Risala*. Ahmad may have adopted this from ash-Shafi'i when listening to him in Makka. In defence of the position of Imam Ahmad, Ibn al-Qayyim states:

> If it were permissible to reject the *Sunna* of the Messenger of Allah in favour of someone else's understanding of the probable texts of the Book, then many *sunnas* would be rejected and completely invalidated. So no one whose position is countered by a sound *sunna* is permitted to hold to the general and undefined texts and refuse to accept the *Sunna* in the way that the Rafidite Shi'ites reject the *hadith*. 'We, the company of Prophets, leave no inheritance' in favour of the general sense of the *ayat* '*Allah instructs you regarding your children: a male receives the same as the share of two females.*' (4:11)

The *Sunna*

This is the second principle of Imam Ahmad or, to be more precise, the second half of the first principle. You know that when Ibn al-Qayyim reported the principles of Ahmad, he considered the sound texts to be a single principle and made the Book and sound *Sunna* a single joint principle. The wisdom behind that has been explained above: the *Sunna* expounds and supplements the Qur'an, and there cannot be any contradiction between them because the one explains the other. This does not contradict the fact that the Qur'an is the primary source because it is clear that it is the foundation on which all laws are based.

But we are studying the Imam of the *Sunna*, to which he held for his entire life, so we must mention above all the position of the *Sunna* in Hanbali *fiqh* alongside the Book in some small detail. That will further clarify the views of the Imam. He often stated that knowledge of the Book is only gained by way of the *Sunna*; that knowledge of the *deen* comes by way of the *Sunna*; and that the easy way to seek the *fiqh* of Islam and its laws is by means of the *Sunna*. Those who confine themselves to the Book without seeking the assistance of the *Sunna* in explaining its laws will be misguided from the Straight Path. There are several reasons for this.

• The text of the Qur'an states that it is obligatory to obey the Messenger, and obedience can only mean following his *Sunna* and taking judgement from the Messenger in what he did during his life and what was related from him after his death. That is established in the *deen* because Allah Almighty says, *"No, by your Lord, they are not believers until they make you the judge in the disputes that break out between them."* (4:65) This was revealed when the Messenger of Allah judged in favour of az-Zubayr ibn al-'Awwam in a dispute with an Ansari about who would get water first from a canal. Az-Zubayr's land was closer to the water. When the Ansari was vexed by this judgement, this was revealed. There are many *ayats* which indicate this obligation, such as *"Obey Allah and obey the Messenger"* (5:93) and *"Anything the Messenger gives you you should take and anything He forbids you you should leave alone."* (59:7)

• The second reason is the evidence found in the *hadiths* which affirm the obligation to follow the *Sunna* and not confine oneself to the Book. It is related that the Prophet said, "One of you is about to say, 'This is the Book of Allah: what is lawful in it we consider lawful and what is unlawful in it we consider unlawful.' Whoever is told a *hadith* from me and denies it has cried lies to three: Allah, His Messenger, and the one who reported it." He also said "The time is approaching when one of you will be reclining on his coach and will be told a *hadith* from me and will say, 'Between us and you is the Book of Allah. We consider what is lawful in it to be lawful and what is unlawful to be unlawful.'" These texts indicate that it is mandatory to seek the laws of the *deen* in the *Sunna* of the Messenger of Allah and that confining oneself to the Book alone is an innovation.

• The third reason is that many Islamic rulings on which most of the Muslims agree are taken from the *Sunna,* or are greatly reliant on the *Sunna*. The prohibition of marriage with those related to one by suckling and of marrying a woman and her aunt at the same time are part of the *Sunna*. The details of the prayer, *zakat* and *hajj* are part of the *Sunna*. The amounts of blood money and other things are detailed in the *Sunna*. Anyone who ignores *fiqh* from the *Sunna* loses nine-tenths of Islamic *fiqh* or more.

Nevertheless, that it must be made clear that the *Sunna* is not all the same in respect of the authority of its *isnads* and it is necessary for us to clarify their relative status, the amount of deduction which may be based on them, the ruling when there is a conflict, and what was Ahmad's position on the subject. The *fuqaha'* divided *hadiths* into four categories with regard to their *isnads*: *mutawatir hadiths*, well-known or famous *hadiths*, *hadiths* with a single transmitter, and *hadiths* whose *isnad* is not complete but broken at some stage.

Mutawatir hadiths are related from such a large number of people and in so many disparate places that it is impossible to imagine that they could be untrue. There are many such *hadiths*. A *mutawatir hadith* entails incontrovertible knowledge. Well-known *hadiths* are those which the second or third generation accepted and which are famous among them, even if they are single *hadiths* related by only one narrator. Single Traditions do not constitute definite evidence. Ahmad was imbued with love of the Prophet and his Companions and so he was content to accept anything

481

which was ascribed to the Prophet. The fourth category of *hadiths* is those which are *mursal*. *Mursal* can mean two things: one is a *hadith* whose *isnad* stops at a Follower without mentioning the Companion from whom he received it, and the second is any *hadith* in which the *isnad* does not connect directly and continuously to the Prophet. Their acceptance by the *fuqaha'* varied.

Malik and Abu Hanifa accepted *mursal hadiths* to the extent which they thought correct. It is clear from studying the *Muwatta'* and the books of Traditions associated with Abu Hanifa that they considered the *mursal* to have the rank of the single *hadith*. When there was a conflict between them, they applied the same criteria as when two reports contradicted. Their strength in relation to a single ascription was in their opinion the same. Ash-Shafi'i, however, did not give the *mursal* the same status in his *Musnad*. He did accept *mursal hadiths*, but imposed certain conditions for doing so.

Ahmad considered *mursal hadiths* to be evidence, but put them below the *fatwas* of the Companions, placing them on a par with weak *hadiths*, and thus he both differed from his shaykh, ash-Shafi'i, and agreed with him. He differed by putting *mursal hadiths* after the *fatwas* of the Companions because he considered the latter to be part of the *Sunna*, as we will explain. Where there was nothing else he accepted *mursal hadiths* as he accepted weak *hadiths* because he preferred using them for making rulings to analogy and opinion, which he applied only as a last resort.

But it is clear that Ahmad considered *mursal hadiths* to be weak reports whose evidence can sometimes be refuted and not accepted, which is why he put the *fatwas* of the Companions first. He never, however, put a *fatwa* of a Companion ahead of a sound *hadith*, so the fact that he did place such *fatwas* before *mursal hadiths* is evidence that he considered them to be weak *hadiths*, not sound *hadiths*. He used them for making rulings in cases of necessity because he did not want to give any *fatwa* about the *deen* on his own accord when there was any tradition he was familiar with. So he accepted them as long as he did not have an alternative in the form of a *fatwa* from the Companions. Hence we can say that Ahmad's acceptance of *mursal hadiths* was certainly no greater than that of his shaykh ash-Shafi'i; it was, if anything, less since he rejected them more on the basis of their being in the category of weak *hadiths*.

Ahmad did not report from liars but only from reliable people of known integrity. He related from those known for being godfearing and truthful. Regarding his position on the *Sunna*, he said in a letter to Musaddad ibn Mufassara al-Basri: "We consider the *Sunna* to be transmission from the Messenger of Allah, may Allah bless him and grant him peace. The *Sunna* explains the Qur'an and is the arbiter of the Qur'an. Analogy does not apply in respect of the *Sunna* and it cannot be made subject to people's opinions and whims. It is a matter of following what has come down and abandoning whim." He did not make it a precondition for the acceptance of the *Sunna* that it should agree with any set of precepts or be measured against them. He did not reject any of it except when there was a *sunna* which conflicted with one which was stronger and more reliable than it and had more reliable transmitters.

We see that Ahmad only forbade transmitting from those who were known to be deliberate liars. He related from the godfearing and accepted their *hadiths* even if they were not completely accurate. But if he found someone more reliable, he took their version. As we have seen, Ahmad used to accept weak *hadiths* – but it is clear that he accepted only those relaters who were not known for lying. He advised his son 'Abdullah, "Almost no one resorts to his own opinion who does not have some defect in his heart. I prefer weak *hadiths* to opinion." 'Abdullah said, "I asked him about situations where the only alternatives are a person with knowledge of *hadith* who does not know the sound from the weak and someone who is known to use opinion: which one should be asked for a ruling? He said one should ask the one with *hadith*, not the one with opinion."

Ahmad put weak *hadiths* before analogy. He said to his son 'Abdullah, "My son, I do not oppose a weak *hadith* unless there is something definite to refute it. Ahmad preferred a middle course between opinion, which he disliked in respect of the *deen*, and *hadiths* lacking *isnad* connected to the Messenger. He preferred to act in accordance with a *hadith* out of cautious concern for his *deen*, assuming its authenticity if there was no evidence to the contrary. Ahmad also avoided having to use his own opinion by accepting the *fatwas* of some earlier *fuqaha'* who were known for following tradition rather than innovation, such as Malik, ash-Shafi'i, ath-Thawri and other jurists who had great knowledge of Tradition. He followed this course when exercising *ijtihad*.

The *Fatwas* of the Companions

Each of the Imams transmitted from a particular group of the *Salaf* in their legal studies, preferring to act like them and follow the path they followed. Abu Hanifa studied Iraqi *fiqh* largely ascribed to Ibn Mas'ud and some Makkan fiqh, and he extrapolated in a particular manner from the *fiqh* of Ibrahim an-Nakha'i, so their methods in deduction were close; and after that he studied *fiqh* with his shaykh Hammad. Malik transmitted the *fiqh* of the seven *fuqaha'* among the *Tabi'un*, Ibn Shihab, Rabi'a ar-Ra'y and others, thus learning it from those who had learned it from the Companions. He preferred deduction using their techniques since his legal training was on the basis of their *fiqh*. Ash-Shafi'i transmitted from Ibn 'Uyayna in *hadith* and then the *fiqh* of Malik, compared that with Iraqi *fiqh* when he met Muhammad ash-Shaybani, and then transmitted to posterity a complete system which was a combination of all of them. That system was the science of the fundamental principles of *fiqh* with precise criteria for deduction.

Ahmad ibn Hanbal had a school which reached back to the time of the Messenger of Allah and his Companions, and produced in *fiqh* a legal collection which transmits the decisions and rulings of the Prophet and those of his Companions as well, whether they referred to the Book of Allah, the *Sunna* of His Messenger or their own *ijtihad* in making them. That is the collection which he transmitted. Ahmad went to all regions of Islam to collect the material for the legal school which he developed and which supported his various legal deductions and extrapolations. He was able to learn from ash-Shafi'i the rules and methods of deduction so as to extrapolate from that material and to assign to each text its appropriate strength.

The legal collection transmitted from the Companions is not an insignificant one from which only a little *fiqh* was derived. It is large and varied and dispersed and forms an immense collection of partial rulings in respect of different events transmitted by disparate individuals. The *fatwas* of the Companions reflect their environment and they varied greatly in the number of *fatwas* they issued. Some gave many *fatwas* and some few. Those who gave many were 'Umar, 'Ali, 'Abdullah ibn Mas'ud, 'Abdullah ibn 'Abbas, Zayd ibn Thabit and 'A'isha. Those six are responsible for the greatest number. After them come ten others: Abu Bakr, 'Uthman, Mu'adh, Sa'd ibn Abi Waqqas, Talha, az-Zubayr, 'Abdullah ibn 'Amr ibn al-'As, Salman al-Farisi, Jabir, and Umm Salama.

Ahmad used that legal collection as a guiding light and a torch of Prophethood from the knowledge of the Messenger of Allah and the knowledge of the Companions. He clung tenaciously to it and consulted it in all that he was asked about. That is why he considered the statements and *fatwas* of the Companions to be evidence which came second only to the sound *hadiths* of the Prophet and before that of *mursal hadiths* and weak reports. The scholars who transmit his *fiqh* are in complete agreement on that point. All of them concur that he accepted the *fatwas* of the Companions and did not exercise his own *ijtihad* as long as there was a *fatwa* transmitted from one of the Companions on the matter in question.

He placed the *fatwas* of the Companions in two categories: those about which there was no known disagreement, and those about which they disagreed and there were two or three positions. With the first category he took the position of the Companions but did not call that consensus, thus agreeing with ash-Shafi'i. For instance, he took the position of Anas about the testimony of a slave because it is reported that he said, "I do not know of anyone who rejects the testimony of slaves." As for the second category, when there was disagreement Ahmad took note of the different positions and considered them all to be his own, so that he would have two or three statements according to the various positions. He did so to avoid preferring his own opinion to that of any of the Companions as they all had light and guidance from the Messenger of Allah.

Ibn al-Qayyim reports another view: "One of Ahmad's principles was that when the Companions differed, he chose from them the position which was closest to the Book and *Sunna*. He did not depart from their statements." There is another report that he referred first to the positions of the Rightly-guided Khalifs. Ibn al-Qayyim mentioned that: "When a Companion made a statement, it either was countered by another Companion or was not. If someone equal to him countered it, neither is evidence against the other. If it is countered by someone with more knowledge, as when the Rightly-guided Khalifs differed from other Companions on a ruling, there are two statements by scholars about that – and both are transmitted from Imam Ahmad." He goes on to point out that the sound position is to prefer the Khalifs, especially Abu Bakr and 'Umar.

It is clear that when Ahmad knew the opinions of the Rightly-guided Khalifs he chose them first. If he did not know them he chose the opinions closest to the Book of Allah and the *Sunna* of the Messenger of Allah. If none was close in any way, he gave two positions on the matter. Of Imam Ahmad's successors, some related the *fatwa* he chose which was the position of the khalifs and another transmitter only related the choice of what was closest to the sources. A third related that he left all the positions as his own, and transmitted all of them.

The rank of the *fatwas* of the Companions in the order of evidence is that it comes after the firm texts, namely the Qur'an and sound *hadiths*. Some scholars claim that when Ahmad found a *fatwa* of a Companion he did not turn to the texts at all because the *fatwa* of the Companion removed the necessity for deduction since the decision had already been made. Since Ahmad took the *fatwas* of the Companions as a source of *fiqh* and applied them, how did he consider them? Did he take them as being part of the *Sunna* or simply as *ijtihad* on the part of the Companions, and consider that it was better to take their *ijtihad*?

The four *fuqaha'* who founded the well-known schools all accepted the *fatwas* of the Companions, but they differed in how they considered them. Ash-Shafi'i, as he stated in his *Risala*, took their *fatwas* as being *ijtihad* but accepted them because he considered their *ijtihad* more fitting than his own. Malik considered their *fatwas* to be part of the *Sunna* and compared them against other reports when there was a contradiction, which differed from ash-Shafi'i. In the case of Ahmad, he did absolutely put the sound *hadiths* before the *fatwas* of the Companion and did not compare them as Malik did. We also find that he put them before *mursal* and weak *hadiths*.

I do not think that we can say that Ahmad considered all the *fatwas* of the Companions as transmission, but he certainly accepted their statements as the second source of understanding of the *deen* and the Muslim *Shari'a* after the statements of the Prophet, may Allah bless him and grant him peace, because they were closest to the Prophet. If there had to be opinion, then the best opinion was that directly taken from the guidance of the Messenger of Allah. Ibn al-Qayyim clearly states in *I'lam al-Muwaqqi'in* that this is an aspect of the *Sunna:*

> When a Companion makes a statement or gives a judgement or a *fatwa,* it may stem from discernment which he has and we do not, or from discernment in which we share. As for what is particular to him, it is likely that he heard it directly from the mouth of the Prophet, may Allah bless him and grant him peace, or from another Companion narrating from the Messenger of Allah. The knowledge which they possessed and to which we do not have access is more than will ever be known, for none of them related all that they heard. How much Abu Bakr as-Siddiq, 'Umar al-Faruq and the other great Companions, may Allah be pleased with them, must have heard, compared to what they related!
>
> There are not even a hundred *hadiths* related from the Siddiq of the Community [Abu Bakr], despite the fact that he was not absent from the Prophet, may Allah bless him

487

and grant him peace, in any of his battles and he accompanied him from the time of his prophetic mission, or indeed even before that, until his death. Abu Bakr was the most knowledgeable of the Community about him, may Allah bless him and grant him peace, and about his words, actions, guidance and conduct. The same applies to the majority of the Companions: the amount that they transmitted from the Prophet is very little indeed in comparison with what they actually heard and witnessed from him. If they had related all that they heard and witnessed, it would have been many times more than what Abu Hurayra transmitted. He was only a Companion for about four years and yet related a great deal from him.

The statement "If the Companions had known anything about this matter..." can only be made by someone who does not understand the behaviour and states of people. They were in awe of transmitting from the Messenger of Allah, may Allah bless him and grant him peace, and attached great importance to it. They did not often do so, fearing to add to, or subtract from, his words.

Any *fatwa* which one of the Companions gave will be based on one of six foundations:

• He heard it himself directly from the Prophet, may Allah bless him and grant him peace.

• He heard it from someone else who heard it.

• He understood it from an *ayat* of the Book of Allah in a manner which is unknown to us.

• It is something which all the Companions were agreed upon but only the statement of the one who gave the *fatwa* has been transmitted to us.

• He understood it through his complete knowledge of the language and what the phrase indicates, in a manner to which he had access and we do not, or by direct knowledge of the actual circumstances which were being addressed; or by the sum of things which he understood over the passage of time through seeing the Prophet, may Allah bless him and grant him peace, and witnessing his actions, states and behaviour and listening to his words, knowing his aims and witnessing the arrival of Revelation and witnessing its interpretation through action. Because of all this, the Companion was able to understand things which we cannot.

If the *fatwa* is based on any of the above five criteria, it is authoritative for us and must be followed. There is one more possibility:

• It was based on an individual understanding of something that the Messenger, may Allah bless him and grant him peace, did not say and the Compan-ion was wrong in his understanding.

Fatwas of the *Tabi'un*

We know the course followed by Ahmad regarding the *fatwas* of the Companions – how he accepted them when nothing contrary to them was known, and how he chose between them when they differed. Now we want to ascertain his view about the *fatwas* of the *Tabi'un* when he found no earlier text or report on a matter. Did he accept them in the same way that he accepted the *fatwas* of the Companions, merely giving them a lesser rank, or did he exercise *ijtihad*?

The majority of *fuqaha'* who stated that they did not take the *fatwas* of the *Tabi'un* as a source in general used nevertheless to accept the *fatwas* of some of the great *Tabi'un*. Abu Hanifa used sometimes to take the position of Ibrahim an-Nakha'i even though did not consider the statements of the *Tabi'un* to be one of the principles of deduction. He clearly stated that they were merely men and that he was as able to come to a judgement as they were. Malik used sometimes to take the position of Sa'id ibn al-Musayyab, Yazid ibn Aslam, and al-Qasim ibn Muhammad ibn

Abi Bakr. Ash-Shafi'i used to sometimes take the position of 'Ata'. This was on the understanding that some of them were renowned for knowledge and were thus accepted on that basis.

This was the view of the three Imams before Ahmad. As for Ahmad, reports disagree about his opinion on the evidentiary status of their *fatwas*. Some say that he accepted them and some that he did not and that, in his view, the *fiqh* of the *Tabi'un* was like commentary. If there was no text on the subject and no statement of a Companion or *mursal hadith*, then he accepted a *fatwa* from one of the *Tabi'un* if it was not disputed.

People say that the Hanbalis disagree about whether the *fatwas* of the *Tabi'un* should be given precedence over analogy. One group put it before analogy because analogy is only resorted to in emergency. Another group put analogy first. In any case we know that Ahmad disliked exercising *ijtihad* by his own opinion and that when there was no Tradition he often took the *fatwas* of scholars of Tradition like Malik, at-Thawri, Sufyan ibn 'Uyayna, al-Awza'i and others. Therefore it is more likely he would have accepted the *fatwas* of well-known and reliable *Tabi'un*.

Consensus (*Ijma'*)

Ibn al-Qayyim did not consider consensus to be one of the principles of Hanbali *fiqh*. He did not mention it and it has been reported that he said, "Whoever claims the existence of consensus is a liar." He often denied its existence, or knowledge of its existence outside of the Companions. We basically accept his opinion regarding consensus in respect of its evidentiary status and its rank as evidence. We will not delve into the words of the legists on consensus. They differ a great deal regarding its universal and particular questions and its place in the knowledge of the basic principles of *fiqh*.

To define consensus we should explain what was meant by those who used it as a legal principle. But the truth is that we cannot find anyone who taught it as a principle except ash-Shafi'i, and we know what he understood by consensus. Ash-Shafi'i mentions the reality of consensus in his *Book on the Invalidation of Istihsan*:

"Neither I nor any of the people of knowledge would say 'this is agreed on' except concerning facts about which you would never find any scholar who would fail to repeat them to you and relate them from a predecessor, such as the *Dhuhr* prayer being four *rak'ats*, wine being unlawful, and similar matters."

There is no doubt that Ahmad adjudged such consensus to be very tenuous on most questions. Ahmad ascertained all the claims and counter-claims about consensus and studied the subject with his shaykh, ash-Shafi'i in his first stay in Makka. That is why we prefer the view that he found the existence of consensus unlikely outside well-known matters of the *deen*. He was keen not to impute to scholars things that they had not said or to make unsound claims, and so out of scrupulousness when he mentioned a position about which no dispute was known, he did not say that there was consensus about it, but used to say, "I do not know of anyone who opposes it."

Ibn al-Qayyim mentioned that Ahmad used to dislike a claim of consensus without evidence, his position in that regard was like that of ash-Shafi'i. He said that Ahmad refuted those who claimed consensus and would not allow it to be put before a sound *hadith*. Ash-Shafi'i said the same in his *New Treatise*: when he said that something about which there is no known dispute should not be called consensus. 'Abdullah ibn Ahmad ibn Hanbal said, "I heard my father say, 'Anything that anyone claims consensus on is a liar. Anyone who claims consensus is a liar. People may disagree without him knowing about it. He should say, "We do not know of any disagreement between people on this."'"

Imam Ahmad and all Imams of *hadith* have too much respect for the texts of the Messenger of Allah to prefer to them the illusion of consensus when there is no known disagreement. If that were allowed, then texts would become unnecessary and anyone who did not know of any disagreements about a ruling could use his ignorance of any disagreement to overrule sound texts. This is what Imam Ahmad and ash-Shafi'i sought to avoid by rejecting claims of consensus.

Two things should be noted here. The first is that Ahmad did not completely deny the existence of consensus; he denied the claims made for it by some scholars of his generation, in the same way that Abu Yusuf denied the claim made by al-Awza'i that consensus denotes the opinion of the general mass of the people of knowledge. Ash-Shafi'i also denied it with those he debated with and did not use the evidence of consensus to refute a sound *hadith*. The second point is that Ahmad affirmed that there are questions about which no disagreement is known of and that such questions are accepted when there is no *hadith* on the subject. But he does not claim in such cases that that is perfect consensus, but says that he does not know of any disagreement. That is scrupulousness in the *deen*.

Thus we can say that the opinion of Ahmad regarding consensus was that he divided it into two categories. The first, which is the higher, is the consensus of the Companions, or rather the consensus of everyone on the principal obligations of the *deen*, and the consensus of the Companions on the questions which they examined and on which they exchanged opinions until they reached a specific view. Such a consensus is evidence and relies on a text of the Book or sound *Sunna*. It is strong evidence and there is no sound *hadith* which opposes it because the Companions transmitted the words, actions and decisions of the Prophet. It is not possible that their consensus be criticised or there be a *hadith* contrary to it.

The second category comprises well-known opinions no one is known to oppose. It is this second type which is generally called consensus. In the view of Ahmad this is less strong than a sound *hadith* but ranks above analogy, because if there is even one *faqih* who opposes it there is no consensus – and how much more is that the case if there is a contrary text.

Analogy

In Islamic *fiqh*, analogy means connecting a matter without a text giving a ruling for it to another matter with a text which does give a ruling, on the basis that they both have the same cause. Ibn al-Qayyim said, "The essence of all deduction is based on considering two similar things as having a correspondence and separating those which are dissimilar. If it were not allowed to compare similar matters in this way, all deduction would be vitiated and the doors to it locked." This is the true nature of analogy. Since events are endless, there must necessarily be some use of analogy in Islamic *fiqh*, be that little or much. The Qur'an indicates this, as do the *hadiths* of the Prophet. Allah mentions rulings and mentions their causes or states the correspondence, as He says, *"They will ask you about menstruation. Say, 'It is an impurity, so keep apart from women during menstruation and do not approach them until they have purified themselves'"* (2:222) and *"They will ask you about menstruation. Say, 'It is an impurity, so keep apart from women during menstruation and do not approach them until they have purified themselves."* (5:9)

There was, however, one group of scholars who totally rejected analogy and another group who went to excess in it. The first group denied the causes, meanings and qualities of similar situations, while the second expanded the scope of analogy beyond all reason and connected together things which were in reality dissimilar.

Ahmad, the *hadith* scholar and *faqih*, held a position between these two. He did not completely reject analogy as did the Dhahirites, who judged only by texts and were not concerned with giving people *fatwas,* so that people did not go to them as they did to Abu Hanifa, Malik, ash-Shafi'i and Ahmad. He was not excessive in analogy as were the Iraqis who followed Abu Hanifa and his students: they contrived unlikely similarities when there was a conflict between the texts and the *fatwas* of the Companions. Ahmad accepted analogy and affirmed it, as Ibn Qudama al-Hanbali states in *ar-Rawda*: Ahmad said about it, "No one can dispense with analogy." That is a true statement in respect of the *mufti* who must give *fatwa* and must use analogy at some point when there is no text or precedent about a particular matter.

The Hanbalis all affirm that Ibn Hanbal used analogy, and support their words with what he said. In this he was not an innovator but a follower. The Companions deduced according to their understanding, using analogy to compare new events with prior events. Al-Muzani said, *"Fuqaha'* from the time of the Messenger of

Allah until today have applied criteria in *fiqh* to all kinds of rulings in their *deen* and they agree that the like of the truth is true and the like of the false is false. It is not allowed for anyone to reject analogy out of hand."

Ahmad made use of analogy and thus it has a place in Hanbali *fiqh*. It may be true that the Hanbalis accord it more weight than Ahmad himself did, owing to the needs of the time. It is new events which necessitate the use of analogy to arrive at rulings through deduction.

Istishab (Presumption of Continuity)

This is a legal principle on which all the four Imams and those who follow them agree. They vary, however, in the amount they use it. It is used least by the Hanafis and most by the Hanbalis, then the Shafi'ites, and the Malikis are in the middle. It is clear that the amount of *istishab* used by the Imams depends on the amount of scope they allow to other evidence. Those who allow wide scope to analogy and *istihsan* and consider custom to be part of the evidence of the *Shari'a* use *istishab* less, considering the number of situations where it is observed as minimal. These are the Hanafis, next to whom come the Malikis because they also expanded the arena of deduction by applying the principle of public interest, *masalih*, which was a means of reducing the rulings in which they relied on *istishab*. The Hanbalis and Shafi'is, who did not consider analogy a valid course to pursue except in necessity, expanded the means of deduction by means of *istishab*. The Shi'ites used it the most.

We will now explain exactly what *istishab* is. Ash-Shawkani explained it as follows: "It means that the basic position established in the past remains in the present and the future. It is derived from '*musahaba*', which means that the matter remains as it is as long as nothing comes about to change it." According to Ibn al-Qayyim, it means that what is proven continues to be proven and what is denied continues to be denied unless there is definite evidence to the contrary. For instance, ownership by a purchaser is deemed to continue unless there is definite evidence of a change. There are several forms of *istishab* which Ahmad ibn Hanbal and the Hanbalis affirmed.

- Continuity of what a contract or the Law affirms. A loan, for instance, is presumed to continue unless there is evidence to the contrary; and a marriage is presumed to continue to exist unless there is evidence of divorce.

- Presumption that a state of affairs does not exist unless there is definite evidence that it does. This is like presumption of innocence and original freedom from liability.

- Continuity of original attributes, so that pure water is presumed to remain pure unless the contrary is definitely established and a missing person is presumed to be alive unless there is clear evidence of his death.

- Presumption of the continuity of consensus about general rules and principles of the law.

It is clear that the Hanbalis accepted *istishab* as one of the principles on which a *fatwa* may be based and used it more widely than did the Hanafis and Malikis, and about the same amount as the Shafi'is. What can be observed is that whenever *fuqaha'* want to expand the scope of deduction by the use of opinion, they rely less on *istishab* and whenever they want to minimise deduction by the use of opinion, they give more consideration to *istishab*. For instance, the Zahirites wanted to prevent the use of any opinion whatsoever and so they made frequent use of *istishab* and were the people who used it most. Shafi'ites, who forbade deduction by *masalih, istihsan, dhara'i*, and other means, used it as a principle and relied on it more than did the Hanafis and Malikis. It was the Hanbalis who inclined to Traditions the most and considered their *fiqh* to be the *fiqh* of Traditions, so they applied the principle of *istishab*.

Masalih (Public Interest)

We have mentioned the principles which Ibn al-Qayyim cited as the principles of deduction used by Ahmad; he did not mention *masalih* among them. The fact that it is not mentioned is not proof that it is not used. Hanbali *fuqaha'* do consider public interest to be one of the principles of deduction, and all attribute that principle to their Imam. Ibn al-Qayyim himself considered it to be one of the principles of deduction. He stated that all that the Lawgiver prescribed is in keeping with the best interests of people and that those commands of the *Shari'a* which are connected to behaviour with other people are based on the principle of bringing benefit and preventing harm and corruption. That is repeated in all the books which he wrote: it is affirmed in *I'lam al-Muwaqqi'in*, *Miftah Dar as-Sa'ada*, *Zad al-Ma'ad* and other books. He ascribed that principle to Imam Ahmad, but he did not include it when enumerating his principles because he thought that it merely constituted part of sound analogy.

The scholars of legal principles state unanimously that Ahmad ibn Hanbal and Malik utilised the principle of consideration of public interest. Indeed some of the books of the Hanbalis go very deeply into the consideration of public interest, excessively so in our view, particularly at-Tufi.

Applying the consideration of public interest (*masalih mursala*) and considering it to be a legal principle on which deduction can be based is found in many places in Ahmad's *fiqh*. It is consistent with his following the *Salaf* in their legal reasoning and not deviating from their path, to such an extent that he was considered one of the *Tabi'un*. For the *Salaf* followed the Companions and extrapolated from their *fatwas* by adopting the principle of public interest. Here are some examples.

- They collected the Noble Qur'an into a bound book – something which had not been done during the lifetime of the Messenger – because of the inherent benefit in it, dictated by the fear that the Qur'an might be forgotten as a result of the death of those who had memorised it. When 'Umar, may Allah be pleased with him, saw many of the memorisers of the Qur'an fall in the Ridda War,[1] he feared that the Qur'an

---

1. The War of Apostasy, the defection of various Arab tribes after the death of the Prophet, may Allah bless him and grant him peace, brought about the Ridda War in which large numbers of Muslims were slain.

might be lost because of their deaths and so he suggested to Abu Bakr that it should be collected together into a book. The Companions agreed to that and were pleased with it.

- The Companions of the Messenger agreed after his death that the *hadd* for wine-drinking should be eighty lashes using the principle of *masalih mursala*, since they observed that one of the consequences of intoxication was the slander of chaste women.

- The Rightly-guided Khalifs agreed to make artisans responsible for any goods of other people they were working on, even though the basic position is that things in one's possession are a trust (under Islamic law trustees are not responsible for unintentional damage to goods in their keeping). They did so because it was found that if they were not made liable for them they would make light of guarding other people's goods and property. So in this case public interest demanded that artisans should be made liable.

- 'Umar ibn al-Khattab, may Allah be pleased with him, used to confiscate half of the wealth of governors who combined their personal wealth with government assets and then used their position as governor to make a profit on it. The benefit involved in that ruling was that he thought that it would reform governors and keep them from exploiting the office of governorship for their own ends.

- It is also related that 'Umar ibn al-Khattab had a group of people executed for the murder of one person when they all participated in it, because public interest demanded that even though no text existed to support it. The benefit in this lies in the fact that it would otherwise become possible to shed inviolable blood with impunity, resulting in a loophole in the principle of retaliation. People would then use cooperation and partnership as a means to commit murder since it would be known that no retaliation would be demanded. If it be argued that this is an innovation by which other parties than the killer are executed even when they were not all actually involved in the act of killing, the argument refuting this is

497

that the group responsible is a collective and so collective execution is the same as executing the individual, since killing is ascribed to the collective in the same way as for one murder to an individual. Therefore individuals who join together with the aim of killing are considered as a single person. Public interest demands this since it involves the prevention of bloodshed and the protection of society.

Ahmad saw that the *fatwas* of the Companions were frequently based on the principle of public interest and, indeed, that perhaps most of the *fatwas* in which they make use of opinion were based on that principle. Since he adhered to the *Salaf* in their *fatwas*, if he did not find a text he likewise followed their methodology so that he would be illuminated by their light. For that reason he used public interest as one of the means of *fatwa* and felt it right to do so. Let us take some examples.

He used *masalih* in legal policy in a general way. It is the means by which a ruler proceeds in putting people right and encouraging them to what is beneficial for them and distancing them from what is corrupting for them. He orders punishments in order to correct people, even if there are no texts sanctioning those punishments, to punish people for certain crimes so as to defend society from the evil of those crimes. We find many instances of such uses of *masalih*, including exiling corrupt people and increasing the punishment for drinking wine in daytime in Ramadan, and punishing those who curse the Companions.

The principle of *adh-Dhara'i'* (Judgement of the Means)

This is a legal principle on which the Hanbalis rely, following their Imam, since he considered it to be one of the principles of *fatwa*. For when the Lawgiver has obliged people to do something, anything which helps it to be achieved is desirable, and when He has forbidden people something, whatever leads to the occurrence of that prohibited action is also unlawful. This can be demonstrated by examining legal obligations in obliging and forbidding. We find that where Lawgiver forbade something He forbade all that leads to it, and where He commanded something He commanded all that leads to it. For instance, because the *Jumu'a* prayer is an obligation, going to it is also an obligation, and leaving off trading to go to it is also obligatory.

He commanded love between people and forbade mutual hate and division and so all that leads to the latter is also forbidden. Therefore, the Prophet, may Allah bless him and grant him peace, forbade one to make a marriage proposal when his brother has made one, and to bid against the bid of his brother. Such actions are a means of engendering bad feeling between people. The Lawgiver divided inheritance shares between the heirs and forbade anything that would lead to someone altering his share, and so He has forbidden a bequest to an heir or denying an heir his share. That is also why the first *Muhajirun* and *Ansar* confirmed that a wife divorced during a man's final illness should still inherit, since there is suspicion that the divorce may have been performed with the aim of depriving her of her inheritance.

There are two areas in the *Shari'a:* ends and means. Ends are things which are benefits or harms in themselves, and the ways are the means of achieving them. Means can be examined in two ways. One is by looking at the incentive which moved the person to act and whether what was intended is lawful or unlawful, and the second is to look at the results without looking into motives or intentions. The principle of *sadd adh-dhara'i'* does not consider personal intentions and objectives but aims for general benefits or the general removal of harm. Hence it examines the objective and end, or simply the end.

Ahmad's position in this was similar to that of Malik. He considered and established the ends, forbade what led to an unlawful end, and confirmed what led to a desirable end. He regarded that as a general principle and applied it to specific questions. For instance, he forbade meeting a caravan before it arrived so that it would not lead to a rise in prices for the public and hence to general harm.

Conclusion

These are the principles of the Hanbali school which the
Hanbalis ascribe to their Imam. All of them are derived from the
Sunna. Although they branch out and subdivide, they come from a
single source: Traditions. He either obtained a text from the traditions, and if he did not find a text for the case in hand he emulated
the means used in the Tradition, adopting its method. In either
case, he followed the path of the *Salaf* or adopted that position.

If we examine the principles one by one, we will find that
Ahmad followed the path of the *Salaf* and did not overstep it or
travel by any other route. He found that the *Salaf* compared cases
with others like them and gave similar rulings in similar cases, and
so he used analogy in the absence of a text. He found that the
Companions considered that something continued to have the
same ruling until the situation or thing changed and so he gave
fatwa by what later scholars called *istishab* on the assumption that
in the absence of any definite alteration rulings would continue
unchanged.

He found that the Companions in the time of the Rightly-guided Khalifs took note of public interest and considered that alone as
sufficient basis enough for a ruling when there was no text. For
instance, the Companions agreed to collect the Qur'an into one
copy; they executed a group of accomplices for one murder; and
they gave a guarantee to public employees because they saw that
public welfare lay in doing so. So Ahmad used *masalih mursala*
for *fatwa* as they did and selected it as one of his principles of
deduction since they had initiated it; and so he followed them in it,
directed by their guidance to their method. He found that they
applied to the means the same ruling as to their end, and so he
adopted the principle of judgement of means, negative and
positive.

Thus in his all *fiqh* he was a *Salafi* and a *Tabi'i*, whether he
exercised his own *ijtihad* or transmitted a ruling from his predecessors. He constantly took from the *Salaf* in his *fiqh*. That did not
make his *fiqh* rigid and inflexible, but rather fertile and luminous.

Imam Ahmad stated what are the necessary qualifications of a *mufti*. He said, "A man should not set himself up to give *fatwa* unless he possesses five qualities. He must have a clear intention: unless he does, he will have no light. He must have knowledge, forbearance, gravity and tranquillity. He must be firm in his knowledge. He must be independent and not dependent on other people. And he must be known to people." As we have seen, he himself admirably fulfilled all these requirements in every way.

Glossary

Abbasids: the dynasty of khalifs who ruled from 750 to 1258 and had their capital in Baghdad. They based their claim to power on their descent from al-ʿAbbas, the uncle of the Prophet, may Allah bless him and grant him peace.

adab: correct behaviour, inward and outward.

ʿadat: customary usage.

adhan: the call to prayer.

ʿAlawites: partisans of ʿAli ibn Abi Talib.

ʿamm: generally applicable, in reference to a Qurʾanic ruling.

Ansar: the "Helpers", the people of Madina who welcomed and aided the Prophet.

asbab an-nuzul: the historical circumstances leading to a Qurʾanic revelation; situational exegesis.

ʿAsr: the Afternoon prayer.

ayat: a verse of the Qurʾan.

Badr: a place near the coast, about 95 miles to the south of Madina where, in 2 AH in the first battle fought by the newly established Muslim community, 300 Muslims led by the Messenger of Allah overwhelmingly defeated more than 1000 Makkan idolaters.

balagha (plural *balaghat*): a *hadith* in which the isnad is not mentioned but the reporter quotes the Prophet directly.

Deen: the life-transaction, lit. the debt between two parties; in this usage, between the Creator and created.

dhahir: apparent; a *dhahir* text can have two or more meanings.

dharaʾiʿ: means, used in the legal principle "judgement of the means".

Dhuhr: midday prayer.

faqih, pl. **fuqahaʾ:** a man learned in the knowledge of *fiqh* (see below) who by virtue of his knowledge can give a legal judgement.

fard al-kifaya: something which is obligatory for each community of Muslims as a whole but is fulfilled if one adult performs it.

fatwa: an authoritative statement or decision on a point of law.

fiqh: the science of the application of the *Shari'a*. A practitioner or expert in *fiqh* is called a *faqih*.

firasa: the science of recognising a person's inward qualities by studying the outward appearance; intuitive knowledge of human nature and understanding of situations.

Follower: see *Tabi'un*.

fuqaha': plural of *faqih*.

Fustat: Egyptian garrison town in early Islamic times; later an administrative center, within modern Cairo.

hadd: see *hudud*.

hadith: reported speech of the Prophet.

hajj: the annual pilgrimage to Makka, which is one of the five Pillars of Islam.

halal: lawful in the *Shari'a*.

haram: unlawful in the *Shari'a*.

Haram: Sacred Precinct, a protected area in which certain behaviour is forbidden and other behaviour necessary. The area around the Ka'ba in Makka is a *Haram*, and the area around the Prophet's Mosque in Madina is a *Haram*. They are referred to together as *al-Haramayn*, 'the two *Haram*s'.

Hijaz: the region along the western seaboard of Arabia in which Makka, Madina, Jidda and Ta'if are situated.

Hijra: emigration, especially for the Cause of Allah. Islamic dating begins with the *Hijra* of the Prophet Muhammad from Makka to Madina in 622 AD.

hudud: plural of *hadd*, Allah's boundary limits for the lawful and unlawful. The *hadd* punishments are specific fixed penalties laid down by Allah for specified crimes.

huffaz: plural of *hafiz*. A *hafiz* is a *hadith* master who has memorised at least 100,000 *hadiths* – texts, chains of transmissions and meanings.

Iblis: the personal name of the Devil. He is also called Shaytan or the enemy of Allah.

'Id: a festival, either the festival at the end of Ramadan or at the time of the *Hajj*.

'Id al-Adha: a festival at the end of the *Hajj*.

'idda: a period after divorce or the death of her husband for which a woman must wait before re-marrying.

ihram: the conditions of clothing and behaviour adopted by someone on *hajj* or *'umra*.

ijaza: a certification, by a teacher, that a particular student is qualified to teach a particular subject or to transmit a specific text or collection of traditions.

ijma': consensus.

ijtihad: to exercise personal judgement in legal matters.

irja': suspending or postponing judgement on whether or not someone is a believer.

'Isha': the obligatory evening prayer.

isnad: a tradition's chain of transmission from individual to individual.

istishab: Presumption of continuity, or presuming continuation of the *status quo ante*.

istihsan: to deem something good, juristic preference; to decide in favour of something which is considered good by the jurist, over against the conclusion that may have been reached by analogy.

istikhara: a prayer for Divine guidance performed by someone faced with a choice or decision.

Jahiliyya: the Time of Ignorance before the coming of Islam.

jihad: struggle, particularly fighting for the Cause of Allah to establish or defend Islam.

Jumu'a: the day of gathering, Friday, and particularly the *Jumu'a* prayer which is performed instead of *Dhuhr* by those who attend it.

kaffara: atonement, prescribed way of making amends for wrong actions, especially missed obligatory acts.

kalam: 'theology' and dogmatics. *Kalam* begins from the revealed tradition and employs rationalistic methods in order to understand it and resolve contradictions.

khalifa: the khalif or caliph. The Arabic word from which khalif is derived is khalifa while *khilafa* means the khalifate.

kharaj: taxes imposed on revenue from land or the work of slaves.

Kharijites: the earliest sect, who separated themselves from the body of the Muslims and declared war on all those who disagreed with them, stating that a wrong action turns a Muslim into an unbeliever.

khass: specifically applicable, particular.

khilafa: the office of khalif.

Khurasan: Persian province southeast of the Caspian Sea; a centre of many dissident movements in early Islamic history.

khutba: a speech, and in particular a standing speech given by the Imam before the *Jumu'a* prayer and after the two *'Id* prayers.

kitaba: a contract by which a slave acquires his freedom against a future payment, or payment by instalments, to his master.

kunya: a respectful but affectionate way of addressing people as "the father of so-and-so" or "the mother of so-and-so."

Madinat as-Salam: "the City of Peace", meaning Baghdad.

Maghrib: the sunset prayer.

marfu': 'elevated', a narration from the Prophet mentioned by a Companion, e.g. "The Messenger of Allah said..."

masalih mursala: Considerations of public interest, human welfare, or utility not explicitly supported by a text.

mawali: the plural of *mawla*, a person with whom a tie of clientage has been established, usually by having been a slave and then set free. It was also used for a type of political patronage.

mawquf: 'stopped,' narration from a Companion. It can be elevated to marfu' if it is of the nature of "We were commanded to..." and the like.

Mihna: the Inquisition instituted by the Abbasid khalif, al-Ma'mun, which required all important people to state publicly that they believed that the Qur'an was created, not uncreated.

mihrab: the prayer-niche, a recess in a mosque wall indicating the direction of *qibla*.

minbar: steps on which the Imam stands to deliver the *khutba*, or sermon, on Friday.

mu'adhdhin: (English, muezzin) someone who calls the adhan or call to prayer.

Mudar: The northern Arab tribes fell into two groups: Mudar, under the leadership of the tribe of Tamim, and Rabi'a. Opposing them were the southern, Yemeni tribes under Azd. The tribes of Rabi'a came to side with the Azdites.

mufti: someone qualified to give a legal opinion or fatwa.

muhaddith: a scholar who transmits and/or studies hadith.

Muhajirun: Companions of the Messenger of Allah who accepted Islam in Makka and emigrated to Madina.

mujtahid: a scholar who is qualified to carry out *ijtihad*.

munqati': a *hadith* in the *isnad* of which a link is omitted.

Murji'ites: the opponents of the Kharijites. They held that it is faith and not actions which are ultimately important. They also have a political position which suspends judgement on a person guilty of major sins.

mursal: a *hadith* where a man in the generation after the Companions quotes directly from the Prophet without mentioning the Companion from whom he received it.

Musnad: a collection of *hadiths* arranged according to the first authority in its isnad.

mutakallimun: those who study the science of *kalam*, the science of investigating theological doctrine.

mutawatir: a *hadith* which is transmitted by a large number of narraters at all stages of the *isnad*.

Mu'tazilite: someone who adheres to the school of the Mu'tazila which is rationalist in its approach to existence. Originally they held that someone who commits a wrong action is neither a believer nor an unbeliever. They also hold the Qur'an to be created.

muttasil: a *hadith* which has an uninterrupted *isnad*.

Nasibite: a group of people who dislike 'Ali and his family; they are the counterpart of the Rafidites.

nass: unequivocal, clear injunction or prohibition; an explicit textual meaning.

Qadar: "power". The Qadariyya were a sect who said that people have power (*qadar*) over their actions and hence free will.

Qadariyya: a sect who believed d that people have complete power (*qadar*) over their actions and hence free will.

qadi: a judge, qualified to judge all matters in accordance with the *Shari'a* and to dispense and enforce legal punishments.

qibla: the direction faced in the prayer, which is towards the Ka'ba in Makka.

Rafidites: group of the Shi'a known for rejecting Abu Bakr and 'Umar as well as 'Uthman.

rak'at: a unit of the prayer consisting of a series of standings, bowing, prostrations and sittings.

Rashidun: the first four khalifs of Islam: Abu Bakr, 'Umar, 'Uthman and 'Ali.

ra'y: opinion, personal discretion.

sadaqa: charitable giving for the Cause of Allah.

sadd adh-dhara'i': the blocking of a means which might lead to undesired consequences.

shahada: bearing witness, particularly testifying that there is no god but Allah and that Muhammad is the Messenger of Allah. It is one of the pillars of Islam.

Salaf: the early generations of the Muslims.

sharif: descendant of the Prophet, may Allah bless him and grant him peace, through Fatima and 'Ali.

Shari'a: The legal modality of a people based on the Revelation of given to their Prophet. The final *Shari'a* is that of Islam.

shaytan: a devil, particularly Iblis.

shirk: the unforgiveable sin of worshipping something or someone other than Allah or associating something or someone as a partner with Him.

Shura: "consultation"; this term also designates the board of selectors that was constituted by 'Umar to elect his successor.

Siddiq: 'the veracious"; a title given to Abu Bakr.

sira: biography of the Prophet.

Subh: the dawn prayer.

sunan: plural of *sunna*.

Sunna: the customary practice of a person or group of people. It has come to refer almost exclusively to the practice of the Messenger of Allah as understood and imitated by the first generation of Muslims.

Tabi'i: singular of *Tabi'un*.

Tabi' at-Tabi'in: the generation after the *Tabi'un*.

Tabi'un: the Followers, the second generation of early Muslims, who did not meet the Prophet Muhammad, may Allah bless him and grant him peace, but learned the *Deen* of Islam from his Companions.

tafsir: commentary or explanation of the meanings of the Qur'an.

taqiyya: concealment of one's views to escape persecution.

tasawwuf: Sufism, the Islamic science of attaining *ihsan* or spiritual excellence.

tawhid: the doctrine of Divine Unity.

tayammum: purification for prayer with clean dust, earth, or stone.

Umayyads: the Muslim dynasty of khalifs who ruled in Damascus from 661 until they were overthrown by the Abbasids in 750.

umm walad: a slavegirl who has borne her master's child: she cannot be sold and becomes free upon her master's death.

'urf: common acknowledgement, customary practice.

usul: plural of *asl*, the basic principles of any source, used in *fiqh*.

wudu': ritual washing, performed to be pure for the prayer.

zakat: a wealth tax, one of the five Pillars of Islam.

Zaydites: a branch of the Shi'a deriving its name from Zayd ibn 'Ali and hence called Fivers as its adherents have five Imams.

zindiq: a term used to describe a heretic whose teaching is a danger to the state. Originally under the Sasanids it meant a free-thinker, atheist or dualist.

zuhd: asceticism.

Index

509

510

511

513

514